Cannington Bypass, Somerset
Excavations in 2014
Middle Bronze Age enclosure at Rodway and Roman villa at Sandy Lane

Cannington Bypass, Somerset Excavations in 2014

Middle Bronze Age enclosure at Rodway and Roman villa at Sandy Lane

by

Jonathan Hart and Andrew Mudd

with contributions from

Philip L. Armitage, Stephen Armstrong, Kayt M. Brown, Sharon Clough, Sarah Cobain, Frances Healy, David Gould, Kevin Hayward, Katie Marsden, E.R. McSloy, Henrietta Quinnell, Stephen Rippon, Ruth Shaffrey, Jacky Sommerville, Peter Warry, Imogen Wood, Sarah F. Wyles, Tim Young

Illustrator

Aleksandra Osinska

Cotswold Archaeology Monograph No. 10

Cirencester 2018

Cotswold Archaeology Monograph No. 10

Published by Cotswold Archaeology
Copyright © authors and Cotswold Archaeology 2018
Building 11, Kemble Enterprise Park, Cirencester, Gloucestershire GL7 6BQ

All rights reserved. No part of this publication may be reproduced, stored in a retrieval system, or transmitted in any form or by any means, electronic, photocopying, recording or otherwise, without the prior permission of the copyright owner.

ISBN 978-0-9934545-4-7

Mapping in Figs 1.1, 1.3, 1.4, 2.2, 2.4, 3.3, 3.4, 3.6, 3.9, 3.10, 3.12, 3.14, 3.16, 3.19, 3.20, 3.22, 3.23, 3.27, 3.31 and 3.32 reproduced from the Ordnance Survey on behalf of The Controller of Her Majesty's Stationery Office, © Crown Copyright and database rights 2018 Ordnance Survey 100031673

Geological information in Fig. 1.3 contains British Geological Survey materials ©NERC 2018

Fig. 4.1 Down Farm Enclosure (from Barrett *et al.* 1991, fig. 5.41) and Thorny Down (Ellison 1987, fig. 1), Fig. 4.2 South Lodge Enclosure (from Barrett *et al.* 1991, fig. 5.13), Fig. 4.7 Langton Roman villa, East Yorkshire (from Finberg 1972, fig. 35) and Fig. 4.8 Pitney Roman villa, Somerset (from Finberg 1972, fig. 38), are reproduced by courtesy of Cambridge University Press. Fig. 4.2 Black Patch, East Sussex (from Drewett 1979, fig. 1) and Fig. 4.12 Stroud Roman villa, Hampshire (from A Moray Williams 1909, plate 1) © Royal Archaeological Institute, reprinted by permission of Taylor & Francis Ltd, http://www.tandfonline.com on behalf of Royal Archaeological Institute. Fig. 4.4 Yewden Roman villa, Buckinghamshire (from Eyers 2011, fig. 3.40) is reproduced courtesy of Chiltern Archaeology. Fig. 4.5 Bath-house at Feltwell, Norfolk (from Gurney 1986, fig. 10) is reproduced courtesy of Norfolk Archaeological Unit. Fig. 4.6 Detail of amphitheatre at Caerleon (from *Archaeologia* vol. 78, plate XXIV 1) is reproduced by permission of the Society of Antiquaries of London. Fig. 4.9 Winterton Roman villa, Lincolnshire (from Stead 1976) is reproduced with the permission of the Controller of HMSO and the Queen's Printer for Scotland. Figs 4.10 and 4.15 Frocester Roman villa (from Price 2000a, figs 5.3 and 6.4) are reproduced courtesy of Gloucestershire Archaeology. Figs 4.16 and 4.17 Poundbury, Dorset (from Sparey Green 1987 figs 55 and 56) are reproduced courtesy of Dorset Natural History and Archaeology Society.

Front cover: Hypocaust in Roman building at Sandy Lane
Back cover: Public Open Day at Sandy Lane (courtesy of South West Heritage Trust); Middle Bronze Age jar from Rodway (drawing by Jane Read)

Cover design by Aleksandra Osinska, Cotswold Archaeology
Produced by Past Historic, Kings Stanley, Gloucestershire
Printed by Henry Ling Ltd, Dorchester

CONTENTS

List of Figures	vii
List of Tables	x
Acknowledgements	xi
Preface	xiii
Foreword	xv
Summary	xvi
Chapter 1 Introduction	1
Project background	1
Location, topography and geology	3
Archaeological background	3
Methods and standards	7
Results summary and structure of report	8
Chapter 2 A Middle Bronze Age Enclosure at Rodway and other Bronze Age Features	9
Introduction	9
The Rodway Enclosure *by Jonathan Hart*	10
Middle Bronze Age trough at Sandy Lane *by Jonathan Hart*	14
Prehistoric pottery *by Henrietta Quinnell with* Fabrics *by Imogen Wood*	15
Lithics from Rodway and Sandy Lane *by Jacky Sommerville*	21
Charred plant remains *by Sarah F. Wyles*	22
Charcoal *by Sarah Cobain*	25
Radiocarbon dating *by Sarah Cobain*	27
Chapter 3 Iron Age Settlement, Roman Villa and post-Roman Structure at Sandy Lane	29
Introduction	29
Iron Age, Roman and post-Roman settlement at Sandy Lane *by Jonathan Hart*	30
Human remains *by Sharon Clough*	61
Radiocarbon dating *by Sarah Cobain and Frances Healy*	62
Iron Age and Roman pottery *by E.R. McSloy*	68
Ceramic building material *by Peter Warry*	79
Mortar and plaster *by Kevin Hayward*	82
Painted wall plaster *by Kayt M. Brown*	84
Stone *by Ruth Shaffrey*	87
Metals *by Katie Marsden*	89
Metallurgical residues *by Tim Young*	92
Charred plant remains *by Sarah F. Wyles*	93
Charcoal *by Sarah Cobain*	99
Animal bones *by Philip L. Armitage*	105

Chapter 4 Discussion 112
    Introduction 112
    Bronze Age settlement at Rodway in its context *by Andrew Mudd and Jonathan Hart* 112
    Iron Age and Roman settlement chronology *by Andrew Mudd and Jonathan Hart* 116
    Design and purpose of the buildings *by Andrew Mudd and Jonathan Hart* 118
    The character of the Iron Age and Roman occupation *by Andrew Mudd and Jonathan Hart* 128
    The Sandy Lane villa: its wider context *by Stephen Rippon, Stephen Armstrong and David Gould* 133
    The post-Roman occupation *by Andrew Mudd and Jonathan Hart* 137
    The early medieval territory associated with Cannington *by Stephen Rippon* 140
    Conclusions *by Andrew Mudd* 142

References 144

Index 153

List of Figures

1.1 The development area in its topographic context, with selected nearby archaeological sites — 2
1.2 Landscape setting looking north-east from the Sandy Lane site across the Parrett Valley — 3
1.3 Simplified geology map of the development area and environs (contains British Geological Survey materials ©NERC 2018) — 4
1.4 Archaeological investigations within the bypass footprint — 6
1.5 The Sandy Lane site after topsoil removal, looking north-east with Cannington Park Quarry to the left — 7
2.1 Rodway Middle Bronze Age enclosure, looking south-west — 9
2.2 Rodway Middle Bronze Age enclosure: plan of archaeological features — 10
2.3 Rodway Middle Bronze Age enclosure: Section 1, north-west facing section through Ditch B; Section 2, south-east facing section through Ditch A; Section 3, south-west facing section through pit 10137; Section 4, south facing section through pit 10263 — 12
2.4 Rodway Middle Bronze Age enclosure: finds density distribution — 13
2.5 Rodway Enclosure and Sandy Lane Middle Bronze Age trough: radiocarbon dating multiplot — 14
2.6 Sandy Lane Middle Bronze Age trough 20871, looking north (scale 1m) — 14
2.7 Middle Bronze Age pottery, nos 1–5 (drawing by Jane Read) — 18
2.8 Middle Bronze Age pottery, nos 6–10 (drawing by Jane Read) — 19
2.9 Flints, nos 1–2 — 22
2.10 Middle Bronze Age charcoal identifications from Rodway and Sandy Lane — 27
3.1 Sandy Lane, looking north-east from Roman Building A — 29
3.2 Sandy Lane, looking north-west towards Cannington Camp hillfort — 30
3.3 Sandy Lane overall site plan — 31
3.4 Sandy Lane Iron Age settlement: plan of Iron Age enclosure. Roman Ditch W probably re-cut an Iron Age ditch on the same alignment — 32
3.5 Sandy Lane Iron Age settlement: Section 5, south-west facing section through Ditch O; Section 6, north-west facing section through Ditch O; Section 7, west facing section through Ditch L — 33
3.6 Sandy Lane Iron Age settlement: detail plan of Structures A–C — 34
3.7 Sandy Lane Iron Age settlement: ditches of Structure B, looking south (scale 1m) — 35
3.8 Sandy Lane Iron Age settlement: Section 8, north-west facing section through the ditches of Structure B — 35
3.9 Sandy Lane Iron Age settlement: detail plan of possible beam-slot building (Structure D) and pits — 37
3.10 Sandy Lane Roman villa: plan of the enclosure — 38
3.11 Sandy Lane Roman villa: Section 9, north-west facing section through Ditch W; Section 10, north-east facing section through Ditch K; Section 11, north-west facing section through Ditch DI — 39
3.12 Sandy Lane Roman villa: plan of Building A, Phase 1 — 41
3.13 Building A Phase 1: Room 1 wall 20472 running north/south: Room 2 foundation 20484 in foreground (scale 1m) — 42
3.14 Building A, Phase 2. The north-west corner is conjectural — 43
3.15 Building A looking east — 44
3.16 Building A Phase 3 — 45
3.17 Building A Room 3, looking south, with the *opus signinum* surface of Phase 4 removed. Wall 20471 to left and wall 20462 to right. Between them, east–west wall 20473, shortening the original room, dates to Phase 3 (scales 2m) — 46

3.18	Building A Phase 3. External face of wall 20473 showing 'bastard pointing' above the pitched stone course (scale 2m)	46	3.43	Painted wall plaster: 1 colour code 8; 2 colour code 11; 3 colour code 11; 4 colour code 13	86
3.19	Building A Phase 4	47	3.44	Stone artefacts: 1 square Lias slab; 2 possible weight; 3 sandstone spindle-whorl	88
3.20	Building A Phase 5	48			
3.21	Building A Phases 4 and 5 hypocaust built on Phase 2 *opus signinum* floor 20475, looking south	49	3.45	Metal artefacts: 1 copper-alloy tweezers; 2 copper-alloy brooch; 3 iron latch lifter; 4 iron cleaver or knife	89
3.22	Building A Phase 6	50	3.46	Late Iron Age/Early Roman and Roman charcoal composition	103
3.23	Plan of Building B	51			
3.24	Building B during excavation, looking south-east	53	3.47	Charcoal assemblage from early medieval pit 20020	103
3.25	Building B, sub-surface 20298 and stone-capped T-shaped drain 20300, looking south	53	3.48	Charcoal from Building D	103
			4.1	Comparative plans of Middle Bronze Age settlements (Down Farm Enclosure after Barrett *et al.* 1991, fig. 5.41; Thorny Down after Ellison 1987, fig. 1)	113
3.26	Building C, looking west	55			
3.27	Plan of Building C, showing infant burials and other depositions	56			
3.28	Building C Room 1 after removal of wall 20616, looking south	57	4.2	Comparative plans of Middle Bronze Age settlements (South Lodge Enclosure after Barrett *et al.* 1991, fig. 5.13; Black Patch after Drewett 1979, fig. 1)	115
3.29	Building C Room 1, wall 20616 overlying remodelled foundations, looking west (scale 0.4m)	57			
3.30	Building C Room 1, detail of surviving wall 20616 (scale 1m)	58	4.3	Reconstruction of Sandy Lane Roman villa in its landscape	119
3.31	Building C, plan of overlying rubble deposits	58	4.4	Yewden, Hambleden Valley (Bucks.) Roman villa in 4th century (after Eyers 2011, fig. 3.40)	120
3.32	Plan of post-Roman Building D	59			
3.33	Building D foundation Trench DL, looking north (scale 2m)	60	4.5	Detached bath-house at Feltwell (Little Oulsham Drove), Norfolk (after Gurney 1986, fig. 10)	121
3.34	Neonatal skeleton Sk 20706	62			
3.35	Neonatal skeletons Sk 20747, 20746 and 20735	62	4.6	Detail of amphitheatre at Caerleon, showing 'bastard pointing' picked out with red paint (from *Archaeologia* 78 (1928), plate XXXIV 1, by kind permission of the Society of Antiquaries)	122
3.36	Sandy Lane radiocarbon dating multi-plot. Blue indicates residual material. (Ditch DM not illustrated)	63			
3.37	Probability distributions for radiocarbon dates from burials in Building C	66	4.7	Langton (East Yorkshire) Roman villa (after Applebaum 1972, fig. 35)	123
3.38	Estimated durations and interval from the model shown in Fig. 3.37. Highest posterior density intervals are given in Table 3.2	68	4.8	Pitney (Somerset) Roman villa (after Applebaum 1972, fig. 38; Haverfield 1906 fig. 83)	124
			4.9	Winterton Roman villa (Lincolnshire) (after Stead 1976; Hingley 1989, fig. 34)	126
3.39	Later Iron Age pottery nos 1–15. Structure B, 1–3; Ditch O, 4–9; other features, 10–15	73	4.10	Frocester Roman villa (Gloucestershire) (after Price 2000a, fig. 5.3)	128
3.40	Roman pottery nos 16–37. Building A, 16; Building B, 17–18; Building C, 19; Ditch DI, 20–22; Hollow-way DC, 23; Ditch W, 24–26; Ditch DZ, 27; Ditch DW, 28–29; post-medieval quarry, 30–37	78	4.11	Cannington in the context of Roman north Somerset	130
			4.12	Stroud Roman villa (Hampshire) (after Williams 1909, plate 1)	133
			4.13	Distribution of Roman villas across South West Britain (research and drawing by David Gould)	134
3.41	Ceramic object and conjectural reconstruction as a spacer bobbin	81			
3.42	Ceramic chimney pot and suggested fitting	82	4.14	Plans of selected villas from Somerset, all redrawn at the same scale (research and drawing by Stephen Armstrong)	136

4.15 Frocester (Gloucestershire) Building E, 5th century or later (after Price 2000a, fig. 6.4) 138
4.16 Poundbury (Dorset) Structure PR2a, 5th–6th century (after Sparey Green 1987, fig. 55) 139
4.17 Poundbury (Dorset) Structure PR3, 5th–6th century (after Sparey Green 1987, fig. 56) 139
4.18 The early folk territory between the Quantock Hills and Parrett Estuary (research and drawing by Stephen Rippon) 141

List of Tables

2.1	The Trevisker-related pottery assemblage from Rodway Enclosure; sherd numbers and weight (g) by contexts and fabrics	15
2.2	The lithics assemblage	22
2.3	Charred plant identifications from Rodway Enclosure	23
2.4	Middle Bronze Age charcoal from Rodway and Sandy Lane	26
2.5	Bronze Age radiocarbon dating results	28
3.1	Radiocarbon dating results from Sandy Lane	64
3.2	Results of the model shown in Figure 3.37. The highest posterior density intervals are rounded outwards to five years	67
3.3	An ordering of dates for deposits in pits inside the villa gallery derived from the model shown in Figure 3.37	68
3.4	Iron Age type pottery. Fabric codes and summary quantification	69
3.5	Roman pottery. Fabric codes and summary quantification	71
3.6	Late prehistoric stratified pottery summary by feature group. Quantities as number of sherds (NOSH)	72
3.7	Roman stratified pottery summary by feature group. Quantities as number of sherds (NOSH)	76
3.8	South-east Dorset Black-burnished ware. Summary showing form incidence by period	77
3.9	Forms summary and comparisons with sites in area	79
3.10	Overall ceramic building material (CBM) quantification by form	80
3.11	Painted wall plaster type series	84
3.12	Painted wall plaster quantification of types by fragment count and estimated surface area	85
3.13	Painted wall plaster quantification by context by count, weight and estimated surface area	85
3.14	Stone catalogue	87
3.15	Metalwork catalogue	90
3.16	Charred plant identifications from Sandy Lane: Late Iron Age–Roman Transition features	94
3.17	Charred plant identifications from Sandy Lane: Roman and post-Roman features	95
3.18	Late Iron Age/Early Roman and Roman charcoal identifications	100
3.19	Charcoal identifications from early medieval features	102
3.20	Summary counts of the identified animal bone elements/fragments (NISP)	104
3.21	Summary counts of numbers of loose animal teeth	105
3.22	Associated/articulating bone groups	105
3.23	Ages of the sheep mandibles (after Payne 1973)	106
3.24	Spatial distributions of the skeletal remains of small vertebrates	107
3.25	Percentage frequencies of the cattle, sheep/goat and pig remains based on NISP data	109
4.1	Quantity of object types by settlement category expressed as mean number of objects per hectare of excavation	131

Acknowledgements

Cotswold Archaeology would like to thank EDF Energy for funding and supporting the fieldwork and post-excavation work through their consultants, AMEC (now Wood PLC). Thanks are particularly due to Rebecca Calder, Planning Manager and Andy Gibbon, Construction Lead (both EDF) and Sean Steadman and Neil Wright (both AMEC). The work at all stages was encouraged and monitored by Steven Membery Senior Historic Environment Officer with South West Heritage Trust, acting on behalf of Somerset County Council, who provided valuable insights throughout the duration of the project. Bob Croft, Historic Environment and Estates Manager, South West Heritage Trust, led public outreach for the project, supported by Rachel Bellamy, Marc Cox and Jane Hill of the South West Heritage Trust.

Many field and post-excavation staff members of Cotswold Archaeology contributed to the project's success and all are thanked for their assistance. Particular thanks go to Richard Young and Kelly Saunders who respectively managed and supervised the evaluation stages; Richard Young also managed the excavation fieldwork and Mark Brett directed the excavations, with the assistance of supervisors Charlotte Haines, Sian Reynish, Steve Sheldon and Tom Weavill. Geomatics was undertaken by Anthony Beechey. The finds, sample and archive processing was directed by Hazel O'Neill and the post-excavation analysis was undertaken by Jonathan Hart with management by Andrew Mudd. Cleaning, stabilisation and x-rays of the metal finds was undertaken by Karen Barker, Antiquities Conservation Service. Ancient DNA analysis on the infant skeletons was undertaken by Konstantina Drosou and Terry Brown of the Manchester Institute of Biotechnology.

The publication illustrations are by Aleksandra Osinska with a contribution by Jane Read (prehistoric pottery). Social media releases and video presentations of the excavations and associated outreach have been compiled and managed on Cotswold Archaeology's Facebook and YouTube pages by Rosanna Price. The South West Heritage Trust would like to thank Alyn Jones and Andy Coupe of Somerset County Council for their support, and also thank Justin Owen for his work on the archaeological films that captured an important phase of the fieldwork. Thanks also to David Eccles of EDF and his communications team for help with outreach and the open day.

The draft publication text was reviewed and edited by Martin Watts, Head of Publications at Cotswold Archaeology, and was academically reviewed by Stephen Rippon of the University of Exeter. Particular thanks are due to Stephen Rippon and colleagues for their additional research into the geography of Roman and early medieval Cannington and its region. The inclusion of this work here has made a significant contribution to the context of the archaeological discoveries. Rachel Tyson undertook the copy editing.

The authors contributing to the publication are individually acknowledged in this volume.

Preface

EDF Energy welcomes the publication of the first archaeological report compiled by Cotswold Archaeology covering the sites found during the construction of the Cannington bypass. The archaeological discoveries were carefully recorded and investigated, and this volume provides a valuable record of this detailed analysis and research.

Further volumes on the archaeological work at Hinkley Point C are planned and they will be published in the next few years. EDF Energy is delighted to have been associated with the production of this report and the archaeological programme, coordinated by Somerset County Council, the South West Heritage Trust and Cotswold Archaeology, because we see our stewardship of the Hinkley Point C sites as being but a fragment of a story spanning thousands of years.

Nigel Cann, Delivery Director HPC, EDF Energy

Foreword by Bob Croft FSA MCIFA
South West Heritage Trust

This volume pulls together all the archaeological work on the route of the Cannington bypass, which took place over a five-year period from 2009 through to 2014. As part of the development proposals linked to the construction of the Hinkley Point C nuclear power station EDF Energy funded the construction of a new road to take traffic away from the middle of Cannington village. This road runs for 1.6km on the west side of the village close to several known archaeological sites, notably the famous Cannington Dark Age cemetery excavated by Philip Rahtz and others in 1962-63.

Cotswold Archaeology, in collaboration with archaeologists from AMEC and Somerset County Council, delivered an extensive programme of investigation and recording through this project. The team of field archaeologists worked through several seasons, coping with weather conditions ranging from snow-filled trenches in the winter of 2010 through to dry and dusty conditions in the summer of 2014.

The now well-established process of desk-based assessments, geophysical surveys, trial trenches and three set-piece excavations revealed a range of archaeological sites along the line of the bypass dating from the Bronze Age, Iron Age and Roman periods through to medieval times. The Bronze Age site at Rodway was an unusual find and has added to the map of Bronze Age Somerset.

One of the key sites found, just off Sandy Lane, was an Iron Age farm that was later occupied by several stone-founded buildings — part of a Roman villa complex. Much of this one-time substantial Roman building had been robbed away in medieval and later periods. The remains of an underfloor heating system did survive and, along with evidence of painted wall plaster, provided some evidence of the quality of the building that once occupied this site. As part of the final phase of recording several of the Red Sandstone walls were salvaged and subsequently built into a replica Roman dining room at the Avalon Marshes Centre, Westhay, near Shapwick.

A programme of outreach work and filming, along with a public open day ensured that the archaeological story from the Cannington bypass was captured and presented to the public. This report now presents that information in a detailed report that can be used by local people and researchers for many years to come.

Summary

This report presents the results of excavations on two archaeological sites undertaken in 2014 in advance of the construction of a bypass road around Cannington in Somerset. The road formed part of enabling works connected with the development of the new nuclear power station at Hinkley Point C by EDF Energy. The route is 1.6km (1 mile) long skirting the north-west side of the village.

At the northern end of the route, near Rodway, was found a Middle Bronze Age settlement defined by a ditch enclosing groups of pits and postholes interpreted as the remains of two roundhouses. Features yielded Trevisker-related pottery and charred plant remains with few other finds of note. The site is similar to small farmsteads of this date more commonly found further east, with examples from Cranborne Chase and the South Downs.

In the central part of the route, straddling Sandy Lane, was discovered an enclosed ridge-top settlement with its origins in the 1st century BC, and evidence of circular or crescent-shaped buildings. In the Roman period the settlement developed into a villa complex and, although the site had been truncated by post-medieval quarrying, the remains of three stone-founded buildings of different forms were identified. The main villa residence showed an arrangement of rooms either side of a corridor containing a line of four infant burials and deposits of sheep bones. To the north stood a building showing several phases of construction and an inserted hypocaust, which may have been a bath-house or for agricultural use. Nearby, the third building with a pitched stone floor to one side was probably a barn.

Pottery, ceramic building material and animal bones were plentiful, although coins, metalwork and exotic finds were rare and, notwithstanding a small quantity of painted wall plaster, the settlement was not a grand one compared with other villas. It was abandoned by the fourth century AD. Within the context of Roman Somerset and the South West the villa is shown to have been somewhat peripheral. Discussion of the findings suggest that the material remains are not altogether typical of sites classed as villas and much of the architecture of the complex may have been concerned with agricultural production and storage rather than the trappings of Roman culture.

In the early medieval period the site was reoccupied. There were no associated artefacts but there was slight evidence of a timber building whose date and form, while difficult to resolve, are not untypical of evidence from the post-Roman West Country. Discussion is brought to bear on the importance of Cannington as an early medieval centre, known for its large Roman and post-Roman cemetery, which had become a royal estate by the 8th century, and was probably the centre of an early folk territory at this time.

Chapter 1
Introduction

The village of Cannington in the district of Sedgemoor, Somerset, is nationally well-known in archaeological circles as the location of a major cemetery in use from at least Late Roman times until the 7th or 8th centuries, and is indeed something of a type-site for cemeteries of this period. The cemetery, which was at Cannington Park Quarry, was the subject of intermittent excavations of one sort or another over the past 100 years and more, which are now concluded as the site has been completely lost to stone extraction. The most recent and largest excavations, undertaken in 1962 and 1963, were published as a major monograph by the Society for the Promotion of Roman Studies, a work that included an assessment of many of the earlier findings (Rahtz *et al.* 2000).

Not far away, the recent construction of a bypass around Cannington was undertaken by EDF Energy as part of their wider infrastructure works associated with the construction of the new nuclear power station at Hinkley Point C. This new development afforded archaeologists a rare opportunity to investigate a large slice of land which approached within 300m of the former cemetery and lies almost as close to other sites of historical importance, including the Iron Age hillfort at Cannington Camp to the north-west, and the village Cannington itself, which was the centre of a royal estate by the 9th century and probably earlier (Rippon 1997, 133; Costen 2011, 58–9). Apart from stone quarrying at Cannington Park and at Castle Hill Quarry further north, the area has seen relatively little commercial development and in recent times there has been little opportunity for development-led archaeological investigation until the work reported on here.

Project background

EDF Energy undertook to build a bypass on land west of Cannington (centred on National Grid Reference 32511400; Fig. 1.1) as part of a scheme of road improvements associated with the construction of the new nuclear power station at Hinkley Point C. The bypass route is 1.6km long and was opened to traffic in December 2015.

Archaeological investigations of the bypass and environs began in July 2009 when AMEC, the archaeological advisor to EDF Energy, was commissioned to undertake an assessment of the cultural heritage on behalf of EDF Energy (AMEC 2010). This assessment identified the known archaeological sites along the route, and those within 500m of it, and was used as a baseline for identifying the archaeological potential of the proposed bypass construction works and the consequent need for mitigation strategies. A geophysical survey of the route in January 2010 identified a number of anomalies of possible archaeological origin (Stratascan 2010) and these were included in the Cultural Heritage Assessment (AMEC 2010). From November 2010 to January 2011 a trial trench evaluation by Cotswold Archaeology targeted the geophysical anomalies, as well as testing blank areas as a control on the geophysical survey results (CA 2011).

Based on these preliminary works, three archaeological sites were identified lying within the footprint of the proposed bypass. Since none were deemed of such significance so as to require preservation *in situ,* and all would be destroyed by the groundworks, it was agreed with Steven Membery, Senior Historic Environment Officer, Somerset County Council Historic Environment Service (SCCHES), that 'preservation by record' would be an appropriate mitigation strategy. Following this, EDF Energy commissioned AMEC to produce a *Written Scheme of Investigation* for three set-piece excavations (SPEs 1–3) targeted on the three areas of archaeological interest (AMEC 2011). SPE 1 lay at the northern end of the route at Rodway and was the site of an enclosure and associated features of Middle Bronze Age date. SPE 2 in the centre of the route, straddling Sandy Lane, contained ditches and buildings of a Roman villa with Late Iron Age antecedents. These sites form the main subject of this report. SPE 3 contained

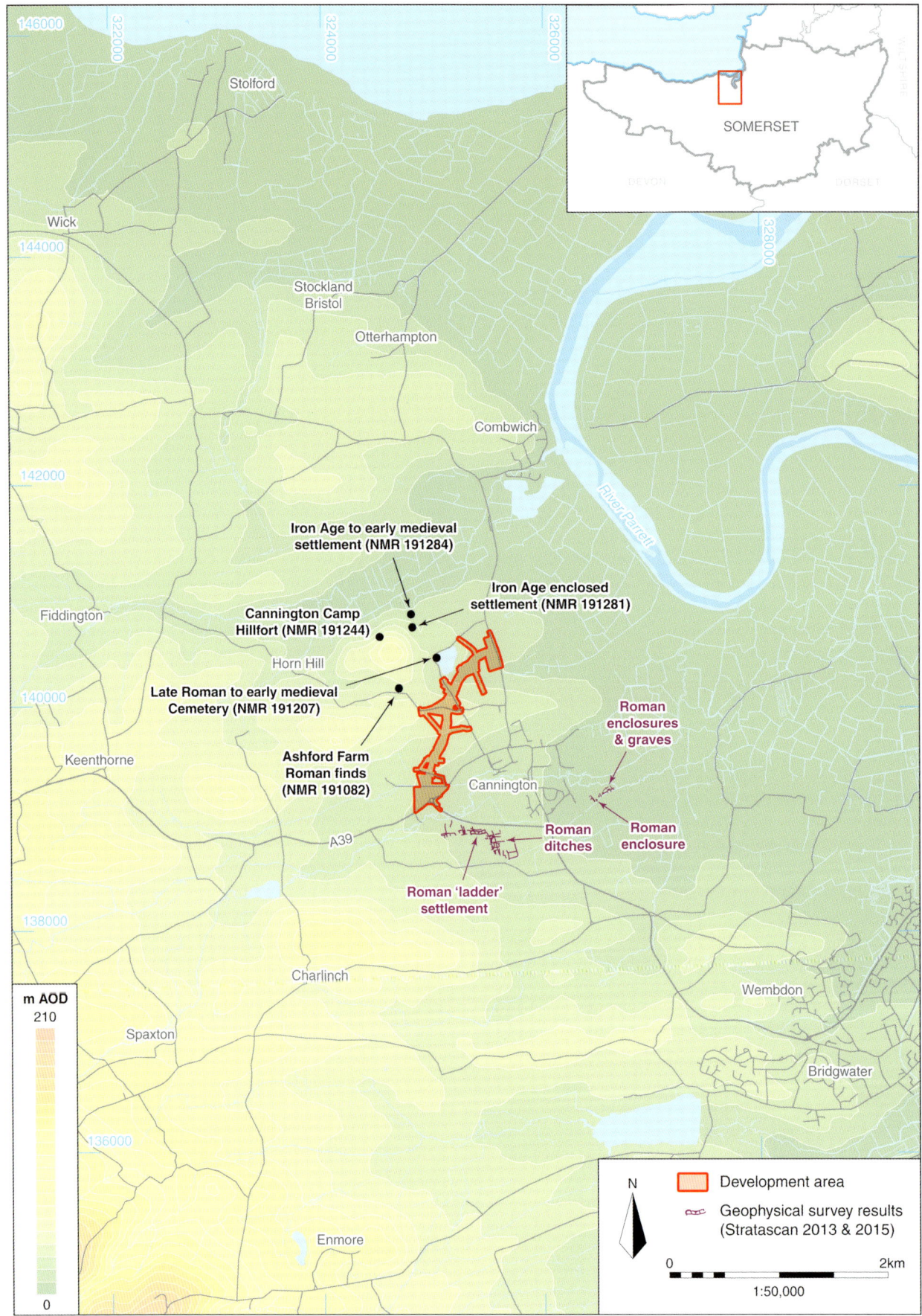

Fig. 1.1 The development area in its topographic context, with selected nearby archaeological sites

a medieval hollow-way which, while of value for the history of the landscape of the area, is a very small part of a much wider topic and is judged not to warrant publication here.

The excavations were undertaken by Cotswold Archaeology between June and November 2014 at the request of AMEC on behalf of EDF Energy. The archaeological work was completed ahead of road construction without any significant effects on the construction programme. Following fieldwork, the archaeological results were assessed by Cotswold Archaeology (CA 2016a) and this was followed by an Updated Project Design (CA 2016b) which together summarised the archaeological results and set out a methodology for bringing them to wider public and academic attention through publication in this monograph. This methodology was agreed with Steven Membery and with AMEC acting on behalf of EDF Energy.

The archaeological fieldwork and this publication form part of a wider programme of fieldwork and reporting being undertaken by Cotswold Archaeology in connection with the development of Hinkley Point C, and this is to be the subject of future publications.

Location, topography and geology

The bypass runs along the western side of Cannington village. Cannington itself occupies an elevation on the eastern fringe of the Quantocks, overlooking the River Parrett and its floodplain to the east (Figs 1.1 and 1.2). The village lies at 20–40m OD adjacent to Cannington Brook, while the Parrett floodplain, here lying at around 6m OD, forms part of the Somerset Levels, which is the second most extensive area of wetland in England. The bypass itself climbs from 20m OD at its southern end to a little over 30m at Sandy Lane, and then falls away to the north to 14m OD at Rodway.

The area has a largely rural character. Local settlements occupy the higher ground above the floodplain and consist of scattered farms and a number of villages, including Cannington. Today, the high ground, including that traversed by the bypass, is primarily used for arable farming while the river floodplain is characterised by pasture.

The underlying geology beneath the southern, higher, end of the route, comprises Triassic deposits of the Mercia Mudstone Group, laid down 251–200 million years ago (Fig. 1.3; BGS 2017). At the centre of the route, an older band of the Carboniferous Rodway Siltstone Formation runs more or less parallel to Sandy Lane. This formation comprises siltstone and limestone deposits laid down 315–313 million years ago. A parallel band of younger rocks runs to the immediate north, comprising sandstone of the Triassic Otter Sandstone Formation laid down 246–229 million years ago. Both of these parallel bands form the substrate beneath SPE 2. The route then skirts the south-eastern edge of an outcrop of the Carboniferous Limestone Supergroup, the site of modern quarrying at Cannington Park and at Castle Hill adjacent to Cannington Camp. The Carboniferous Limestone here is recorded as containing secondary quartz as well as barytes veins, some of which contain small amounts of copper ore (Anderson 2000). The northern end of the route lies on Triassic deposits of the Mercia Mudstone Group, which, where the level of the route falls away at the edge of the Quantocks, are overlain by Quaternary River Terrace deposits of sand and gravel associated with the River Parrett.

Archaeological background

The archaeological context of excavations is detailed below. The information comes from the Cultural Heritage Assessment (AMEC 2010), comprising a study area of sites within *c.* 500m of the bypass, and published

Fig. 1.2 Landscape setting looking north-east from the Sandy Lane site across the Parrett Valley

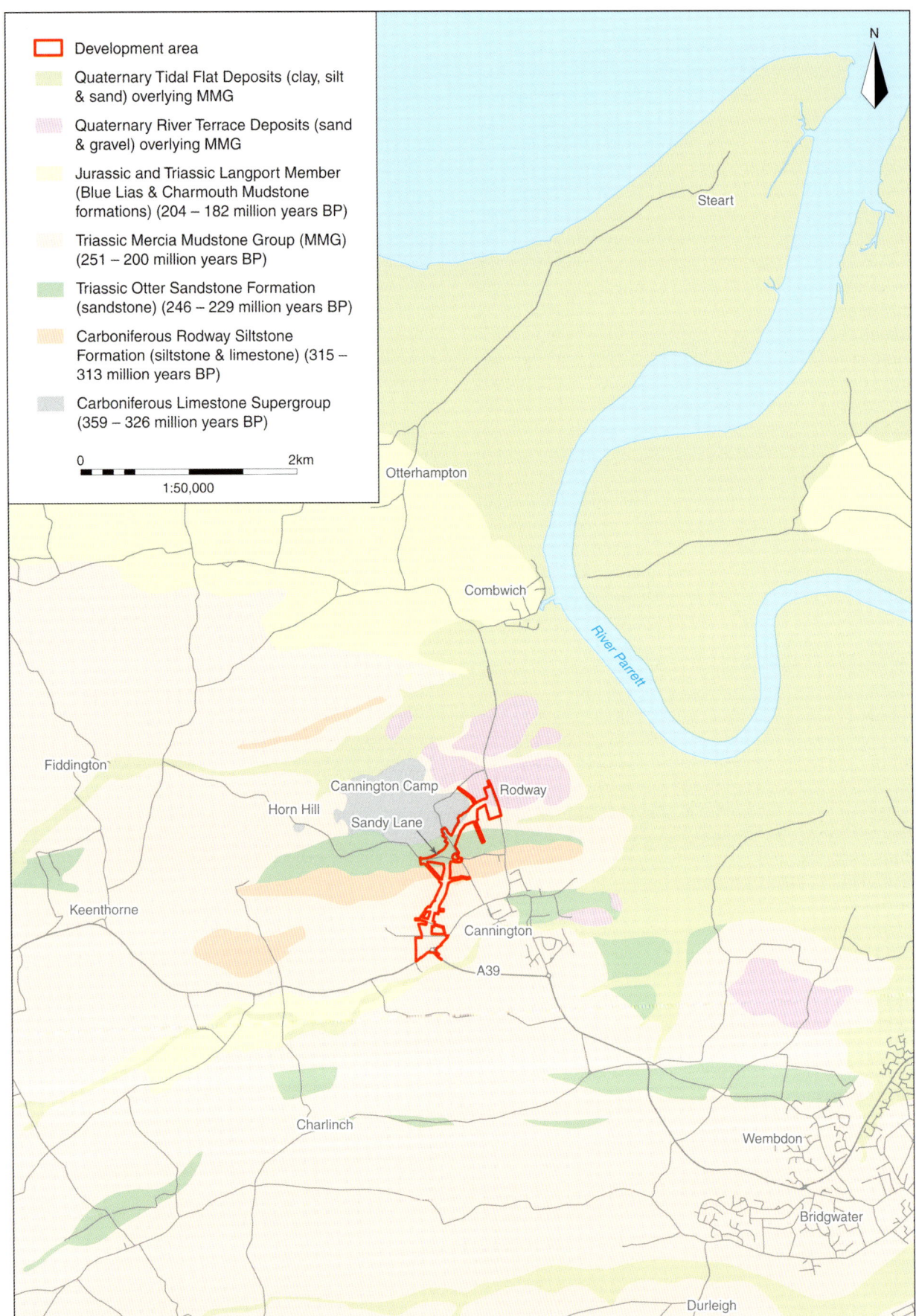

Fig. 1.3 Simplified geology map of the development area and environs (contains British Geological Survey materials ©NERC 2018)

sources. Sites listed in the National Monuments Record (NMR) are referenced below with their NMR number and those detailed in the Somerset Historic Environment Record (SHER) are also referenced with their SHER number.

Rich collections of fauna came from caves at both Cannington Park Quarry and Castle Hill Quarry, recovered during stone extraction (Rahtz *et al.* 2000, 20). It is possible that Cannington Park Cave contained Pleistocene fauna; mineralised bones of lion and bear in features from the much later cemetery may support this suggestion (ibid.). Human remains from this cave amounted to around seven individuals and include some reported as 'of *Homo erectus* affinity', but the age and derivation of this material is unsubstantiated and it is considered possible that all derived from the cemetery above (ibid.). To date, therefore, no unequivocally Palaeolithic finds have been made in the locality. The earliest finds date to the Mesolithic period (between 9000 and 4000 BC) and consist entirely of scatters of flintwork. At this time the retreat of the ice sheets led to rising sea levels which inundated much of the Levels. The higher ground, including that around Cannington, was gradually colonised by woodland and associated fauna which, along with the water, would have provided a range of resources for hunter-gatherer groups, whose traces include scatters of Mesolithic flint flakes and blades in Cannington Park, now in Taunton Museum (NMR 191299). The claim that Cannington Park Cave was occupied during the Mesolithic is unverified and the site was de-scheduled in the 1970s following an exploration by the University of Bristol Speleological Society (NMR 191292; SHER 103101). Uncertainty also exists about the provenance of a group of Mesolithic flints found near Brymore School in the centre of Cannington (NMR 191073; SHER 10296). Material of this date is attested from the region more generally (Rahtz *et al.* 2000, 394). Evidence from the Neolithic period, *c.* 4000–2400 BC, has not been recognised in the local area except as a small number of diagnostic pottery sherds and flint artefacts from Cannington Park Quarry (ibid., 394). There was also Bronze Age (*c.* 2400–700 BC) pottery from Cannington Park Quarry, including complete Beakers and numerous sherds of Biconical Urn, which may suggest the site of a prehistoric barrow or cemetery here (ibid., 394). Elsewhere, reported finds are restricted to a tanged bronze knife (NMR 191293; SHER 16250) found at Cannington Camp.

It is from the later prehistoric period (*c.* 700 BC to AD 43) that archaeological remains become more widely attested. The most prominent of these is the Iron Age hillfort known as Cannington Camp or Cynwit Castle (NMR 191244; SHER 10439; Fig. 1.4). This Scheduled Monument occupies a limestone outcrop 0.6km northwest of the bypass and survives as a rock-cut ditch with an internal bank. Limited excavations in 1905, 1913 and 1963 recovered prehistoric finds, including Iron Age pottery. A circular Iron Age enclosure north of the hillfort was first identified as a cropmark and was partially excavated in 1963, when it was shown to be defined by a shallow rock-cut palisade (NMR 191281; SHER 10302 and 28899; Fig. 1.1). The interior of the enclosure was not investigated and the entire site has subsequently been quarried away, so it is uncertain whether or not this was a settlement (Rahtz 1969, 60). Unexcavated earthworks on the south side of the hillfort are preserved in the scheduled area and seem to consist of rectangular houses and the remains of fields and lynchets, although whether these are prehistoric, Roman or medieval is uncertain (NMR 191284; SHER 10444).

The 1963 excavations at Cannington Camp identified evidence for occupation during the Roman period in the form of a layer and a possible structure, as well as Roman pottery (Rahtz 1969). Roman burials excavated at Cannington Park Quarry are generally late, but earlier ones cannot be ruled out and the concentration of Roman finds may indicate some other form of occupation here as well (Rahtz *et al.* 2000, 398). A circular temple or mortuary enclosure occupied the summit (ibid., 50–1). Further Roman settlements are suggested by concentrations of Late Roman pottery found west of the bypass at Ashford Farm (NMR 191082; Fig. 1.1), while on low ground south of Cannington a spread of Roman enclosures and associated features, discovered in connection with the Cannington Flood Alleviation Scheme, would appear to represent the margins of extensive settlement (CA 2018) (Fig. 1.1). The Roman settlement at Combwich, 2km north-east of the bypass, may have been a port although this is uncertain and it may have simply been a river crossing. Roman levels lie beneath 1.3–1.5m of alluvium (Rahtz *et al.* 2000, 21–2). The River Parrett was navigable in Roman times and featured a transhipment port at Crandon Bridge, located 5.5km east of the bypass on a former course of the Parrett and linked to the town at Ilchester by a road along the Polden Hills (Rippon 2008a, 90). Ilchester lies 36km south-east of the bypass. Its hinterland contained a dense network of villas, but Cannington lies on the western edge of the 'villa belt' that ran through southern Britain (Allen and Smith 2016, 33–7 and figs 2.19, 2.21).

The cemetery at Cannington Park Quarry is thought to have been used between *c.* AD 350 and 800, although only a small fraction of it was excavated to modern standards and much remains uncertain (Rahtz *et al.* 2000; NMR 191207; SHER 10503; Figs 1.1, 1.5). The excavations in 1962–3 recorded over 500 individuals, with the original cemetery population a matter of speculation but estimated to have been between around 1500 and 5000 (Rahtz *et al.* 2000, 401, 420) depending upon the assumed density of graves across the site. The continued use of the cemetery following the end of the Roman administration in Britain supports the suggestion made by Rippon (2006a, 62) of a degree of

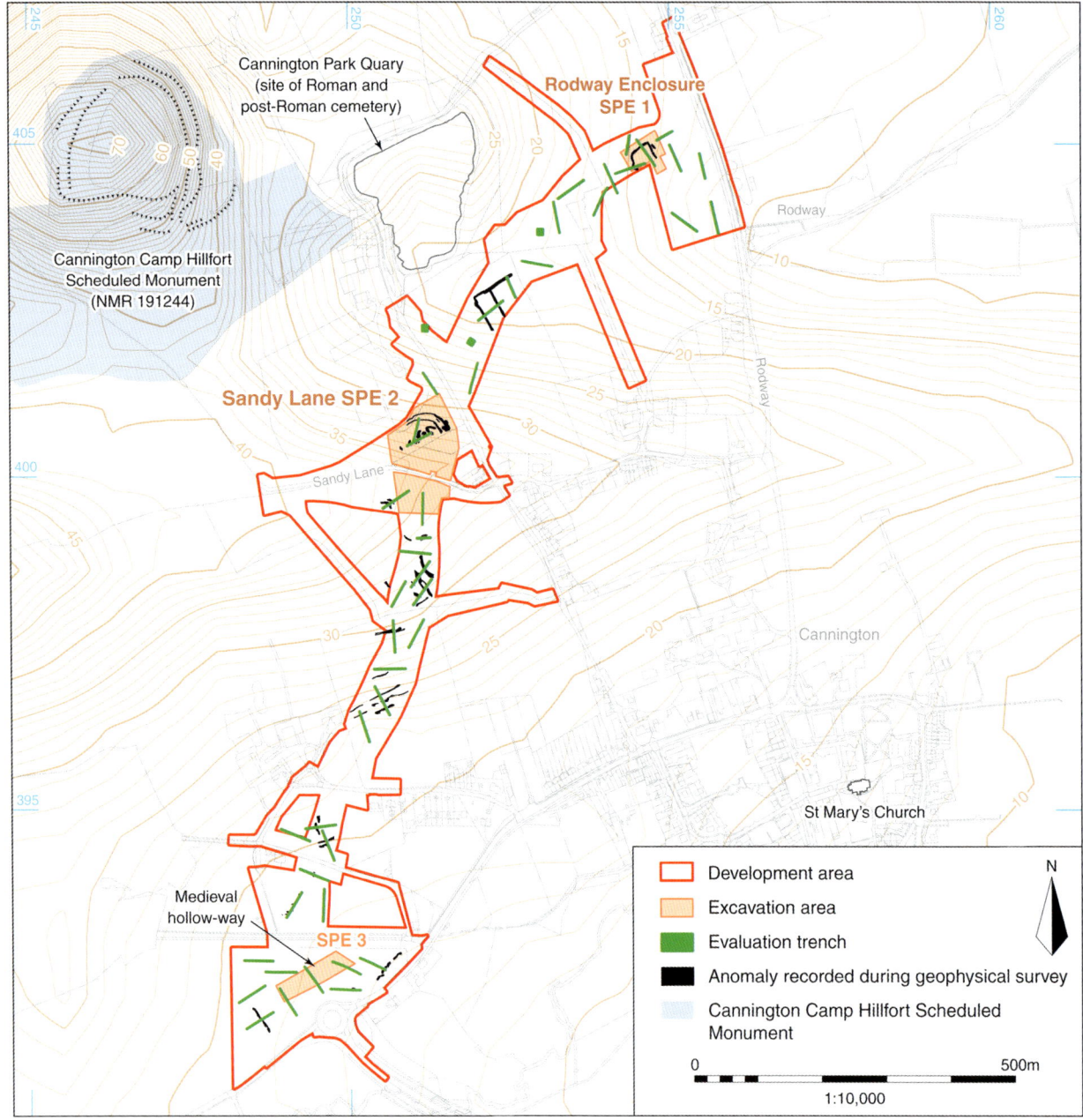

Fig. 1.4 Archaeological investigations within the bypass footprint

continuity in the rural settlement of South West Britain into the 6th and 7th centuries. The presence of such an extensive cemetery suggested that it served a number of early medieval settlements in the area, although none have been securely identified.

Documentary evidence indicates that Cannington was politically important in post-Roman times, although, with the exception of the cemetery, there is almost nothing by way of supporting archaeological information. The earliest form of its name is *Cantūctūn* ('Quantock Town', possibly referring to its location at the 'gateway' to the Quantocks) and is first mentioned in *c*. AD 900 in King Alfred's will as a royal possession which he left to his son Edward. This probably implies that it was a royal estate at least as early as the 8th century (Rahtz *et al*. 2000, 23 and references; Rippon 1997, 133; Costen 2011, 58–60). The early medieval territory associated with Cannington is further explored by Rippon in Chapter 4 of this volume.

A Saxon military road (or *herepath*) is believed to have crossed the Parrett at Combwich, the location of the Roman settlement, leading from there to pass to the south of Cannington Camp, although, if it existed, its precise route is uncertain. Cannington Camp is associated with a battle in AD 878 in which a Danish force besieged an earthwork (*Arx Cynwit*) but were repelled by the

Fig. 1.5 The Sandy Lane site after topsoil removal, looking north-east with Cannington Park Quarry to the left

English levies led by Odda, Eolderman of Devon. The name Cynwit Castle is often used as an alternative name for the hillfort. The identification was apparently based on the similarity between the names Cynwit and Combwich, with an assumption that the graves on the nearby hill were battle victims (Rahtz 1969, 58) and so the association must be considered unreliable. There are a number of other possible contenders for the site (HER 10439), and there is currently no suggestion of 9th-century occupation in the hillfort. The medieval and later landscape has had a largely rural character, as it does today. Of greatest significance for the archaeology is the exploitation of the local geology for construction materials, which means that several areas in the locality, including land on the present site north of Sandy Lane, have been affected by quarrying for building stone and lime.

Methods and standards

The three set-piece excavations together amounted to 1.6ha: SPE 1 was 0.23ha; SPE 2 was 0.95ha; and SPE 3 was 0.42ha. The excavations were undertaken in accordance with the *Written Scheme of Investigation* (AMEC 2011), Cotswold Archaeology's technical manuals, and the appropriate professional standards including the Chartered Institute for Archaeologists' *Standards and Guidance for Archaeological Excavation* and *Code of Conduct* (2008), and Somerset County Council's *Heritage Service Archaeological Handbook* (2008). Soil sampling for palaeo-environmental remains and their subsequent treatment followed English Heritage guidelines (English Heritage 2002). All fieldwork was undertaken by staff of Cotswold Archaeology and monitored by AMEC and Steven Membery (SCCHES).

Fieldwork commenced with the removal of topsoil and subsoil deposits from the excavation areas using a mechanical excavator equipped with a toothless grading bucket, under archaeological direction. The archaeological features thus exposed were hand-excavated to the bottom of archaeological stratigraphy based on the following sampling levels: a minimum of 10% by length of all linear features, including key intersections to investigate stratigraphic relationships, and sections located at all ditch terminals; discrete features, such as postholes and pits less than 1m in diameter were at least half-sectioned (50% by area); discrete features greater than 1m in diameter were excavated to at least 25% of their surface area; structural remains and burials were 100% excavated. The extensive quarry pits at Sandy Lane were not treated as archaeological features; they were selectively hand- and machine-excavated to establish their limits and retrieve indicative dating evidence. Survey was undertaken electronically using a Leica Viva GPS. Building foundations and other stonework was recorded by georectified photography.

All radiocarbon dating was undertaken by Scottish Universities Environmental Research Centre and calibrated to the current internationally agreed standard (IntCal13; Reimer *et al.* 2013). Dates are quoted to the 2-sigma calibrated range (95%) unless otherwise stated. Bayesian modelling was undertaken for the group of infant and associated burials at Sandy Lane and the modelled dates (respecting convention) are italicised; they are also rounded out to the nearest five years.

The archaeological archive, comprising finds and records, is to be deposited for long-term curation with Somerset County Museums Service (SCMS Accession no. TTNCM 4/2010) subject to the implementation of the SCMS retention policy. The digital archive is to be deposited with the Archaeology Data Service (University of York) in line with best practice (CIfA 2014).

Results summary and structure of report

The results from Rodway (SPE 1) and Sandy Lane (SPE 2) are presented in Chapters 2 and 3 respectively, within which reports detailing the artefactual, ecofactual and dating evidence are also presented. Chapter 4 presents a discussion of the results and places them within their wider context. Details of the findings from SPE 3 are to be found in the Assessment Report (CA 2016a), available via the Cotswold Archaeology website Archaeological Reports Online.

At Rodway a Middle Bronze Age enclosure contained two posthole structures and a number of pits. The remains were associated with Trevisker-style Middle Bronze Age pottery and radiocarbon determinations in the mid to late second millennium BC. A single tree-throw hole yielded a radiocarbon date falling within the Early Bronze Age. A Bronze Age trough at Sandy Lane was without artefacts but was dated by radiocarbon to the mid second millennium BC and was therefore possibly contemporary with the Rodway Enclosure.

The majority of the remains at Sandy Lane related to an enclosed settlement dating to the Late Iron Age and Roman periods. The settlement had been truncated by post-medieval quarry pits but in the Late Iron Age included enclosure ditches surrounding distinct areas of activity, the best preserved of which comprised three curvilinear structures, perhaps crescent-shaped buildings. Possible rectangular buildings were also present. Occupation was continuous into the Roman period, when the settlement took on a Romanised appearance, including the provision of stone-founded buildings, evidence for underfloor heating, stone and ceramic roofing, and painted plaster. The complex included a recognisable villa residence, a probable barn and a bath-house and/or additional residence. A series of special deposits within the villa corridor included burials of neonatal infants, sheep and lambs, and other placed deposits. Although the settlement was of villa form, the material assemblage lacked many Roman-style cultural markers and was in many ways more characteristic of a non-villa rural farmstead. A mixed agricultural basis to the settlement is implied throughout its existence, and it is suggested that the uptake of Roman culture followed particularly local rural agenda. The site is located towards the margin of the distribution of villas in the region but there were strong links to the Dorset pottery production area. It is possible that contacts extended across the Severn Estuary via the River Parrett with riverside local centres nearby at Combwich and a little further away at Crandon Bridge. The finds and radiocarbon dates from the villa site indicate abandonment by the 4th century AD. Post-Roman reoccupation is indicated and there are traces of a timber building dating to perhaps the 7th/8th centuries, although this evidence is very fragmentary.

Chapter 2
A Middle Bronze Age Enclosure at Rodway and other Bronze Age Features

Introduction

Archaeological remains at Rodway were first identified by the geophysical survey, which recorded a sub-rectangular enclosure (Stratascan 2010; Fig. 1.4). Subsequent trial trenching confirmed that this was an archaeological feature, probably of Bronze Age date, and that further remains were concentrated within the enclosure itself (CA 2011). Consequently, the enclosure was selected for recording within one of the set-piece excavations, SPE 1. The enclosure lay at approximately 14.4m OD on a broad plateau that forms a palaeo-terrace of the River Parrett (Fig. 1.3). To the east, the enclosure site overlooks the broad valley of the river, with the current flow some 1.7km to the north-east (Fig. 1.1). Westwards, the plateau continues for some 0.5km before ascending higher ground outlying the Quantocks. The enclosure lies on a substrate of sand and gravel river terrace deposits overlying the Triassic Mercia Mudstone Group (BGS 2017; (Fig. 1.3).

The majority of the enclosure lay within the footprint of the proposed bypass, and a rectangular area 58m by 34m in extent was excavated around the enclosure, including a buffer area around its western, northern and eastern sides, to test for the presence or absence of archaeological remains outside the enclosure. The southernmost edge of the enclosure was outside the footprint of the bypass, but its alignment was confirmed within three small test pits, each of which identified the inner edge of the enclosure ditch, and within an extension to the excavation area at the enclosure's south-eastern corner (Figs 2.1 and 2.2).

Fig. 2.1   Rodway Middle Bronze Age enclosure, looking south-west

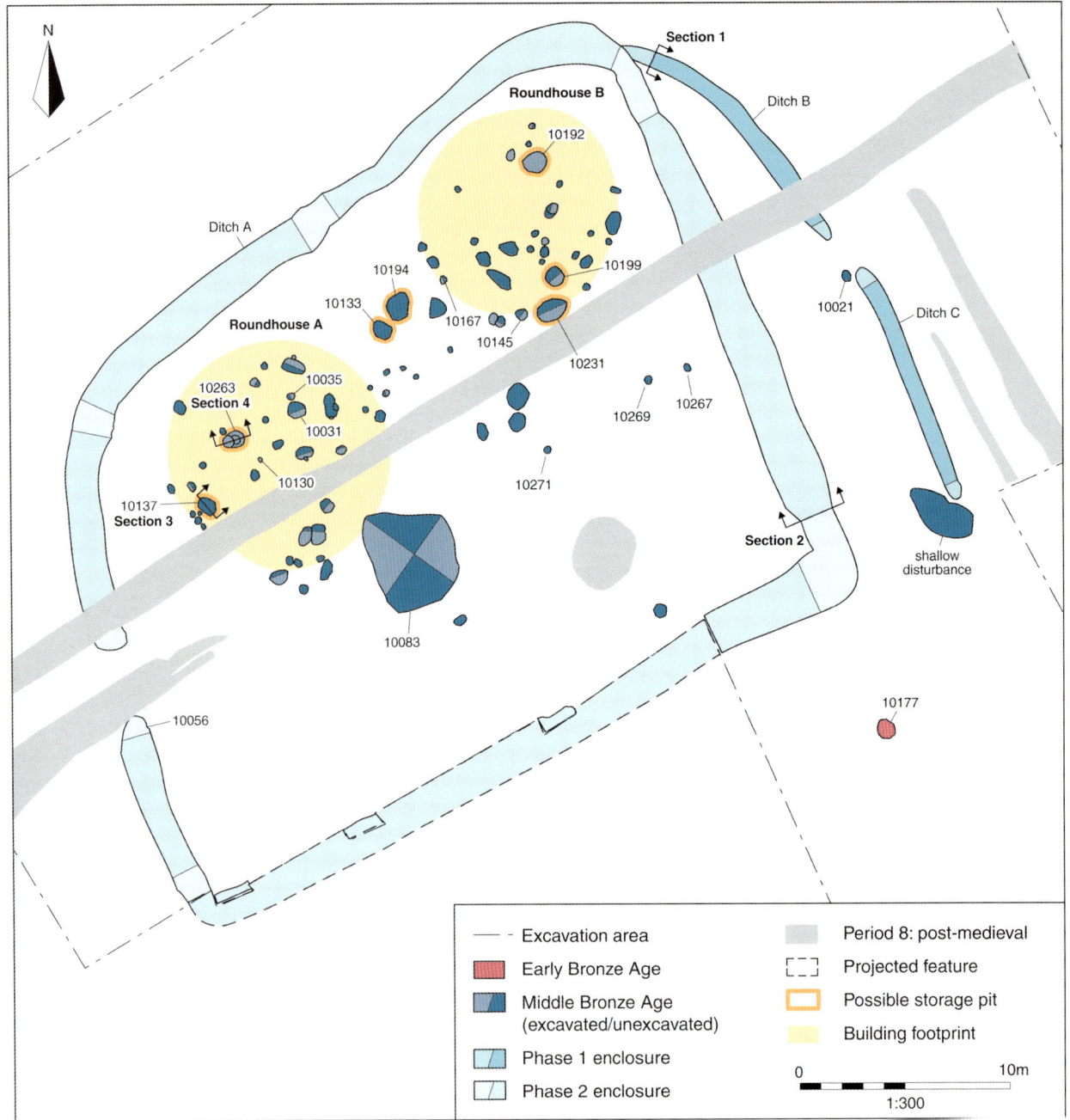

Fig. 2.2 Rodway Middle Bronze Age enclosure: plan of archaeological features

Excavation confirmed that the majority of the features were of Bronze Age date and were contained within the enclosure. Later remains comprised paired ditches which would have flanked hedge-bank boundaries. These were largely unexcavated, but the north/south-aligned boundary was associated with 16th to 17th-century pottery and may correlate to a boundary depicted on the 1st Edition 1:2500 Ordnance Survey map of 1889. Together, these field boundaries probably defined one corner of a rectilinear field, and a circular feature between the two, identified as post-medieval during the excavation on the basis of having been cut through the subsoil, was possibly an infilled water-hole or pond.

At Sandy Lane (SPE 2) there was just one feature identified as Bronze Age (a rectangular pit containing burnt stones) and dating was only confirmed by radiocarbon dating since it was without artefacts (see Fig. 3.10). It lay to the south of the Roman villa and does not seem to have had any associated features.

The Rodway Enclosure
Jonathan Hart

Early Bronze Age (1800–1600 BC)
A single feature, 10177, was found to the south-east of the enclosure (Fig. 2.2). This was a somewhat irregular

cut up to 1m wide and 0.2m deep and was perhaps a tree-throw hole, although it might have been a pit with edges disturbed by roots. It contained two sandy silt/silty clay fills, both of which produced charred hazelnut shells. One fragment was radiocarbon dated to 1885–1696 cal. BC (SUERC-69950; Fig. 2.5; Table 2.5). A grain of wheat was also identified (Table 2.3). A flint flake and two flint chips from the upper fill are not closely dateable.

Middle Bronze Age (1600–1150 BC)

All other prehistoric remains were dated to the Middle Bronze Age, either through the presence of Trevisker-style Middle Bronze Age pottery, or as a result of five radiocarbon determinations, or through spatial relationships with features so dated. These features were focused on the enclosure identified during the preliminary works (Figs 2.1 and 2.2). The enclosure as it survived (Ditch A) seems largely to represent a later phase (Phase 2) following slight remodelling. The enclosure's earliest phase (Phase 1) was only partially recoverable.

Phase 1 enclosure

Ditches B and C formed the easternmost extent of the Phase 1 enclosure. An alternative possibility, that Ditches B and C defined an eastern annexe to the Phase 2 enclosure, seems less likely given that there seems to have been little usable space within this putative annexe, and that the layout in plan is more suggestive of the original eastern edge of an enclosure, the remaining (northern, western and southern) edges of which were superseded by Ditch A of the Phase 2 enclosure. If this is accepted, then the earliest manifestation of the enclosure would have been as a D-shaped space, 38m by 24m in extent and defined by a fairly slight ditch up to 0.75m wide and 0.3m deep, assuming Ditches B and C to have been representative (Fig. 2.3, section 1). Stony deposits within Ditches B and C suggest that the ditch may have been accompanied by a bank which, based on analogy with the later form of the enclosure (see below) would have been internal. A 2m-wide gap between Ditches B and C was partially due to truncation of the latter, slighter ditch, but was opposite a convincing 3m-wide entrance along the western edge of the Phase 2 enclosure, which must also have been present during Phase 1, suggesting that the original enclosure was furnished with opposing entrances. The south-eastern corner of the enclosure was either open to provide a third entrance, or was bounded by a bank or other barrier with no associated ditch. The stony fills of Ditches B and C suggest that the associated bank was deliberately slighted into the ditch prior to the enclosure's remodelling. Finds from the ditches comprised a few Middle Bronze Age pottery sherds from each.

A single posthole, 10021, was found just inside the eastern entrance to the enclosure. This perhaps supported a gatepost, although it is possible that it formed part of a fence-line continuing westwards, with other posts held in postholes 10267, 10269 and 10271. Other features within the enclosure could not be ascribed to a particular phase and are described as part of the Phase 2 enclosure below.

Phase 2 enclosure

The enclosure was reduced to a slightly smaller, more rectangular area, 30m by 24m in extent, defined by Ditch A. The ditch appeared continuous, with the exception of a 3m-wide entrance along its western side, defined by butt-ended ditch terminals. The southern corners of this remodelled enclosure were right angles whereas the northern corners, located close to possible roundhouses (see below), were more rounded, perhaps suggesting that the houses were the primary features around which the enclosure was modelled. The Phase 2 enclosure ditch was notably more substantial than previously, comprising a steep-sided, flat-based cut up to 1.8m wide and 0.65m deep (Fig. 2.3, section 2). There was some evidence for an associated bank; the majority of the fills were stony sandy silt deposits that may have been slighted bank material. Tip lines within these fills, which might have pointed to the former location of the bank, were absent but a dearth of features along the ditch's inner edge may reflect the former presence of an internal bank, up to 2m wide. There was no evidence from the ditch fills for re-cutting along Ditch A, but the stepped profile of its edges observed within some excavated sondages suggested that some re-cutting was undertaken, perhaps along the ditch's inner edge where bank material may have slumped in (Fig. 2.3, section 2). The presence of an upper sandy silt in one section, likely to have accumulated naturally, suggests that the ditch remained visible as an earthwork after the ditch had been largely backfilled and the enclosure presumably abandoned.

Finds from the ditch fills mostly came from the terminals, although the majority of the excavated sections produced several sherds of pottery as well as flints, the latter mainly flakes but with a possible blade also present. In contrast, the only animal bone recovered comprised a few scraps retrieved from soil samples, a paucity that can be for the most part attributed to the acidic soil. The southern terminal yielded a few flint and Greensand flakes and a flint chip, as well as three flint scrapers, 37 sherds of pottery, a little animal bone and a burnt stone. In contrast, flints were absent from the northern terminal, but which produced 86 sherds of pottery.

Features within the enclosure

Pits and postholes within the enclosure lay almost entirely to the north of its long central axis. None could be assigned to a particular phase of the enclosure, although all were probably contemporary with it. These internal features included two concentrations of postholes, in the north-eastern and north-western

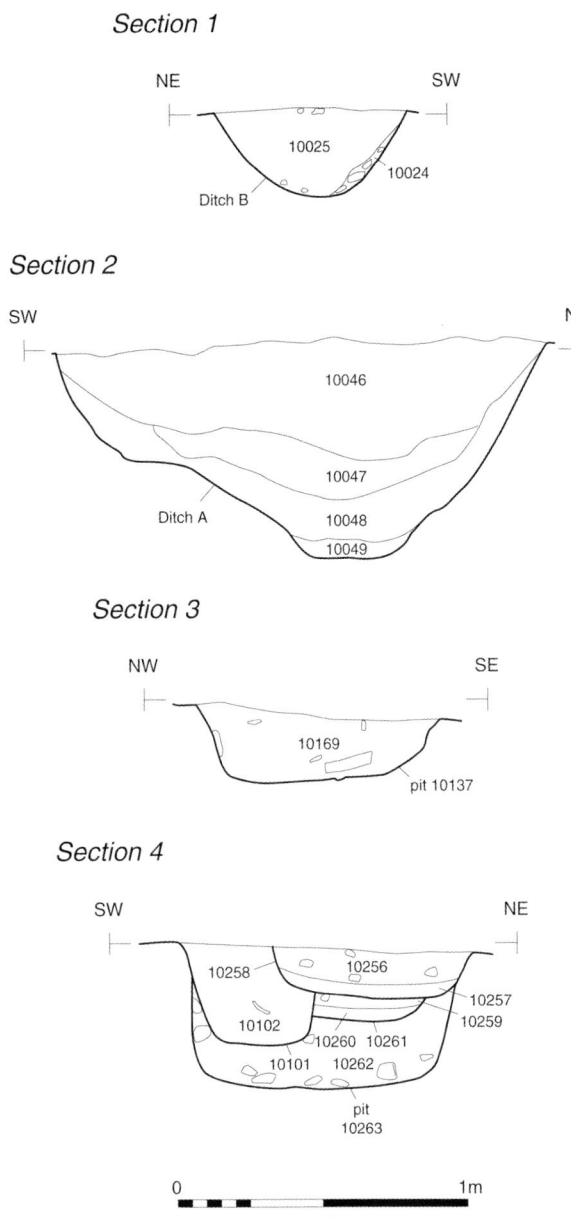

Fig. 2.3 Rodway Middle Bronze Age enclosure: Section 1, north-west facing section through Ditch B; Section 2, south-east facing section through Ditch A; Section 3, south-west facing section through pit 10137; Section 4, south facing section through pit 10263

corners of the enclosure. Although it has proved impossible to suggest structural ground plans from these postholes, it seems likely that each cluster represents the footprint of a building, here labelled Roundhouses A and B (Fig. 2.2). The material culture assemblage recovered from these features is suggestive of domestic occupation, and includes pottery, animal bone, charred plant remains and fuel ash slag, the latter a residue indicative of features such as hearths and ovens.

Roundhouse A was approximately 9m in diameter.

There was no obvious entrance, but one would have presumably faced broadly southwards into the enclosure's interior, or eastwards towards Roundhouse B. The postholes occasionally included packing stones used to hold the posts in place and most produced a few charcoal flecks, some of which were identifiable as charred cereal grains, in addition to which two produced Middle Bronze Age pottery, finds suggestive of floor sweepings (cf. Reynolds 1995, 24). Figure 2.4 shows the distribution and density of pottery, flint and charred plant remains within the enclosure, from which a focus is suggested to lie within Roundhouse A, raising the possibility that this was a dwelling whilst Roundhouse B was an ancillary structure.

Several pits lay within the footprint of Roundhouse A, although they may have been earlier or later features. Of these, pit 10031, a bowl-shaped cut up to 0.9m wide and 0.35m deep, contained 57 sherds from a single biconical vessel, which would have been a large storage jar, and was associated with a radiocarbon date of 1495–1300 cal. BC on a fragment of associated cherry-wood charcoal (SUERC-63442; Table 2.5 and Fig. 2.5). Soil samples from this pit contained large quantities of charred cereal grains, with all of those identifiable being emmer wheat, the main wheat species grown in the Bronze Age (Table 2.3). Also within the assemblage was a smaller quantity of cereal chaff, as well as weed seeds from species associated with grassland, arable fields and field margins. The seed from a Celtic bean is also likely to represent a weed, given its occurrence as a single item, although the species could have been cultivated.

Pits 10137 and 10263 were steep/vertical-sided, flat-based cuts up to 0.9m wide and 0.45m deep (Fig. 2.3, sections 3 and 4). Both contained homogeneous deposits with pottery, flint debitage and animal bone. Pit 10137 produced a small assemblage of charred cereal remains, mainly of emmer wheat, while pit 10263 contained large numbers of charred flax seeds as well as small number of charred emmer wheat grains and weed seeds (Table 2.3). The pottery from pit 10137 amounted to 97 sherds of Trevisker-type ware, whilst a charred emmer/spelt wheat grain from this pit produced a radiocarbon date of 1371–1118 cal. BC (SUERC-69951) and a charred flax seed from pit 10263 was radiocarbon dated to 1418–1266 cal. BC (SUERC-62337). The dates are all mutually consistent (Fig. 2.5; Table 2.5). There was evidence for reuse of these pits, with pit 10263 having been re-cut up to three times, each by another vertical-sided pit.

Other pits within the footprint of Roundhouse A were broad, bowl-shaped cuts, the functions of which were unclear. Two of these along the north-eastern perimeter of Roundhouse A were shallow and rather irregular and might have been caused by animals digging up against the inner edge of the wall line.

Roundhouse B was 8m north-east of Roundhouse A. It survived as a cluster of postholes, among which it

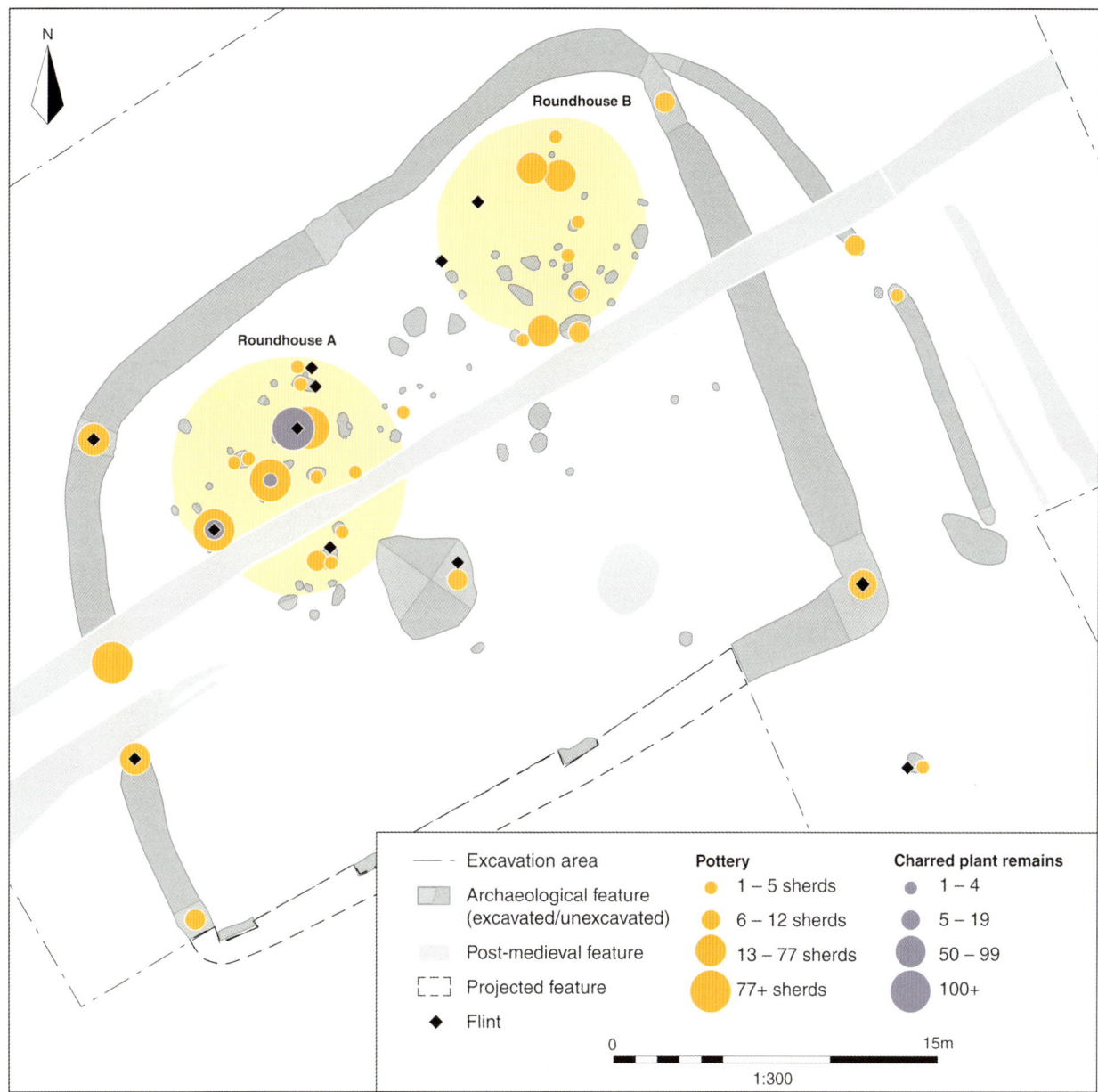

Fig. 2.4 *Rodway Middle Bronze Age enclosure: finds density distribution*

was possible to trace the southern part of an outer arc, approximately 9m in diameter, with postholes within the internal area perhaps representing house fittings or parts of the structure. If the enclosure had included an internal bank, as suggested above, then the rear part of the roundhouse must have been cut into it if the building's footprint was as indicated (Fig. 2.2). As with Roundhouse A there was no evidence for the location of an entrance, but one facing towards Roundhouse A, or into the southern half of the enclosure might be envisaged. One of the outer postholes produced a blade-like Greensand flake, whilst others collectively produced charcoal flecks, a few pottery sherds, animal bone fragments and a flint. An alder/hazel charcoal fragment from posthole 10145 was radiocarbon dated to 1426–1276 cal. BC (SUERC-62336; Table 2.5 and Fig. 2.5).

As with Roundhouse A, a number of pits were present within the structure's footprint, although it is not apparent whether or not these were contemporary with Roundhouse B. Among these, pits 10192, 10199 and 10231 had vertical sides and flat bases and were perhaps grain stores, although at just 0.2–0.3m deep they would have been shallow ones. None contained stored material, but had been backfilled with material that produced a small assemblage of animal bone and burnt stones. A large number of pottery sherds came from pit 10192 and a charcoal fragment from pit 10199 was radiocarbon dated to 1393–1135 cal. BC (SUERC-69952; Table

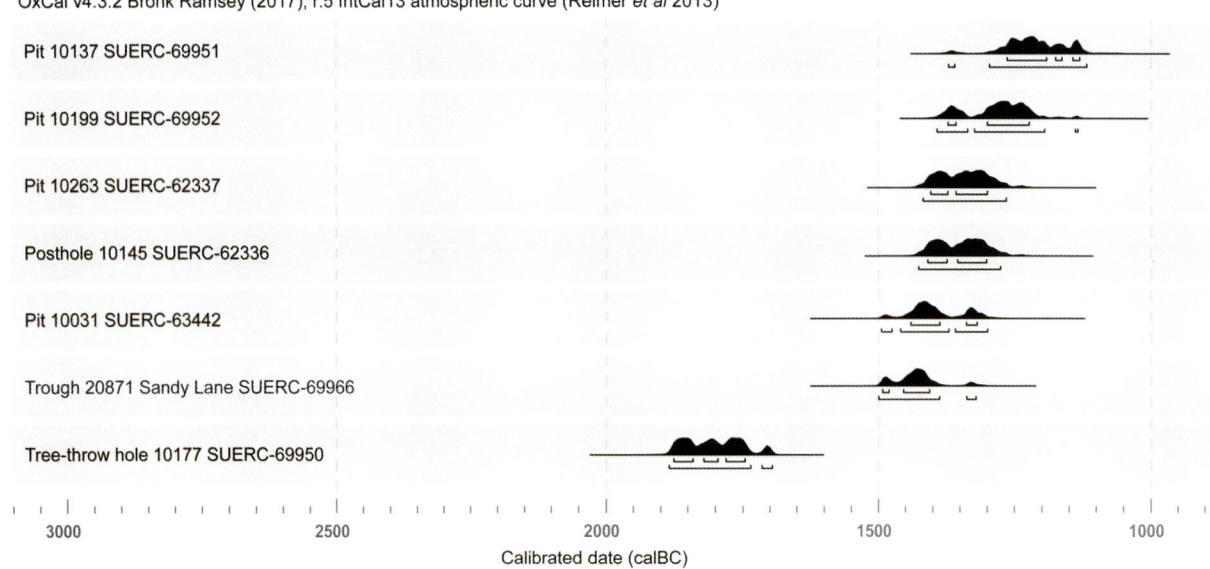

Fig. 2.5 Rodway Enclosure and Sandy Lane Middle Bronze Age trough: radiocarbon dating multiplot

2.5; Fig. 2.5). Other pits within the roundhouse were shallow bowl-shaped features, some of which were fairly irregular and may have been erosion hollows caused by human or animal activity.

The area between the two roundhouses contained further features, suggesting that this may have been a yard or working/storage area. These included a few postholes and two further vertical-sided, flat-based pits, 10133 and 10194, each infilled with sandy silt.

The southern half of the enclosure was more open. A large, shallow feature lay just off the central point, and along the axis between the opposed entrances of the first phase enclosure. This feature, 10083, was an irregular cut, 4.4m to 5m wide and 0.1m deep, oval in plan and with indistinct sides sloping gently to a flattish base. It contained a single dark silty clay fill which produced two flint flakes and seven sherds of pottery.

Middle Bronze Age trough at Sandy Lane
Jonathan Hart

A single Middle Bronze Age feature was found at Sandy Lane (SPE 2), where the majority of the remains dated to the later prehistoric and Roman periods (see Chapter 3). The feature was a rectangular pit (20871), 2.15m long and 1.45m wide with vertical sides leading to a flat base (Fig. 2.6). It survived to a depth of 0.3m and contained four horizontal fills, the lowest of which was rich in charcoal and scorched stones, with the later fills having these inclusions in smaller quantities. A cherry-wood

Fig. 2.6 Sandy Lane Middle Bronze Age trough 20871, looking north (scale 1m)

charcoal fragment from the lower fill was radiocarbon dated to 1500–1321 cal. BC (SUERC-69966; Table 2.5; Fig. 2.5). The scorched stones suggest that this was a trough relating to Bronze Age hot-stone technology. Although no stream or palaeochannel lay nearby, it was noted on site that the pit retained rain water, and it is possible that a spring, since disturbed by quarrying, may have lain nearby.

Prehistoric pottery
Henrietta Quinnell
(with Fabrics, by Imogen Wood)

The prehistoric features at Rodway produced 897 sherds (8686g) of pottery, with a mean sherd weight of 9.7g (Table 2.1). All the pottery can be identified as Trevisker-related material and occurs in five fabrics, all but one of which contain grog (fired-clay fragments used as filler). Most vessels are reduced but with patchy spreads of oxidisation across both inner and outer surfaces. Most sherds are fresh: where some abrasion is present it is usually only on part of the perimeter, suggesting that most were buried soon after breakage with abrasion related to bioturbation.

Fabrics
Imogen Wood

All sherds were examined macroscopically with a hand lens at x2 magnification to identify initial fabric groups; these groups were then examined under a binocular microscope at a magnification of x10 to x40. This enabled large areas of the surface and edges of sherds to be examined and, in many cases, useful diagnostic mineral and rock components to be identified.

Table 2.1: The Trevisker-related pottery assemblage from Rodway Enclosure; sherd numbers and weight (g) by contexts and fabrics. P-numbers refer to illustrated vessels

Context	Feature	Fabric 1		Fabric 2		Fabric 3		Fabric 4		Fabric 5		Totals	
		Count	Weight	Count	Weight	Count	Weight	Count	Weight	Count	Weight	Count	Weight
10004	Ditch C	-	-	2	8	-	-	-	-	-	-	2	8
10008	Ditch A	45 P1–2	491	-	-	2 P3	66	39 P4	179	-	-	86	736
10014	Ditch B	9	46	-	-	1	41	-	-	-	-	10	87
10016	Ditch A	-	-	-	-	8	86	-	-	-	-	8	86
10030	Ditch A	6	7	-	-	-	-	-	-	-	-	6	7
10033	pit 10031	57 P5	2158	-	-	-	-	-	-	-	-	57	2158
10036	Ditch A	1	4	-	-	-	-	-	-	-	-	1	4
10037	Ditch A	16	32	-	-	-	-	-	-	-	-	16	32
10039	post-med. ditch 10038	2	33	-	-	-	-	-	-	-	-	2	33
10046	Ditch A	6	50	3	20	-	-	-	-	-	-	9	70
10051	Ditch A	4	63	-	-	-	-	-	-	-	-	4	63
10053	posthole 10044	1	19	-	-	-	-	-	-	-	-	1	19
10055	pit 10054	4	19	-	-	-	-	-	-	-	-	4	19
10057	Ditch A	14	8	-	-	-	-	-	-	-	-	14	8
10058	Ditch A	-	-	1	4	-	-	-	-	-	-	1	4
10059	Ditch A	21	37	-	-	-	-	-	-	1	8	22	45
10076	pit 10075	7	63	-	-	-	-	-	-	-	-	7	63
10078	pit 10077	2	2	-	-	-	-	-	-	-	-	2	2
10080	posthole 10079	-	-	1	14	-	-	-	-	-	-	1	14
10082	posthole 10081	4	21	-	-	-	-	-	-	-	-	4	21
10084	hollow 10083	7	86	-	-	-	-	-	-	-	-	7	86

Table 2.1 (cont.): The Trevisker-related pottery assemblage from Rodway Enclosure

Context	Feature	Fabric 1		Fabric 2		Fabric 3		Fabric 4		Fabric 5		Totals	
		Count	*Weight*	*Count*	*Weight*	*Count*	*Weight*	*Count*	*Weight*	*Count*	*Weight*	*Count*	*Weight*
10102	pit 10101	6	57	-	-	-	-	-	-	-	-	6	57
10123	pit 10119	2	3	-	-	-	-	-	-	-	-	2	3
10129	posthole 10128	-	-	-	-	1	9	-	-	-	-	1	9
10131	pit 10130	78	36	-	-	-	-	-	-	-	-	78	36
10132	pit 10130	28 P6	599	-	-	-	-	-	-	-	-	28	599
10136	posthole 10135	75 P7	1578	106 P8	1890	1	26	-	-	-	-	182	3494
10146	posthole 10145	56	44	4	79	-	-	-	-	-	-	60	123
10157	posthole 10158	-	-	1	4	-	-	-	-	-	-	1	4
10169	pit 10137	-	-	92	115	-	-	-	-	-	-	92	115
10193	pit 10192	8	39	-	-	-	-	-	-	-	-	8	39
10200	pit 10199	1	1	-	-	-	-	-	-	-	-	1	1
10203	pit 10199	-	-	-	-	1	19	-	-	-	-	1	19
10204	posthole 10205	-	-	-	-	2	11	-	-	-	-	2	11
10214	pit 10192	51 P9	145	2	12	-	-	-	-	-	-	53	157
10224	posthole 10223	-	-	4	23	-	-	-	-	-	-	4	23
10232	pit 10231	-	-	12	28	-	-	-	-	-	-	12	28
10236	pit 10235	5	103	72	245	-	-	-	-	-	-	77	348
10242	posthole 10241	-	-	-	-	1	3	-	-	-	-	1	3
10259	pit 10261	-	-	-	-	-	-	-	-	2	9	2	9
10262	pit 10263	22 P10	43	-	-	-	-	-	-	-	-	22	43
Totals		538	5787	300	2442	17	261	39	179	3	17	897	8686

Fabric descriptions

Fabric 1 Grog: 538 sherds (5787g); mean sherd weight 10.8g.
The clay matrix is of fine silty clay with fine muscovite mica and rare fine quartz. The fabric includes 10–15% of very poorly sorted temper and is reduced throughout, with a soapy texture. Two types of grog are present, described below:

Grog: common inclusions of buff to grey grog with a soft texture and 2–6mm in size. In shape, these inclusions are tabular sub-angular, and the aplastic angularity of these suggests they derive from crushed ceramic vessels; large inclusions with relic vessel surfaces were observed in sherds from fill 10033, and the lack of shrinkage around these larger inclusions suggests that the original vessel(s) from which they derived were fired to a similar temperature as that within which they were reused.

Grog: rare inclusions of buff-reddish yellow grog; generally oxidised. These inclusions are well-rounded and 5–7mm in size. Slight shrinkage suggests that their original firing temperature was lower than that of the vessels into which they were incorporated. There are some examples of quartz inclusions within them, suggesting that they came from a different fabric to that from which the more angular grog described above derived.

Comment: This fabric is in a locally derived micaceous clay tempered with well-rounded grog inclusions, as found in the other grog-tempered fabrics (2, 3 and 4), but with the addition of angular pieces of grog with relic boundaries visible suggesting a secondary crushed grog temper.

Fabric 2 Grog, black haematite: 300 sherds (2442g); mean sherd weight 8.1g.
The clay matrix is of fine silty clay with 15–20% very poorly sorted temper and is variably oxidised/reduced with a soapy texture. The temper is described below:

Iron-rich haematite: common inclusions of dark-brown to

black iron-rich haematite; tabular in shape with sub-angular to sub-rounded edges and a soft texture. These inclusions are strongly magnetic and range in size between 1–7mm.

Grog: sparse inclusions of oxidised reddish yellow grog. Rounded tabular and spherical in shape, and ranging between 2–4mm in size.

Quartz: rare inclusions of opaque, angular quartz, 4mm in size.

Comments: this fabric is made using locally derived non-micaceous clay from a different source to that used for Fabrics 1, 3, 4 and 5, although it contains the same well-rounded grog inclusions. The common haematite inclusions suggest a riverine source.

Fabric 3 Grog with sand: 17 sherds (261g); mean sherd weight 15.4g. The clay matrix is of smooth micaceous and quartz-rich clay, tempered with a varying quantity of sand, up to 10–15% of the total fabric and poorly sorted. The fabric overall is variably oxidised/reduced and includes the tempers described below:

Quartz: rare inclusions of well-rounded, river worn, crystal up to 1mm in size.

Quartz: sparse inclusions of sub-angular quartz up to 1mm in size.

Muscovite mica: a scatter of silver cleavage flakes up to 1mm in size.

Grog: sparse inclusions of grey to buff, well-rounded grog, 2–5mm in size.

Feldspar: rare inclusions of off-white/yellow, soft and rounded feldspar up to 1mm in size.

Comment: locally derived micaceous quartz-rich clay with small amounts of river sand added, and well-rounded grog temper similar to Fabrics 1, 2 and 4.

Fabric 4 Grog with rock: 39 sherds (179g); mean sherd weight 4.6g. The clay matrix is of smooth silty clay with some muscovite mica and the fabric includes 15–20% of very poorly sorted temper. Overall, the fabric is variably oxidised/reduced.

Rock: a scatter of angular sandstone inclusions with an epiclastic texture and with quartz in the matrix. Size range 2–5mm.

Rock: a scatter of sub-angular limestone (fine conglomerate of quartz), 2–8mm in size.

Grog: a scatter of dark brown to red rounded grog, 2–7mm in size.

Quartz: a scatter of sub-angular quartz, 1–2mm in size.

Muscovite mica: sparse inclusions of silver cleavage flakes, up to 1mm in size.

Comment: locally derived micaceous quartz-rich clay. The small quartz inclusions are the by-product of crushing sandstone for use as temper, as suggested by their larger angular size and shape.

Fabric 5 Rock: 3 sherds (17g); mean sherd weight 5.7g. The clay matrix is of smooth silty micaceous clay and is variably oxidised/reduced with a soft and sandy texture. The fabric includes 15% poorly sorted temper, as described below.

Rock: a scatter of sub-angular sandstone (quartz in conglomerate with white matrix), 1–5mm in size.

Quartz: a scatter of sub-angular quartz, 1mm in size.

Muscovite mica: a scatter of silver cleavage flakes up to 1mm in size.

Comments: a locally derived micaceous clay tempered with angular crushed sandstone and quartz inclusions, possibly as an added by-product of crushing, suggesting no grading of temper. No grog was used in this fabric.

Provenance of fabrics

The fabrics can be broadly grouped under a 'grog-tempered' fabric, which is common in this period and region. Fabrics 1, 2, 3 and 4 are variations on the same grog-tempered fabric, the exception being Fabric 5, which is tempered with crushed sandstone.

The geology of the Cannington area provides many elements identified in the fabrics and thus suggest the clays and tempers were locally sourced. The micaceous Otter Sandstone formation underlain by beds of reddish brown clay may be a source for the base clay for Fabrics 1, 3, 4 and 5, with Fabric 2 deriving from a nearby riverine source. The absence of fine mica and presence of haematite inclusions in Fabric 2 suggest locally derived riverine clay. There are deposits of haematite which have formed from iron-bearing waters descending from the overlying Triassic rocks and which became trapped in cavities and fissures in the Carboniferous Limestone on nearby Castle Hill.

The grog-tempered Fabrics 1, 2, 3 and 4 are comparable to Woodward's (1989) Fabric group 1 of the Trevisker assemblage from Norton Fitzwarren hillfort; petrographic analysis of this fabric identified grog inclusions in a locally derived clay, which is entirely consistent with the conclusions of this analysis (Williams 1987). Similar grog-tempered fabrics of suggested Early Bronze Age Biconical Urns are known from Cannington Park Quarry (ApSimon 2000, 285, fabric A1). Another Early Bronze Age grog fabric (fabric 1) has been identified in Collared Urns from burials at Wick Lane, Norton Fitzwarren (Alexander and Adam 2013, 7).

The grog is a feature of most of the fabrics suggesting a tradition of crushing old pottery as a temper for new clay. The use of two different types of grog in Fabric 1 suggests that there may have been an accumulated resource of crushed pottery consisting of many vessels of different fabrics which was then mixed and added as temper. The most common form of grog seen in Fabrics 1, 2, 3 and 4 is rounded. This suggests that either it was not freshly crushed before use but had been left to weather, or that it may have been a weathered soft-fired burnt clay material, or that the preparation involved a good deal of rolling after crushing.

Discussion of the assemblage

The assemblage comes from 41 contexts, with some 15 vessels illustrated and/or described below. The large number of contexts with pottery suggests a considerable number of vessels are represented, but only by small amounts of material. Only the contents of pit 10031, with up to a quarter of the distinctive vessel **P5** (Fig. 2.7, no. 5), and with sherds of this vessel alone, could be argued as having been the result of some form of structured deposition. There are no differences apparent in the distribution of the fabrics across the enclosure.

There are five radiocarbon dates from the site that relate to contexts with pottery. Four of these indicate

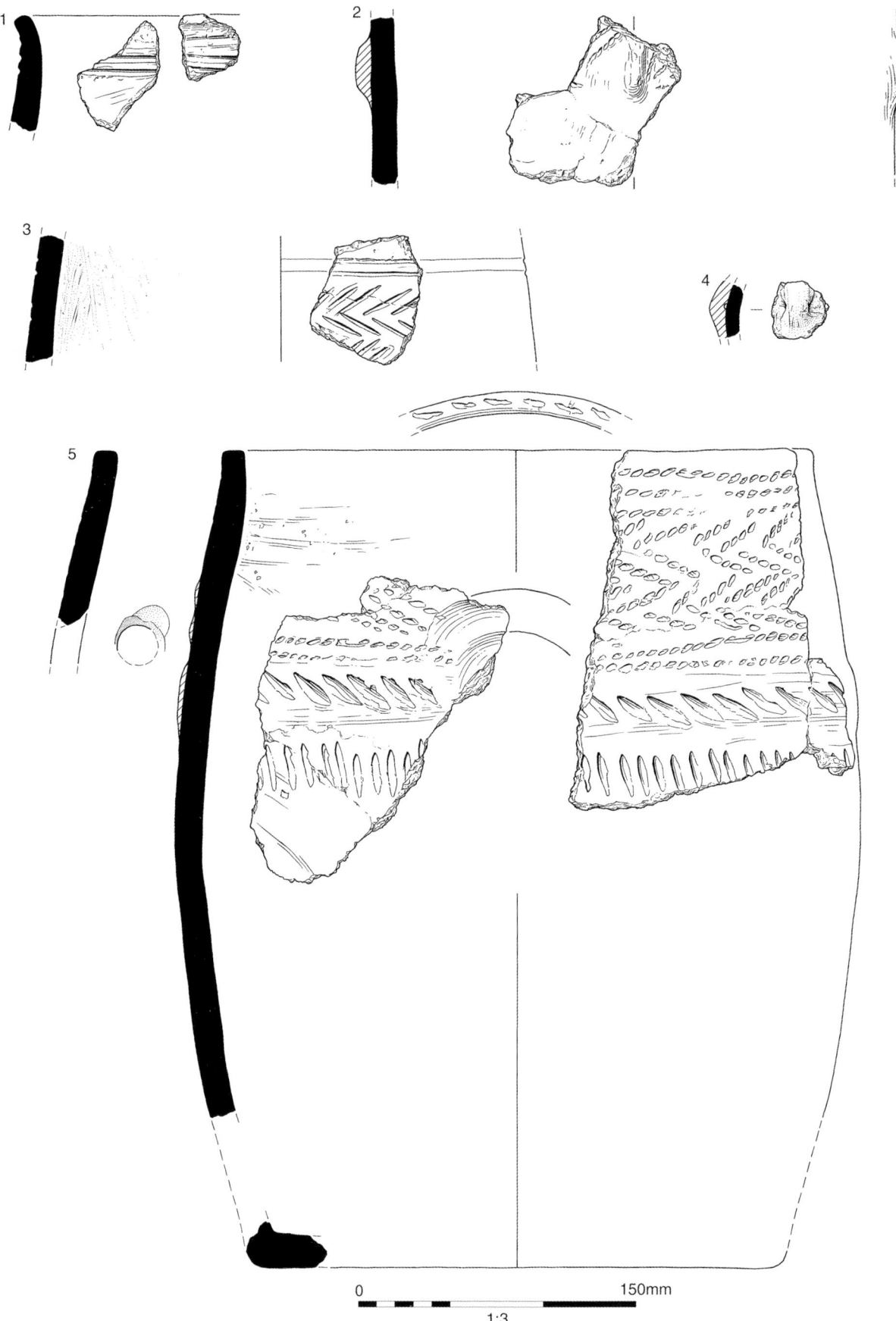

Fig. 2.7 Middle Bronze Age pottery, nos 1–5 (drawing by Jane Read)

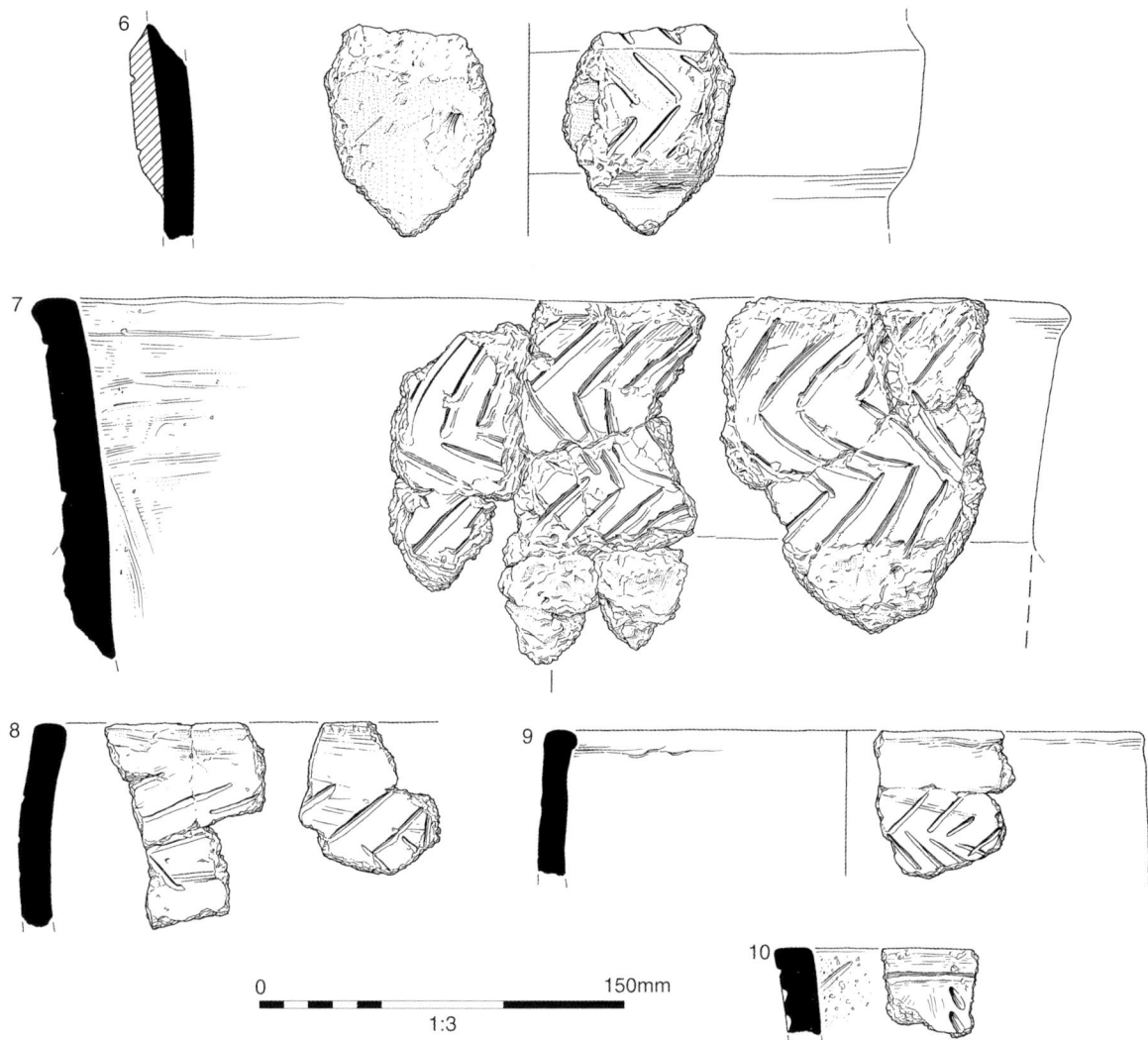

Fig. 2.8   Middle Bronze Age pottery, nos 6–10 (drawing by Jane Read)

activity within the 14th century cal. BC, while the fifth (SUERC-69951) suggests that this extended into the 13th century. This date range is appropriate for the Middle Bronze Age and for the occurrence of Trevisker-related ceramics in Somerset.

The Trevisker ceramic style originated in Cornwall in the Early Bronze Age and is recovered on occasion from sites of that period in Devon, and very occasionally beyond these two counties. These Early Bronze Age occurrences generally relate to barrows and burials. In the Middle Bronze Age the style continued with little stylistic change in Devon and Cornwall but with the finds generally coming from settlement sites, which became common in the landscape just as sites connected with burial decreased (Quinnell 2012; Parker Pearson 1995; Woodward and Cane 1991). Assemblages from Middle Bronze Age sites in the Lower Exe Valley and East Devon do differ in minor ways from those found further to the west, for example in producing larger numbers of undecorated vessels and in greater use of applied cordons, differences which support the use of the term 'Trevisker-related'. There is some influence apparent, particularly in the cordons, from Deverel-Rimbury ceramics further east, emphasised especially for vessels from Old Rydon Lane, Exeter (Raymond 2012). It is appropriate to extend the use of the term 'Trevisker-related' to assemblages in Somerset.

In Somerset, ceramics of the Trevisker style do not appear until the Middle Bronze Age. The only two published sites with this material are the hilltop enclosure at Norton Fitzwarren, 14km to the south-west, which lies beneath the larger Iron Age hillfort (Woodward 1989) and at Unit 5B of the coastal settlement site at Brean Down, 20km to the north (Woodward 1990). The former has no radiocarbon dates whilst dates from the latter (1411–908 cal. BC [HAR-7019 2940 +/- 100 BP], 1263–843 cal. BC [HAR-7018 2870 +/- 80 BP], and 1211–752 cal. BC, 94.4% probability [HAR-7017 2730 +/- 100 BP]) are weighted towards a later date than those for Rodway.

The Norton Fitzwarren illustrated assemblage from the 1968–71 excavations, re-examined by the authors, contains some 20 Trevisker-related vessels (Woodward 1989, figs 18–19; the total assemblage consisted of 209 sherds (4978g), most of it Trevisker-related, but some Late Bronze and Iron Age). We considered that vessels published as of earlier styles (e.g. ibid., fig. 18, no. 1) can now be grouped with the Trevisker material, but that the amount of Late Bronze Age material had been underestimated. We would suggest that none of the ceramics pre-date the Middle Bronze Age: fig. 18, no. 1, described as 'domestic Beaker', has a rim form typical of Trevisker-related ware and is not found in South-Western Beaker assemblages. The Trevisker-related assemblage is mainly of grogged fabrics but with several examples with felspathic tuff and quartzite, possibly derived from the Shepton Mallet area (Williams 1987). Six of the Trevisker-related vessels have cord-impressed decoration, all using cord very much coarser than that found in Cornwall and Devon. Another six have untidy incised decoration; four have fingernail decoration, some of which is combined with incised lines. The remainder are plain. These comments from our re-examination are intended to be used in addition to the very detailed analysis contained in Woodward (1989). The material from the 1908 excavations was not available for re-examination but, from the comments in Woodward's report, also could now be accommodated in the Trevisker-related style. The range of rim forms found at Rodway are paralleled by those at Norton Fitzwarren and overall the style of the two assemblages is similar, but without exact parallels.

The assemblage recovered from Unit 5b at Brean Down in Somerset was much larger, with 1883 sherds weighing 15.859kg (Woodward 1990, table 7), and was mainly of grogged fabrics, with a little local limestone, calcite and sand. Forty-four vessels were illustrated (ibid., figs 89–92). Two vessels are cord impressed; the majority of the remainder have untidy incised designs. Woodward argues convincingly that the style of this material belongs late within the Trevisker sequence. Recent studies of Cornish material have indicated a comparable late stage with only untidy incised decoration, notably at Gwithian and a site at Porthleven (Quinnell 2012, 166). The Brean Down assemblage has general similarities to that from Rodway, but some features, such as flattened and extensively flattened rims, are absent.

The Cannington Roman cemetery at Cannington Park Quarry, 500m south of the Rodway Enclosure, produced pre-Roman finds including grogged fabrics described as 'Biconical Urn' (ApSimon 2000, 286, fig. 196, nos 17–34) but a comment within the Brean Down report (Woodward 1990, 132) refers to the presence of Trevisker material at Cannington Park Quarry. The division between Biconical Urn and Trevisker is not clear cut (Quinnell 2012, 161) and identifications for small and/or unstratified sherds can be uncertain.

A number of sites near Taunton have recorded small quantities of probable Trevisker-related material. Of these, Cambria Farm produced mainly grog-tempered fabrics with an associated radiocarbon date of 1131–923 cal. BC, 89.4% probability [SUERC-29293, 2870 +/- 40 BP] (Context One 2011). The illustrations show a number of Trevisker-type rims but no decoration and the site appears to belong at the end of the Trevisker tradition. Evaluation trenches at Hartnell's Farm, Monkton Heathfield, produced a small quantity of body sherds with grog or quartz/sandstone inclusions (Wessex Archaeology 2008). An enclosure ditch at Nerrols Farm also produced a small grogged assemblage, considered broadly similar to that from Norton Fitzwarren (Mason 2010).

These comments provide background for the Trevisker-related assemblage from Cannington, with the possible exception of vessel **P5** from pit 10031. The slightly biconical shape, girth cordon and herringbone cord-impressed decoration of **P5** are all Trevisker features: the coarse cord especially reflects that at Norton Fitzwarren. However the combination of impressed and applied decoration, especially the 'horseshoe' handle(s), have no current parallels. The horseshoe handle has affinities with the variant of biconical vessels termed Wessex Biconical Urns (Calkin 1962, 35, fig. 14). Biconical assemblages generally belong to the later Early Bronze Age (Woodward 1990, 126). A biconical assemblage was found at Brean Down in Unit 6, which was earlier than Unit 5B with Trevisker pottery: two fragments of possible applied horseshoe handles found in Unit 5B were considered residual in its late Trevisker-related assemblage (ibid., 124). Horseshoe handles are not usually found in Trevisker assemblages. The only two known from Cornwall, from Duloe (Patchett 1944, G.15; Borlase 1972), and from Morvah (Patchett 1944, G.14; Borlase 1972, 248), come from incomplete vessels which do not survive today, whilst only one possible Devon example is known, from Nymet Tracey (Pearce 1973). **P5** is best regarded as a vessel of simple biconical shape with applied horseshoe handle(s), reflecting the earlier horseshoe handle tradition, incorporated in a Trevisker-related design.

Illustrated vessels

P1 (Fig. 2.7, no. 1) Fill 10008 of Ditch A. Fabric 1. Small, everted, slightly rounded rim with surviving decoration of incised broad grooves; two other non-joining sherds with similar decoration.

P2 (Fig. 2.7, no. 2) Fill 10008 of Ditch A. Fabric 1. Three joining sherds from girth of vessel with internal diameter *c.* 280mm, with narrow imperforate vertical lug set within cord-impressed decoration.

P3 (Fig. 2.7, no. 3) Fill 10008 of Ditch A. Fabric 3. Two joining girth sherds from vessel of slightly biconical shape with internal diameter 250mm+. Incised design of herringbone with two horizontal lines above.

P4 (Fig. 2.7, no. 4) Fill 10008 of Ditch A. Fabric 4. Flat-faced small lug with incomplete perforation. Sherds of the same fabric with incised lines from this context may form part of the same vessel.

P5 (Fig. 2.7, no. 5) Fill 10033 of pit 10031. Fabric 1. Large slightly biconical vessel, flat-topped rim with internal diameter of 295mm and height of 310mm. Large possible fingernail impressions along its top. Decoration of impressed very coarse cord forming an irregular herringbone design which incorporates part of an applied horseshoe handle formed by a double cordon or a very wide single cordon with a central broad depression; it is presumed that there would have been a second handle. There is a large pre-firing perforation, part of which survives. Below is a wide girth cordon, decorated with long diagonal slashes and flattening beneath the applied handle. Below this is a second line of long nearly vertical slashes. A single small base angle sherd survives. All 57 sherds (2158g) from this context are probably from this vessel, but they represent less than a quarter of it, so the original vessel would have weighed over 8kg. SUERC-63442: 1495–1300 cal. BC (Table 2.5).

P6 (Fig. 2.8, no. 6) Fill 10132 of pit 10130. Fabric 1. Girth sherd with a wide horizontal cordon and deep incised herringbone lines on the cordon and above it; internal vessel diameter: 280mm.

P7 (Fig. 2.8, no. 7) fill 10136 of posthole 10135. Fabric 1. Flat-topped, slightly expanded rim and upper part of vessel with an internal rim diameter *c*. 340mm. Deeply incised herringbone design and a scar below representing the position of a former cordon. A few Fabric 1 sherds may come from a similar, thinner vessel.

P8 (Fig. 2.8, no. 8) fill 10136 of posthole 10135. Fabric 2. Flat-topped rim and sherds from the upper part of a vessel with untidy herringbone design. Other sherds in Fabric 2 have broader incised lines from a different vessel, and others in this fabric have flat cordons apparently from an undecorated vessel.

P9 (Fig. 2.8, no. 9) fill 10214 of pit 10192. Fabric 1. Rim with slight internal expansion and internal diameter of 225mm. Incised herringbone beneath. Another sherd with a more pronounced in-turn and incised lines may form part of another vessel.

P10 (Fig. 2.8, no. 10) fill 10262 of pit 10263 Fabric 1. Flat-topped rim above two surviving deep stab marks. A similar Fabric 1 rim with two fingernail/stabbed marks set side by side came from fill 10046 of Ditch A. SUERC-62337: 1418–1266 cal. BC (Table 2.5).

Lithics from Rodway and Sandy Lane
Jacky Sommerville

In total, 53 worked lithics (210g) were retrieved from 32 deposits and as unstratified finds. Five (11%) were made using Greensand chert and the remainder are flint (89%). A total of 31 worked lithics came from the Rodway Enclosure, of which 16 were retrieved from the fills of Ditch A. The other 21 lithics came from the Sandy Lane site, where they occurred as residual finds and the remaining find was an unstratified arrowhead (Table 2.2).

Range and variety
Primary technology
The debitage comprises mainly flakes and chips, the majority from the Middle Bronze Age enclosure at Rodway (Table 2.2). Although none of these are closely dateable, attributes associated with the Mesolithic/Early Neolithic periods (e.g. blade technology) are absent.

Secondary technology
A barbed-and-tanged arrowhead, recovered as an unstratified find, is a (Green) Sutton (A)e type (Green 1980, 122), dating to the Beaker/Early Bronze Age period (*c*. 2600–1500 BC). The dorsal face has been reworked around all edges with regular, abrupt to semi-abrupt, slightly invasive retouch; the ventral face features only a few shallow removals.

The four retouched tools from the Rodway Enclosure comprise a miscellaneous piece and three scrapers from Ditch A terminal 10056 (Fig. 2.2). These include an end-and-side scraper from fill 10059 (Fig. 2.9, no. 1); a scraper fragment from fill 10057 featuring an area of steep, rather crude retouch along one convex edge: and a scraper from fill 10060 which appears to be a very small discoidal core with one portion made into a scraper with rather irregular, semi-abrupt retouch. The miscellaneous piece came from fill 10057 and was made on a flake blank with small flakes removed from the ventral face. This type of unsystematic and opportunistic flintworking was most common during the Bronze Age (Butler 2005, 155–8).

Eight retouched items were retrieved from Sandy Lane, all as residual items (Table 2.2). Roman Ditch F produced a probable thumbnail-type scraper (Fig. 2.9, no. 2), a type common to the Early Bronze Age/Beaker periods, although it lacks the domed profile and fully invasive retouch most typical of this type (Butler 2005, 168). The other retouched items were made on flake blanks and are not chronologically diagnostic.

Illustration catalogue (Fig. 2.9)
1   End-and-side scraper. Rodway Enclosure Ditch A terminal (fill 10059): scraper made on a flake blank with an incipient cone of percussion. Dimensions: 28mm by 31mm by 9mm.
2   Thumbnail-type scraper. Sandy Lane Roman Ditch F (fill 20035). Dimensions: 21mm by 26mm by 6mm.

Discussion
The most notable aspect of this assemblage is the material from the Rodway Enclosure, which includes items consistent with Middle Bronze Age dating. Two tools (the arrowhead from an unknown location, and the residual thumbnail-type scraper from Sandy Lane), suggest Early Bronze Age activity.

The lithics from the Rodway Enclosure add to the small corpus of stratified Middle Bronze Age assemblages in Somerset, which includes those from Brean Down. That site produced 15 lithics from Unit 5a, and 54

Table 2.2: The lithics assemblage

	Rodway Enclosure		Sandy Lane			Unstratified
	Middle Bronze Age	Undated	Later Iron Age/ Early Roman	Roman	Undated	
Burnt unworked	7	-	-	-	-	-
Primary technology						
Chip	4	3	1	2	-	-
Flake	17	1	3	3	3	-
Shatter	2	-	-	1	-	-
Secondary technology						
Arrowhead (barbed-and-tanged)	-	-	-	-	-	1
Miscellaneous	1	-	-	-	-	-
Notched flake	-	-	-	-	1	-
Notched/spurred flake	-	-	-	-	1	-
Retouched flake	-	-	1	-	1	-
Scraper	3	-	3	-	1	-
Total	**34**	**4**	**8**	**6**	**7**	**1**

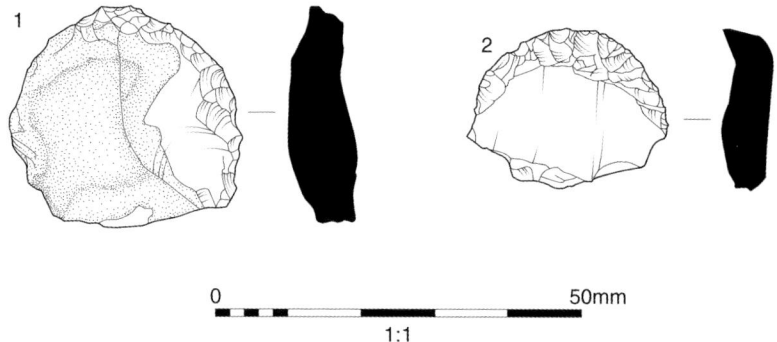

Fig. 2.9 Flints, nos 1–2

from Unit 6, both of which were dated to the Middle Bronze Age, and featured 21 retouched tools including a plano-convex knife, end scrapers, a piercer, a rod and miscellaneous retouched pieces (Saville 1990, 156–7). Although the assemblages from the Rodway Enclosure and Brean Down do not appear closely comparable, this may simply reflect the small size of the assemblages.

Charred plant remains
Sarah F. Wyles

A total of 16 soil samples were taken and assessed from the Rodway Enclosure site. Of these, six were selected for detailed analysis on the basis of their quality: two from Early Bronze Age tree-throw hole 10177 and four from Middle Bronze Age pits and postholes associated with Roundhouse A (Table 2.3). The bulk samples were processed following standard flotation methods, using a 250μm sieve for the recovery of the float and a 1mm sieve for the collection of the residue. All identifiable charred plant remains were identified following nomenclature of Stace (1997) for wild plants, and traditional nomenclature, as provided by Zohary *et al.* (2012) for cereals.

Early Bronze Age
The charred plant assemblages recovered from fills 10178 (sample 107) and 10187 (sample 108) of tree-throw hole 10177 were dominated by hazelnut (*Corylus avellana*) shell fragments. A single hulled wheat, emmer or spelt (*Triticum dicoccum/spelta*) grain was recorded from fill 10178. Hazelnut shell fragments from fill 10178 were radiocarbon dated to 1885–1696 cal. BC (SUERC-69950; Table 2.5). These assemblages are

Table 2.3: Charred plant identifications from Rodway Enclosure

Phase		EBA		MBA			
Group				Roundhouse A			
Feature type/label		Tree-throw hole		Pits			
Cut		10177		10031	10130	10137	10263
Context		10178	10187	10033	10131	10169	10262
Sample		107	108	101	104	106	114
Vol (L)		14	18	36	5	34	36
Flot size (ml)		8	2	288	12	42	23
Cereals	**Common Name**						
Hordeum vulgare L. *s.l.* (grain)	barley	-	-	-	4	-	-
Triticum cf. *dicoccum* (Schübl) (grain)	emmer wheat	-	-	175	1	1	1
Triticum dicoccum (Schübl) (glume base)	emmer wheat	-	-	25	3	6	1
Triticum dicoccum (Schübl) (spikelet fork)	emmer wheat	-	-	2	1	-	-
Triticum spelta L. (glume bases)	spelt wheat	-	-	-	-	1	-
Triticum dicoccum/spelta (grain)	emmer/spelt wheat	1	-	680	5	3	3
Triticum dicoccum/spelta (glume bases)	emmer/spelt wheat	-	-	3	-		1
Cereal indet. (grains)	cereal	-	-	170	8	10	2
Cereal frag. (est. whole grains)	cereal	-	-	220	-	4	1
Cereal frags (culm node)	cereal	-	-	1	3	-	-
Other Species							
Corylus avellana L. (fragments)	hazelnut	38	11	-	-	3	-
Chenopodium sp.	goosefoot	-	-	1	1	-	4
Chenopodium album L.	fat-hen	-	-	2	-	-	1
Atriplex sp. L.	oraches	-	-	-	1	-	1
Persicaria lapathifolia/ maculosa (L.) Gray/Gray	pale persicaria/redshank	-	-	2	-	-	-
Polygonum aviculare L.	knotgrass	-	-	3	-	-	-
Fallopia convolvulus (L.) À. Löve	black-bindweed	-	-	1	-	-	-
Rumex sp. L.	docks	-	-	6	-	-	10
Brassica sp. L.	brassica	-	-	5	-	-	5
Rubus sp. L.	brambles	-	-	-	-	-	1
Prunus spinosa L. (fragments)	sloe stone	-	-	2	-	-	-
Vicia L./*Lathyrus* sp. L.	vetch/wild pea	-	-	44	9	-	23
Vicia faba	Celtic bean	-	-	1	1	-	1
Medicago/Trifolium sp. L.	medick/clover	-	-	13	-	-	69
Linum usitatissimum L. (whole)	flax	-	-	-	-	-	33
Linum usitatissimum L. (frags est. whole)	flax	-	-	-	-	-	35
Plantago lanceolata L.	ribwort plantain	-	-	2	-	-	2
Sherardia arvensis L.	field madder	-	-	1	-	-	-
Galium sp. L.	bedstraw	-	-	-	-	-	1
Galium aparine L.	cleavers	-	-	-	-	1	-
Poa/Phleum sp. L.	meadow grass/cat's-tail	-	-	1	-	-	2
Avena L./*Bromus* L. sp.	oat/brome grass	-	-	2	-	-	-
Monocot. stem/rootlet frag		-	-	-	1	-	5
Bud		-	-	1	-	-	-

likely to be representative of burnt domestic waste and indicative of the exploitation of the local wild food resource.

Middle Bronze Age
The charred plant remains from four pits were analysed. A radiocarbon date of 1495–1300 cal. BC (SUERC-63442) was obtained on *Prunus* (cherry) charcoal from fill 10033 of pit 10031. Hulled wheat grains from fill 10169 of pit 10137 were radiocarbon dated to 1371–1118 cal. BC (SUERC-69951) and flax (*Linum usitatissimum*) seeds from fill 10262 of pit 10263 were radiocarbon dated to 1418–1266 cal. BC (SUERC-62337; Table 2.5).

Pit 10031
A very high number of charred plant remains (1363 items) were recovered from fill 10033 (sample 101) of pit 10031. Cereal remains were predominant, representing over 93% of the assemblage, and grains greatly outnumbered the chaff elements. The identifiable cereal remains were of hulled wheat, with around 200 of them identifiable as emmer (*Triticum dicoccum*). No definite remains of spelt wheat (*Triticum spelta*) were recorded. Emmer wheat was the predominant wheat species during the Middle Bronze Age in southern Britain (Greig 1991). Other potential crops were a single seed of Celtic bean (*Vicia faba*).

The weed seed assemblage included seeds of vetch/wild pea (*Vicia/Lathyrus* sp.), clover/medick (*Trifolium/Medicago* sp.), docks (*Rumex* sp.), knotgrass (*Polygonum aviculare*), brassica (*Brassica* sp.), ribwort plantain (*Plantago lanceolata*), field madder (*Sherardia arvensis*) and fat-hen (*Chenopodium album*). These are species typical of grassland, field margins and arable environments.

This assemblage may be representative of cleaned grain and a small amount of waste from a final stage of crop processing (Hillman 1981; 1984). The grains are generally well preserved which, together with the high number of remains, suggest that the assemblage may have been a deliberate deposit within the pit. There is no indication of any insect damage or germination of these grains, so the charring seems unlikely to have been the result of deliberate firing to sterilise the pit before storing a new harvest.

Pit 10130
Fill 10131 (sample 104) of pit 10130 contained a moderately small number of charred plant remains. Cereal remains were most numerous and included barley (*Hordeum vulgare*) and hulled wheat, with some identifiable as emmer wheat. Grains outnumbered the chaff elements. Other possible crop remains were a single seed of Celtic bean. The weed seeds included vetch/wild pea. This assemblage may be representative of a dump of cleaned grain and final-stage crop-processing waste, or the pit may have been used to store cleaned grain.

Pit 10137
The moderately small assemblage recorded from fill 10169 (sample 106) of pit 10137 was dominated by cereal remains, in particular those of emmer wheat. A glume base of spelt wheat was also noted. The other remains included hazelnut shell fragments. This assemblage appears to be a dump of domestic hearth waste.

Pit 10263
Fill 10262 (sample 114) of pit 10263 contained a large quantity of flax seeds. The small number of cereal remains included those of emmer wheat and the weed seeds included clover/medick, vetch/wild pea, docks and brassica. This assemblage may represent stored remains.

Discussion

Early Bronze Age
Both samples of this date came from tree-throw hole 10177 located outside the enclosure, and were dominated by hazelnut shell fragments. The likely exploitation and general reliance on the wild food resources for significant parts of the diet has been observed in assemblages in southern Britain during the early prehistoric period; hazelnut shells were also recovered from Early Bronze Age contexts at Brean Down, Somerset (Straker 1990).

Middle Bronze Age
The samples richest in crop remains of this date came from pits associated with Roundhouse A. There may have been deliberate deposits of charred remains within pits 10031, 10130 and 10263.

The possible crops included emmer wheat, barley, Celtic bean and flax. Emmer wheat was the predominant wheat during this period and, together with barley, was recovered from assemblages of this period nearby at Brean Down (Straker 1990). Celtic beans have rarely been recorded from deposits of Neolithic and earlier Bronze Age date but are noted more frequently in later Bronze Age assemblages, particularly those from coastal sites (Treasure and Church 2016). They were found in a number of Middle Bronze Age assemblages at Brean Down (Straker 1990). Charred flax (seeds and capsule fragments) is unusual in Bronze Age and earlier assemblages, but flax is thought to have been more widely cultivated than the quantity of charred remains recovered to date would suggest. A large deposit of charred flax seeds was recorded from a Beaker pit at land south of Amesbury, Wiltshire (Wyles and Stevens forthcoming), and of charred flax capsule fragments from a Late Bronze Age/Early Iron Age pit from Saltwood Tunnel, Kent (Stevens 2006). Flax appears to have been cultivated for both linseed oil and fibres during the Bronze Age. The presence of large numbers of capsule fragments in some Late Bronze Age assemblages, such as from Saltwood Tunnel (ibid.) and Cliffs End Farm, Isle of Thanet, Kent (Stevens 2014) would tend to indicate processing for seeds and linseed oil rather than just for fibre, and at Must Farm (Cambridgeshire) there is clear evidence, from preserved textiles and retting tools, for flax fibres being used (Must Farm website).

The weed seeds in these assemblages were generally of species typical of grassland, field margins and arable environments. There is also an indication of the exploitation of a local hedgerow/scrub/woodland edge environment.

Charcoal
Sarah Cobain

A total of 16 bulk soil samples were taken and assessed for charcoal from the Rodway Enclosure and a further sample was taken from the Middle Bronze Age trough at Sandy Lane. Following assessment, six samples from Rodway Enclosure and the sample from Sandy Lane were fully analysed on the basis of the quality of the remains. The aim of the analysis was to identify the charcoal, to determine the wood used for fuel, to provide evidence of woodland management and to infer the composition of the local woodlands. Following flotation (see Wyles, Charred plant remains, above), the residue was dried and sorted by eye, and the floated material was scanned. Up to 100 charcoal fragments were fractured by hand to reveal the wood anatomy on radial, tangential and transverse planes. The pieces were then supported in a sand bath and identified under an epi-illuminating microscope (Brunel SP400) at magnifications from x40 to x400. Identifications were carried out with reference to images and descriptions by Gale and Cutler (2000), Schoch *et al.* (2004) and Wheeler *et al.* (1989). Nomenclature of species follows Stace (1997).

The charcoal was moderately to well preserved and full results are presented in tabular form (Table 2.4).

Middle Bronze Age

Rodway Enclosure
Pit 10263 (fill 10262; sample 114) contained a moderate assemblage of moderately well-preserved charcoal identified as oak (*Quercus*), alder/hazel (*Alnus glutinosa/ Corylus avellana*), ivy (*Hedera helix*), birch (*Betula*), hawthorn/rowan/crab apple (*Crataegus monogyna/ Sorbus/Malus sylvestris*) and maple (*Acer campestre*). This pit also contained an interesting assemblage of plant macrofossils including a large number of charred flax (*Linum usitatissimum*) seeds which are an unusual find in Middle Bronze Age assemblages (Wyles, Charred plant remains, Chapter 2, this volume). The charcoal included small amounts of ivy which was not seen in other Middle Bronze Age features on this site. The assemblage is assumed to represent fuel used in drying flax seeds, which were accidentally burned in the process. There is no evidence that the pit itself contained the fire and it seems more likely that the remains were deposited in the pit.

The charcoal from pit 10130 (sample 104) and posthole 10167 (sample 106) was moderately abundant and moderately well preserved, and identified dominantly as oak, with smaller amounts of elder (*Sambucus nigra*), ash (*Fraxinus excelsior*), hawthorn/rowan/crab apple, alder, alder/hazel, field maple and cherry species (*Prunus*) also recorded. The charcoal is indicative of discarded hearth debris originating from domestic or crop-processing activities, as indicated by the associated charred plants.

A moderate assemblage of poorly preserved charcoal was recovered from pit 10031 (sample 101) identified as predominantly oak, with ash and two fragments of alder/hazel also recorded. The pit also contained a large assemblage of charred cereal grains representative of an assemblage of clean grain. The reason why such a large assemblage of grain had become charred is unclear; it may have happened accidentally or deliberately, and the wood fuel does not help clarify this.

Pit 10192 (sample 111), from the area of Roundhouse B, contained a large assemblage of well-preserved charcoal identified as predominantly oak, with smaller amounts of maple, alder (*Alnus glutinosa*), hawthorn/ rowan/crab apple and alder/hazel also recorded. This material is indicative of discarded hearth debris.

Posthole 10145 (sample 105), also from the area of Roundhouse B, contained a large assemblage of moderately well-preserved charcoal identified as oak with single fragments of alder/hazel and cherry species. It is often the case when a charcoal-rich deposit within a posthole is dominated by a single species that it represents a burnt *in situ* post, but in this instance there was no reddening of the ground to indicate a burning event so it is likely this posthole was backfilled with firing debris from a nearby hearth, where oak also tended to be dominant.

Sandy Lane
A large assemblage of moderately well-preserved charcoal was recovered from trough 20871 (sample 262) and was identified as oak, alder, hazel, ash, hawthorn/rowan/ crab apple, cherry species and blackthorn (*Prunus spinosa*). The feature contained abundant scorched stones, and it is likely the charcoal retrieved from this feature originated from fuel utilised to heat the stones.

Discussion of the Middle Bronze Age assemblages
The mixture of charred waste within the features at Rodway Enclosure appears indicative of burnt domestic refuse, most likely from activities taking place within the enclosure. The burnt mound trough at Sandy Lane contains a similar fuel assemblage to that at Rodway Enclosure. While the Sandy Lane trough has an earlier radiocarbon date, it appears that very similar woodland resources were available in the area at this time.

Fuel utilised is dominated by oak (81.8%) with the odd inclusion of maple and ash (Fig. 2.10). The remainder of the assemblage is made up of hedgerow or shrubby species such as elder, ivy, hazel, birch, hawthorn/rowan crab apple and cherry species. A

Table 2.4: Middle Bronze Age charcoal from Rodway and Sandy Lane

Feature number		10031	10130	10145	10167	10192	10263	20871
Context number		10033	10131	10146	10169	10214	10262	20872
Feature label		Roundhouse A	Roundhouse A	Roundhouse B	Roundhouse B	Roundhouse B	Roundhouse A	Trough 20871
Sample number (SS)		101	104	105	106	111	114	262
Flot volume (ml)		288	12	101	42	405	23	22
Sample volume processed (l)		36	5	30	34	45	36	37
Charcoal quantity >2mm		++++	++++	+++++	++++	+++++	+++	++++++
Charcoal preservation		Poor	Moderate	Moderate	Good	Good	Moderate	Moderate
Family	Species	Common Name						
Aceraceae	*Acer campestre* L.	Field maple	-	-	-	2	1	2	-
Adoxaceae	*Sambucus nigra* L.	Elder r/w	-	2	-	-	-	-	-
Araliaceae	*Hedera helix* L.	Ivy	-	-	-	-	-	3	-
Betulaceae	*Alnus glutinosa* (L.) Gaertn.	Alder	-	-	-	1	5	-	1
	Alnus glutinosa (L.) Gaertn.	Alder r/w	-	-	-	-	6	-	-
	Alnus glutinosa (L.) Gaertn./*Corylus avellana* L.	Alder/Hazel	2	2	1	1	5	2	9
	Alnus glutinosa (L.) Gaertn./*Corylus avellana* L.	Alder/Hazel r/w	-	-	-	-	-	2	-
	Betula L.	Birches	-	-	-	-	-	1	-
	Corylus avellana L.	Hazel	-	-	-	-	3	-	1
Fagaceae	*Quercus petraea* (Matt.) Liebl./*Quercus robur* L.	Sessile Oak/Pedunculate Oak	48	54	98	44	66	16	61
	Quercus petraea (Matt.) Liebl./*Quercus robur* L.	Sessile Oak/Pedunculate Oak r/w	2	-	-	-	3	2	-
	Quercus petraea (Matt.) Liebl./*Quercus robur* L.	Sessile Oak/Pedunculate Oak r.w	4	2	-	10	10	-	3
Oleaceae	*Fraxinus excelsior* L.	Ash	4	1	-	-	-	-	2
	Fraxinus excelsior L.	Ash r/w	-	1	-	-	-	-	-
Rosaceae	*Crataegus monogyna* Jacq./*Sorbus* L./*Malus sylvestris* (L.) Mill.	Hawthorn/Rowans/Crab apple	-	3	-	-	1	3	3
	Crataegus monogyna Jacq./*Sorbus* L./*Malus sylvestris* (L.) Mill.	Hawthorn/Rowans/Crab apple r/w	-	-	-	-	-	-	1
	Prunus L.	Cherries	-	1	1	2	-	-	15
	Prunus spinosa L.	Blackthorn	-	-	-	-	-	-	4
		Indeterminate	-	-	-	9	-	-	-
		Total	60	66	100	69	100	31	100

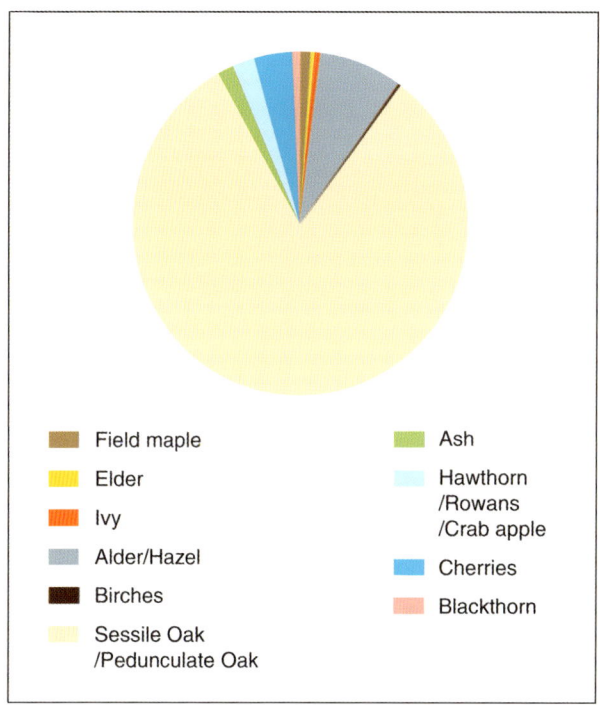

Fig. 2.10 Middle Bronze Age charcoal identifications from Rodway and Sandy Lane

number of the hedgerow/shrubby species exhibited curved growth rings, suggesting twigs were gathered to use within brushwood bundles for use as kindling. Oak is a highly calorific and efficient fuel (Gale and Cutler 2000, 205), and for the period of woodland clearance during the Middle Bronze Age, would have been widely available and used (either as fuelwood or charcoal) in both domestic and industrial contexts (Harris *et al.* 2003, 13). Oak heartwood along with blackthorn roundwood was a common find within a Middle Bronze Age curvilinear ditch at Queen Camel, Somerset (Challinor forthcoming), suggesting a similar use of oak as the main fuel utilised other sites in the area, as well as presumably also being used for construction.

Of interest was the charcoal composition of fill 10262 within pit 10263, which included a mixture of species, including ivy which was not recorded in any of the other Middle Bronze Age samples. It is likely the ivy was an incidental inclusion, included where it had wound around other species chosen as fuelwood.

The charcoal assemblage suggests that the local woodland comprised stands of oak, with smaller numbers of ash and maple, alongside scrub/shrub species such as hawthorn/rowan/crab apple, cherry species, elder and blackthorn perhaps making up hedgerows. Ivy tends not to colonise existing woodland, usually only recorded in areas of newly establishing woodland (Rackham 2001, 133), which may indicate an area of woodland regeneration around the site during this period. The presence of alder suggests wetland areas are present nearby, but not heavily exploited.

Radiocarbon dating
Sarah Cobain

Radiocarbon dating was undertaken in order to confirm the dates of a number of discrete features associated with the Bronze Age enclosure at Rodway, and of the trough containing burnt flint at Sandy Lane. The samples were analysed during November and December 2016 and April 2017 at Scottish Universities Environmental Research Centre (SUERC), Rankine Avenue, Scottish Enterprise Technology Park, East Kilbride, Glasgow, G75 0QF, Scotland.

The uncalibrated dates are conventional radiocarbon ages. The radiocarbon ages were calibrated using the University of Oxford Radiocarbon Accelerator Unit calibration programme OxCal v.4.2.4 (2013; Bronk Ramsey 2009) using the IntCal13 curve (Reimer *et al.* 2013). The methodology employed by SUERC Radiocarbon Laboratory is outlined in Dunbar *et al.* (2016). The results are presented in Table 2.5. Dates from Brean Down and Cambria Farm (Quinnell, Prehistoric pottery, above) have been recalibrated using Oxcal v.4.3.2 (2017) employing the same curve.

The dates fall within the expected range for the features sampled, both those on charred seeds and those on wood charcoal, and are considered to be reliable. Those from the pits and postholes inside the Rodway Enclosure are mutually consistent. Most overlap with the date from the trough from Sandy Lane, although this is a little earlier. Earlier still is the irregular tree-throw hole outside the Rodway Enclosure.

Table 2.5: Bronze Age radiocarbon dating results

Feature	Lab No.	Material	δ 13C‰	Radiocarbon age yrs BP	Calibrated radiocarbon age 95.4% probability	Calibrated radiocarbon age 68.2% probability
Rodway						
Context 10033 Pit 10031	SUERC-63442	Charcoal - *Prunus* (cherry species)	-25.0	3131 ± 31	1495–1476 cal. BC (4.0%) 1460–1371 cal. BC (66.1%) 1359–1300 cal. BC (25.3%)	1441–1388 cal. BC (54.2%) 1339–1319 cal. BC (14.0%)
Context 10146 Posthole 10145	SUERC-62336	Charcoal - *Alnus glutinosa/ Corylus avellana* (alder/hazel)	-26.5	3089 ± 30	1426–1276 cal. BC (95.4 %)	1410–1374 cal. BC (26.8 %) 1355–1302 cal. BC (41.4 %)
Context 10169 Pit 10137	SUERC-69951	Charred grain - *Triticum dicoccum/ Triticum spelta* (emmer/spelt wheat)	-22.2	2987 ± 29	1371–1360 cal. BC (1.5%) 1296–1118 cal. BC (93.9%)	1264–1192 cal. BC (54.3%) 1175–1164 cal. BC (5.9%) 1144–1131 cal. BC (8.0%)
Context 10178 Tree-throw hole 10177	SUERC-69950	Charred seed - *Corylus avellana* (hazelnut shell)	-23.4	3474 ± 28	1885–1737 cal. BC (89.5%) 1716–1696 cal. BC (5.9%)	1877–1841 cal. BC (26.0%) 1821–1796 cal. BC (16.7%) 1782–1747 cal. BC (25.5%)
Context 10200 Pit 10199	SUERC-69952	Charcoal - *Crataegus monogyna/ Sorbus/Malus sylvestris* (hawthorn/rowan/crab apple)	-25.9	3026 ± 28	1393–1366 cal. BC (22.8%) 1324–1195 cal. BC (72.1%) 1139–1135 cal. BC (0.5%)	1372–1358 cal. BC (9.0%) 1300–1224 cal. BC (59.2%)
Context 10262 Pit 10263	SUERC-62337	Charred seed - *Linum usitatissimum* (flax)	-27.5	3082 ± 30	1418–1266 cal. BC (95.4 %)	1404–1373 cal. BC (23.4 %) 1358–1300 cal. BC (44.8 %)
Sandy Lane						
Context 20872 Pit 20871	SUERC-69966	Charcoal - *Prunus* (cherry species)	-24.1‰	3154 ± 29	1500–1388 cal. BC (91.0%) 1338–1321 cal. BC (4.4%)	1493–1481 cal. BC (8.8%) 1454–1407 cal. BC (59.4%)

Chapter 3
Iron Age Settlement, Roman Villa and post-Roman Structure at Sandy Lane

Introduction

A possible enclosure was identified to the north of Sandy Lane at SPE 2 by geophysical survey, which formed part of the pre-construction works (Stratascan 2010; Fig. 1.4). Subsequent trial trenching in this area recorded stone-wall foundations and pits, and recovered Late Iron Age and Roman pottery. Two further trenches to the south of Sandy Lane identified ditches. In view of the clear importance of the features, on the advice of Steven Membery excavation within the trial trenches was kept to the minimum necessary to establish the presence of archaeological features and recover broad dating evidence. Full excavation was required in the two areas to the north and south of Sandy Lane.

The SPE 2 site lay on the edge of higher ground overlooking the Parrett Valley to the east (Fig. 3.1), with the highest part of the site along its western boundary at 37m OD, the level falling away northwards to 29m OD and eastwards to 35m OD. The underlying solid geology is mapped as the Triassic Otter Sandstone Formation (sandstone), with the southern part of the site bordered by the Carboniferous Rodway Siltstone Formation (siltstone and limestone) (BGS 2017; Fig. 1.3). No superficial deposits are recorded within the site (ibid.).

Although the extent of both Iron Age and Roman villa enclosures was probably fully exposed within the site, interpretation of the remains is severely restricted by the effects of truncation. Much of the site had been affected

Fig. 3.1   Sandy Lane, looking north-east from Roman Building A

Fig. 3.2   Sandy Lane, looking north-west towards Cannington Camp hillfort

by post-medieval quarrying, which had truncated parts of Iron Age and Roman buildings, parts of the associated settlement enclosure boundaries, and much of the interior (Figs 3.3 and 3.4). A number of these quarries were linear, following bedding planes. Some remains, including buildings, are likely to have been lost in their entirety. Ploughing had caused additional truncation, with buildings surviving for the most part only at foundation level, and with surfaces and wall courses above historic ground levels rarely present. This has restricted the extent to which the functions of buildings and of the rooms within them can be interpreted, and has also meant that any complex biographies of rebuilding and repair may have been lost, with the notable exception of one building (Roman Building A). Overall, this has restricted the extent to which the spatial organisation of economic and social spaces within each settlement can be reconstructed. The limited survival of the buildings means that reconstructions above ground level must remain largely speculative, and it should be noted that the accompanying reconstruction drawing (Fig. 4.3) depicts generic Roman buildings, the appearances of which should only be taken as a best estimate.

Features have been assigned to periods based on spot dates from finds and radiocarbon dates (Table 3.22) and on spatial and stratigraphic relationships to dated features. Aside from the Bronze Age trough and a small assemblage of residual flints described in Chapter 2, the earliest remains related to an enclosed late prehistoric settlement. This was superseded by a Roman villa, following which there was an apparent hiatus until the construction of a building during the post-Roman period.

Iron Age, Roman and post-Roman settlement at Sandy Lane
Jonathan Hart

Late Iron Age to Roman transition period (c. 100 BC–AD 100)

The late prehistoric settlement was located to the north of Sandy Lane, and below the highest point of the site (Fig. 3.1). It originated in the Late Iron Age and was intervisible with the hillfort at Cannington Camp to the north-west (Fig. 3.2). Dating for the Iron Age settlement is provided by the pottery which comprises handmade wares, including south-west decorated wares dateable to after 400/300 BC, and plain wares dateable to the Iron Age to Roman transition period from the later 1st century BC and into the early or middle decades of the 1st century AD, which, being found together, suggest occupation of the Iron Age site during the later 1st century BC to the mid or later 1st century AD. The features produced a fairly small animal bone assemblage, but sufficient to indicate that livestock were bred, slaughtered and butchered by the inhabitants. This husbandry was dominated by sheep/goat rearing, with cattle in smaller numbers. Pigs were also kept, as were a few domestic fowl, and horses were either bred on site or imported as young animals. Part of a single dog skeleton was also recovered. Crops indicated by charred plants included emmer and spelt wheat, barley and Celtic beans, and there were indications of crop processing within the site.

The Iron Age settlement presumably had been enclosed by ditches (Fig. 3.4), although the southern extents of these had been lost to quarrying. Neither was an Iron

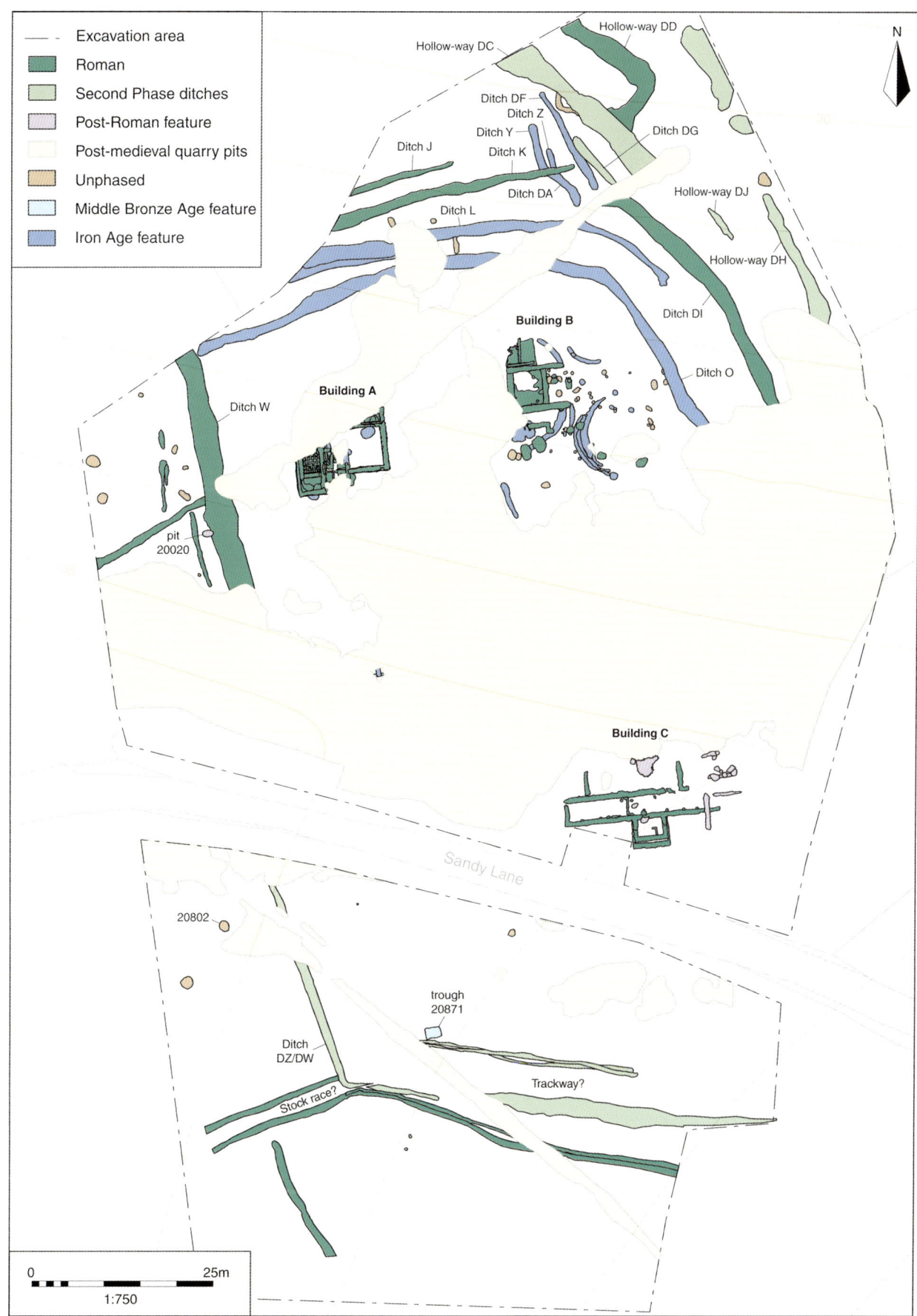

Fig. 3.3   Sandy Lane overall site plan

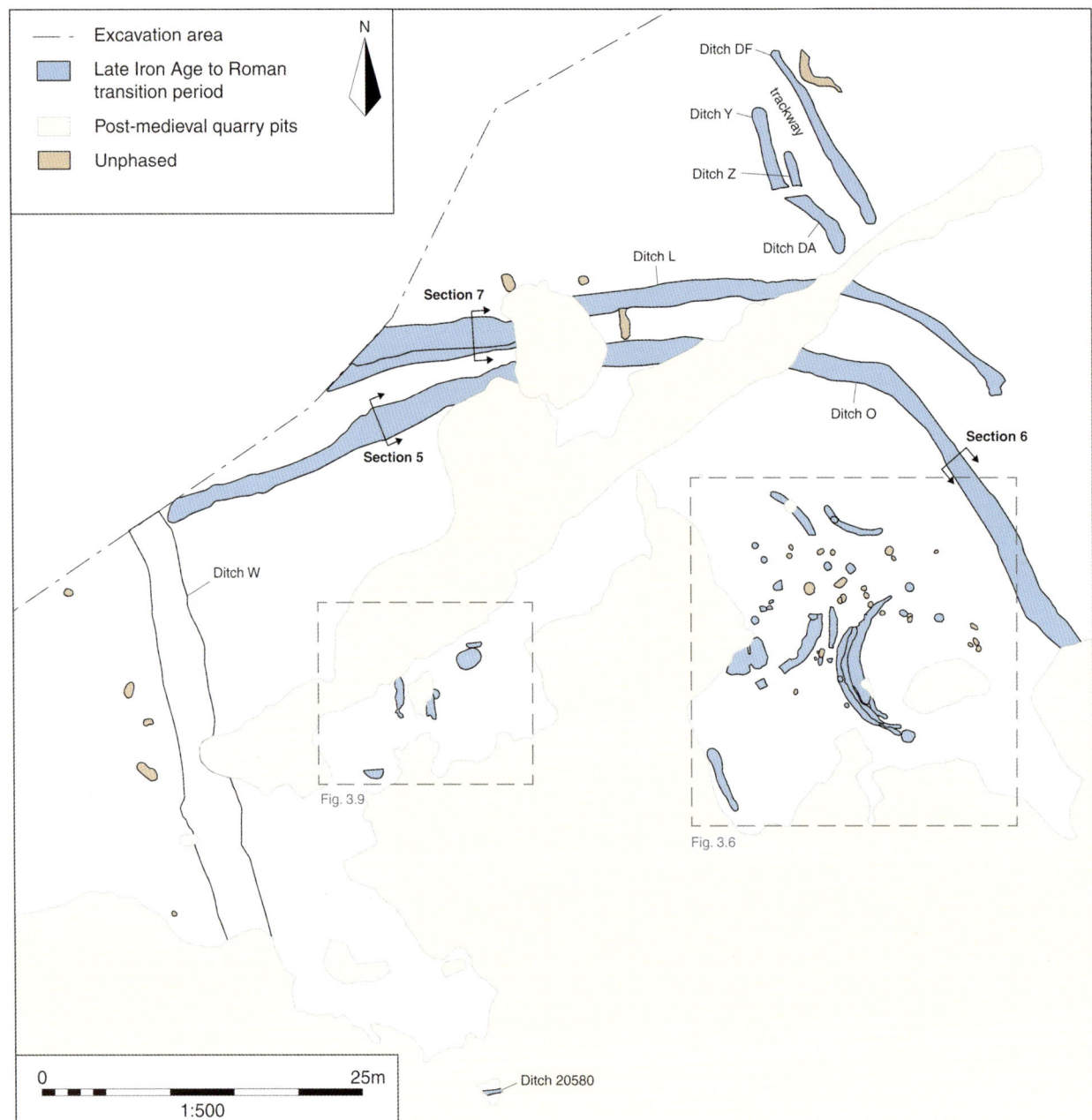

Fig. 3.4 Sandy Lane Iron Age settlement: plan of Iron Age enclosure. Roman Ditch W probably re-cut an Iron Age ditch on the same alignment

Age western ditch identified but it is possible that Roman Ditch W fossilised the line of the western edge of the Iron Age enclosure, entirely re-cutting an Iron Age ditch or some other form of boundary. The inner ditch (Ditch O) was a curvilinear feature bounding the northern and north-eastern sides of the settlement and terminating just short of Ditch W. In profile, it varied between a broad U-shape, up to 3m wide and 0.7m deep, to a steeper-sided cut, 1.4m wide and 0.5m deep (Fig. 3.5, sections 5 and 6). This variable profile may reflect episodes of re-cutting which were also suggested by the stepped profile noted in places along the ditch edges and within some of the fills. The ditch contained a few slumped deposits which suggested the former presence of a bank along its northern edge, although the evidence for this was slight. The uppermost part of the ditch was filled with dark sandy silts which produced frequent cultural debris, including charcoal, pottery and the bones of cattle, sheep/goat and pig, as well as of a young horse and two adult horses. Unworked sandstone within the fills may have derived from a bank or from demolished structures within the settlement. Occasional finds of Roman pottery within the upper fills suggest that the ditch remained as an earthwork into the Roman period.

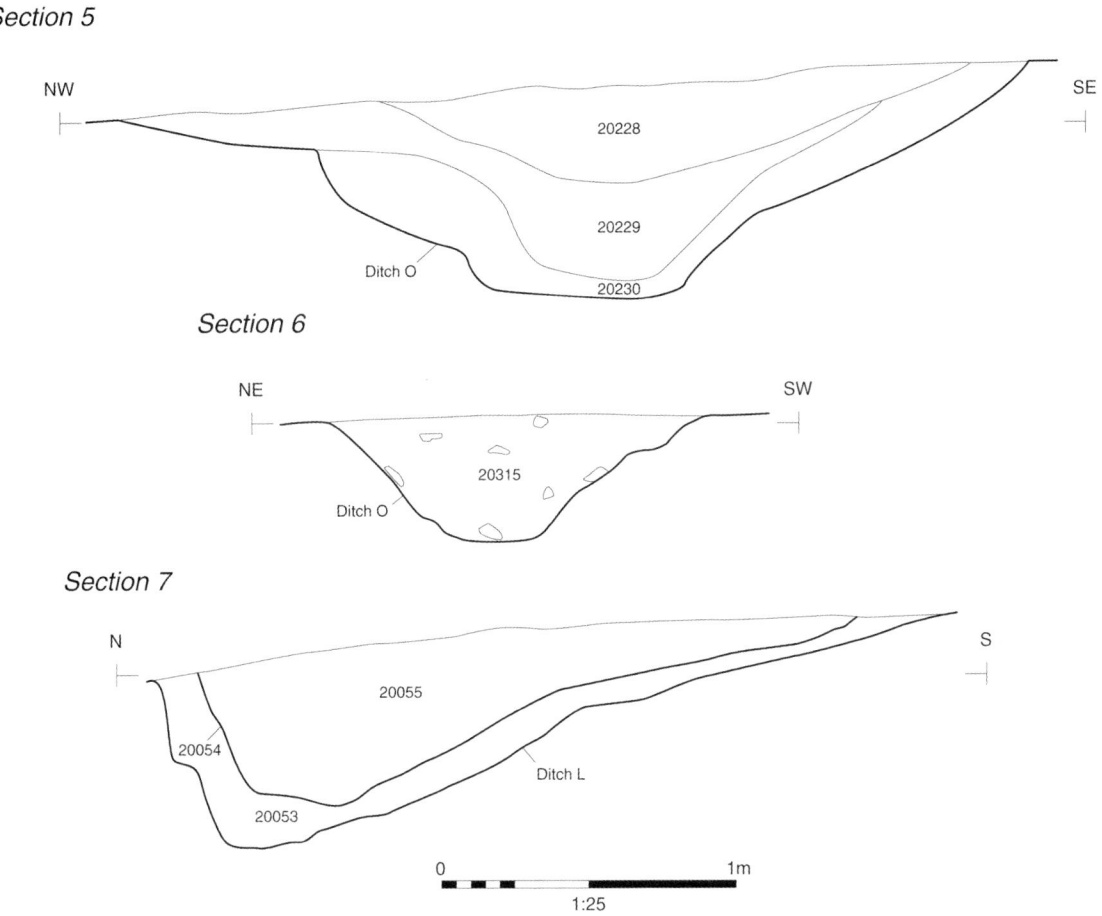

Fig. 3.5 Sandy Lane Iron Age settlement: Section 5, south-west facing section through Ditch O; Section 6, north-west facing section through Ditch O; Section 7, west facing section through Ditch L

Ditch L was between 1.4m and 5m from the outer edge of Ditch O, and ran broadly parallel to it. At its eastern extent, the ditch ended in a convincing butt-ended terminal and it is possible that an entrance to the enclosure was originally at this point, perhaps later obscured by re-cutting along the inner ditch (Ditch O). Ditch L itself showed clear evidence of re-cutting, the re-cutting of both ditches perhaps accounting for the varying distance between them, and their varying profiles, but in its latest form, Ditch L varied between 1.3m wide and 0.4m deep to 2.2m wide and 0.5m deep (Fig. 3.5, section 7). The profile also varied, from a symmetric U-shape to a profile with a steeper outer edge. As with the inner ditch, Ditch L seemed to have been deliberately backfilled with dark silty sand deposits, which produced charcoal, a smithing hearth-cake fragment (a metallurgical residue relating to iron-smithing), pottery, a stone spindlewhorl and sandstone, with some of the pottery dating to the Roman period again suggesting that the ditch persisted as an earthwork.

A possible southern boundary to the Iron Age enclosure was hinted at by the presence of a small east/west-aligned ditch (20580), which survived fortuitously in an area surrounded by extensive quarrying (Fig. 3.4). This ditch produced Iron Age pottery and was the southernmost surviving Iron Age feature within the site, its small size reflecting the fact that only the base of this feature survived the later quarrying. It is possible that the western limit of the settlement lay beyond the excavated area, or that the settlement was unenclosed towards the higher ground to the west, but if Roman Ditch W (which was aligned with the western terminal of Iron Age Ditch O) represents a Roman re-cutting of the Iron Age western boundary, and ditch 20580 represents the southern boundary to the enclosure, then the Iron Age enclosure would have measured 48m north to south and 62m east to west, a total area of some 0.3ha.

The only Iron Age features found outside the enclosure were a series of ditches extending from its north-eastern side (Ditches DA, DF, Y and Z). These flat-based to U-profiled ditches produced few finds aside from several sherds of Iron Age pottery, and seem to have filled naturally, and may have flanked a trackway of variable width (2m to 4m).

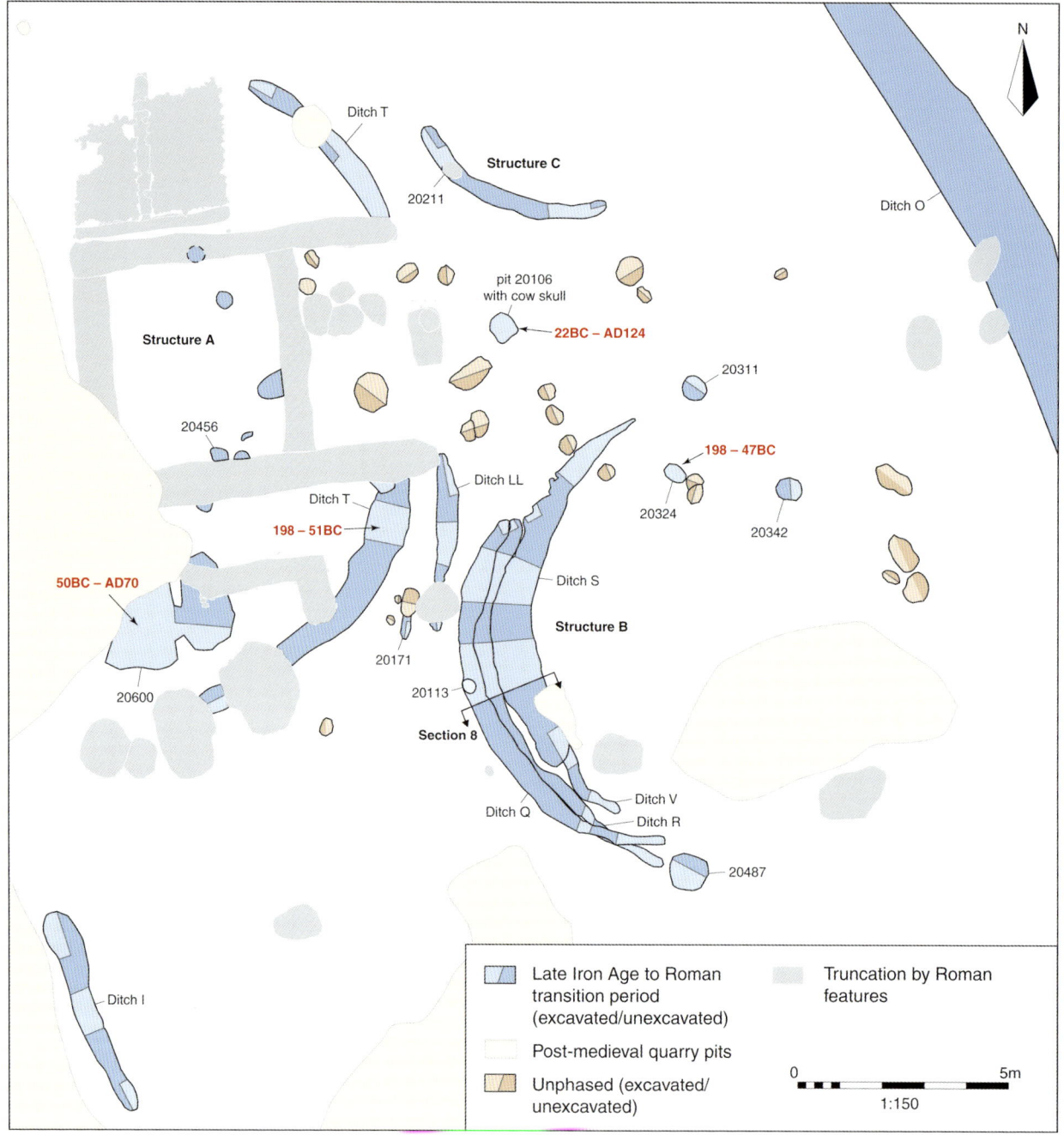

Fig. 3.6   Sandy Lane Iron Age settlement: detail plan of Structures A–C

Internally, the enclosure contained two surviving areas of activity. The eastern of these areas included the settings of curvilinear ditches which seem to have related to structures (Structures A–C; Fig. 3.6).

Structure A survived as segments of a curvilinear ditch (Ditch T) assumed to have marked the setting of a circular or semi-circular structure up to 15m across. That it was never a full ring ditch is suggested by the northern segment, which included a convincing northern terminal; other breaks along the ditch segments were partially or wholly the result of truncation. The ditch segments were 0.5m to 1m wide and 0.25m deep with U-shaped profiles and contained notably compact red-brown sandy silt fills which included frequent sandstones. A hazel twig from Ditch T was radiocarbon dated to 198–51 cal. BC (SUERC-69954) and was found alongside Iron Age/Roman transitional pottery. The bones of a few small mammals (shrew, wood mouse and field vole), and of frogs from Ditch T suggest that these creatures made their home in and around Structure A. A short curvilinear ditch segment (Ditch LL) outside Ditch T was of uncertain function but may have related to drainage or to an earlier form of the structure.

Just inside the southern part of the Ditch T circuit

was a pair of pits (excavated and numbered as a single feature, 20600). These two relatively large pits (up to 2.8m wide and 0.4m deep) were joined by a small ledge, thought during excavation to have been a flue, although it was very unpronounced. The pits contained a series of dark sandy silt fills which included varying quantities of charcoal and occasional burnt clay. Samples from the charcoal produced a moderate assemblage of charred cereal remains, predominantly barley, emmer wheat and spelt wheat grains, but with chaff and weed seeds also present. One of the charred emmer/spelt wheat grains was radiocarbon dated to 50 cal. BC–cal. AD 70 (SUERC-69953), a date which accords with the Late Iron Age to Early Roman pottery from the pits. Further evidence of the site's economy came from the fills of Ditch T which produced the remains of three male pigs ranging in age from one and a half to two years.

Structure B was 1.7m east of the main ditch of Structure A. It survived as a series of intercutting curvilinear ditches partially enclosing an area some 11m in diameter. Stratigraphically, Ditches R and V were the earliest, with Ditches Q and S later. It is possible that the structure comprised paired ditches, although it is equally possible that a sequence of four cuts is represented (Figs 3.7 and 3.8). Ditch R was flat-based, up to 0.35m wide and 0.2m deep, although the terminals were slighter, and had been largely truncated. Its apparent southern terminal was really the result of truncation and the ditch originally may have extended further to the south-east. Ditch V was only slightly larger, and had a more U-shaped profile. Ditch Q was more variable in profile, being U-shaped to flat-based, and was comparable in size to Ditch R, whilst Ditch S was notably more substantial, with a U-shaped profile up to 0.9m wide and 0.4m deep. Its southern terminal was convincing, the northern terminal more probably the result of truncation. All of the ditches contained sandy silt fills, occasionally with charcoal and pottery. Ditch S produced two unsexed pig skeletons, aged 7 to 14 months and 0 to 7 months.

Additional parts of Structure B were suggested by

Fig. 3.7 Sandy Lane Iron Age settlement: ditches of Structure B, looking south (scale 1m)

postholes 20487 and 20311, to either end of the structure ditch terminals. These bowl-shaped features were more suggestive of pits but contained what appeared to be stones used to pack around former posts, and so may have been associated with the wall line of Structure B. Similarly, posthole 20113 may represent a deeper post along the wall line within Ditch Q.

Internally, Structure B enclosed oval pit 20324, which was 0.55m long, 0.25m wide and 0.15m deep with a flat base. It contained a charcoal-rich lower fill, 20325, from which a roundwood charcoal fragment produced a

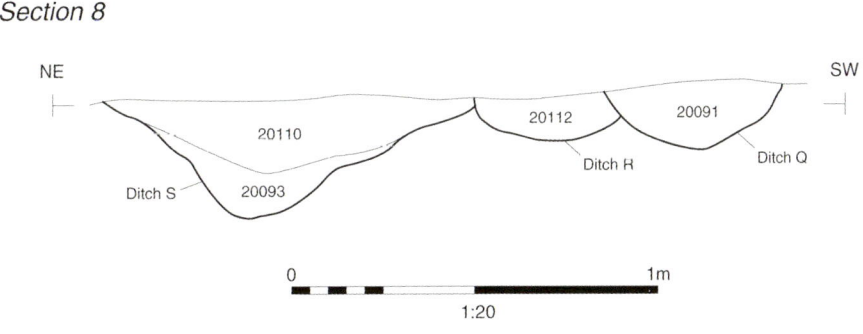

Fig. 3.8 Sandy Lane Iron Age settlement: Section 8, north-west facing section through the ditches of Structure B

radiocarbon date of 198–47 cal. BC (95.4% probability; SUERC-70708). This was sealed by a second charcoal-rich fill and it is possible, although not certain, that this pit was the base of a hearth.

Structure C was 1.5m north-east of Structure A and comprised a curvilinear ditch, of which the north-western terminal was convincing but its south-eastern end was probably caused by truncation, the ditch being only 0.05m–0.1m deep.

Some 11m south-west of Structure B, a fourth possible structure was identified. This survived as Ditch I, a fairly straight ditch segment 5m long, 0.5m wide and 0.15m deep with a flat base. It was found in an 'island' of undisturbed natural surrounded on three sides by post-medieval quarrying, and so is difficult to interpret, but one possibility is that it was a beam slot forming the eastern wall of a building. Small quantities of Late Iron Age pottery came from its single sandy silt fill.

A number of pits and postholes were found within and around Structures A, B and C. Some of these contained Iron Age finds, whilst others were of Roman date and a number could not be phased. The dated Iron Age and undated pits and postholes are shown on Fig. 3.6. Included amongst these were two features (pits 20600 and 20106) that produced radiocarbon dates spanning the Late Iron Age to Roman transition period, and extending into the Roman period. These dates were generally later than the radiocarbon dates from the other Iron Age features, and it is unclear whether they reflect subsequent Roman activity within this part of the site, or point to longevity of the Iron Age features. Given the apparent continuity of occupation within the site, these remains have been included within the Iron Age phase.

That some of these remains belonged to the Early Roman period was evidenced by the presence of an early form of DOR BB1 pottery from pit 20342, 4.6m east of the ditches of Structure B, in the form of a jar with a footring, dateable to the 1st century AD, so perhaps from one of the later deposits associated with the structures. Pit 20106, located centrally between Structures A, B and C, may also have been a late deposit associated with the Iron Age occupation. It was sub-rectangular, 0.7m long, 0.6m wide and 0.15m deep with vertical sides and a flat base. It contained a single green-brown sandy silt fill which included a smithing hearth-cake fragment and a cattle skull radiocarbon dated to 22 cal. BC–cal. AD 124 (SUERC-72465). This skull would seem to represent a deliberate placement, and the location of the pit, centrally between the Iron Age structures, suggests that it was associated with them. However, it should also be noted that the pit would have lain just outside the later Roman building on the site (Building B; Fig. 3.23) and the radiocarbon date would also be compatible with this association.

The second area of surviving Iron Age activity within the enclosure was 18m west of Structures A–C and beneath what was later the site of Roman Building A (Fig. 3.9). Much of this activity had been truncated by the Roman building or by post-medieval quarrying, restricting the extent to which the Iron Age features could be interpreted. Amongst these were two parallel linear features, 20608 and 20751. These had vertical sides and flat bases and were beneath Roman deposits. Feature 20608 was 0.5m wide and 0.3m deep, and survived to a length of 2.9m, although it was truncated at both ends, so was probably longer originally. Its single sandy silt fill produced Iron Age pottery. Feature 20751 was less clearly defined, but may have been similar. It was undated, but was slightly off the alignment of an overlying Roman wall. It is possible that these two parallel features were beam slots for a building (Structure D), in which case the space between them, 2m wide, suggests that they may have flanked a lobby rather than a room, although this cannot be more than speculation.

Three steep-sided, flat-based pits were found around Structure D (20573, 20430 and 20271). They ranged in size from pit 20430, which was 0.55m wide and 0.2m deep, to pit 20271, which was 1.45m wide and 0.45m deep. All had been backfilled and were cut or sealed by Roman deposits, in addition to which pit 20430 produced Iron Age pottery. It is possible that the larger pits were grain stores, whilst pit 20430 may have been a further grain store or a posthole associated with the putative Iron Age Structure D. A fourth pit, 20348, had more sloping sides leading to a flat base, and produced a sherd of transitional pottery and a sherd of wheel-thrown Roman pottery. It is possible that this was a scoured-out storage pit, backfilled prior to the Roman building phase, although it could conceivably belong to the subsequent Roman building.

Early to Mid Roman (c. AD 100–300)

The Iron Age enclosed settlement seems to have been occupied into the Roman period, during which time it was remodelled to become Romanised, including a villa range. The Iron Age enclosure ditches and banks were levelled, although some at least remained visible as earthworks, collecting debris such as pottery into the Roman period, and their general layout influenced that of the Roman period enclosure, at least along its northern side. The pottery assemblage from this period is dominated by South-east Dorset Black-burnished ware (DOR BB1) and reduced coarsewares, the latter probably from Somerset potteries. The DOR BB1 pottery from the site includes early forms of the 1st century AD, although most of the DOR BB1 forms are dateable to after the early 2nd century. A few regional (British) and continental imports are also present, but the assemblage as a whole is utilitarian, with only a few finewares. Overall, the Roman pottery assemblage suggests occupation during the 1st to late 3rd centuries, with no apparent break from the Iron Age occupation and with a focus on the late 2nd to 3rd centuries; Oxfordshire and New Forest finewares, which

Fig. 3.9 Sandy Lane Iron Age settlement: detail plan of possible beam-slot building (Structure D) and pits

indicate 4th-century activity, are largely absent from the assemblage.

The animal bone assemblage from the Roman period showed little change from the Iron Age, with sheep rearing predominating but cattle providing the greatest meat weight, although kept in life principally for traction, breeding and dairying. Horses were also kept, with one horse bone displaying a pathological condition called 'spavin', an indicator that the animal was used for draught work. Fewer pigs were kept than in the Iron Age, and fowl comprised bantam-sized birds, with possible evidence for rearing. A duck may have been domestic or wild; marine and riverine fish were eaten, although in small quantities, whilst bones from one or two hares may have been from hunted animals, although hunting clearly did not contribute significantly to the inhabitants' diet. Dogs and cats were also kept. The charred plants included crops, of which spelt wheat was the most common, although some emmer, free-threshing wheat, barley and oats were also present,

as was flax. There was evidence that cereals had been processed on site, particular from material that had been redeposited in later features but which was shown to have been largely Roman through radiocarbon dating.

As with the Iron Age settlement, the Roman villa was enclosed by boundaries (Fig. 3.10). The western, northern and eastern boundaries comprised Ditches W, J, K and DI, and closely followed those of the Iron Age, although they were built on the external side of the Iron Age boundaries, except in the case of Ditch W which, as discussed above, may have followed the exact line of the Iron Age enclosure ditch. Of these, only Ditch W, the closest to a building, produced much cultural material/building debris. The other ditches were filled with pale silts/clays with few finds and probably served as the boundary between the villa yard and the surrounding fields. Where the southern boundary of the villa was is uncertain. Ditches to the south of Sandy Lane were certainly Roman but were relatively insubstantial and more akin to the field boundaries seen to the west of

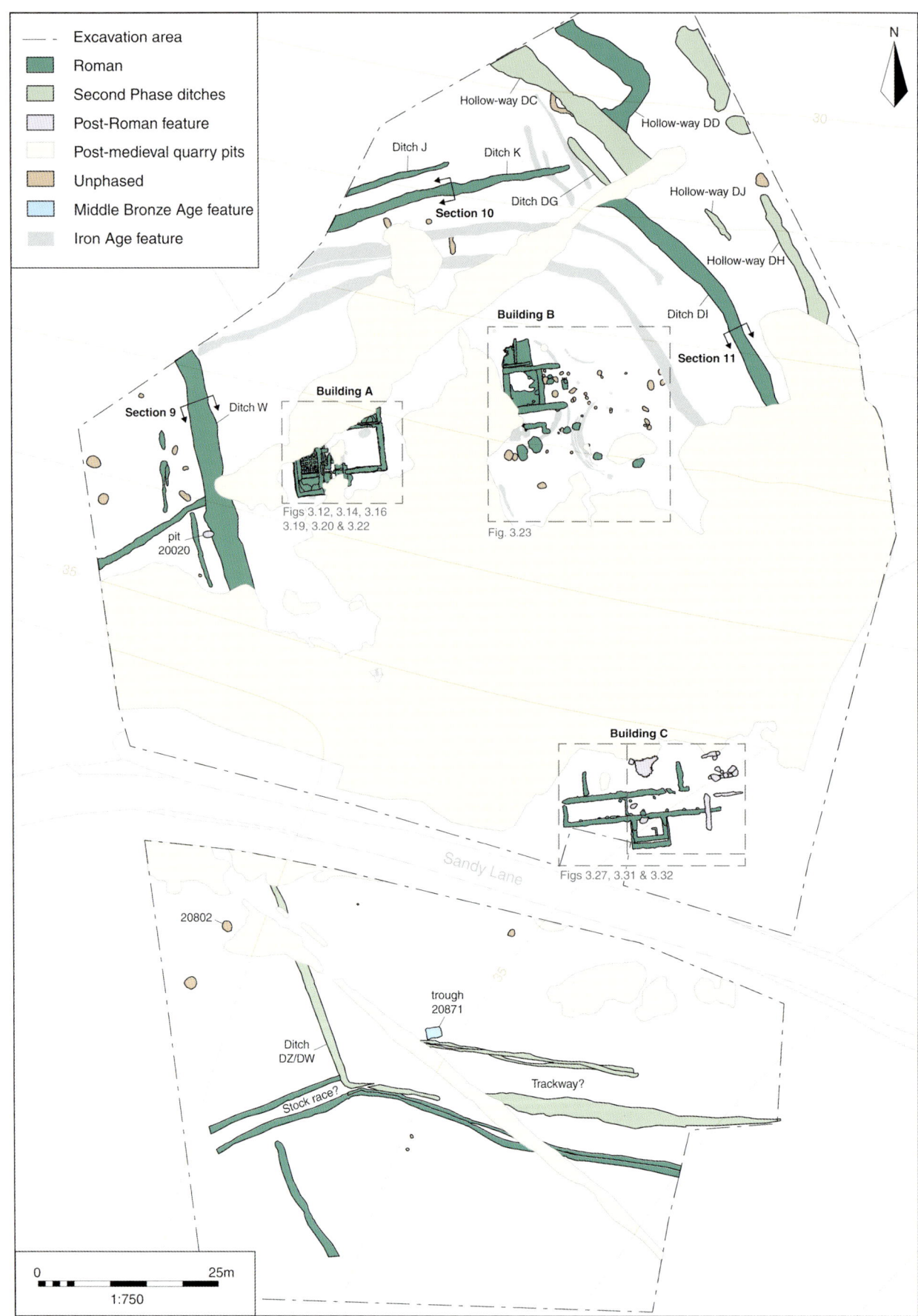

Fig. 3.10   Sandy Lane Roman villa: plan of the enclosure

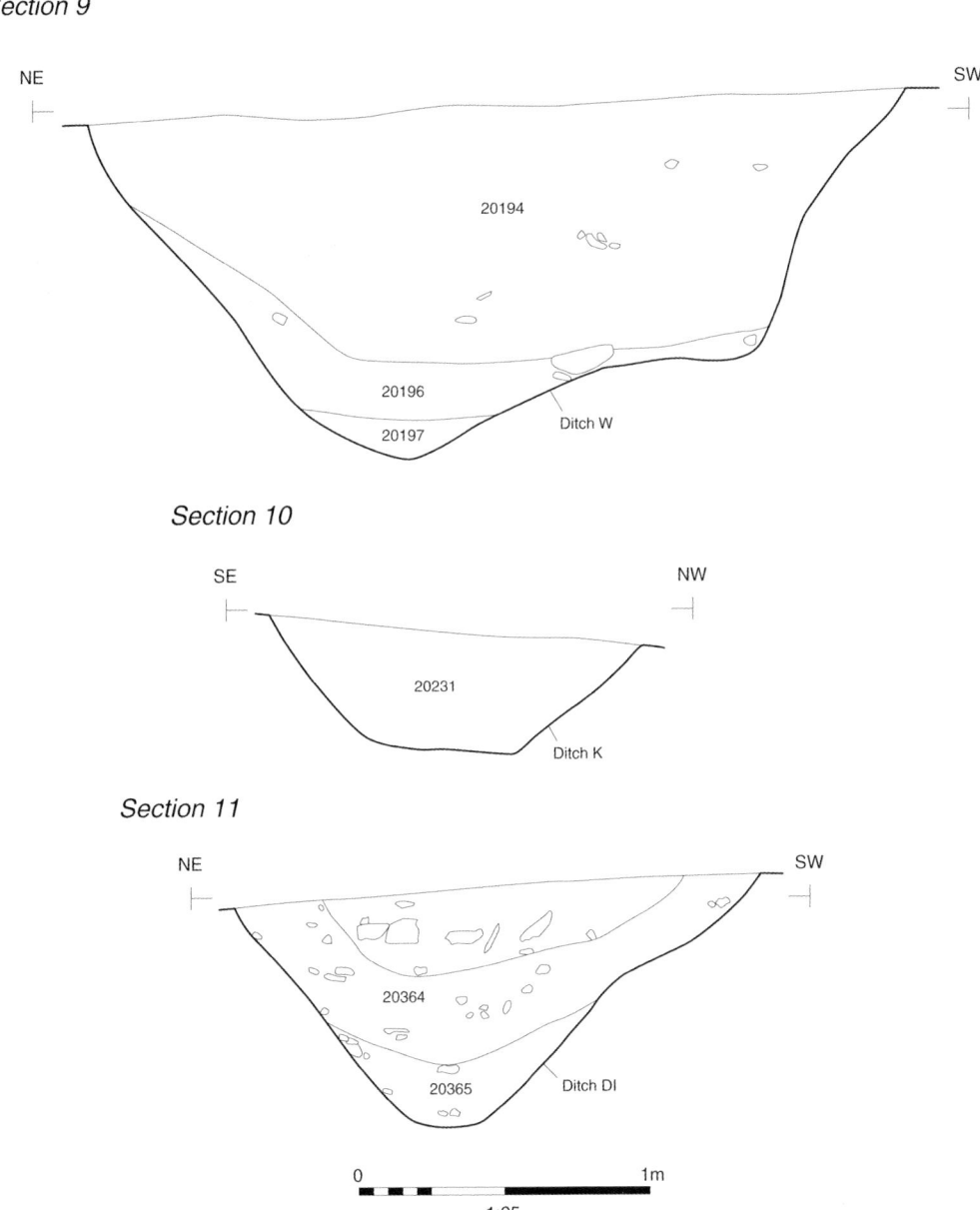

Fig. 3.11 Sandy Lane Roman villa: Section 9, north-west facing section through Ditch W; Section 10, north-east facing section through Ditch K; Section 11, north-west facing section through Ditch DI

Ditch W. It is possible that any southern boundary to the villa ran along the line of Sandy Lane which, on the basis of its alignment relative to the extant field boundaries, would seem to be of post-medieval date (Stephen Rippon, pers. comm.). If the rear of the villa enclosure was along the line of Sandy Lane, then the enclosure would have measured approximately 70m east to west and 75m north to south, an area of some 0.6ha.

The Roman enclosure ditches were generally substantial. Ditch W, the western boundary, was steep-sided and flat-based, up to 2.8m wide and 1.1m deep (Fig. 3.11, section 9). A reddish silty clay basal fill was overlain by a deposit which slumped in from the eastern side of the ditch, perhaps from an internal bank. The northern boundary was provided by Ditches K and J, with U-shaped profiles up to 1.75m wide and 0.45m deep (Fig. 3.11, section 10), separated by a 2.25m-wide gap suggesting that they may have flanked a hedge-bank. Ditch DI, the eastern boundary, was also substantial (Fig. 3.11, section 11) and although its northern terminal was lost to post-medieval quarrying, seems to have turned westwards, leaving a 5.5m-wide gap between itself and Ditch K, suggesting that the villa enclosure was accessible from the north-east.

The ditch fills produced pottery, charcoal, animal bone and ceramic building material (CBM). Ditch

W also contained a Roman-style knife, two smithing hearth-cake fragments and a number of carpentry nails. Unworked stones within the fills of the enclosure ditches may have derived from former banks or buildings (or a mixture of the two) and Ditch DI contained a few probable Lias paving stones. The majority of the finds came from the upper fills of the ditches, relating to their disuse; the recovered pottery spanned the 2nd to 3rd centuries AD. Pottery from the primary fills of Ditch W dated to the 2nd century AD or later, but the ditch itself may have been earlier than this, with the earliest deposits having been scoured out, a suggestion raised by the flat base of the ditch which would have facilitated shovel-scraping. The latest pottery from the ditch included DOR BB1 jars with lattice decoration, dateable to after c. AD 220, and flanged bowls dateable to after c. AD 250, suggesting that the settlement was abandoned no later than the later 3rd or early 4th century AD.

Externally, the north-eastern entrance was accessed via Hollow-way DD, a broad, shallow hollow 3.3m wide and 0.25m deep, which produced Roman pottery. This hollow-way would seem to have followed the gentle zig-zag descent of the earlier Iron Age trackway, and can be seen in plan to have funnelled out as it approached the entrance to the villa enclosure (later cut by Hollow-way DC). The fact that the hollow-way terminated before reaching the entrance raises the possibility that the entrance was paved, although direct evidence for this was absent. The hollow-way fill produced a copper-alloy T-shaped brooch (Fig. 3.45, no. 2), probably dateable to the 2nd century AD. Other elements of the landscape surrounding the villa were also exposed. Narrow ditches to the west of the enclosure were presumably field boundaries. Further such boundaries to the south of Sandy Lane included a pair separated by a 2m-wide gap, perhaps forming a stock race.

There was evidence that this layout was remodelled. The original north-eastern entrance was blocked by the insertion of Ditch DG. Presumably at the same time, the original hollow-way was abandoned in favour of a route (Hollow-way DC) that ran past the former entrance and along the eastern side of the enclosure, presumably to an entrance along the enclosure's eastern side, but now lost to post-medieval quarrying. This later hollow-way produced a copper-alloy *As* coin of Marcus Aurelius (AD 161–180). Other irregular features may have been further hollow-ways (DH and DJ). The pottery from these later features mostly spanned the same 2nd to 3rd-century date range as that provided by the pottery from the original ditches of the enclosure, and Ditch DJ also produced an iron 'latch lifter' key of a type used from the Late Iron Age and throughout the Roman period (Fig. 3.45, no. 3). However, Hollow-way DH produced a pottery sherd from a New Forest beaker, dateable to after c. AD 260, Hollow-way DC contained sherds from two large storage vessels of Middle to Late Roman type, and Ditch DW, a field boundary south of Sandy Lane, produced an Oxford whiteware mortarium dating to the second half of the 3rd century, as well as a red-slipped ware bowl (Fig. 3.40; 28–9), dateable to c. AD 240/270–400. Together, these features probably reflect the latest period of use of the villa, the hollow-ways having filled when the routes fell into disuse. Some evidence that the ditches persisted as earthworks into the post-Roman period was gained from a radiocarbon date from the upper fill of field boundary Ditch DW, to the south-east of the enclosure, which produced an unexpectedly late date of cal. AD 426–582 (SUERC-69956). While it is possible that this was simply an intrusive charcoal fragment (from an oak twig), the date does suggest early post-Roman activity on the site.

Pit 20802, 7m west of Ditch DW, was a bowl-shaped cut 1.3m in diameter and 0.35m deep. Its sides and edges had been lined with stones, which included small and worn fragments of lava, probably the reused remains of broken-up rotary querns. Above these, the pit contained a single brown silty clay fill, seemingly derived from the natural substrate. No finds or botanical remains were found within the fill and the pit is technically undated, but the quern fragments are almost certainly Roman in date and the pit is therefore Roman (or later) in all probability.

The enclosure contained three buildings (Buildings A, B and C). As with the Iron Age remains, it is possible that the extensive post-medieval quarrying had entirely removed the remains of other structures, most notably any that might have been located within the central part of the enclosure.

Building A (Figs 3.12–22)

Building A was the best preserved of the Roman buildings, and provides a sequence of building and rebuilding which seems to have spanned the entire duration of the villa's Roman occupation. As well as the structural remains described below, nine painted wall plaster fragments were recovered from layers, mainly demolition deposits, as were seven ceramic roof tile fragments, together weighing 1.6kg. The possible function of the building is examined in the Discussion (below); the following is a narrative description of the building's development. This development has been assigned to a number of phases, although close dating of each phase is not possible, due to the broad ranges provided by the pottery, dominated by DOR BB1 sherds and with finewares entirely absent. Overall, the Roman pottery assemblage from Building A suggests use during the late 2nd or 3rd centuries. Identifiable rooms have been given numbers (Room 1, Room 2, etc.) which continue through phases where rooms seem to have remained in use in their original or a remodelled form.

Building A, Phase 1

The date of the construction works is uncertain since little dating evidence was recovered. The earliest

Fig. 3.12 Sandy Lane Roman villa: plan of Building A, Phase 1

identifiable building works comprised the construction of two rooms (Rooms 1 and 2; Fig. 3.12) within a small rectangular building *c.* 7.7m by 5m internally.

Room 1
Room 1 was within the south-western corner of Building A. Much had been truncated but surviving wall stubs suggested a room approximately square in plan, measuring 2.7m by 2.5m internally. It was defined by earth-bonded wall foundations built within flat-based construction trenches. In places, the trenches had been levelled with sandy bedding deposits which included occasional sherds of pottery, although these were only broadly dateable as Roman. The surviving foundations included walls 20464 and 20465, forming the room's north-western corner. The western wall, 20465, had been cut back during later remodelling, but wall 20464 survived to its full width of 0.5m and comprised roughly squared sandstone with a rubble core.

The eastern side of the room was partly defined by wall 20472. This was 0.55m wide and 0.26m high and comprised a foundation course of horizontal sandstone slabs with a rubble core. Onto these, a course of pitched sandstone was set, perhaps the lowest course of herringbone-patterned walling above foundation level (Fig. 3.13). The wall projected south of the building to form what for later developments of Building A was the presumed site of a furnace. Although there was no evidence for heating within Phase 1, in the form of hypocaust channels or *pilae*, it seems likely that an external furnace was part of the original build and that the original Room 1 was heated, although how the heat was channelled into Room 1 is uncertain: it might have come through underfloor channels, or from wall flues, but no trace of either remained.

Room 2
Room 2 had an L-shaped floor plan, with Room 1 in its south-western corner, and measured 7.7m by 5m internally. It survived only at foundation level, with the foundations (20484) laid onto a sandy bedding layer within a shallow construction trench. The foundations

Fig. 3.13 Building A Phase 1: Room 1 wall 20472 running north/south: Room 2 foundation 20484 in foreground (scale 1m)

were of earth-bonded stone rubble, mainly sandstone but with some limestone, and survived to a single course, 0.75m wide. The northern extent of the footings had been cut back in a later phase of the building, whilst the north-western and western extents were entirely lost to truncation. One small length of wall, 20485, survived above foundation level and was formed from a single course of limestone blocks laid onto a thin sandy bedding layer above the rubble footings. This sandy bedding layer produced pottery broadly dateable as Roman whilst the bedding layer within the foundation trench produced Late Iron Age to Roman pottery, and the footings themselves pottery broadly dateable as Roman. The room had been cut into the natural substrate at 35.32m OD. No surfaces survived and it is possible that the room had had a beaten earth floor, although any more substantial surfacing might simply have been removed, given the degree of truncation.

Building A, Phase 2

Phase 2 marked extensive remodelling of Building A. The original build formed the core of the remodelled building, which was expanded by the addition of rooms to the north and west (Figs 3.14 and 3.15). The added walls were characterised by the use of reddish gravelly mortars, in contrast to the earth bonding previously employed.

Room 1

The original room was retained, but with a series of channels inserted into the base. These were defined by L-shaped sections of stone wall comprising roughly squared sandstone blocks on the inner faces, backed with sandstone rubble. The sandstone blocks were bonded with reddish gravelly cement mortar, with the rubble within a red-brown sandy silt matrix. Wall 20469 extended south of Room 1, into the housing of the putative Phase 1 furnace, thus creating a flue through which heat from the furnace could enter the room at below-ground level. A sample from the infill of heating channels produced a very small assemblage of charred cereals but an abundance of charcoal, presumably the remains of fuel drawn in from the furnace outside, although this material may have accumulated over the life of the heating channels, which extended as late as Phase 6 of Building 2. Any traces of the furnace itself had been removed by a quarry pit, which extended into the furnace housing. No traces of floor survived above the heating channels.

Room 3

Room 3 was added to the west of Rooms 1 and 2. Direct stratigraphic relationships between the two were absent but the eastern wall of Room 3 must have been a rebuild of the western walls of Rooms 1 and 2, the

Fig. 3.14 Building A, Phase 2. The north-west corner is conjectural

bonding now being of mortar rather than earth. Room 3 was a rectangular space, internally 2.4m wide. Its northern extent was lost to quarrying but the extent of the quarrying in all likelihood defined the upper limit of the northern extent of Room 3, which can have been no more than 10.8m long, and perhaps shorter if Room 4 had occupied this space.

It had been built within a rectangular cut into the natural north-to-south hillslope, within which a series of wall foundations were built. The eastern foundation, 20471, consisted of roughly squared sandstones with a rubble core and was 0.6m wide, surviving to four courses and bonded with a hard red-brown gravelly mortar. Where a gap remained between the wall and the construction cut, this was filled with sandy silt deposits which included Roman pottery, some dateable to the 1st to 2nd centuries AD, along with two sherds of Dorset Black-burnished ware dateable to the later 2nd to 3rd centuries AD, suggesting a construction date during or after the late 2nd to 3rd century.

The western side of the room was defined by foundations 20462, which were of comparable build to foundations 20471 and used the same mortar. They survived to a height of four courses (0.4m) and a notable feature was that the uppermost course included 'bastard pointing' along the mortar of the external face, a decorative feature indicating that the foundations were visible from this height upwards (*c*. 35.65m OD). Below this height, the external face of the foundations was butted by construction cut backfill deposit 20350, which produced broadly dateable Roman pottery. Internally, the walls were covered with a thin wash of lime plaster that extended to the base of the foundations.

Room 4
Room 4 was added to the north of Room 2. Most of this

Fig. 3.15   Building A looking east

space had been lost to quarrying but the northern wall of Room 2 had been cut back and a shallow terrace had been made into the natural slope to accommodate the new room. Only the south-eastern corner of the wall foundations survived (wall 20483), and these were built using roughly squared sandstones with a rubble core. Unlike the other Phase 2 walls, these had earth bonding but this might reflect the fact that only the very lowest part of the foundations survived, or could suggest that this addition was earlier than Room 3 and the heating channels within Room 1. Quarrying had removed much of the floor plan of Room 4, but as with Room 3, the extent of the quarrying defined the upper limit of Room 4's northern side. If flush with the northern edge of Room 3, then Room 4 would have been a corridor, some 1.5m wide (as suggested on Figure 3.14).

Within the surviving corner of Room 4, a small patch of what was probably a sub-floor surface (20440) survived. This was formed from pink-orange mortar which included occasional CBM fragments and was 0.06m thick. This seemed to be a sub-floor layer (possibly for a tiled surface) rather than a surface in its own right as its upper surface was at 35.25m OD, suggesting that an overlying surface (assuming this comprised tiles and mortar some 0.05m thick) might have been at c. 35.3m OD, comparable to the finished floor level presumed for Room 2. This sub-surface overlaid a layer of stone rubble and a sandy layer, probably levelling deposits, of which the sandy layer, 20460, produced late 2nd to 3rd-century pottery.

Building A, Phase 3

Phase 3 saw modification to Room 3, which was shortened (Fig. 3.16). This involved demolishing the southern wall and the southern end of its western wall, the material being used to infill the disused part of the room which now lay outside the building. The southern end of the eastern wall was retained since this formed the western wall of the furnace housing, which continued to supply heat to Room 1. No modifications to Rooms 1, 2 and 4 were apparent.

Room 3

The eastern and western walls of the original build

Fig. 3.16   Building A Phase 3

were partially retained, although in a shortened form. The new southern extent was defined by wall 20473, which was built directly onto the natural substrate (Fig. 3.17). This new wall was formed from roughly squared sandstone with a rubble core. Its internal face was simply coursed, of which three to four courses survived. In contrast, the external face comprised a lower course of horizontal sandstone overlain by a course of pitched sandstone, themselves overlain by a horizontal sandstone (Fig. 3.18). All were bonded with pinkish mortar which differed from that used in earlier walls (20462 and 20471) in having charcoal inclusions. Above the pitched stone course, this mortar included bastard pointing, a decorative feature which shows the external wall face was visible above c. 35.55m OD. To match the internal faces of the existing walls, the internal face of the new wall was plastered with a low density chaff-rich pinkish plaster (20474), possibly the backing for a skim of painted plaster that did not survive. A 2nd-century mortarium sherd from the wall construction cut backfill provides a *terminus post quem* for this construction work.

A deposit (20461) of stone, CBM, wall plaster and mortar rubble within a red-brown silty sand matrix lay directly over wall 20471, which had formerly divided Rooms 1 and 3. The purpose of this layer is unclear, but it cannot have formed a wall and was perhaps a sub-floor. If so, this suggests that there was a continuous floor between Rooms 1 and 3, with no load-bearing wall present. The top of this possible sub-floor was at 35.56m OD which, allowing for an overlying floor surface, would indicate a finished floor level at c. 35.6m OD.

Fig. 3.17 Building A Room 3, looking south, with the opus signinum surface of Phase 4 removed. Wall 20471 to left and wall 20462 to right. Between them, east–west wall 20473, shortening the original room, dates to Phase 3 (scales 2m)

Fig. 3.18 Building A Phase 3. External face of wall 20473 showing 'bastard pointing' above the pitched stone course (scale 2m)

Building A, Phase 4

Phase 4 saw further developments to the western side of Building A associated with the provision of underfloor heating within adjoining rooms (Fig. 3.19). A new cross wall, 20463, was inserted within Room 3, creating two smaller rooms (5 and 6). The wall survived to a height of two courses and was of sandstone with a rubble core and was bonded with a pinkish mortar. Much of Room 6 had been lost to truncation, but the full floor plan of Room 5 survived. Internally, it measured 2.5m by 2.5m and its base was formed by an *opus signinum* surface, 20475, which was laid onto a make-up layer of sandstones overlain by a thin bedding layer of red sand. The *opus signinum* was 0.08m thick, providing a

Fig. 3.19 Building A Phase 4

surface at 35.35m OD, a height comparable to the level to which Room 1 had been cut.

Within Room 5, a series of *pilae* (collectively numbered as 20448) were built onto *opus signinum* surface 20475. Due to later remodelling, only five of these *pilum* stacks survived, but the south-easternmost had been cut into wall 20471. Each stack was formed from CBM tiles measuring 200mm by 200mm, and was bonded with pale brown lime mortar. The full height of the *pilae* did not survive, and the floor above these had been entirely removed during later remodelling, but is assumed to have been formed from tiles bridging the gaps between the *pilae*, sealed with *opus signinum*. If the floor of Room 5 was flush with a floor above 'sub-floor' 20461, the *pilae* stacks would have been c. 0.25m high.

Wall 20463 between Rooms 5 and 6 included a gap along its length that formed a flue channel, the base of which was at the same level that the *pilae* in Room 5 were built from. Little of Room 6 survived, but the fortuitous survival of a further *pilum* stack in its south-eastern corner indicates that it was part of this heated suite of rooms, the stack itself having used tiles comparable to those within Room 5, and thus presumably having been laid at the same time.

Building A, Phase 5

In Phase 5 the heating system beneath Room 5 was rebuilt (Fig. 3.20). It is not known if comparable rebuilding occurred within Room 6, since too little of the room survived. No further modifications to the remainder of Building A were evident.

Room 5

A new arrangement of *pilae* (collectively numbered as

Fig. 3.20 Building A Phase 5

20447) was inserted into Room 5 in a 5 by 5 arrangement of 25 stacks, with the outermost *pilae* up against the walls (Fig. 3.21). Several of the original stacks were retained, although there was no obvious structural reason for this; they may simply have been left behind for convenience, or it may be that the overlying floor was retained and that the construction was undertaken by crawling beneath this, from the room's northern side, for which removal of the more northerly of the earlier pilae stacks would have been required, but which would have meant that the remainder could have been left in situ for convenience. The south-easternmost *pilum* incorporated reused tiles from the demolished earlier *pilae*, their smaller size enabling this *pilum* to be squeezed into the corner of the room. With the exception of this smaller *pilum*, the new *pilae* were built using ceramic tiles measuring up to c. 320mm by 320mm, with some of the earlier smaller tiles having been reused. All were bonded with lime mortar, lumps of which found adhering to the upper surface of the *opus signinum* onto which the stacks were built, no doubt represent spillages during the construction of one or other phase of the hypocaust.

A thin ashy layer, 20398, between the *pilae* probably represents material drawn in from the furnace via the flue, and a sample of this material produced only small and unidentifiable charcoal fragments, presumably those small enough to have been drawn into this space by the air flow. The layer also included fragments of wall-backing plaster which perhaps fell from the surrounding walls as a result of the heat, as well as the bones of a few microvertebrates, all unburnt with the exception of a mouse femur, and presumably representing house fauna attracted to the warm sub-floor area around the *pilae*.

Fig. 3.21 Building A Phases 4 and 5 hypocaust built on Phase 2 opus signinum floor 20475, looking south

Building A, Phase 6
Phase 6 saw further work within Room 5 during which the floor above the hypocaust was removed and the *pilae* themselves were partially reduced. The spaces between were infilled with demolition debris and this was used as the make-up for an *opus signinum* floor (Fig. 3.22). Underfloor heating therefore ceased to be provided within Room 5.

Room 5
The spaces between the *pilae* were filled to a thickness of 0.15m, flush with the tops of the reduced *pilae*, with rubble 20375 comprising tile, stone and plaster fragments, mortar and clay lumps, and pottery broadly dateable as Roman, all within an orange-red silty clay matrix. Above these a pinkish *opus signinum* sub-floor, 20240, was laid to a thickness of 120mm, extending partially over the divide between Room 5 and Room 1, indicating that this divide was not present at sub-floor level between these rooms. Above this sub-floor, a polished *opus signinum* surface, 20344, was laid. This survived only as patches, but those surviving thickness were 0.05m thick, providing a surface at 35.67m OD.

Building A, Phase 7 (demolition/collapse)
The end date of Building A is uncertain. Within Room 1, a series of demolition deposits filled the underfloor heating channels, indicating that any overlying floor or covering structure had been demolished. The demolition deposits within the Room 1 heating channels included stone, CBM, charcoal, wall plaster and mortar; one wall plaster fragment (from layer 20413) may have been a repainted piece. Amongst one of these deposits were disarticulated and incomplete remains of three puppies whilst two other deposits contained the remains of a single adult cat. One of the puppy bones was radiocarbon dated to cal. AD 132–325 (SUERC-69960), whilst the rubble deposits generally produced late 2nd to 3rd-century pottery.

Further rubble deposits found across the building produced a small smithing hearth-cake fragment as well as pottery dating no later than the late 2nd to 3rd

Fig. 3.22   Building A Phase 6

centuries, and most likely dateable to no later than c. AD 250, and abandonment of Building A by the mid 3rd century is likely.

Building B (Figs 3.23–25)
Building B was 18m east of Building A and had been built on the footprint of Iron Age Structure A. At least some of Building B had been lost to post-medieval quarrying, but it does seem that its plan at foundation level was largely intact (Figs 3.23 and 3.24). The building survived as a series of wall foundations built into foundation trenches forming a rectangular structure, open to the east and with an internal partition dividing it into two cells. The eastern cell was 4.7m by 2.55m internally and accessible from the east, whilst the western cell was 4.7m by 4.3m internally and had no surviving entrance at foundation level, although one may have been situated along the internal partition, at least part of which could have been at sub-floor level, or which could have provided a raised floor within the western cell, otherwise resting on wooden supports which have left no trace. The Roman pottery assemblage associated with Building B amounted to only 29 sherds, mostly from rubble deposits post-dating the building's disuse. No closely dateable material came from the construction levels of the building, although the rubble layers did contain a more varied assemblage than that recovered from Building A, with Gaulish amphora and Oxfordshire products accompanying the ubiquitous DOR BB1 ceramics.

For the most part, the foundation trenches were 0.6m wide and 0.15m deep, but the trench for the southern wall was notably deeper, at 0.75m. The walls (20509) were at foundation level and were of a comparable build throughout, comprising uncoursed and unfaced

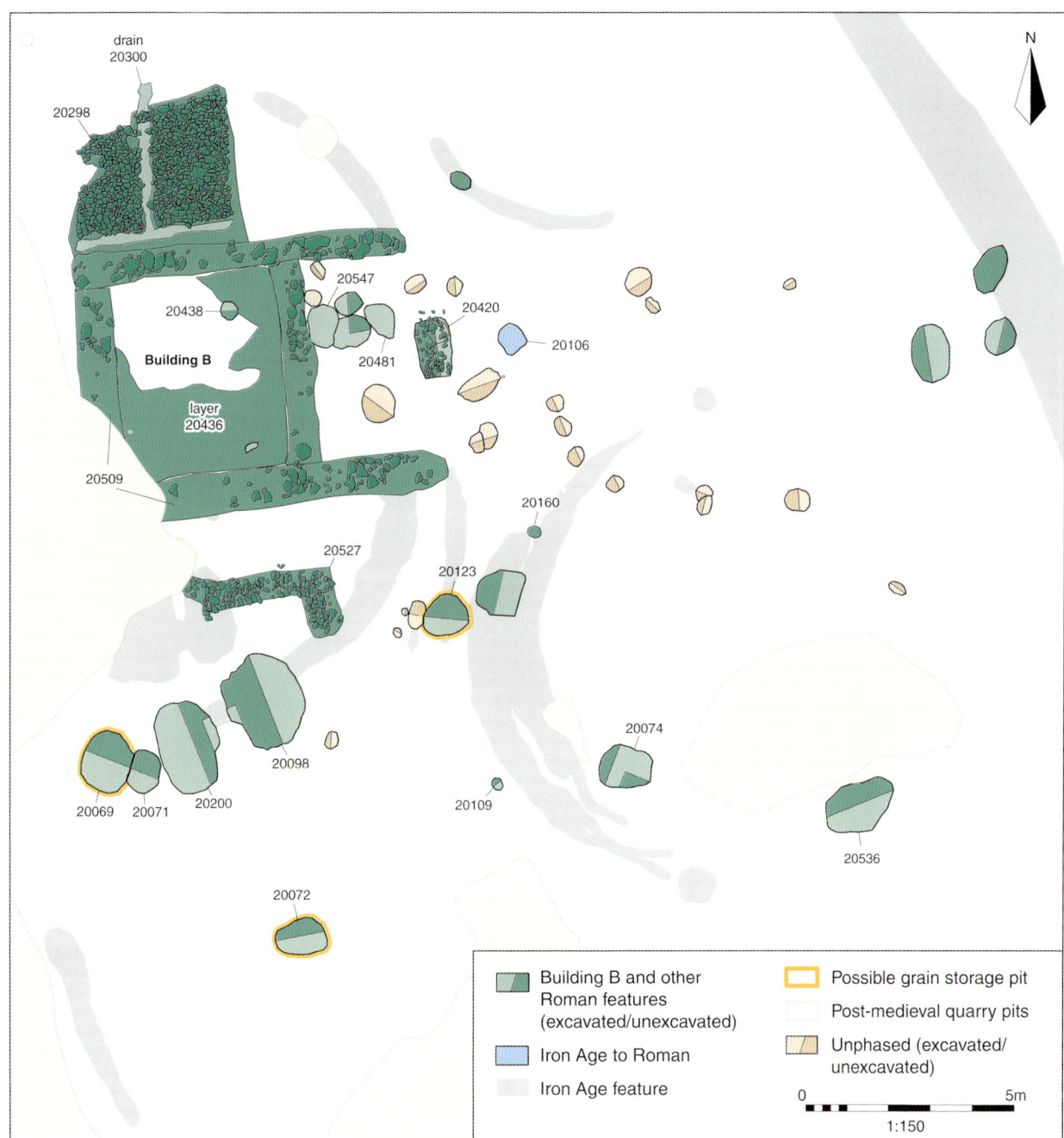

Fig. 3.23 Plan of Building B

sandstone rubble bonded with yellow-red clay. In places, the stones were sparse and these parts of the foundations were more accurately described as compacted clay with stone rubble. The only evidence for a wall level above these came from three stones along the edge of the northern foundations which perhaps suggest that roughly faced rubble core walls were used. The majority of the foundations were 0.6m wide and 0.125m deep, but in the deeper southern trench were 0.85m wide and 0.7m deep. Eight fragments of ceramic roof tile (1.4kg) may indicate the type of roofing used.

An additional structural element was found offset from the open eastern end of Building B. this comprised a small construction trench into which a rectangular pad of limestone rubble in a sandy silt matrix (20420) had been laid. The pad was 1.6m long, 0.8m wide and 0.05m thick. Assuming this supported a pillar or door post, it would have divided two east-facing entrances at least 1.3m wide (to the north) and 1.7m wide (to the south).

Internally, the western end of Building B contained a dark brown silty sand layer, 20436, 0.04m thick. This contained no finds but was cut through by a few postholes, some of which contained Iron Age pottery. Conceivably, this represents the remains of an

Fig. 3.24 Building B during excavation, looking south-east

occupation layer within Iron Age Structure A, preserved beneath the later Roman building. Alternatively, the layer could, for example, have been a construction deposit associated with the Roman building, with the postholes representing construction features containing residual pottery. Amongst the features cut through layer 20436, pit/posthole 20438, 0.4m wide and 0.1m deep with vertical sides and a flat base, contained a blackish clay sand fill which included lumps of scorched natural clay, suggesting that some heating process had occurred, although this might not represent *in situ* burning and could easily represent a dump.

South of Building B, an L-shaped wall foundation, 20527, survived, 1.65m from Building B. This comprised uncoursed limestone and sandstone rubble laid within a foundation trench to a width of 0.65m and a depth of up to 0.25m. The longer part of this construction was parallel to Building B and would seem to have been related. An angled turn at the western end of these foundations perhaps joined them to the rear (western) end of Building B, but any such relationship had been destroyed by post-medieval quarrying.

The north side of Building B was adjoined by a drain and surface (Fig. 3.23). These were built into a rectangular construction cut into which a sandy gravel bedding layer, 20559, had been laid. Above this, a T-shaped drain (20300) was formed from a single width of limestone slabs placed end to end to form the base of a 0.35m-wide drain emptying down to the north. On either side of the drain was a sub-surface (20298) formed from limestones, with occasional CBM fragments (Fig. 3.25).

These were roughly laid which, along with the absence of the sides and capping of the drain, suggests that they were below the finished surface level. Finds from the bedding layer and sub-surface were sparse, but included two white-painted wall plaster fragments from the latter and, from both, a few fragments of Roman ceramic roof tiles (*tegulae*), possibly made using an inverted former, a technique introduced in the mid 3rd century AD and therefore a possible indication that the surface was a later addition to Building B. The drain base was slightly below the upper level of the surface and retained brown-green silty sand fills likely to represent silting within the drain. These drain fills produced pottery of the 2nd to 4th centuries AD, as well as bones from a magpie and a jackdaw, as well as micromammals, predominantly house mice, but also house/wood mice, bank voles, a common shrew, and numerous bones from common frogs. These were probably part of the background fauna living in and around Building B; the possibility that they were in mammal faeces washed into the drain, or from owl pellets, are both considered less likely (see Armitage, Animal bones, Chapter 3, this volume, for a discussion of this evidence). The charred plants suggest that the dehusking of semi-cleaned grain took place in the vicinity.

Pits and a few postholes were found within and close to Building B (Fig. 3.23). Some contained Roman pottery, whilst others were undated. Inside the eastern cell of the building, a cluster of pits and postholes included two with post-packing (postholes 20481 and 20457) and it is possible that some of these supported a ladder or staircase set up against the inside of the northern wall.

Fig. 3.25   Building B, sub-surface 20298 and stone-capped T-shaped drain 20300, looking south

Other pits and postholes were external to the building. The possibility that pit 20106, which contained a cattle skull, was Roman rather than Iron Age has been raised above. The majority of the other pits were bowl-shaped, varying in size and without readily apparent functions. Some were shallow (0.05m deep) and may have been caused by animals, including livestock. Three of the pits (20069, 20072 and 20123) were distinctly different, comprising vertical-sided, flat-based cuts 1m to 1.35m wide and 0.25m to 0.6m deep. All contained single fills which seem to relate to backfilling, but it is possible that they were used originally to store grains or other materials. Others among the larger but more bowl-shaped pits were perhaps further examples, the edges of which had been eroded when the pits were last scoured out.

The foundations of Building B were overlain by deposit 20257, a layer of demolition or collapse debris, amongst which were stone roof tiles, ceramic roof tile fragments, plaster and mortar flecks. The layer was fairly extensive, covering an area 3.6m by 3m and up to 0.15m thick, and produced 3rd to 4th-century pottery suggesting, as with Building A, abandonment by the later 3rd or early 4th century AD.

Building C (Figs 3.26–31)

Building C was a villa range and was located 47m south of Buildings A and B at the crest of the north-facing slope. Its alignment allowed it to face northwards, possibly a compromise that allowed the building to look across the villa enclosure whilst still affording views towards the Parrett Valley (Fig. 3.10). The northern side of the building, which was presumably the frontage, given the direction of the view, had been truncated by quarrying. The eastern end of the surviving remains had also been lost to truncation due to the level of the underlying bedrock, which rose up at that point, meaning that any deposits not within deeper features had been ploughed away. The irregular nature of the underlying bedrock accounts for the earliest remains associated with Building C, which comprised a terrace on its northern side to level the natural slope. This terracing was up to 0.7m deep where it had been cut by post-medieval quarry backfill. It contained silty sand levelling layers which produced pottery broadly dateable to the 2nd to 4th centuries AD.

Building C, Phase 1

The villa building was constructed within and to the south of this terrace and survived only at foundation level with no surviving surfaces or sub-floors, restricting the extent to which the functions of different rooms, and indeed the locations of different rooms, could be determined (Figs 3.26 and 3.27). Thirty-four ceramic roof tile fragments, together amounting to 9.9kg, suggest the nature of the roofing. A further 11 flue tile fragments (together weighing 3.4kg) suggest the provision of underfloor heating, although no traces of this were found *in situ*. In its surviving form, the villa comprised a corridor/gallery with rooms lying to the

Fig. 3.26   Building C, looking west

north and south. The corridor had been truncated at its eastern end where the underlying bedrock was higher, and the foundation trenches themselves shallowed to the east until they had been entirely removed.

Assuming symmetry based on the southern room, the corridor would have been 22m long and 2.5m wide internally, and was defined by flat-based foundation trenches into which the foundations had been laid. The foundations (20610 and 20611) comprised earth-bonded sandstone and limestone rubble, 0.6m wide along the southern foundations and 0.7m wide along the northern side of the corridor, and surviving to a maximum thickness of 0.25m (four 'courses'). Finds from these foundation deposits were sparse, restricted to two very small sherds of DOR BB1 pottery of 2nd to 4th-century date from the foundations (20611) along the northern side of the corridor, while a large sherd of this pottery from the southern foundations (20610) was from a conical flanged bowl dating to after *c*. AD 250.

The southern foundations of the corridor were contiguous with those of a structure adjoining its southern side. Here, the foundations were indistinguishable in build and width from those along the corridor, and defined a space 3.6m long and 2.35m wide internally (Room 1 on Figs 3.26 and 3.27). Internally, this room contained an L-shaped trench (20731), 0.2m wide and 0.1m deep with almost vertical sides. Pit/posthole 20726, also within Room 1, was a steep-sided feature 0.4m wide and 0.4m deep that produced four sherds of Dorset Black-burnished ware pottery.

Truncation by quarrying had removed much to the north of the corridor. What survived comprised the remains of two parallel foundations, defining a space 12.5m across (Room 4). The western foundations, 20612, were built within a flat-based construction trench and comprised earth-bonded sandstone rubble up to 0.7m wide. The eastern foundations, 20614, survived more partially but were also within a construction trench, and were built from limestone and sandstone rubble, earth-bonded and 0.5m wide. Their southern end was contiguous with the northern foundations of the corridor, indicating that all were of one build, although no surviving relationship was present between the western foundations of Room 4 and the corridor foundations.

Internally, the corridor contained a trench, 20707, which crossed its width. This trench was 0.2m wide and 0.05m deep with a V-shaped profile and perhaps supported a non-load-bearing internal division. The stony fill of this contained a sherd of Dorset Black-burnished ware pottery of the 2nd to 4th centuries. No other partitions were evident along the corridor.

Features beneath the villa corridor

A number of features were found against the internal face of the wall foundations along the corridor's southern side that contained evidence for special deposition. These included four neonate burials, the burial of lamb/sheep remains, and the placement of a ceramic vessel (Fig. 3.27).

The burials were all in earth-cut graves and were

Iron Age Settlement, Roman Villa and post-Roman Structure at Sandy Lane

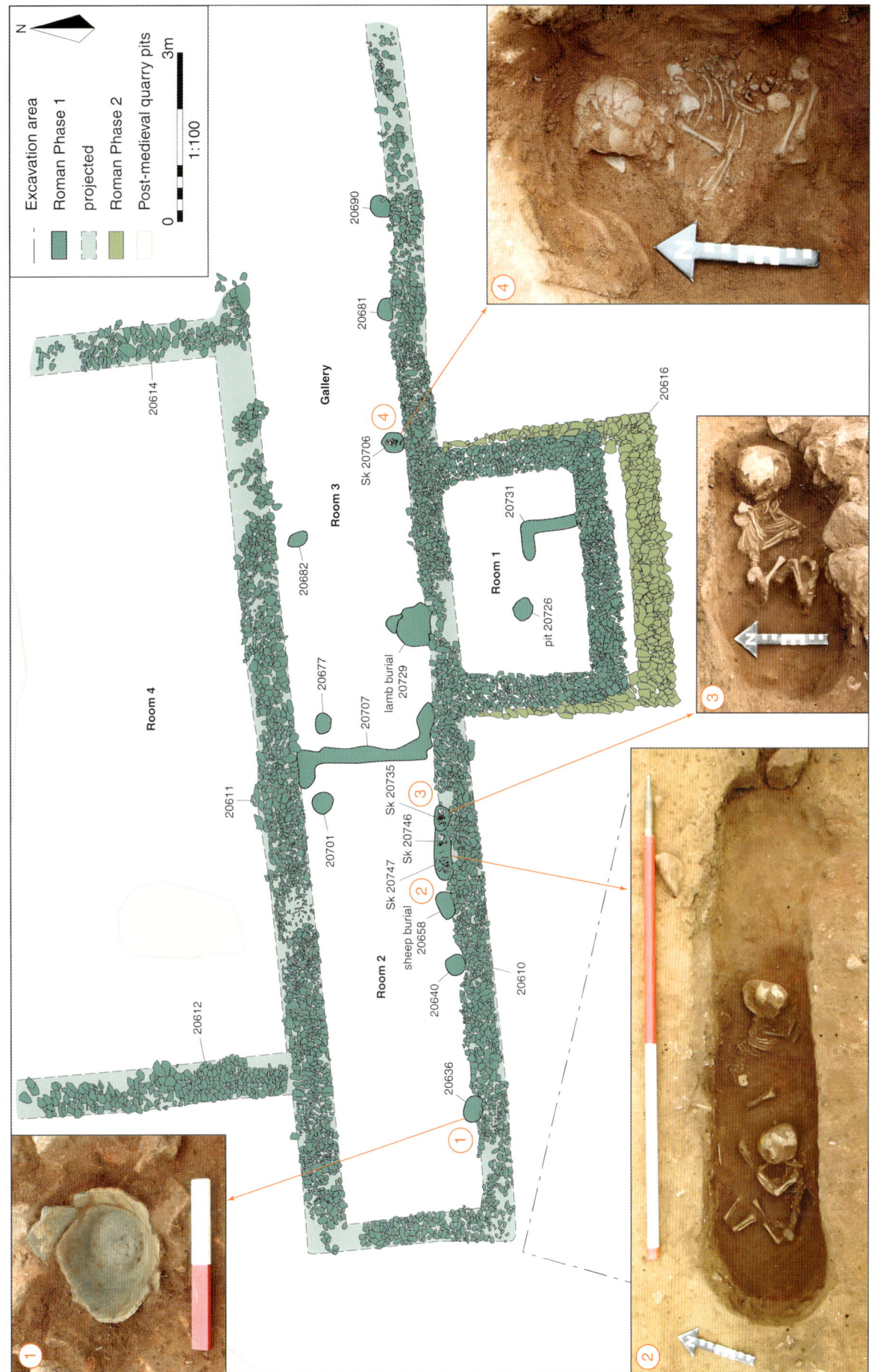

Fig. 3.27 Plan of Building C, showing infant burials and other depositions

radiocarbon dated. In addition, since there are no accepted methodologies for sexing neonate burials from analysis of the skeletal development, the sex of each was determined through DNA analysis from a sample of bone (Clough, Human remains, below).

Bayesian analysis of radiocarbon dates from the human and animal remains has allowed the sequence of their burial to be suggested (Healy, Bayesian analysis, below; Tables 3.2 and 3.3). The dates quoted below are in italics where derived from the Bayesian modelling. All other dates are simple calibrations. It is probable that the earliest burial was of a sheep in pit 20658, which took place *cal. AD 95–235* (SUERC-69974). The animal may have been killed with a cut through the neck, although whether or not this decapitated the sheep is not known and the skull had been interred with the rest of the carcass. Next in the sequence came three neonate burials found immediately east of the slaughtered sheep. Stratigraphically, Sk 20746, a neonatal girl, was the earliest of these, with a modelled date of *cal. AD 125–230* (SUERC-69972). She had been placed into a small grave cut into the edge of the corridor foundations, presumably beneath the corridor floor (which did not survive), and was laid out alongside the foundations in a foetal position, with her head to the east and facing south towards the foundations. A salmon/trout bone within her grave fill represents the only surviving find from any of the graves. The girl's lower legs and one femur were missing suggesting that the burial in the western part of the same grave (Sk 20747) was later.

The following burials might equally have been of Sk 20747 or Sk 20735, buried at either side of neonatal girl Sk 20746. Sk 20747, a neonatal boy with a modelled date of *cal. AD 135–260* (SUERC-75151), had been placed within a small grave cut into the western end of that belonging to Sk 20746, and had been laid out in a crouched position parallel to the foundations, with his head to the east, but facing north, into the corridor. Sk 20735, another neonatal girl, has a modelled date of *cal. AD 140–240* (SUERC-69971) and had been placed within a small grave at the eastern end of Sk 20746. Her grave had also been cut up against the foundations, so that the three graves formed a continuous line and her burial position, aligned along the foundations, with her head to the east, looking south, mirrored that of the earliest burial, Sk 20746.

Subsequent burials took place within the eastern part of the corridor where Sk 20706, a neonatal boy, was dated to cal. AD 135–332 (SUERC-69970; modelled *cal. AD 135–265, 88% probability*). In contrast to the other burials, which had been aligned along the foundations, this boy had been placed within a small oval grave at right angles to the foundations, with his head to the north, facing west. Unlike the other graves, which had simply been backfilled with sandy silts, the backfill of this grave was covered with sandstone, perhaps making good any floor surfaces.

The last dated event in the sequence was the burial of at least seven lambs within pit 20729, with a modelled date *cal. AD 205–330* (79% probability; SUERC-72468). The lambs were aged six months to one year at death and superficial knife marks on their bones suggest that they had been skinned, with only their heads and limbs placed in the pit.

A further pit cut into the corridor foundations contained what may have been another special deposit. This pit, 20636, was cut through several of the foundation rubble stones, and a Dorset Black-burnished ware jar (dateable to before *c.* AD 250/70) had been placed upright within the pit. Only the base of this vessel survived and it was in a fragmentary condition. Had it been buried with its rim flush with the ground, a loss in the ground level of 100–150mm can be suggested, although this would have been less if the vessel had protruded through the floor. A limey residue on the interior surfaces was probably left by evaporating water.

Three more small pits were cut along the inner edge of the southern corridor foundations. At the western end of the corridor, pit 20640 was small and bowl-shaped without notable remains within its fill. Towards the eastern end, pit 20690 was also bowl-shaped and contained nothing notable other than a few pieces of sandstone, conceivably packing for a post, or remains of an overlying surface. Also in the eastern half of the corridor, a steeper-sided but rounded pit, 20681, 0.5m wide and 0.15m deep, had two large stone roof tile fragments on its base, along with a couple of horizontal stones but contained no finds.

Three small pits (20701, 20677 and 20682) lay along the northern side of the corridor, none of which cut into the foundations. Of these, bowl-shaped pits 20701 and 20677 contained silty sand fills with a few tile fragments and stones, while pit 20682, more irregular with steep sides and a rounded base, contained a stony fill which produced two sherds from a Dorset Black-burnished ware dish.

Building C, Phase 2

Evidence for modification to the villa was restricted to Room 1, which was remodelled at foundation level along its outer walls (Figs 3.27 and 3.28). This involved digging a foundation trench with an unusual V-shaped profile for the new wall. Along the western and eastern sides, the existing foundations were slightly widened by the addition of extra stone rubble, the outermost face of which was of roughly pitched stones. Onto this, the lower course of a sandstone wall had been laid (wall 20616) formed by roughly faced stones with a rubble core and bonded with pink-orange mortar (Fig. 3.29). The southern part of the foundations projected beyond the original footprint of the earlier foundations, and were 0.75m wide and 0.2m deep, again, with the outer edge of roughly pitched stones, backed by stone rubble, all bonded with the same mortar. The enlarged Room 1 was still 3.6m long but was now 3.15m wide. A small

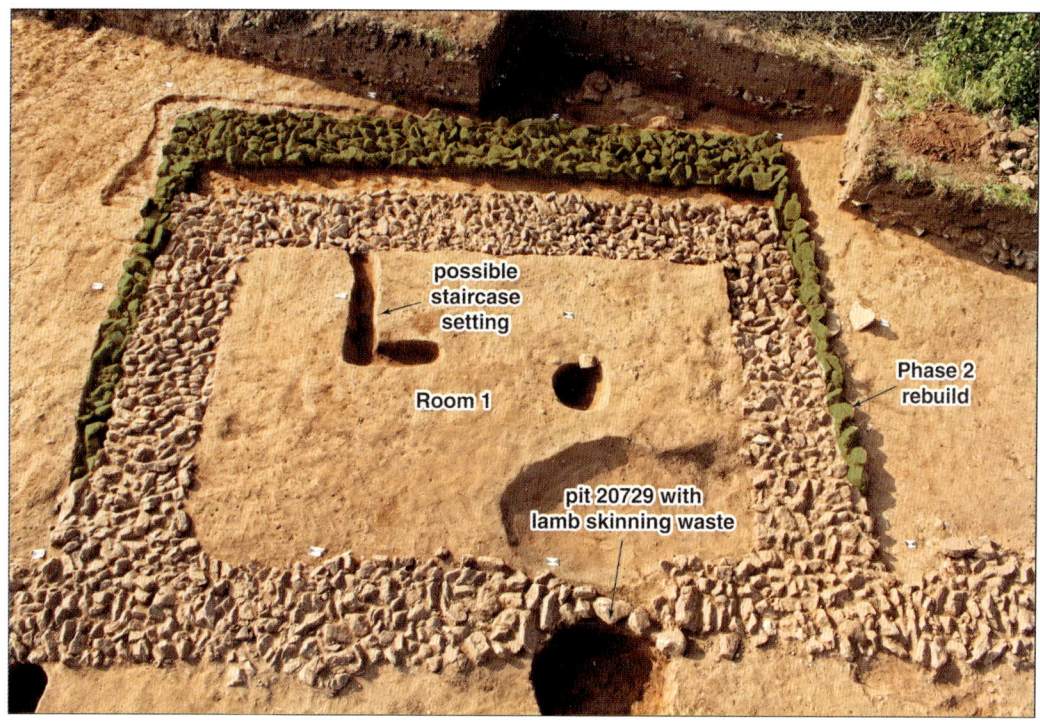

Fig. 3.28 Building C Room 1 after removal of wall 20616, looking south

Fig. 3.29 Building C Room 1, wall 20616 overlying remodelled foundations, looking west (scale 0.4m)

section of these foundations was also overlain by coursed stonework wall 20616, which was probably the lowest level of visible walling (Fig. 3.30).

The Roman pottery assemblage recovered from Phase 2 features was small (36 sherds) but includes material dating to after AD 150, and with a focus on the 3rd century. The absence of Oxfordshire and New Forest finewares suggests abandonment by the end of the 3rd century. Deposits relating to the post-abandonment demolition or collapse of the Roman villa were heavily truncated (Fig. 3.31). Layer 20673, a small rubble deposit within the villa corridor, included stone and charcoal. Layers 20618 and 20626 were within the former Room 4 of the villa. The earliest of these, 20618, was up to 5m wide and 0.1m thick and contained stone, CBM and mortar flecks. It was overlain by a smaller layer, 20626, which contained similar debris alongside the largest assemblage of painted wall plaster to have been recovered from the site. This amounted to 107 fragments, all of high quality although with an estimated coverage of only 0.026m^2 (Brown, Painted wall plaster, below). Analysis revealed monochrome pink elements, possibly from a plain dado, but with most fragments likely to originate from middle zone panels, including red, white and black panel schemes characteristic of Flavian–Trajanic designs in Britain (Davey and Ling 1982, 33; Fig. 3.43, no. 1). A second scheme of blue panels delineated with black and white bands probably contained figurative elements, with garments represented by blue brush strokes (Fig. 3.43, no. 3), and foliate designs in yellow and white over maroon with possible green tendrils (Fig. 3.43, no. 4). Unfortunately none of these fragments survive in sufficient size or

Fig. 3.30 Building C Room 1, detail of surviving wall 20616 (scale 1m)

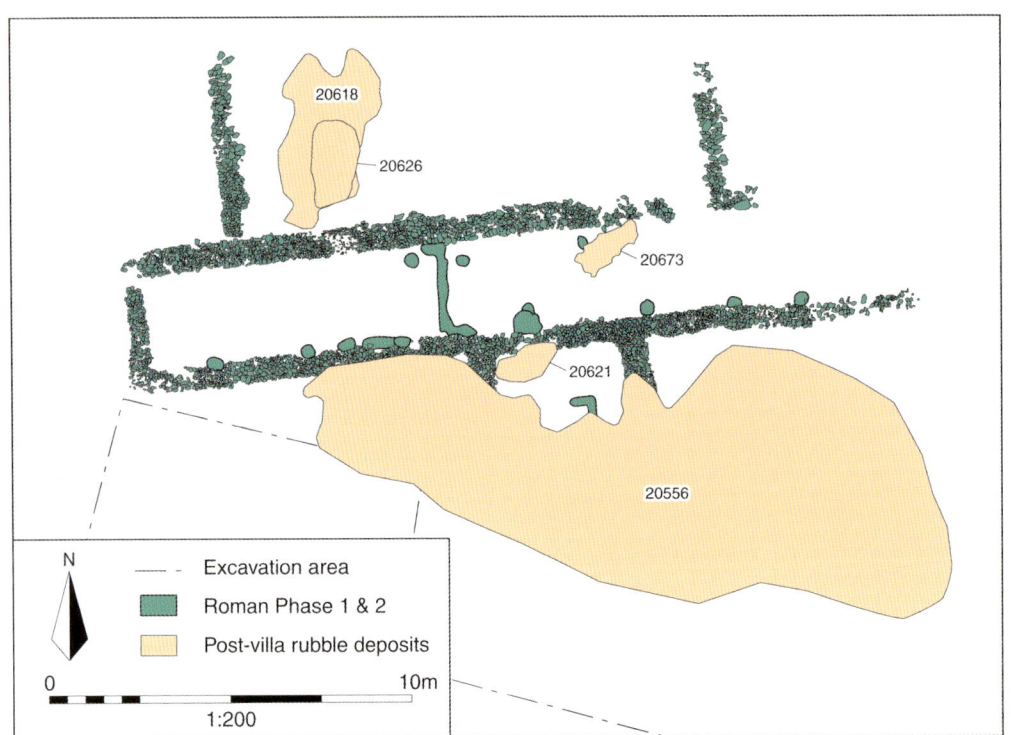

Fig. 3.31 Building C, plan of overlying rubble deposits

quantities to elaborate more on these designs. The absence of an underlying floor surface in Room 4 suggests that they may represent a dump of robbing debris, rather than resulting from the collapse of the walls.

More extensive rubble layers were found along the southern side of the villa range, and covering Room 1. The most extensive of these, layer 20556, was 0.1m thick and contained stone, including a sandstone roof tile fragment, 6.9kg (29 fragments) of ceramic roof tiles, ceramic flue tiles, a Roman brick fragment, in excess of 60 carpentry nails and charcoal, along with a relatively large pottery group, a radiate coin of Tetricus II (Caesar of the Gallic Empire, AD 270–274), copper-alloy tweezers and a painted wall plaster fragment. The tweezers are comparable to a set from Kingscote, Gloucestershire, there dated to c. AD 353–360, although this form of artefact is poorly dated and the current example need not be contemporary with that from Kingscote (Marsden, Metals, below). An overlying layer, 20639 (not illustrated), within Room 1 produced CBM, stone, mortar flecks and charcoal.

Early medieval to medieval (c. AD 400–AD 1250)

Aside from poorly dated demolition/collapse deposits relating to the Roman structures, remains belonging to the centuries post-dating the villa and into the early medieval period were identified through radiocarbon dating. These included a possible building, and two pits.

A possible post-Roman building (Building D) was found at the eastern end of the former villa range (Fig. 3.32). Its alignment was similar to that of Building C (and indeed the other buildings), suggesting that the villa at the least remained visible. However, the fact that Building D was built across the eastern end of the former villa corridor indicates that the villa must have been at least partially ruinous. It should be noted that there was no clear stratigraphic relationship between the two structures: stones noted 'above' the fill of Trench DL of Building D undoubtedly derived from the villa corridor foundations but seem either to have been dragged over during machining, or to have tumbled in when Trench DL was filled. Building D has however been assigned to a post-Roman phase on the basis of a radiocarbon date and on the presence of other post-Roman dated features.

Building D survived as a series of foundation trenches. In places these were deep, but they had suffered from truncation due to the higher levels of the underlying bedrock, and much of the building's ground plan was not recoverable, particularly along its eastern side, which was entirely absent. However, enough survived to suggest that Building D was of post-in-trench construct-

Fig. 3.32 Plan of post-Roman Building D

ion, and was aligned broadly north/south–east/west. The trenches seemed to indicate a rectangular building, 9.85m long (north to south) and at least 5.5m wide, with a three-bay ground plan consisting of two larger rooms (1 and 3) either side of a smaller room (2).

The surviving outer foundation trenches were Trenches DL and ED. Trench DL was vertical-sided and flat-based and was 0.6m wide and 0.2m deep. Its southern terminal was real, and probably marks the south-western corner of the building (Fig. 3.33). However, its northern 'terminal' was in fact simply where truncation had extended to the full depth of the trench, the projected continuation of which is shown on Fig. 3.32. No postholes were noted along its length, and the trench had been filled with greyish sandy silt which included fairly frequent sandstone towards the base of the fill; none of these were in positions suggestive of *in situ* post-packing or postpads, but they could represent the disturbed remains of such structural elements. The fill also contained a large amount of grain, among which was a barley grain radiocarbon dated to cal. AD 134–326 (SUERC-69955), and a range of wood charcoal from which a fragment of alder charcoal produced a date of cal. AD 658–769 (SUERC-72472). It is judged that the earlier date came from residual material, and that two sherds of Roman pottery within the fills were also residual, because the date is similar to others from the villa building.

Fig. 3.33 Building D foundation Trench DL, looking north (scale 2m)

Building D's northern extent is assumed to be represented by Trench ED. This was 2.6m long, although it may originally have been more extensive. Its eastern surviving end was marked by posthole 20644, which had vertical sides and a flat base and was 0.45m wide and 0.15m deep. This posthole was recorded as having cut through the trench fill, but may in fact reflect the location of a post that was held within the trench, and excavation of the long axis of the foundation trench revealed a further two postholes (20879 and 20881), one at the trench's western terminal, and thus at the presumed north-western corner of Building D. The construction trench was filled with a greyish sandy silt which included occasional stone, as well as two sherds of Roman pottery, assumed to be residual. A sample from one of the trench fills (fill 20648) produced birch charcoal that was radiocarbon dated to cal. AD 132–326 (SUERC-72473). The fill of posthole 20644 was also sampled and included a hazel charcoal fragment dated to cal. AD 86–239 (SUERC-72474). The dating is contemporary with the range of the other radiocarbon dates from the Roman villa, and both fragments are assumed to have been residual material.

Building D was divided into its three rooms by two internal east/west partitions represented by Trenches DO and DP. The northern trench, DP, was 4m long although each 'terminal' shallowed out and both probably represent truncation. It was 0.4m wide and up to 0.15m deep and included three postholes (20661, 20671 and 20666) set at regular intervals along its surviving length, all recorded as having cut through the trench fill. These postholes were broad and fairly shallow, up to 0.8m wide and 0.3m deep, but it is possible that this reflects removal of the posts after Building D was abandoned, with the original cuts having been narrower. Posthole 20671 had a tabular stone on its base which may have been a postpad whilst other stones were probably post-packing, although they were largely disturbed. Stones within posthole 20666 may also have been post-packing, but, if so, were heavily disturbed. The trench and postholes contained sandy silt fills. Samples from the fills of postholes 20671 and 20666 produced cereals and charcoal. A charred spelt wheat grain from posthole 20671 was radiocarbon dated to cal. AD 80–228 (SUERC-69964) and another charred spelt wheat grain from posthole 20666 was dated to cal. AD 86–241 (SUERC-69965). These grains are assumed to have been residual, along with Roman pottery which was found in the trench and postholes, generally in small quantities, although posthole 20666 produced 37 sherds.

The other internal partition was provided by Trench DO. This was heavily truncated, and survived to no more than 0.1m depth, with its 'terminals' both resulting from truncation rather than having been the real ends of the trench. No postholes were seen and the trench contained a silty sand fill which included occasional stone and charcoal.

Internally, the building contained three rooms. The northernmost of these, Room 1, was approximately 2.7m (north/south) by at least 5m (east/west) internally and contained several broad, shallow pits. Amongst these, oval pit 20715 was 0.85m long and 0.1m deep with steep sides and flat base. Two upright stones along one of its sides suggest that it may have been stone-lined, and was perhaps a hearth. The remaining pits were shallow and poorly defined, and their status as archaeological features is uncertain. Room 2, the central room, was 2m wide (north/south) internally, whilst Room 3 to the south was some 4.3m wide (north/south) internally; neither contained any features.

Several features found west of Building D and within the footprint of the former villa suggest further post-Roman activity. Amongst these was an irregular surface, 20613, built from roughly laid sandstone and limestone rubble mixed with a few CBM fragments (Fig. 3.32). These fragments included what may have been part of a ceramic chimney pot. The stones appeared slightly worn on the upper surfaces, perhaps suggesting that this was once a surface, and one that would seem to have been inappropriate within a Roman villa room and therefore more likely to reflect post-Roman activity, although post-Roman dating for the layer was absent and the only finds comprised CBM fragments and a small assemblage of Roman pottery. An adjacent posthole 20712 with vertical sides and a flat base contained a possible packing stone and fragments of CBM, again perhaps derived from the former villa. It is possible that this supported a post relating to a structure associated with surface 20613, but truncation by quarrying to the north may have removed further elements of this.

More certainly dated post-Roman features comprised two pits. Pit 20625 had been dug into the foundations of Room 1 of the former villa range. It was oval in plan with a shallow bowl-shaped profile and was 1.15m long and 0.2m deep. It contained a greyish silty sand fill, a sample from which yielded mostly weed seeds and hedgerow-type material, including sloe stones. A wood charcoal fragment was radiocarbon dated to cal. AD 407–538 (SUERC-72467), a cherry pip was radiocarbon dated to cal. AD 667–770 (SUERC-69961), and a charred barley grain was dated to cal. AD 1042–1220 (SUERC-72466). While the date of the feature is ambiguous, it was clearly post-Roman.

The second pit, 20020, was found 75m north-west of Building D, cut into the outer edge of Roman enclosure Ditch W (Fig. 3.10). It was oval in plan with a bowl-shaped profile and was 1.45m long and 0.45m deep. Its single dark silty sand fill contained frequent charcoal flecks and a sample from this produced cereals including rye, which is more typically post-Roman. A charred barley grain was dated to cal. AD 665–853 (SUERC-69963) and a fragment of alder charcoal to cal. AD 682–866 (SUERC-72475), confirming a 7th/8th-century date.

Post-medieval to modern (AD 1500+)

Remains post-dating the early medieval period were restricted to the extensive quarry pits seen across the site (Fig. 3.10). These were left largely unexcavated and were poorly dated, but where excavated yielded small quantities of pottery of the 16th to 18th centuries AD. The quarry is not depicted on the 1839 Tithe Map of Cannington (The Genealogist website) and must have been levelled up before then. The stone appears to be of relatively poor quality compared with Carboniferous Limestone outcrop to the north (Fig. 1.3) and quarrying was perhaps short-lived.

Human remains
Sharon Clough

Four inhumations were found along the villa range (Building C; Fig. 3.27). The skeletal remains were all of neonates interred within earth-cut graves inside the corridor of Building C, apparently cut up against the wall foundations. All were examined and recorded in accordance with national guidelines (Hillson 1996; Brickley and McKinley 2004; Mays *et al.* 2004). The completeness of each skeleton was classified as a percentage of the whole and divided into four groups: 0–25%; 26–50%; 51–74%; and 75+%. The condition of the bone surface of each skeleton was recorded in detail with reference to different anatomical areas (skull, arms, hands, legs and feet) after McKinley (2004, 16) and given an overall summary score. Measurements of long bones were used to estimate age. As the remains were neonatal, dentition was recorded for development only. The presence or absence of frequently recorded non-metrical cranial and post-cranial traits was scored (Berry and Berry 1967; Schwartz 1995; Hillson 1996). Evidence for skeletal pathology and/or bony abnormality was assessed, but no such evidence was present. Sex identification of four skeletons was carried out at the Manchester Institute of Biotechnology, University of Manchester, through aDNA analysis by typing the amelogenin gene, which is present on the X and Y chromosomes with diagnostic features that enable the X and Y versions to be distinguished, and by detection of the SRY gene, which is only present on the Y chromosome (Drosou and Brown 2017). Two individuals were male and two female.

Burial catalogue

Sk 20706 (Fig. 3.34)
Sex: male
Age: neonate 36–44 weeks
Long bone length: right femur 73mm
Completeness: 75+%
Condition: (McKinley 2004) grade 1
Pathologies: none
Dental: 11 unerupted
The cranium, mandible, arms, legs and torso were present, representing over 75% of the skeleton, and the bone was in excellent

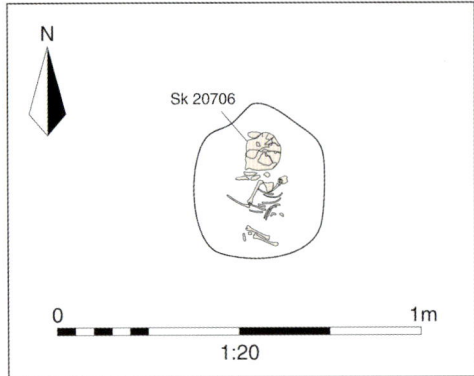

Fig. 3.34   Neonatal skeleton Sk 20706

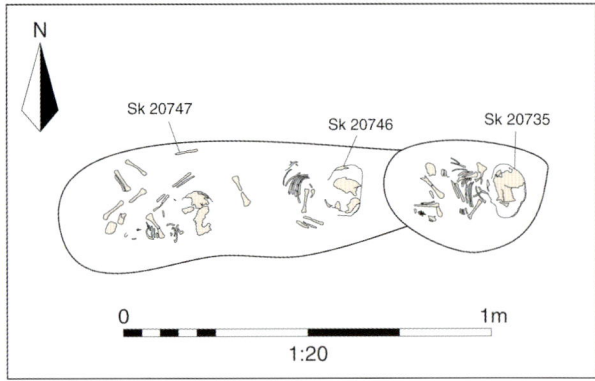

Fig. 3.35   Neonatal skeletons Sk 20747, 20746 and 20735

condition, grade 1. This individual was male and is estimated to have died at 36–44 weeks' gestation (normal gestation is 38–42 weeks), so during or around the time of birth.

Sk 20735 (Fig. 3.35)
Sex: female
Age: neonate 38–46 weeks
Long bone length: right humerus 66.7mm
Completeness: 75+%
Condition: (McKinley 2004) grade 1
Pathologies: None
Dental: 6 unerupted
This individual, a female, had all parts of the skeleton represented, apart from the left lower leg, left hand and facial area, 75% was considered present with the bone surface in excellent condition, grade 1. The age at death is estimated at 38–46 weeks' gestation.

Sk 20746 (Fig. 3.35)
Sex: female
Age: neonate 36–44 weeks
Long bone length: left femur 75.7mm
Completeness: 51–74%
Condition: (McKinley 2004) grade 1
Pathologies: none
Dental: 2 unerupted
This individual had 51–74% of the skeleton present which comprised most of the upper half and the left femur. The bone surface had slight and patchy erosion, but can be considered as grade 1, although all the bones were fragmented. The individual was female and age at death is estimated at 36–44 weeks' gestation.

Sk 20747 (Fig. 3.35)
Sex: male
Age: neonate 38–48 weeks
Long bone length: left tibia 69.4mm, right tibia 68.4mm, left humerus 67.9mm
Completeness: 75+%
Condition: (McKinley 2004) grade 1
Pathologies: none
Dental: 5 unerupted
This individual had 75%+ of the skeleton present, although the skull was very fragmented with the facial area and maxilla and mandible absent. Fragmentation continued across the post-cranial skeleton and the ends of the long bones had suffered post-mortem damage. The individual was male and age at death is estimated at 38–48 weeks' gestation.

The remains represent four neonate burials. Neonate (also called perinate, 'at around the time of birth') is defined as up to the age of one month (Lewis 2007). Average gestation is 40 weeks, but commonly falls two weeks either side of this (38–42 weeks). These babies are likely to have been either stillborn, or to have lived for no more than a few weeks after birth. Two boys and two girls were present: a small sample, but within the expected male : female ratio for natural deaths. The absence of pathological or other distinguishing skeletal characteristics is entirely to be expected with neonate skeletons.

Radiocarbon dating
Sarah Cobain and Frances Healy

Radiocarbon dating was undertaken in order to confirm the dates of key deposits associated with the Iron Age and Roman settlements. The programme included dating several samples associated with the enigmatic post-Roman Building D. Most of these features were found to contain residual Roman grain and charcoal and were unhelpful for dating the building. Just one date from this structure (SUERC-72472) from Trench DL, was post-Roman. Pit 20625, cutting the wall of Roman Building C west of Building D, yielded three incompatible dates from different samples of material. Dates were also obtained from the four neonates buried within Building C and the associated deposits of sheep bones. Radiocarbon modelling was undertaken to help understand the probable sequence and timescale of these deposits. One of the original samples of skeleton 20747 (SUERC-69973) yielded an anomalously early date and the re-run measurement (SUERC-75151) is preferable because of its consistency with the other dates.

The methods and standards were the same as those used for the Bronze Age radiocarbon samples (Cobain, Chapter 2, Radiocarbon dating, this volume).

The results are shown in Table 3.1 and are plotted together as a single multiplot in Figure 3.36, which indicates the dates considered to be from samples

Iron Age Settlement, Roman Villa and post-Roman Structure at Sandy Lane

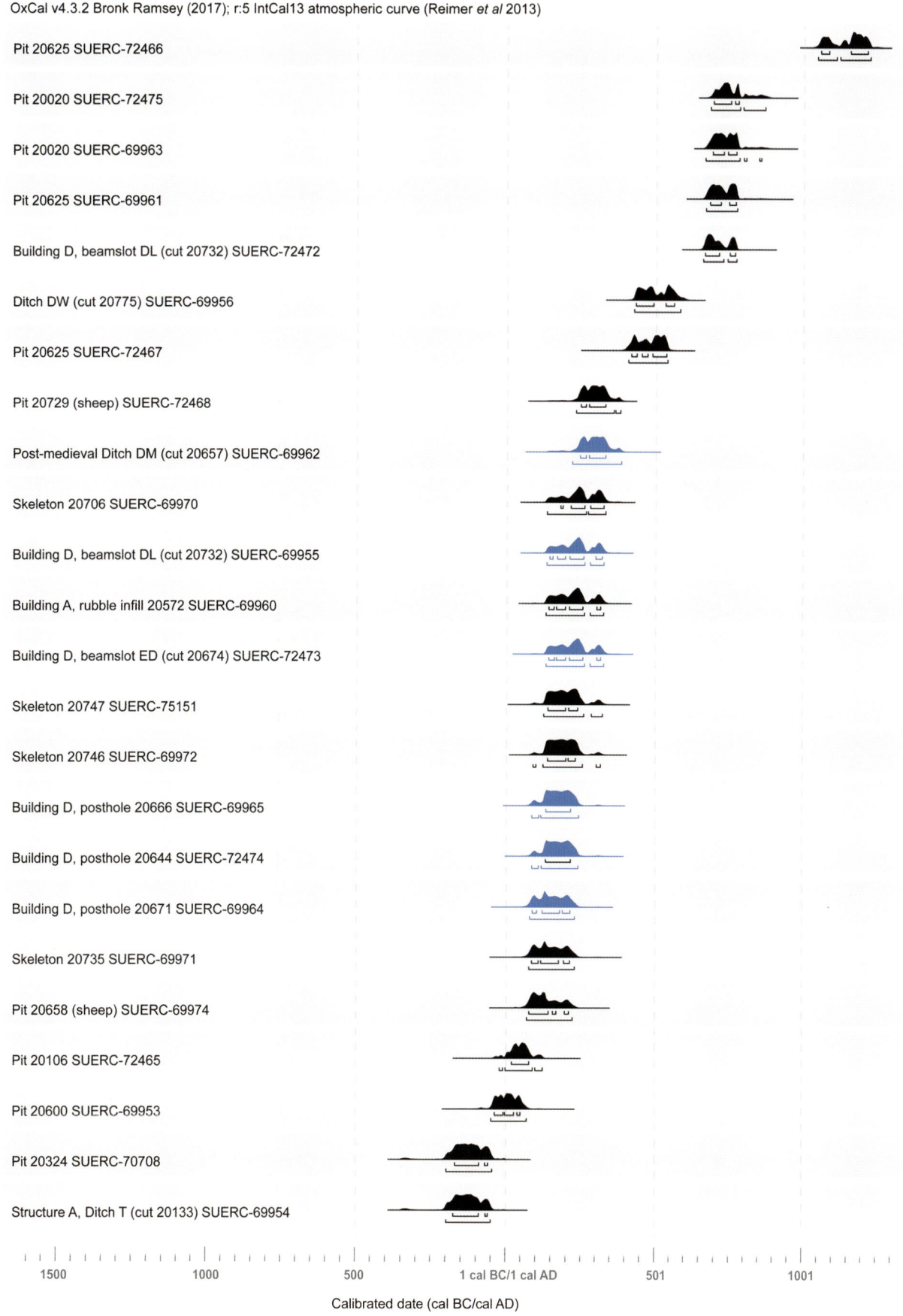

Fig. 3.36 Sandy Lane radiocarbon dating multiplot. Blue indicates residual material. (Ditch DM not illustrated)

Table 3.1: Radiocarbon dating results from Sandy Lane

Feature	Lab No.	Material	δ¹³C	δ¹⁵N	C/N ratio	Radiocarbon age yrs BP	Calibrated radiocarbon age 95.4% probability	Calibrated radiocarbon age 68.2% probability
Context 20019 Pit 20020	SUERC-69963	Charred grain *Hordeum vulgare* (barley)	-21.0‰	-	-	1269 ± 28	665–778 cal. AD (94.0%) 793–801 cal. AD (0.8%) 846–853 cal. AD (0.6%)	689–725 cal. AD (38.9%) 739–767 cal. AD (29.3%)
Context 20019 Pit 20020	SUERC-72475	Charcoal *Alnus glutinosa* (alder)	-26.6	-	-	1246 ± 22	682–779 cal. AD (80.3%) 791–866 cal. AD (15.1%)	691–749 cal. AD (56.5%) 762–774 cal. AD (11.7%)
Context 20107 Pit 20106	SUERC-72465	Animal bone *Bos taurus* (cattle skull)	-21.7‰	8.5‰	3.4	1952 ± 27	22–11 cal. BC (2.4%) 2 cal. BC–90 cal. AD (86.1%) 99–124 cal. AD (6.9%)	20–78 cal. AD (68.2%)
Context 20134 Ditch T	SUERC-69954	Charcoal *Corylus avellana* (hazel, twig 1–4 years)	-25.3‰	-	-	2106 ± 28	198–51 cal. BC (95.4%)	175–91 cal. BC (63.9%) 69–61 cal. BC (4.3%)
Context 20325 ?hearth 20324	SUERC-70708	Charcoal Indeterminate (roundwood, non-ring porous)	-27.7‰	-	-	2100 ± 30	198–47 cal. BC (95.4%)	170–91 cal. BC (61.5%) 71–61 cal. BC (6.7%)
Context 20572 Building A (channel backfill)	SUERC-69960	Animal bone *Canis lupus* (dog, long bone)	-21.2‰	12.8‰	3.5	1797 ± 28	132–260 cal. AD (77.4%) 280–325 cal. AD (18.0%)	142–158 cal. AD (8.3%) 166–196 cal. AD (16.5%) 209–254 cal. AD (36.2%) 302–315 cal. AD (7.2%)
Context 20603 Pit 20600	SUERC-69953	Charred grain *Triticum dicoccum/Triticum spelta* (emmer/spelt wheat)	-25.0‰ assumed	-	-	1994 ± 29	50 cal. BC – 70 cal. AD (95.4%)	38–9 cal. BC (27.2%) 4 cal. BC–28 cal. AD (31.9%) 39–49 cal. AD (9.1%)
Context 20624 Pit 20625	SUERC-69961	Charred seed *Prunus* (cherry species pip)	-27.0‰	-	-	1285 ± 28	667–770 cal. AD (95.4%)	680–716 cal. AD (40.8%) 743–766 cal. AD (27.4%)
Context 20624 Pit 20625	SUERC-72466	Charred grain *Hordeum vulgare* (barley)	-23.1‰	-	-	884 ± 29	1042–1105 cal. AD (30.1%) 1117–1220 cal. AD (65.3%)	1053–1080 cal. AD (19.0%) 1152–1210 cal. AD (49.2%)
Context 20624 Pit 20625	SUERC-72467	Charcoal *Crataegus monogyna/Sorbus/Malus sylvestris* (hawthorn/rowan/crab apple)	-26.2%	-	-	1595 ± 26	407–538 cal. AD (95.4%)	417–435 cal. AD (14.5%) 452–471 cal. AD (12.5%) 487–534 cal. AD (41.2%)
Context 20645 Posthole 20644	SUERC-72474	Charcoal *Corylus avellana* (hazel)	-26.5%	-	-	1843 ± 26	86–109 cal. AD (5.4%) 118–239 cal. AD (90.0%)	132–214 cal. AD (68.2%)
Context 20648 Construction cut 20674	SUERC-72473	Charcoal *Betula* (birch)	-28.3%	-	-	1797 ± 29	132–260 cal. AD (76.9%) 279–326 cal. AD (18.5%)	141–159 cal. AD (9.0%) 166–196 cal. AD (16.9%) 209–254 cal. AD (35.2%) 302–315 cal. AD (18.5%)
Context 20656 Ditch DM (cut 20657)	SUERC-69962	Charred grain *Triticum spelta* (spelt wheat)	-23.2‰	-	-	1754 ± 29	217–384 cal. AD (95.4%)	244–264 cal. AD (17.4%) 274–330 cal. AD (50.8%)

Feature	Lab No.	Material	δ¹³C	δ¹⁵N	C/N ratio	Radiocarbon age yrs BP	Calibrated radiocarbon age 95.4% probability	Calibrated radiocarbon age 68.2% probability
Context 20659 Pit 20658	SUERC-69974	Animal bone *Ovis aries* (sheep tooth)	-21.9‰	8.0‰	3.3	1876 ± 28	70–221 cal. AD (95.4%)	78–142 cal. AD (55.7%) 156–167 cal. AD (5.4%) 195–209 cal. AD (7.1%)
Context 20667 Posthole 20655	SUERC-69965	Charred grain *cf Triticum spelta* (spelt wheat)	-24.2‰	-	-	1841 ± 28	86–110 cal. AD (5.6%) 117–241 cal. AD (89.8%)	133–215 cal. AD (68.2%)
Context 20672 Posthole 20671	SUERC-69964	Charred grain *cf Triticum spelta* (spelt wheat)	-25.0‰ assumed	-	-	1862 ± 28	80–228 cal. AD (95.4%)	88–103 cal. AD (10.1%) 122–179 cal. AD (40.7%) 188–213 cal. AD (17.5%)
Context 20738 Pit 20729	SUERC-72468	Animal bone *Ovis aries* (sheep metacarpal)	-21.7‰	7.2‰	3.3	1751 ± 26	230–359 cal. AD (92.3%) 364–381 cal. AD (3.1%)	246–264 cal. AD (15.7%) 274–330 cal. AD (52.5%)
Context 20733 Ditch DL (cut 20732)	SUERC-69955	Charred grain *Hordeum vulgare* (barley)	-24.2‰	-	-	1793 ± 28	134–260 cal. AD (73.3%) 279–326 cal. AD (22.1%)	144–154 cal. AD (4.5%) 168–195 cal. AD (13.4%) 210–257 cal. AD (37.3%) 298–320 cal. AD (13.0%)
Context 20733 Ditch DL (cut 20732)	SUERC-72472	Charcoal *Alnus glutinosa* (alder)	-26.7‰	-	-	1308 ± 28	658–725 cal. AD (67.6%) 739–769 cal. AD (27.8%)	664–710 cal. AD (49.6%) 746–764 cal. AD (18.6%)
Context 20773 Ditch DW (cut 20775)	SUERC-69956	Charcoal *Quercus* (oak twig, 1–3 years)	-23.7‰	-	-	1542 ± 28	426–582 cal. AD (95.4%)	432–490 cal. AD (44.7%) 531–560 cal. AD (23.5%)
Skeleton 20706 Grave 20697	SUERC-69970	Human bone Right tibia	-19.4‰	14.4‰	3.4	1785 ± 29	135–265 cal. AD (62.5%) 272–332 cal. AD (32.9%)	179–187 cal. AD (3.1%) 213–260 cal. AD (36.0%) 280–325 cal. AD (29.1%)
Skeleton 20735 Grave 20736	SUERC-69971	Human bone Right radius	-19.8‰	12.3‰	3.4	1865 ± 29	77–228 cal. AD (95.4%)	86–109 cal. AD (15.5%) 117–175 cal. AD (39.5%) 192–212 cal. AD (13.2%)
Skeleton 20746 Grave 20748	SUERC-69972	Human bone Right ulna	-20.3‰	13.3‰	3.4	1824 ± 28	90–100 cal. AD (1.0%) 124–254 cal. AD (92.7%) 302–316 cal. AD (1.7%)	139–198 cal. AD (48.1%) 206–230 cal. AD (20.1%)
Skeleton 20747* Grave 20748	SUERC-69973	Human bone Right femur	-20.0‰	14.1‰	3.3	1967 ± 29	43 cal. BC –85 cal. AD (95.4%)	5–67 cal. AD (68.2%)
Skeleton 20747 Grave 20748	SUERC-75151	Human bone Ulna shaft	-20.3‰	13.6‰	3.3	1815 ± 30	140–197 cal. AD (43.1%) 207–238 cal. AD (25.1%)	126–258 cal. AD (88.9%) 284–322 cal. AD (6.5%)
Context 20872 'Trough' 20871	SUERC-69966	Charcoal *Prunus* (cherry species)	-24.1‰	-	-	3154 ± 29	1500–1388 cal. BC (91.0%) 1338–1321 cal. BC (4.4%)	1493–1481 cal. BC (8.8%) 1454–1407 cal. BC (59.4%)

* date considered to be erroneous

residual in their context (blue). The erroneous date (SUERC-69973) on infant 20747 is omitted from Figure 3.36. Despite the extended calibrated date ranges inherent in this period, the results illustrate a general focus in the 1st to 3rd centuries AD with little indication of activity here in the 4th to 6th centuries.

Bayesian analysis
Frances Healy

Radiocarbon dates were obtained for two deposits of sheep bone and four human neonate burials within Building C. When the six measurements were received, the 1st century cal. BC to 1st century cal. AD date from Sk 20747 was substantially earlier than the dates for the other samples, which all fell in the 1st to 3rd/4th centuries cal. AD. The early date seemed implausible in this particular context, especially as the measurements for the other three neonates were statistically consistent as determined by a chi-square test (Ward and Wilson 1978; T'=3.8; T'(5%)=6.0; ν=2). Despite increasingly effective laboratory procedures and increasingly high standards, radiocarbon dates can sometimes be inaccurate (Bayliss *et al.* 2011, 45–56). A second bone from skeleton 20747 was therefore submitted for dating, providing a measurement which is statistically consistent with those for the other neonates (T'=3.9; T'(5%)=7.8; ν=3). Since it is highly probable that the first measurement is inaccurate it is excluded from the model described below (Fig. 3.37: *SUERC-69973?*) and the second measurement is employed (Fig. 3.37: *SUERC-75151*).

Due to plateaux in the radiocarbon calibration curve for the Romano-British period the calibrated age ranges for all six samples are extended, often fragmented, and estimates based on them are therefore relatively imprecise.

In an attempt to determine the sequence of these deposits and the overall length of the period in which they were buried, the dates were the subject of Bayesian modelling, in which absolute dates are combined with other relevant information to refine individual age estimates and to calculate further parameters which are not directly dated. The method is described by, among others, Bronk Ramsey (2009) and Buck and Juarez (2017). The model presented here were constructed using the program OxCal v.4.2 (OxCal website; Bronk

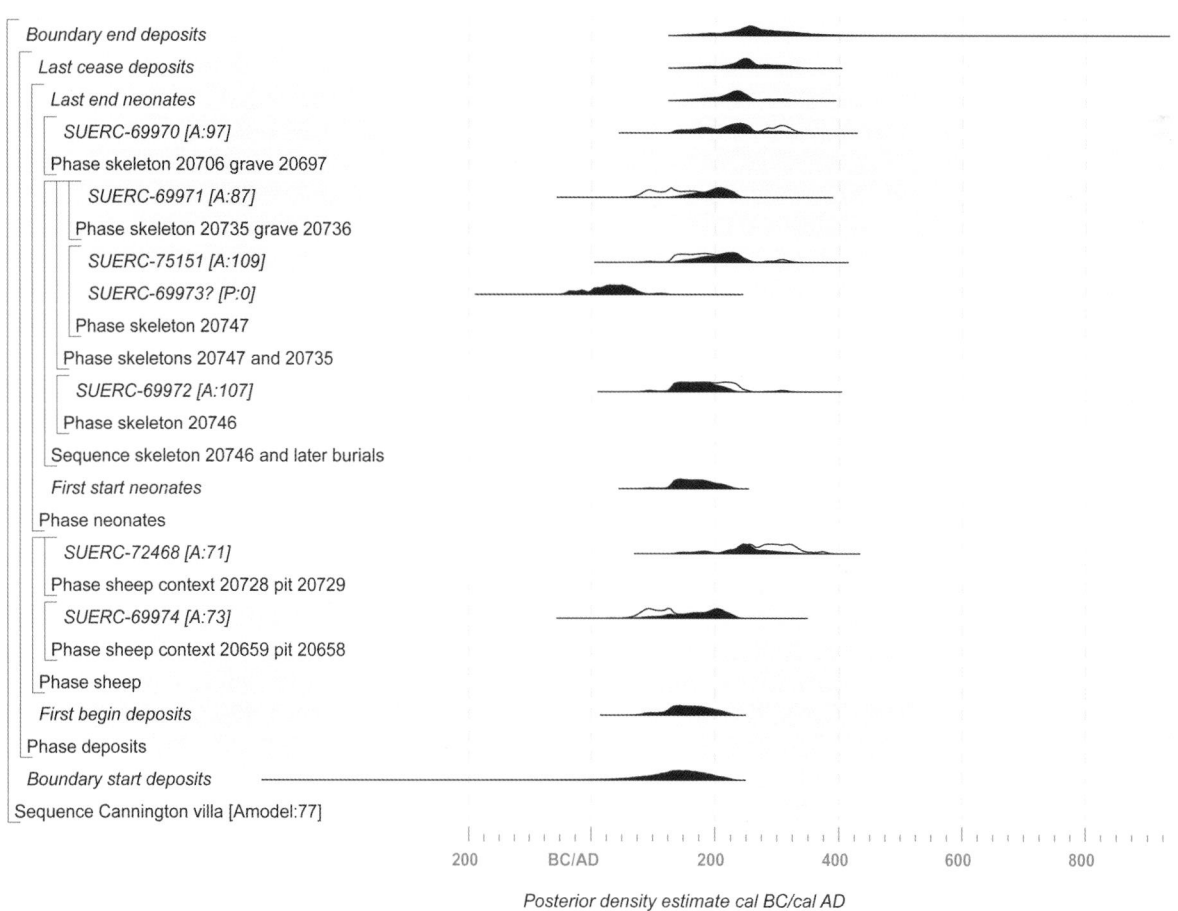

Fig. 3.37 Probability distributions for radiocarbon dates from burials in Building C

Ramsey and Lee 2013) and the internationally agreed calibration curve for terrestrial samples from the northern hemisphere (IntCal13; Reimer *et al.* 2013).

The statistical consistency of measurements for all four neonates, noted above, means that they could have died at the same time, although it is not demonstrable that they did, especially given the wide calibrated age ranges. The measurement for the earlier of the two sheep deposits (Fig. 3.37: *SUERC-69974*) is also statistically consistent with those for the four neonates (T'=6.8; T'(5%)-9.5; ν-4).

The model shown in Figure 3.37 treats all six deposits as part of a single episode of activity. Following the stratigraphic evidence, skeleton 20746 is modelled as earlier than both skeleton 20747 in the same grave (since 20747 seemed to have truncated the legs of 20746), and skeleton 20735 in grave 20736. It also estimates a start, end and duration for the neonate burials alone. The model has good overall agreement (Amodel 77). The

'highest posterior density intervals' generated by the model are printed in italics to distinguish them from simple calibrations and are listed in Table 3.2.

According to this model, the first deposit would have been made in *cal. AD 90–225* (*95% probability*), probably in *cal. AD 125–195* (*68% probability*: Fig. 3.37: *begin deposits*) and the last in *cal. AD 165–335* (*95% probability*), probably in *cal. AD 215–305* (*68% probability*; Fig. 3.37: *cease deposits*). Neonate burials would have ended sooner, in *cal. AD 160–270* (*84% probability*) or *275–325* (*11% probability*), probably in *cal. AD 195–260* (*68% probability*; Fig. 3.37: *end neonates*). The whole process would have occupied *1–195 years* (*95% probability*), probably *15–130 years* (*64% probability*; Fig. 3.38: *duration deposits*). Neonates would have been buried over *1–155 years* (*95% probability*), probably *1–85 years* (*68% probability*; Fig. 3.38: *duration neonates*). The difference between these two estimates is mainly due to the later of the two sheep

Table 3.2: Results of the model shown in Figure 3.37. The highest posterior density intervals are rounded outwards to five years

Sample or estimated parameter	Lab No.	δ ¹³C	δ ¹³N	C/N ratio	Radiocarbon age yrs BP	Weighted mean	*Highest posterior density interval (95% probability)*	*Highest posterior density interval (68% probability)*
begin deposits	-	-	-	-	-	-	*cal. AD 90–225*	*cal. AD 125–195*
start neonates	-	-	-	-	-	-	*cal. AD 125–230*	*cal. AD 135–190*
Sheep tooth, context 20659 Pit 20658	SUERC-69974	−21.9‰	8.0‰	3.3	1876 ± 28	-	*cal. AD 95–235*	*cal. AD 155–230*
Sheep metacarpal, context 20728 Pit 20729	SUERC-72468	−21.7‰	7.2‰	3.3	1751 ± 26	-	*cal. AD 140–200 (16%) 205–330 (79%)*	*cal. AD 180–190 (1%) 215–295 (67%)*
Skeleton 20746 Grave 20748 R ulna, pre-dating skeletons 20747 and 20735	SUERC-69972	−20.3‰	13.3‰	3.4	1824 ± 28	-	*cal. AD 125–230*	*cal. AD 135–195*
Skeleton 20735 Grave 20736 R radius	SUERC-69971	−19.8‰	12.3‰	3.4	1865 ± 29	-	*cal. AD 140–240*	*cal. AD 180–235*
Skeleton 20747 Grave 20748 R femur from same individual as SUERC-75151	SUERC-69973	−20.0‰	14.1‰	3.3	1967 ± 29	1895 ± 21 T'=13.3; T'(5%)=3.8; ν=1	Excluded from model	
Ulna shaft from same individual as SUERC-69973	SUERC-75151	−20.3‰	13.6‰	3.3	1815 ± 30	-	*cal. AD 135–260*	*cal. AD 180–245*
Skeleton 20706 Grave 20697 R tibia	SUERC-69970	−19.4‰	14.4‰	3.4	1785 ± 29	-	*cal. AD 135–265 (88%) 275–315 (7%)*	*cal. AD 165–200 (19%) 205–260 (49%)*
end neonates	-	-	-	-	-	-	*cal. AD 160–270 (84%) 275–325 (11%)*	*cal. AD 195–260*
cease deposits	-	-	-	-	-	-	*cal. AD 165–335*	*cal. AD 215–295*
duration neonates	-	-	-	-	-	-	*1–150 years*	*1–80 years*
duration deposits	-	-	-	-	-	-	*1–195 years*	*1–10 years (4%) 15–130 years (61%)*
end neonates/cease deposits	-	-	-	-	-	-	*−90 to +125 years*	*−25 to +85 years*

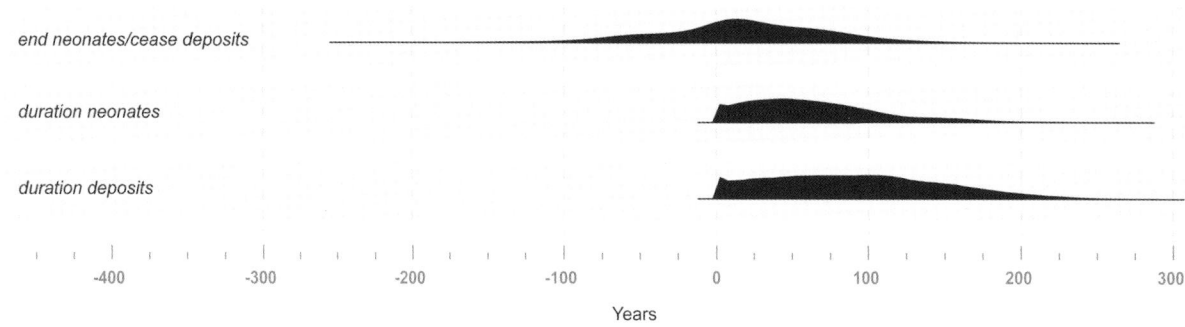

Fig. 3.38 Estimated durations and interval from the model shown in Fig. 3.37. Highest posterior density intervals are given in Table 3.2

Table 3.3: An ordering of dates for deposits in pits inside the villa gallery derived from the model shown in Figure 3.37. Each cell shows the % probability that the deposit in the left-hand column is earlier than the deposit in the top row. It is, for example, 100% probable that Sk 20746 died before Sk 20735

	Sk 20746 SUERC-69972	Sheep in pit 20658 SUERC-69974	Sk 20735 SUERC-69971	Sk 20747 SUERC-75151	Sk 20706 SUERC-69970	Sheep in pit 20729 SUERC-72468
Sk 20746 SUERC-69972	-	61	100	100	87	94
Sheep in pit 20658 SUERC-69974	39	-	71	78	79	89
Sk 20735 SUERC-69971	0	29	-	63	67	84
Sk 20747 SUERC-75151	0	22	37	-	58	78
Sk 20706 SUERC-69970	13	21	33	42	-	71
Sheep in pit 20729 SUERC-72468	6	11	16	22	29	-

deposits, in pit 20729. Some years may have elapsed between the last neonate burial and this final deposit, since the estimated interval between *end neonates* and *cease deposits* is *–90 to +125 years* (95% probability), probably *–25 to +85 years* (*68% probability*; Fig.3.38: *end neonates/cease deposits*).

The sequence in which the deposits were made, as calculated by the Order function in OxCal, is shown in Table 3.3. Sk 20746 and the sheep in pit 20658 were earlier than the other burials; it is, however, unclear which of them was first, since it is 61% probable that Sk 20746 was, 39% probable that the sheep was. The remaining burials are also difficult to sequence, although they were all probably earlier than the multiple sheep deposit in pit 20729.

Iron Age and Roman pottery
E.R. McSloy

Pottery amounting to 3214 sherds (54.6kg) was recovered from Sandy Lane, the large majority dating to the Roman period. The assemblage derived from 183 stratified contexts, with further small quantities of unstratified finds. Quantification is according to fabric within context and by sherd count, weight and rim EVEs (Estimated Vessel Equivalent). Codes utilised for the pottery fabrics are for late prehistoric types primarily related to primary/secondary inclusion types. Fabric codes used for recording the late prehistoric and Roman pottery types are defined in Tables 3.4 and 3.5; full fabric descriptions are included in the archive. For the widely traded regional or continental imports, codes

Table 3.4: Iron Age type pottery. Fabric codes and summary quantification

Code	Description	Count	Weight (g)	EVEs
ARG1	Argillaceous (mudstone?) inclusions	3	27	0.00
ARGQ1	Argillaceous (mudstone?) and quartz inclusions	3	69	0.10
GR1	Grog	40	453	0.35
GRLI1	Grog/limestone	1	39	0.00
GRQZ1	Grog/quartz	4	81	0.03
GRVES1	Grog/vesicular (limestone?)	1	3	0.00
LI1	Limestone	109	851	0.26
LI2	Fine limestone (wheel-thrown)	2	8	0.00
LIcalc	Limestone (including calcitic)	18	135	0.08
QT1	Coarse quartzite	21	100	0.10
QT2	Finer quartzite	2	40	0.00
QZ1	Quartz (sandstone-derived)	194	1528	1.15
QZ2	Quartz (sandstone-derived) wheel-thrown	33	763	0.25
QZ3	Fine quartz/silty	1	9	0.05
SS1	Polycrystalline quartz (sandstone)	174	2136	1.87
SS2	Fine/sparse sandstone	1	18	0.02
VES	Vesicular (limestone?)	1	5	0.00
Total		**608**	**6265**	**4.26**

matching those of the National Roman Fabric Reference Collection have been utilised (Tomber and Dore 1998). The assemblage is discussed below by period.

Late Prehistoric

The late prehistoric pottery component describes handmade 'native style' pottery, use of which almost certainly continued into the period following the Roman conquest. Pottery categorised as such amounted to 608 sherds, weighing 6265g (rim EVEs value of 4.26).

The bulk of the assemblage is considered to belong to the later Iron Age (after *c*. 400/300 BC), and probably continuing into the early decades of the Roman period. For a small proportion of less diagnostic material (mainly unfeatured body sherds), dating potentially spans a longer period and the term 'later prehistoric' is most appropriate.

The largest stratified groups are those from Ditches O (121 sherds) and T (41 sherds) and Ditch S of Structure A. A significant proportion of the assemblage is residual, having been recovered from Roman walls and robber trenches (79 sherds or 13%) and from post-medieval quarry pits (40 sherds or 7%).

This notwithstanding, the late prehistoric pottery survives in moderately good condition, reflected in a moderately high mean sherd weight (10.3g) and by good surface survival. Surface preservation has occasionally permitted survival of evidence for use in the form of carbonaceous and other residues, although the incidence of this is restricted to 40 sherds.

Assemblage composition: fabrics

The range of the late prehistoric group (according to fabric) is set out in Table 3.4. The largest proportion (Types QZ1–3: 228 sherds or 38%) occurs in fabrics containing abundant quartz inclusions. These are likely to have used local clays, although determining the precise source is impossible due to the ubiquity of quartz sand-bearing clays in Somerset (Morris 2007, 569). A proportion might derive from the same Mendip source as the polycrystalline quartz-bearing (sandstone-tempered) types SS1 and SS2, which amount to 175 sherds or 29% of the total. A smaller, but relatively sizeable proportion (129 sherds or 21%) occurs as calcareous (limestone/calcite) fabrics, the source for which is also likely to have been the Mendip Hills (below). For the remainder of the group, occurring in a mix of grogged/argillaceous, coarse quartz/quartzite-tempered and vesicular types, local origins are likely or possible.

Forms and decoration/surface treatment

The late prehistoric group includes rim sherds from a minimum of 64 vessels. Rim forms are mainly simple: shorter-everted/simple rounded and squared and bead-like (Fig. 3.39, nos 1–9 and 11–15). The fragmentation within the assemblage has made reconstruction of vessel profiles difficult in most instances. The decorated fineware bowls occur with a high-shouldered profile featuring an everted rim (Fig. 3.39, no. 1) or with a probably rounded/globular profile (Fig. 3.39, no. 2). Most of the minimally decorated or plain forms

Table 3.5: Roman pottery. Fabric codes and summary quantification

Source	Code*	Description	Count	Weight (g)	EVEs
Local/	BS1	Fine/medium sandy dark grey/black-fired	271	2913	3.31
unsourced	BS1m	Fine, black-fired, micaceous	1	6	0.00
	BS2	Coarse black-firing (late BB imit.)	64	634	0.75
	GGW1	Grogged greyware	37	675	0.49
	GGW2	Grogged greyware (finer)	17	715	0.00
	GRQZ1	Coarse grogged with quartz	7	349	0.20
	GW1	Greyware, sparse quartz, red core	343	6297	3.87
	GW2	Greyware, coarse quartz, with common iron	422	13658	2.04
	GW3	Sandy greyware	153	1900	2.88
	GW4	Hard, grey with red margin	34	511	1.06
	GWf	Fine (silty) greyware	2	46	0.20
	buff1	Buff-firing	3	79	0.00
	OX1	Fine oxidised (sparse quartz)	10	64	0.04
	OX2	Coarse, sandy oxidised	1	4	0.00
	OXRS3	Fine oxidised/micaceous with red wash	1	1	0.00
	LOC CC	Unsourced colour-coated ware	1	20	0.31
	SVW OX	Severn Valley ware (Shepton Mallet?)	3	23	0.07
	WHf	Fine whiteware (Oxford?)	3	23	0.00
(mortaria)	MORT1	Gritty pink/white mortaria	1	114	0.12
	MORTRS	Shepton Mallet red slipped mortaria	1	31	0.05
Regional	DOR BB1	South-east Dorset Black-burnished ware	1142	12209	13.47
	NFO CC	New Forest slipped colour-coated ware	3	65	1.00
	OXF RS	Oxford red-slipped ware	5	30	0.15
(mortaria)	OXF WH	Oxford whiteware	5	182	0.22
Imports	CNG BS	Central Gaulish black-slipped	2	5	0.00
	MOS KER	Trier black-slipped (Moselkeramik)	4	7	0.00
(samian)	LEZ SA2	Central Gaulish (Lezoux) samian	21	314	0.40
	EG SA	East Gaulish samian	16	296	0.24
(amphorae)	BAT AM2	Baetican amphorae	31	7214	0.00
	GAL AM	South Gaulish wine amphorae	2	7	0.00
Total			**2606**	**48392**	**30.87**

* types in bold conform to National Roman fabric Reference Collection codes (Tomber and Dore 1998)

are probably jar-profiled and neck-less; the fully reconstructable vessel no. 7 having a squat, barrel-like profile. The undecorated bead-rim jar forms (Fig. 3.39, nos 3 and 7–9) are amongst the latest elements in the late prehistoric assemblage. Notably, such vessels occur in a wider range of fabrics compared to the decorated forms, including calcareous and grogged types.

Decoration (including burnishing) was recorded on 94 sherds (9.5%), representing 26 vessels and was limited to fabrics QZ1/2 and SS1. In its most complex form, the decoration occurs with fineware bowls and consists of incised or incised and stamped curvilinear patterns, commonly incorporating hatched infill (Fig. 3.39, nos 1, 4 and 10). The designs used are close to the La Tène-inspired designs recorded on pottery from Glastonbury and Meare (in Peacock 1969, fig. 4) and characterised in the region as the *south-western decorated* style (below). Other vessels, probably bowls, in this style exhibit less complex geometrical decoration at the shoulder (Fig. 3.39, nos 6 and 12), or single, paired or multiple horizontal grooves below the rim. The simple grooved decoration may be confined to jar-proportioned vessels (Fig. 3.39, nos 13 and 15) and can be combined with zones of horizontal and vertical burnish (nos 11 and 15).

The incised decoration described falls within the

south-western decorated tradition which characterises Iron Age assemblages in the region. Peacock's (1969) study of what had been termed 'Glastonbury ware' found that the style occurred in a range of fabrics across the South West, and that distribution of the fabric groups reflected geological variation and the availability of mineral 'fillers'. A later study by Rouillard (1987) of undecorated (Iron Age) pottery recorded similar results, with assemblages dominated by sandstone (Peacock's Group 2) and limestone/calcite-tempered fabrics (Peacock's Group 3). The source for both groupings is almost certainly the Mendip Hills and the sandstones of the Old Red series (ibid., 46). The origin of the limestone-tempered fabrics (Peacock's Group 3) is the palaeozoic limestones of the Mendip or hills extending northwards to the Bristol area (Allen 1998).

Dating/discussion

The difficulties that persist in the application of absolute scientific dating to this period mean that the south-western decorated style remains ill-defined in its chronological range. The La Tène-inspired designs imply dating no earlier than *c.* 400 BC and an inception date of *c.* 300 BC has been argued (H. Quinnell pers. comm.). It remains unclear, but is likely, that the elaborate decorated wares in this style occur contemporaneously with more simply decorated or undecorated vessels. In common with other regions in lowland Britain it appears that the use of complex decoration was no longer common by the time of the Roman conquest, and it has been suggested that the south-western decorated style had been discontinued by *c.* 50 BC (Coles and Minnitt 1995). The plain styles characterising assemblages across the later 1st century BC and into the early or middle decades of the 1st century AD are common to the Somerset littoral extending northwards and to both sides of the Severn Estuary (Allen 1998). Such groups are made up of handmade forms, commonly comprising jars with bead rims and incorporating small numbers of wheel-thrown vessels in the 'Belgic' tradition.

Incidence in the Cannington group both of vessels in the south-western decorated style and of the plain bead-rim forms characterising transitional styles suggests a date range spanning the earlier 1st century AD (or a little earlier) to the mid or later 1st century AD. Refinement of dating based on separation of 'early' decorated elements and later plain styles is made difficult by the scarcity of larger and well-stratified groups. However, an assessment of the limited evidence for such a refinement is detailed below.

Late Iron Age to Early Roman transition period

Pottery relating to the main features of the Iron Age settlement is set out in Table 3.6. Structures A and B produced 42 sherds and 78 sherds respectively. These are compositionally discrete, with the exception of one sherd in wheel-thrown fabric BS1, comprising handmade 'native style' pottery primarily in quartz/sandstone-tempered fabrics. Both groups contain a mix of decorated, minimally decorated and plain elements. The presence of elaborately decorated vessel no. 1 from Structure B implies origins before *c.* 50 BC. Significantly, although some plain or sparsely decorated vessels are present (Fig. 3.39, nos 2 and 3), the bead-rim forms most typical of the 'transitional' styles are absent.

That the larger pottery groups from Enclosure Ditches O and L contain certainly Roman elements is unsurprising given the non-closed nature of the context. The presence in Ditch O of vessels in the south-western decorated style (Fig. 3.39, nos 4, 5 and 10) is nevertheless consistent with construction and initial use which might be contemporaneous with Structures A and B. Evidence for occupation extending later than the disuse of Structures A and B, comes from the presence in Ditch O of undecorated bead-rim vessels occurring in limestone-tempered and other fabrics (Fig. 3.39, nos 8 and 9).

Collectively the pottery from the pits and postholes close to Structures A–C resembles that from these structures and the rest of the Iron Age assemblage in the preponderance (84%) of native style types. Notably the limestone-tempered types sparse from Structures A and B, but common from Ditch O, are well-represented within the postholes and pits. Amongst these sherds, complex La Tène-style decoration is absent and such decoration as occurs is limited to simple motifs (Fig. 3.39, nos 12 and 13) and as vessels with bead-like rims. Indications that activity extends into the later 1st or 2nd centuries AD are from Roman elements, including a few sherds in South-east Dorset Black-burnished ware (DOR BB1), wheel-thrown reduced wares (types GW1 and BS1), and a single sherd of samian.

Illustration catalogue (Fig. 3.39)

Structure B

1. Shouldered bowl; everted rim. Complex incised curvilinear and impressed decoration in south-western decorated style. Fabric QZ1. Ditch S (fill 20093).
2. ?Jar; short, squared rim. Single groove at neck. Fabric QZ1. Ditch S (fill 20092).
3. Globular jar; short, upright/simple rim. Undecorated. Fabric LI1. Ditch S (fill 20186).

Ditch O

4. ?Globular bowl; short upright rim. Incised curvilinear decoration with crosshatch infill. Fabric SS1. (Fill 20315).
5. ?Globular bowl; short everted rim. Cordon at neck with zone of incised oblique line infill and burnished below. Fabric SS1. (Fill 20346).
6. ?Globular bowl; bead-like rim. Horizontal incised lines below neck defining zone of incised oblique at opposing angles. Fabric SS1. (Fill 20065).
7. Jar; barrel-shaped profile, with bead rim. Horizontal burnish lines at shoulder and vertical below. Fabric QZ1. (Fill 20254).

Table 3.6: Late prehistoric stratified pottery summary by feature group. Quantities as number of sherds (NOSH)

Date	Fabric	Structure A Ditch LL	Structure A Ditch T	Structure B Ditch Q	Structure B Ditch R	Structure B Ditch S	Structure D	Pits adjacent to Structure D	Ditch 20580	Ditch I	Ditch L	Ditch N	Ditch O	Ditch DF	Structure A Ditch DQ	NOSH	Weight (g)	Pits adjacent to Structures A–C (NOSH/weight)
Lpre./trans.	ARG1	-	1	-	-	-	-	-	-	-	-	-	-	-	-	1	13	1 / 8
	ARGQ1	-	-	-	-	-	-	-	-	-	-	-	-	-	-	-	-	2 / 2
	GR1	-	-	-	1	6	-	-	-	-	2	-	5	-	-	14	152	- / -
	GRLI1	-	-	-	-	-	-	-	-	-	-	-	1	-	-	1	39	- / -
	GRQZ1	-	-	-	-	-	-	-	-	-	-	-	-	-	-	1	6	- / -
	LI1	-	-	-	2	1	-	3	-	-	6	-	53	-	-	65	562	8 / 50
	LIcalc	-	-	-	-	-	3	-	-	-	-	-	1	-	-	4	44	- / -
	QT1	-	-	-	1	2	-	-	-	1	-	-	-	-	-	4	43	4 / 7
	QT2	-	-	-	2	-	-	-	-	-	-	-	-	-	-	2	40	- / -
	QZ1	-	23	18	-	41	-	7	-	-	7	1	36	2	1	136	649	12 / 89
	QZ2	1	-	-	2	-	-	-	-	-	10	-	2	-	-	15	524	4 / 63
	SS1	-	17	-	-	-	1	1	1	1	1	-	23	-	7	52	720	45 / 477
	VES	-	-	-	1	-	-	-	-	-	-	-	-	-	-	1	5	- / -
Subtotal		1	41	18	9	50	4	11	1	2	27	1	121	2	8	296	2797	76 / 696
Roman	BS1	-	-	-	-	1	-	-	-	-	1	-	1	-	-	3	22	4 / 37
	GGW1	-	-	-	-	-	-	-	-	-	-	-	-	-	-	1	16	- / -
	GRQZ1	-	-	-	-	-	-	-	-	-	-	2	-	-	-	2	145	1 / 85
	GW1	-	-	-	-	-	-	-	-	-	17	-	1	-	-	18	442	1 / 6
	GW2	-	-	-	-	-	-	-	-	-	2	-	-	-	-	2	474	- / -
	BB1	-	-	-	-	-	-	-	-	-	6	-	15	-	-	21	257	7 / 21
	LEZ SA2	-	-	-	-	-	-	-	-	-	2	-	-	-	1	3	107	1 / 2
	SVW OX2	-	-	-	-	-	-	-	-	-	-	-	1	-	-	1	12	- / -
Subtotal		-	-	-	-	1	-	1	-	-	28	2	18	-	1	51	1475	14 / 151
Total		1	41	18	9	51	4	12	1	2	55	3	139	2	9	347	4272	90 / 847

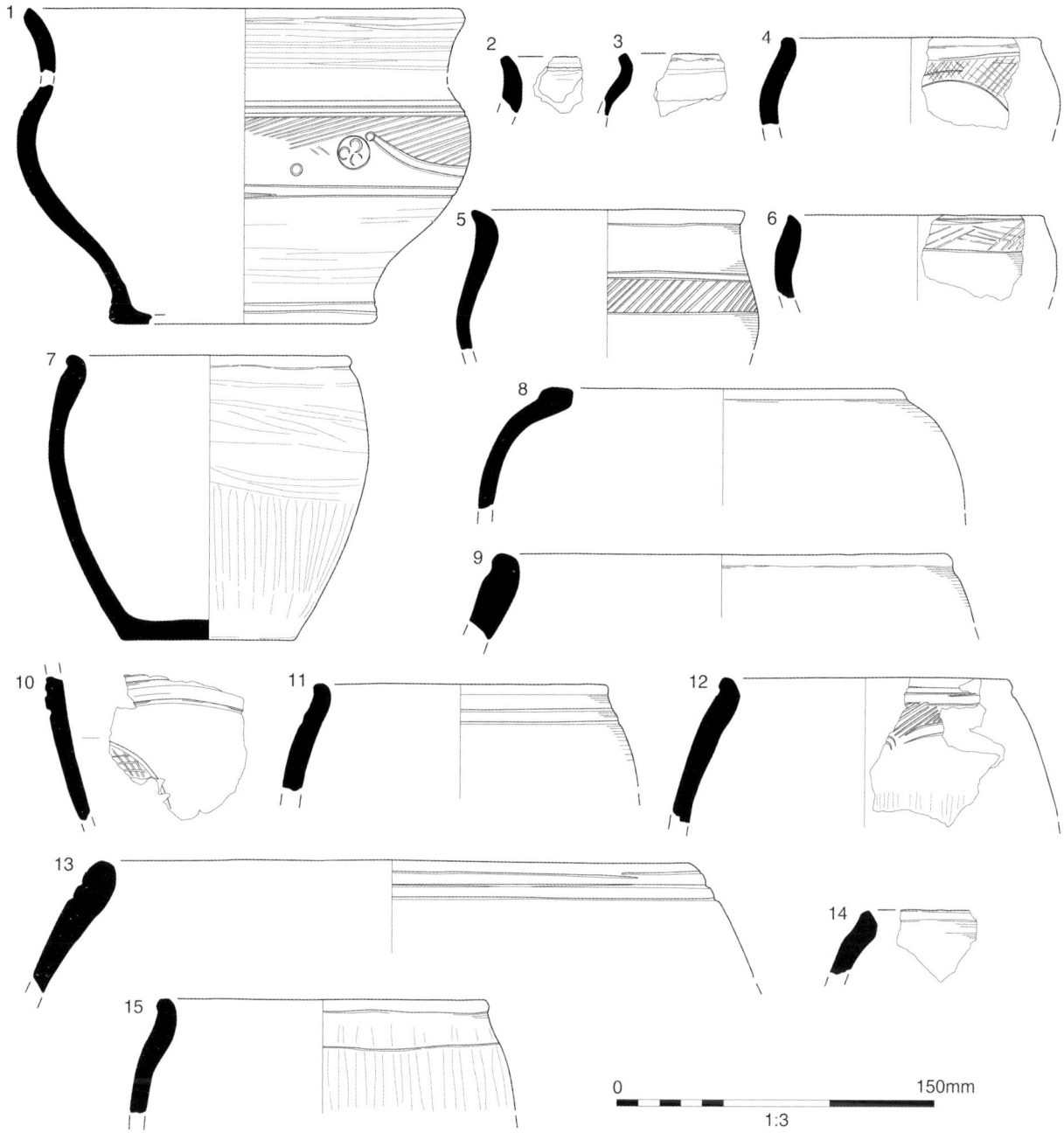

Fig. 3.39 Later Iron Age pottery nos 1–15. Structure B, 1–3; Ditch O, 4–9; other features, 10–15

8   Ovoid jar; bead rim. Burnished. Fabric LI1. (Fill 20229).

9   Ovoid/barrel-shaped jar; bead rim. Fabric GR1. (Fill 20229).

Other features

10 ?Bowl sherd. Deep-grooved curvilinear design with crosshatch infill. Orientation is uncertain. Fabric QZ2. Posthole 20456 (fill 20457).

11 Globular jar or bowl. Pulled 'bead' rim. Double incised horizontal line decoration at neck. Vertical burnish lines below. Fabric QZ1. Hollow-way DF (fill 20327).

12 Globular jar or bowl. Pulled 'bead' rim. Double incised horizontal line decoration below rim and oblique or curving incised decoration at neck. Burnished. Fabric SS1. Pit 20071 (fill 20070).

13 Globular or barrel-shaped jar. Simple, thickened rim. Double incised horizontal line decoration at neck. Fabric GRQZ1. Pit 20098 (fill 20099).

14 Ovoid/barrel-shaped jar; bead rim. Fabric SS1. Pit/posthole 20487 (fill 20488).

15 Globular jar or bowl. Pulled 'bead' rim. Single incised horizontal line decoration at neck. Vertical burnish lines below. Fabric QZ2. Unphased natural feature 20244 (fill 20245).

Roman

A total of 2606 sherds (48.4kg) of Roman pottery was recovered, the majority by hand but including 198 sherds retrieved from soil samples. The condition of the hand-collected Roman assemblage is good with minimal surface loss resulting from abrasion or from the burial environment. The mean sherd weight of 18.6g is fairly high for a Roman assemblage and is not suggestive of a well broken-up group, although this is likely to have been elevated somewhat by the quantities of amphora and thick-walled storage jar sherds (below).

Pottery relating to phased Roman deposits is set out in Table 3.5. The largest proportion derived from pits/postholes with the remainder mostly from ditches. Relatively little material (less than 25%) was recorded from structural deposits relating to the villa buildings or associated demolition rubble. Further material was derived from unphased robbing activity (39 sherds) and from rubble layer 20556 above Building C (253 sherds).

Composition

South-east Dorset Black-burnished ware is the single most common type, amounting to 1142 sherds or 43% of the total (Table 3.5). Next most common are reduced coarsewares (types BS1–2; GGW1–2; GW1–4 and GWf), which collectively make up 51% of the total (1351 sherds). Most or all of the reduced coarsewares are considered of local manufacture (below).

South-east Dorset Black-burnished wares (hereafter DOR BB1) are typically abundant from sites in Roman Somerset. A small number of vessels from Sandy Lane are possible examples of early output (Brailsford 1958), dating to the 1st century AD. Examples include a jar from upper fill 20346 of Iron Age Ditch O, and an open vessel with a footring from Iron Age pit 20342 (fill 20343). The large bulk of material can be expected to date to the period of expansion of the industry beginning in the earlier 2nd century. Forms represented in the assemblage are set out in Table 3.8. Jars and open classes are most abundant, with non-utilitarian vessel classes confined to flagons, represented by ribbed 'strap' handle fragments from two deposits (Iron Age enclosure Ditch L fill 20055 and Roman Building A rubble layer 20313). Dishes are overwhelmingly of plain-rimmed type, common to the period after the mid or later 2nd century (Holbrook and Bidwell 1991). Bowls comprise conical forms with flat, grooved rims (Fig. 3.40, no. 21), with fewer 'dropped' flange vessels.

Variability in fabric among the local reduced coarsewares almost certainly reflects origins from a number of sources. In common with the pre-Roman quartz-bearing types described above, conventional visual/microscopic examination is unable to narrow source with certainty. A source for a proportion of the harder, sandy greywares (GW1, GW3–4) is however likely to be the important kilns at Congresbury *c*. 25 km to the north (Usher and Lilly 1964). The coarser grey (GW2) and grogged/argillaceous types (GGW1–2 and GRQZ1) may include products from kilns known at Norton Fitzwarren to the south (Timby 1989). Dominant forms among the reduced wares are necked jar classes. Some (neck-less) jars and open forms including plain-rim dishes demonstrate influence from Black-burnished ware; however, necked jar or bowl forms, lids and bag-shaped or indented beakers (Fig. 3.40, nos 24, 25 and 31–4) reflect other influences. With knowledge of local ceramic traditions limited by an absence of published production sites, close dating of the reduced coarsewares is possible only through association with better-understood types (below). A form which is common among coarse Greyware fabric GW2 is the distinctive large storage jar class (Fig. 3.40, nos 19 and 23). This form, typically with heavy, bifid rim and fingertip/thumb impressions to the rim top and shoulder zones is abundant from Somerset and Devon in the later 2nd to the 4th centuries (Holbrook 1991). A likely source is the kilns at Norton Fitzwarren, Somerset where closely comparable forms are known (Timby 1989, 58, fig. 22).

The remainder of the assemblage is limited in its range; the small number of sherds in sandy oxidised types cannot be assigned to a particular source. The few body sherds of Severn Valley ware type (SVW OX2) are similarly only broadly dateable. The likely source for this type is Shepton Mallet, where kilns representing an offshoot of the main Gloucestershire/Worcestershire group are known to have operated in the 2nd and 3rd centuries AD (Webster 1976). An oxidised and red-slipped mortarium fabric (MORTRS), represented by a base sherd residual in a Period 8 quarry fill, is also probably from this source (Hartley 2001). Colour-coated fabric MSC CC is present as a single bag-shaped vessel with a well-formed cornice rim (Fig. 3.40, no. 36). Its source is unknown, although similar material recorded from Ilchester was thought to be local (Leach 1982, 138) and typologically the vessel form should date to the 2nd or earlier 3rd centuries.

Regional fineware/specialist types (mortaria, flagons) are poorly represented, comprising mainly products from the New Forest and Oxfordshire. A Verulamium-region mortarium (VER WH; Fig. 3.40, no. 16) is rare evidence for the use of Romano-British traded wares before *c*. AD 150/200. Whiteware mortaria from Oxfordshire (OXF WH) are mid/later 3rd-century flanged classes (Fig. 3.40, nos 18 and 29). The few identifiable forms in Oxford red-slipped ware (OXF RS) are fineware bowls and beakers (Fig. 3.40, nos 17 and 28) for which only broad dating after *c*. AD 240/270 can be asserted. The few sherds of New Forest slipped colour-coated ware (NFO CC) come from beakers of indented form and a bottle (Fig. 3.40, no. 37), all dating to after *c*. AD 260.

Imported continental wares are present most commonly as Gaulish samian (below). Non-sigillata finewares are present as small sherds from Gaulish Black-slipped wares (MOS KER; CNG BS), all probably from beakers/cups. They share dating corresponding to that of the samian, in the range *c.* AD 150–200/250. One sherd in fabric CNG BS exhibited evidence for repair using rivets.

Amphorae types occur as southern Spanish (BAT AM2) and Gaulish (GAL AM) types. Both types are representative of the most common forms found within Romano-British deposits of the mid 1st to 3rd centuries AD. Sherds of Baetican type (BAT AM2) from Roman Ditch W (fill 20194) are notable in having been reworked/ground to form a rudimentary rim and in a manner suggesting reuse following partial breakage (Fig. 3.40, no. 26).

Samian

The samian group amounts to 37 sherds, equivalent to 1.4% of the assemblage total. All are plain forms in Central (LEZ SA2) and East Gaulish (EG SA) fabrics. Three vessels among the East Gaulish samian exhibit evidence for repair. The relative abundance of the East Gaulish material (16 sherds) signifies this being a late group, dateable after *c.* AD 140 and as late as *c.* AD 250. Identifiable forms among the East Gaulish group comprise a Dressel (Dr.) 45 wall-sided mortarium (one or more vessels from Ditch W fill 20165 and subsoil 20001) which is dateable after *c.* AD 170, and Dr. 31r bowl sherds, dateable after *c.* AD 160 from Ditch W fills 20165, 20198 and 20334. A more varied range of vessels characterises the Central Gaulish assemblage, although forms dating after *c.* AD 150 still dominate: dishes/bowls Dr. 31 and Dr. 31r, and mortarium Dr. 45.

Stratigraphy

Some 1537 sherds (32300g) sherds were recorded from Roman deposits. The stratified material, summarised by feature group in Table 3.7, includes 123 sherds of late prehistoric type, all of which can be considered residual. The largest Roman groups and those most useful for the refinement of dating are those from Ditches DE, DI and DW. Most groups relating to the villa buildings are of small size and rarely permit close dating. In addition to material from Roman deposits, 567 sherds (9163g) of late prehistoric and Roman pottery were recorded from post-medieval quarry fills (Fig. 3.40, nos 31–7).

Roman material associated with Building A (all phases) amounts to 122 sherds; approximately half comprising handmade Iron Age type material which is presumably redeposited from precursive activity. A (2nd-century) mortarium sherd (Fig. 3.40, no. 16) from the construction cut for wall 20473 is among few, more closely dateable individual pieces. There are no clear compositional differences comparing groups from the different building phases; among the Roman material, finewares are entirely absent, this assemblage comprising mainly DOR BB1 and local reduced coarsewares. Few rim sherds were present; the (DOR BB1) plain-rim dishes and flat, grooved rim bowls however suggesting dating probably in the late 2nd or 3rd centuries range.

Only small quantities of pottery (29 sherds) were associated with Building B, with the majority (23 sherds) from collapse/demolition deposits. A slightly more varied range of material is represented compared with Building A, with a Gaulish amphora sherd and Oxfordshire products (OXF WH; OXF RS) recorded from among the 'disuse' layers. Nothing which is closely dateable was recorded from the 'use' deposits associated with this structure. Material from demolition layer 20257 included an Oxfordshire mortarium of form M18 dating *c.* AD 240–300 (Young 1977, 72) and a red-slipped ware beaker from the same source dateable after *c.* AD 240/270 (Fig. 3.40, nos 17–18).

Building C also produced only modest quantities of pottery (36 sherds) and again a group largely composed of coarsewares. A conical flanged bowl in DOR BB1 from masonry 20610 provides evidence for dating after *c.* AD 250. Significantly larger quantities of pottery (334 sherds) were recorded from unphased demolition deposits overlying this building. Most again from this group comprises DOR BB1 and other coarseware types (Fig. 3.40, no. 19). Among the DOR BB1 plain-rim dishes and bowls with flat, grooved rims support a 3rd-century focus.

A moderately large group (224 sherds) from Ditch DI largely comprises coarseware types, including 69 sherds from one DOR BB1 jar. Central Gaulish samian is present as two sherds, including from a plainware dish (form Dr. 31 or 31r), probably dating after *c.* AD 150. Similar dating and as late as the earlier 3rd century is suggested by jar and bowl forms in BB1. Ditch DE (231 sherds) and small groups from Ditches K and DG also located to the north and northeast of Iron Age Ditches O and L, are all compositionally similar, the more closely dateable elements suggestive of a later 2nd to 3rd-century range.

Hollow-way DC produced a group of 70 sherds which was unusual in containing mainly local reduced coarsewares and only four sherds of DOR BB1. This group included sherds from two large storage jars (Fig. 3.40, no. 23) of distinctive regional type and common to the Middle and Late Roman periods (*c.* AD 160/180–400). A smaller group (20 sherds) from Hollow-way DH included a further example of this class, and a sherd from a New Forest indented beaker; this suggesting dating after *c.* AD 260. Given the presence of storage vessels amongst the assemblages from these hollow-ways, it is possible that these finds represent accidental losses from carts.

Ditch W, located 9m to the west of Building A, produced the largest pottery group (606 sherds) from the Roman deposits. Untypically for the site, continental wares are moderately well-represented, present as quantities of East Gaulish samian (fabric

Table 3.7: Roman stratified pottery summary by feature group. Quantities as number of sherds (NOSH)

Date	Fabric	Building A	Building B	Building B rubble	Building C	Ditch D	Ditch DE	Ditch DG	Ditch DI	Ditch DS	Ditch DU	Ditch DW	Ditch DZ	Ditch EC	Ditch F	Ditch K	Ditch W	Features within Building C	Hollow-way DC	Hollow-way DD	Hollow-way DH	NOSH	Weight (g)
Lpre		59	2	-	1	1	-	-	16	20	-	1	-	-	3	2	17	-	-	1	-	123	1081
Roman	BS1	1	1	5	5	-	16	-	15	-	11	2	-	-	-	1	63	7	-	-	4	131	1530
	BS1m	1	-	-	-	-	-	-	-	-	-	-	-	-	-	-	-	-	-	-	-	1	6
	BS2	-	-	1	-	-	-	-	10	-	-	-	-	-	-	-	11	-	2	1	1	26	304
	GGW1	-	-	-	-	-	-	-	6	-	-	-	-	-	-	-	5	-	-	-	1	12	167
	GRQZ1	-	-	-	-	-	-	-	-	-	-	-	-	3	-	-	3	-	-	-	-	3	91
	GW1	53	-	3	1	-	-	-	2	-	-	-	-	-	-	1	79	6	21	-	1	170	3553
	GW2	10	1	1	2	-	201	-	18	-	-	3	-	-	-	-	15	1	42	1	7	302	9970
	GW3	5	-	-	1	-	3	1	20	-	-	4	1	-	-	-	42	-	1	-	-	78	1050
	GW4	-	-	-	1	-	-	-	-	-	-	-	-	-	-	-	-	1	-	-	-	2	7
	GWf	1	-	-	-	-	-	-	-	-	-	-	-	-	-	-	-	-	-	-	-	1	33
	buf1	-	-	-	-	-	-	-	-	-	-	-	-	-	-	-	2	-	-	-	-	2	78
	OX1	-	-	-	-	-	1	-	-	-	-	1	-	-	-	-	2	-	-	-	-	4	13
	WHf	-	-	-	-	-	-	-	-	-	-	3	-	-	-	-	-	-	-	-	-	3	3
	MORT1	1	-	-	-	-	-	-	-	-	-	-	-	-	-	-	-	-	-	-	-	1	114
	DOR BB1	50	2	7	25	-	9	7	134	-	2	1	1	-	-	3	323	44	4	-	5	617	6895
	NFO CC	-	-	-	-	-	-	-	-	-	-	-	-	-	-	-	-	-	-	-	1	1	12
	OXF RS	-	-	4	-	-	-	-	-	-	-	1	-	-	-	-	-	-	-	-	-	5	30
	OXF WH	-	-	1	-	-	-	-	-	-	-	4	-	-	-	-	-	-	-	-	-	5	182
	CNG BS	-	-	-	-	-	1	-	-	-	-	-	-	-	-	-	-	-	-	-	-	1	2
	MOS KER	-	-	-	-	-	-	-	-	-	-	-	-	-	-	-	2	-	-	-	-	2	2
	LEZ SA2	-	-	-	-	-	-	-	2	-	-	1	-	-	-	-	-	-	-	-	-	3	33
	EG SA	-	-	-	-	-	-	-	-	-	-	-	-	-	-	-	13	-	-	-	-	13	217
	BAT AM2	-	-	-	-	-	-	-	1	-	-	-	-	-	-	-	29	-	-	-	-	30	6923
	GAL AM	-	-	1	-	-	-	-	-	-	-	-	-	-	-	-	-	-	-	-	-	1	4
Sub-total		122	4	23	35	1	231	8	208	-	13	20	2	3	-	5	589	59	70	2	20	1414	31219
Total		181	6	23	36	1	231	8	224	20	13	21	2	3	3	7	606	59	70	3	20	1537	32300

Table 3.8: South-east Dorset Black-burnished ware. Summary showing form incidence by period

Form	Profile	Classification* H&B	Classification* SS&D	Late Iron Age to Roman transition No. V	Late Iron Age to Roman transition EVEs	Early to Mid Roman No. V	Early to Mid Roman EVEs	Post-medieval and unphased No. V	Post-medieval and unphased EVEs	Totals *No. V*	Totals *EVEs*
flagon	indet.	-	29	1	-	1	-	-	-	**2**	**-**
jar	everted rim	11–20	1–3	-	-	6	0.13	4	0.23	**10**	**0.36**
	upright/everted rim	12–13	1	2	0.09	8	0.73	5	0.37	**15**	**1.19**
	everted rim (early)	17	2	-	-	16	1.89	13	1.60	**29**	**3.49**
	everted rim (indet.)	17/20	2/3	-	-	2	0.69	3	0.37	**5**	**1.06**
	everted rim (late)	20	3	-	-	5	0.47	9	0.68	**14**	**1.15**
bowl/	footring	-	15?	-	-	1	-	-	-	**1**	**-**
dish	flat rim	38/39	22	-	-	2	0.20	1	0.03	**3**	**0.23**
	flat rim with groove	43.1	24	-	-	8	0.90	13	1.09	**21**	**1.99**
	flanged	45	25	-	-	4	0.45	7	0.57	**11**	**1.02**
dish	bead rim	34	22/23	-	-	-	-	1	0.09	**1**	**0.09**
	indet.	-	-	-	-	-	-	1	0.02	**1**	**0.02**
	plain rim	56–59	20	-	-	20	1.20	22	1.53	**42**	**2.73**
Totals				**3**	**0.09**	**73**	**6.66**	**79**	**6.58**	**155**	**13.33**

* alternative classifications are provided: Holbrook and Bidwell 1991; and Seager-Smith and Davies 1993

EG SA), 'Moselkeramik' (MOS KER) and Baetican amphora (BAT AM2). The latter type is present largely as an 'adapted' vessel, cut down from its original size for reuse as a large container (Fig. 3.40, no. 26). The East Gaulish samian, including forms Dr. 31R and (mortarium) Dr. 45, and provide a *termini post quem* of c. AD 160/170. Forms represented in DOR BB1 include jars with obtuse-angled lattice suggestive of dating after c. AD 220. Also present are bowls with flat, grooved and flanged form, the latter indicating dating after c. AD 250. Significantly the Oxfordshire and New Forest finewares which might evidence continuance into the 4th century are absent.

The ditch and other context groups located south of Sandy Lane for the most part produced only small quantities of material and are poorly dated. The largest group of 21 sherds from Ditch DW included an Oxford whiteware mortarium of Young's form M17, dating to the second half of the 3rd century and a red-slipped ware bowl (Fig. 3.40, nos 28–9), dateable c. AD 240/270–400.

Dating summary and discussion

The coarseware-dominated assemblage commonly provides only broad context-level dating and means that meaningful comparisons across structures or other features to determine close contemporaneity is challenging. In summary, the assemblage provides evidence for activity across the 1st to late 3rd centuries AD, with a focus of activity relating to the villa structures in the late 2nd and 3rd centuries. There is no equivocal evidence for continued occupation into the 4th century and a near absence of coins from this period further supports the site abandonment before c. AD 300.

The assemblage appears unexceptional within its regional context with the bulk of the pottery comprising coarsewares supplied from regional and local sources. There is no clear evidence from the pottery, either from 'exotic' or specialist ceramic forms, to reflect the wealth/'high status' which is elsewhere apparent from the Romanised buildings. Access to olive oil and wine is however evidenced by the quantities of Baetican and Gallic amphorae. Finewares from all sources are poorly represented, with samian representation only 1.3% by NOSH (number of sherds): 2.4% of EVEs total. In part this may be a reflection of the chronological focus of the assemblage, which is later than the main periods of samian importation. The low incidence nevertheless accords with a wider pattern of low samian incidence for rural sites, and with little or no difference apparent between villa and non-villa sites (Willis 2005). Some need for 'curation' of pottery vessels is apparent from the instances of repair or adaptation and hints at an inconstant supply. Mortaria are similarly poorly represented and whilst this may be partly related to chronology (mortaria tend to be more common from 4th-century groups) it implies only limited adoption of Roman styles of food preparation.

The utilitarian character of the Roman assemblage is apparent from the dominance of forms where use for cooking/storage or food preparation is likely. Jars are heavily dominant (67.2% of EVEs total) with the majority of the remainder made up of coarseware

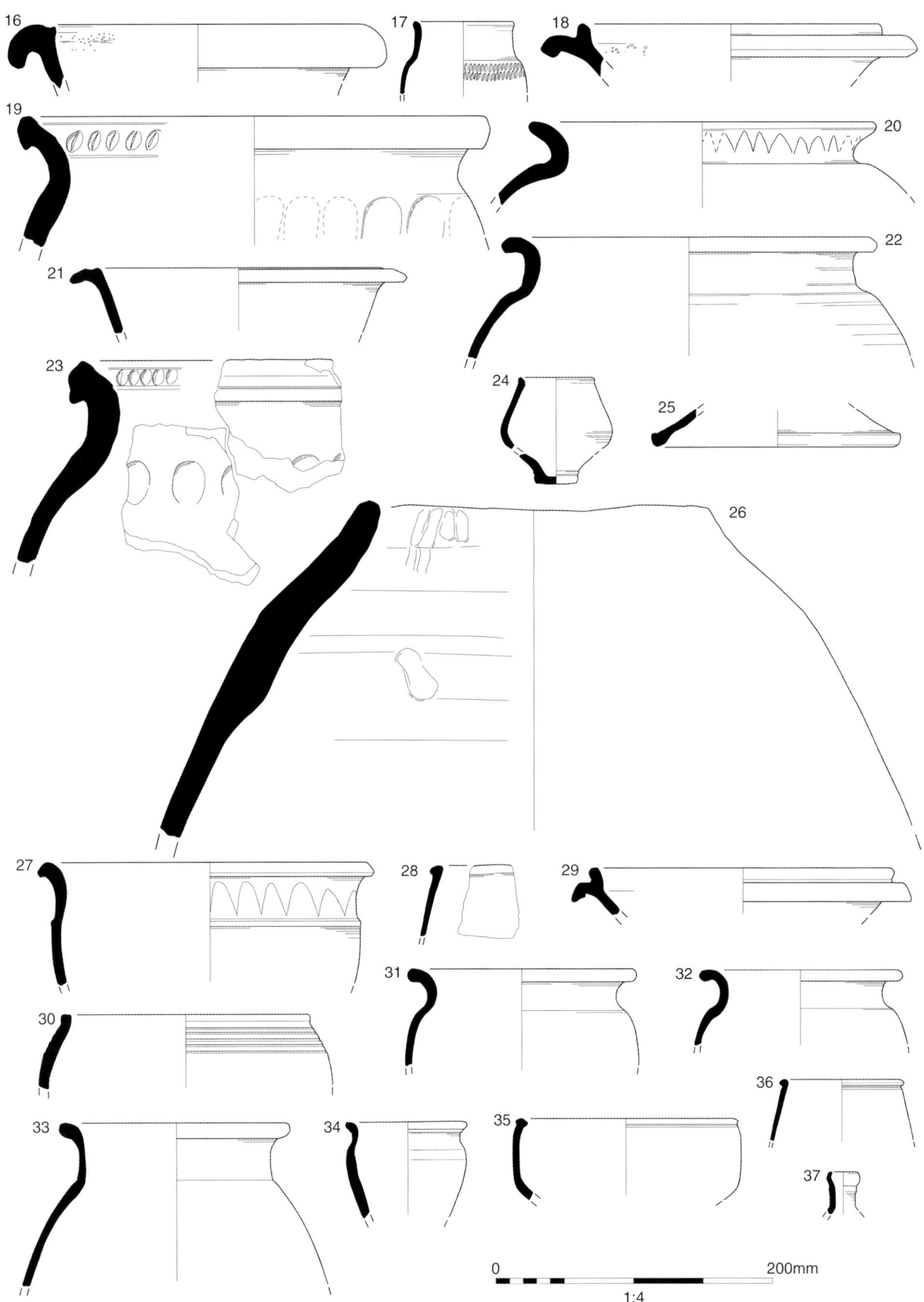

Fig. 3.40 Roman pottery nos 16–37. Building A, 16; Building B, 17–18; Building C, 19; Ditch DI, 20–22; Hollow-way DC, 23; Ditch W, 24–26; Ditch DZ, 27; Ditch DW, 28–29; post-medieval quarry, 30–37

Table 3.9: Forms summary and comparisons with sites in area (Crawford and McSloy forthcoming)

	Cannington Bypass		Cannington Flood Allev.		Hinkley Point	
	EVEs	*%EVEs*	*EVEs*	*%EVEs*	*EVEs*	*%EVEs*
Flagon/bottle	1.00	*3.30*	0.10	*<1.00*	-	-
Beaker/cup	0.73	*2.40*	0.18	*1.20*	0.29	*<1.00*
Tankard	-	-	0.51	*3.50*	0.30	*<1.00*
Jar	20.42	*66.40*	10.56	*71.80*	30.75	*78.60*
Bowl/dish	3.81	*12.40*	1.98	*13.50*	2.61	*6.70*
Dish/platter	3.91	*12.70*	1.27	*8.60*	4.54	*11.60*
Mortarium	0.61	*2.00*	0.10	*<1.00*	0.64	*1.60*
Lid	0.26	*<1.00*	-	-	-	-
	30.74		14.70		39.13	

dishes/bowls, mostly in DOR BB1. Comparisons with site assemblages from within the area (Table 3.9) shows a similar range of forms. Perhaps significantly, the dominance of jars is far less pronounced when compared with the large assemblage from Hinkley Point which derived from several small (non-villa) rural sites (Crawford and McSloy forthcoming). The imbalance results from a significantly larger component of coarseware bowls and dishes at Cannington Bypass. The greater presence of such forms, which individually cannot be seen as high-status items or associated with refinement or display, might reflect different cooking practices or other kitchen usage, perhaps one directed at the bulk feeding of estate workers.

Illustration catalogue (Fig. 3.40)

Building A
16   Mortarium with hooked-over flange and low bead. Fabric VER WH. Construction cut 20341 (fill 20239).

Building B
17   Beaker. Funnel neck and rouletted shoulder. Probably as Young's form C24 (Young 1977, 152). Fabric OXF RS. Demolition layer 20257.
18   Mortarium. Young's form M18 (Young 1977, 72). Fabric OXF WH. Demolition layer 20257.

Building C
19   Large storage jar. Thumbing at shoulder and rim interior. Fabric GW2. Demolition layer 20556.

Ditch DI
20   Jar. Burnished wavy decoration to neck. As Holbrook and Bidwell 'Cooking pot' Class B/Type 12–13 (Holbrook and Bidwell 1991, 95–6). Fabric DOR BB1. Fill 20363.
21   Dish/bowl. Flat rim with groove to top. As Holbrook and Bidwell 'Class F/Type 43.1' (ibid., 235). Fabric DOR BB1. Fill 20363.
22   Jar, necked, medium mouth. Fabric GW2. Fill 20363.

Hollow-way DC
23   Large storage jar. Thumbing at shoulder and rim interior. Rim complex. Fabric GW2. Fill 20262.

Ditch W
24   Beaker. Bag-shaped with short everted rim. Fabric BS1. Fill 20198.
25   Lid. Fabric BS1. Fill 20198.
26   Globular amphora (Dressel 20). Neck crudely reworked with ground 'rim'. Fabric BAT AM2. Fill 20194.

Ditch DZ
27   Wide-mouthed, necked bowl or jar. Burnished wavy decoration to neck. Fabric GW3. Fill 20772.

Ditch DW
28   Bowl. Young's form C45 (Young 1977, 158). Fabric OXF RS. Fill 20773.
29   Mortarium. Young's form M17 (Young 1977, 72). Fabric OXF WH. Fill 20773.

Post-medieval quarry pits
30   Globular jar or bowl. Short, upright/squared rim. Multiple scored horizontal decoration at neck. Fabric SS1. Quarry 20411 (fill 20412).
31   Medium-mouth, necked jar; thickened, out-curved rim. Fabric GGW1. Quarry 20442 (fill 20443).
32   Medium-mouth, necked jar; out-curved rim. Fabric GW4. Quarry 20442 (fill 20443).
33   Medium-mouth, necked jar; thickened, out-curved rim. Fabric GW1. Quarry 20442 (fill 20443).
34   Small jar; thickened, everted rim with external groove. Sooted. Fabric GW1. Quarry 20442 (fill 20443).
35   Bowl; carinated, with beaded rim. Fabric GW3. Quarry 20442 (fill 20443).
36   Bag-shaped(?) beaker with cornice rim. Fabric MSC CC. Quarry 20442 (fill 20443).
37   Flagon or bottle. Possibly as Fulford disc-necked Type 11 (Fulford 2000, 46). Fabric NFO CC. Quarry 20411 (fill 20412).

Ceramic building material
Peter Warry

Just over 100kg of ceramic building material (CBM) was examined from the Sandy Lane site. The materials include *tegulae* of 2nd/3rd-century date, of two forms to which can be added the stone tile (see Shaffrey, Stone, below). There were also two varieties of box flue tile

Table 3.10: Overall ceramic building material (CBM) quantification by form

	Tegulae	*Imbrices*	Brick	Flue	Unid.	Total
Weight (kg)	16.00	4.70	26.40	23.30	32.80	103.20
% of total	15.00	5.00	25.00	23.00	32.00	100.00
% of identifiable	23.00	7.00	37.00	33.00		
No. pieces	54.00	34.00	48.00	97.00		
Av. weight (kg)	0.30	0.14	0.55	0.24		
No. of contexts	**19**	**18**	**11**	**28**		

present, possibly together with a third, 1st/early 2nd-century form.

The CBM is analysed in aggregate in Table 3.10; a detailed listing by context is retained in archive. The proportion of brick and flue tile is far higher than normal and although the bulk of this derives from *in situ pilae* within Building A, the proportion of flue tile remains unusually high which may reflect the inclusion of combed *pedalis* tiles which are discussed later.

Roofing

The average weight of the *tegula* sherds at 0.3kg is a little over twice the average sherd weight of the *imbrices* and quite close to the expected ratio of 2.5 times, which is the average of a complete *tegula* weight to that of a complete *imbrex*. However, both the number of *imbrex* sherds compared to *tegula* sherds, and the ratio of their aggregate weights, are far lower than expected. Most sites suffer from preferential robbing of the flat *tegulae* for reuse in walls and floors leaving a disproportionate quantity of *imbrices*, but the opposite is the case here. This would suggest that the sample of CBM recovered is unrepresentative of the building as a whole or that many *tegulae* were used to form drainage channels etc. rather than all being on the roof.

Nine *tegulae* with diagnostic cutaways were noted; all of these were Group C types (Warry 2006) which normally date between the mid 2nd and mid 3rd centuries. These divided into two groups: the first group had chunkier flanges and deeper cutaways of which two examples came from Building B rubble layer 20257 and other examples of chunky flanges but without cutaways were noted from rubble layer 20239 and construction cut backfill 20352 (both Building A), fill 20364 of Ditch DI and fill 20395 of Hollow-way DH. The second, and probably later, group forms were observed in fill 20165 of Ditch W and rubble layers 20556 and 20626 (both Building C). Some of this latter group had smooth undersides and squarish flanges which are typical of production using an inverted rather than upright former. This method of production started around the middle of the 3rd century, and this group may represent later material than that of the first group. Other possible examples of inverted formed production were noted in surface 20298 and underlying bedding layer 20559, both associated with the surfacing and drain adjoining the northern side of Building B. It is not known whether the different tiles types used (including stone tiles), reflects purely chronological differences in building construction and repair/rebuilding, or reflects use within different buildings.

Flue tile and brick

The majority of the flue tile and brick came from hypocaust *pilae* 20447 within Building A, which included one complete *pedalis* and 14 further fragments, in total weighing 10.9kg, and one partially complete *bessalis* together with 33 further probable fragments, in total weighing 17.7kg. The complete *pedalis* measured 325mm by 315mm by 30mm and weighed 7.2kg. This is consistent with Brodribb's average measurement of 281mm square and thickness ranging from 25 to 70mm (Brodribb 1987, 36). One side of the *pedalis* was combed with a saltire cross pattern stretching from corner to corner. All the fragmentary *pedales* appeared similar. The partially complete *bessalis* had a side of 210mm and a thickness of 45mm; the fragmentary *bessales* appeared to be similar. Other deposits no doubt contained further fragments of these tiles which could not be so easily identified, but a definite example of a *pedalis* was recovered from the fill of a post-medieval quarry pit, and a further fragment of a *bessalis* came from mortar 20490, which was part of the *pilae* build within Building A.

Hypocaust *pilae* were typically constructed using a *pedalis* as a base followed by a stack of around ten *bessales* with a further *pedalis* to cap the *pilum*. A large *bipedalis* was then placed on top to bridge across four *pilae*. Only one possible fragment of *bipedalis* was seen (Ditch W, fill 20334) and this was 65mm thick and scored on its upper surface. It is unusual to find proportionately so many *pedalis* fragments relative to *bessalis* ones.

Fig. 3.41 shows an unusual piece of Roman fired clay found as a residual item in a post-medieval deposit. Although broken it appears to have originally been part of a thick and roughly formed squat cylinder. It is just possible that this was a spacer bobbin used to create an air gap between a wall and flat tiles (*parietales*) set against the spacer bobbins which would allow heat from a hypocaust to be conducted up a wall. The flat tiles would have been locked in position by T-shaped

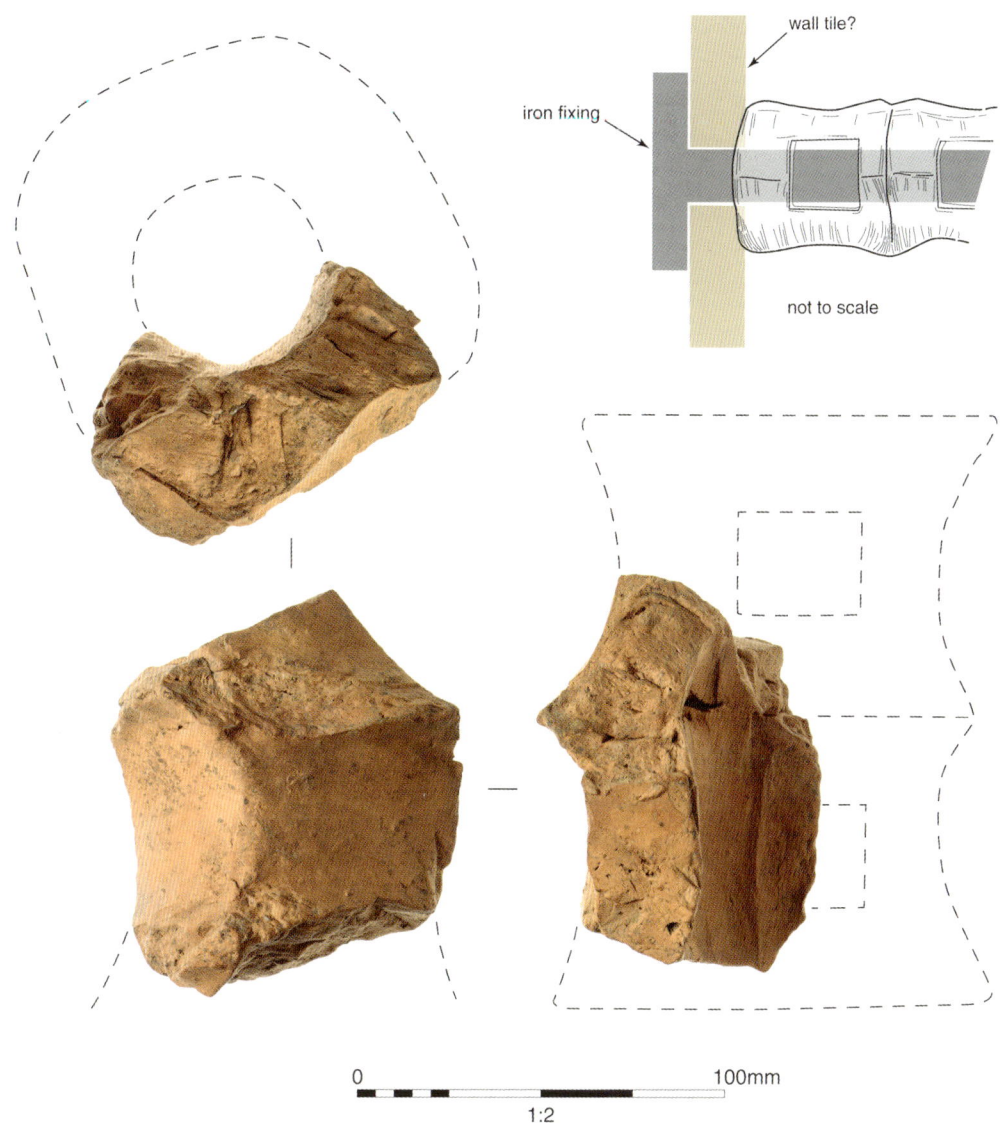

Fig. 3.41 Ceramic object and conjectural reconstruction as a spacer bobbin

fixings (none of which were found), inserted through spacer bobbins and hammered into the wall. If this interpretation is correct then the *pedales,* instead of being used in the *pilae,* might actually have been used as *parietales* to form the air gap. The combing on the *pedales* (which is slightly unusual) would have provided a key for the plaster which would have been spread over them. *Parietales* normally have notches in their sides to allow the tiles to butt against each other, whilst still leaving space for the metal fixings. No notches were observed on the *pedales* but it is not crucial that they should butt seamlessly, as any gap would have been plastered over. However, such a heating system would likely date to the 1st or early 2nd century, so does not appear to be related to any of the buildings that survived within the site.

By number (but not weight) most of the flue tile observed was conventional box flue tile. At least two varieties were present; one fragment with the normal rectangular vent hole came from the subsoil and the other, with an offset triangular vent, came from (unillustrated) post-Roman Ditch DM (fill 20656). The width of the vent side of this latter tile was 115mm. A complete combed side measuring 170mm by 95mm was noted along a fragment from a post-medieval quarry. Fill 20156 of Iron Age Structure B Ditch R, included a combed waster, although this would seem to have been either intrusive or the result of late infilling of this Late Iron Age ditch; no other wasters were noted in the assemblage.

An enigmatic but carefully formed fragment came from the rubble 20613 of Building C (Fig. 3.42). Its presumed lower surface had a series of preformed

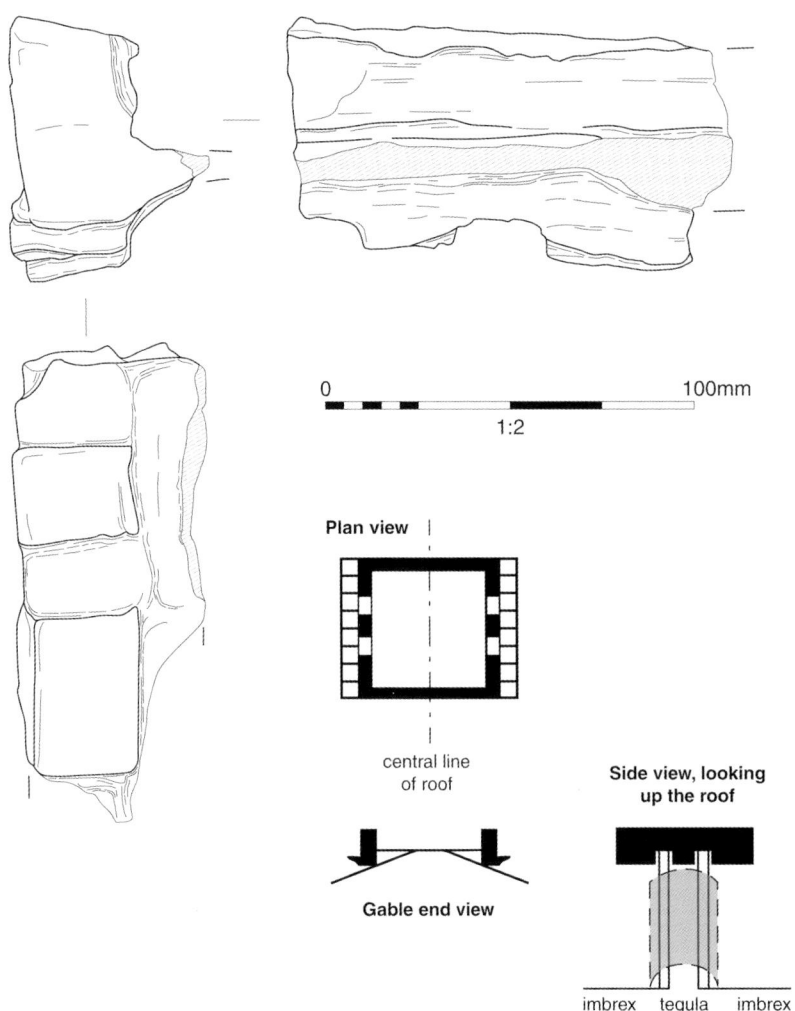

Fig. 3.42   Ceramic chimney pot and suggested fitting

notches; the width of the one complete notch was 28mm which would have fitted neatly over the flange of one of the later *tegulae* described above. There was then a space of 23mm before the next (incomplete) notch. *Tegulae*, particularly later *tegulae*, were trapezoidal rather than rectangular in plan being wider at the top than the bottom. When rows of *tegulae* were placed on a roof there would have been a varying gap between the rows – if each pair of horizontally adjacent *tegulae* abutted at the top then a widening would develop towards the bottom of the tiles; for Group C *tegulae* of average dimensions this gap would grow to 22mm (Warry 2006, 136, table 9.1). This gap equates to the spacing between the notches on the sherd and therefore implies it may have been designed to be placed on top of the tiles when laid on a roof (Fig. 3.42). This suggests that it could be a fragment of a chimney pot although all the known Romano-British chimneys are circular whereas the sherd was straight which would have created a rectangular base for the chimney. Above the notched section of the sherd there was an ornamental rim which further reinforces the idea that it came from a chimney pot.

Mortar and plaster
Kevin Hayward

A large group of 345 fragments (7207.63g) of mortar and plaster was obtained from different parts of Building A, along with one large example of *opus signinum* (5120g). These were assessed macroscopically and are described below.

Mortars

Mortar Type 1a
Light red-brown 2.5YR 6/4 heterogeneous very coarse gravelly mortar with yellow calcareous marl and large dark brown 5YR 3/2 new red sandstone and siltstone fragments.

This, by far the most common mortar type from

the site, consists of a very hard cement-like bedding mortar (*opus caementatum*), present in the Phase 2 wall foundations 20462 and 20471 of Room 3 where it was used to bond the regularly coursed roughly squared sandstone rubble walls (Fig. 3.14). A comparable mortar was also used to bond the Phase 2 masonry hypocaust in Room 1.

In detail, these mortars are characterised by a relatively low percentage of inclusions (5–7%) set within a fine light red-brown sandy matrix. However, this low number of inclusions is more than made up for their sheer size, being large angular lumps of hard country rock as big as 40mm across. These are dominated (80%) by red-brown fine sandstones comparable in their lithology to descriptions to the locally outcropping Permo-Triassic Otter Sandstone (Edmonds and Williams 1985, 38). Other inclusions (15%) include smaller (15mm) fine pale yellow marls that could well derive from weathered clay and marl particles from the Mercia Mudstone Group (Blue Anchor Formation) (ibid., 27) as could the white inclusions (5%). The red-brown colour of the mortar should be seen more in terms of the oxidised red-brown lithology of the local bedrock rather than any effect of oxidation caused by the high temperatures associated with the *pilae*. In essence this heterogeneous, relatively dense, mixture bonded with a hard cement (probably from lime extracted from the local marl or Carboniferous Limestone slightly further away) would have been suitable for bonding masonry foundations.

Mortar Type 1b

A further example of *opus caementatum* was recorded from a sample taken from Phase 3 wall 20473 (Fig. 3.16). This is similar to the Type 1a mortars, having the same colour and large inclusions of country rock. However, the presence of small rods of charcoal, together with finer red silty laths of what may be cuboidally splitting red mudstones and grey-green sandstones and siltstone from the Mercia Mudstone, suggest a slightly different recipe and are thus in accordance with a later build. Some of these pieces are smoothed and included evidence for incision or cut marks perhaps to paste or smear the mortar onto the sandstone walling.

Mortar Type 2

Red-brown 2.5YR 4/4 concretionary sandy mortar with new red sandstone and siltstone fragments, chalk and charcoal.

This second type of hard concretionary mortar was only identified from the backfill of a post-medieval quarry pit excavated through Building A. It has a slightly higher proportion of inclusions than Type 1, but these are much smaller in size (5–10mm). The red-brown sandstones so prevalent in Type 1 only form a quarter of all inclusions within Type 2, with white lime (75%) far more common and supplemented by small black charcoal rods (5%).

Plaster

Light-red to salmon-pink 2.5YR 7/6 low density mottled chaff-rich crushed tile coarse plaster backing *(arriccio)*.

This plaster was present in three samples, from wall plaster 20474 found adhering to wall 20473, from ashy deposit 20398, and from a deposit surrounding hypocaust *pilae* (20447), and is a coarse wall plaster backing (*arriccio*). It has an entirely different composition and character to the *opus caementatum*, being of a much lower density, with numerous voids and chaff marks suggesting that vegetation and twigs were very important in its production. The voids and the rather globular or cellular structures are reminiscent of impressions left by inclusions of a low density Holocene spring water deposit (calcareous tufa), and such material might perhaps have been found alongside the River Parrett. The second key characteristic is the light red mottled colour, a product of numerous crushed ceramic roof tile or brick inclusions, lumps of a lighter marly rock, and paler lime. These produce a much higher proportion of inclusions (30%), typically forming a homogeneous angular to sub-angular mosaic, with each inclusion typically 8–12mm across.

Combing on examples from ashy layer 20398 and *pilae* 20447, both of Phase 5, Room 5 (Fig. 3.20), suggests preparation of a flat surface for an upper fine plaster layer *intonaco* which itself would have been a suitable surface for a paint layer (*fresco*). Extensive wafer-thin (2–3mm) layers of crushed tile on the upper surface of wall plaster 20474 (Phase 3 Room 3) may represent further attempts at preparing the upper surface for plaster and paint.

Opus signinum

This material was a light-red to salmon-pink 2.5YR 7/6 dense, concretionary aggregate (*opus signinum*) used as sub-flooring (20240) within Room 5 during Phase 6 (Fig. 3.22). It was 120mm thick with frequent large chunks (up to 50mm across, though typically 15–20mm) of broken-up angular pink-red ceramic building material. These inclusions account for 90% of the fabric. A further 5% had been vitrified black whilst 5% consisted of dark brown 5YR 3/2 rock inclusions of Otter Sandstone. These were set in a hard pale cream-grey vuggy calcareous matrix with chaff and wood inclusions, as well as small concretionary, nodular lumps of what may be tufa. The scraping or smoothing of the regular upper surface would have been treated whilst the mixture was still in a semi-fluid state, almost certainly set within a mould.

The fabric of this sizeable chunk of pink *opus signinum* is a recipe typical of this type of flooring material. The large angular chunks of Roman tile and brick had evidently been collected from discarded, broken-up or burnt material from the villa and it is possible that the vitrified material may simply be burnt recycled hypocaust material. The recipe, albeit much denser, coarser and concretionary, appears to be comparable to the wall plaster backing 20474 (Phase 3, Room 3), especially in terms of its colour and inclusions.

Summary

Phase 2 walls 20462 and 20471 of Room 3 consist of much harder red-brown concretionary mortars (Type 1) defined by their high inclusion content of local country rock and their red-brown colour which is the result of the local red sandstone Permian lithologies rather than the effects of burning.

Later additions to the structure of the bath-house represented by Phase 3 wall 20473 have a slightly different mortar recipe whilst it is possible that the dump of mortar (20237; Type 2) found within a post-medieval quarry pit reflects further rebuilding/remodelling.

The wall plaster backing or *arriccio* from 20474, 20398 and 20447 on the other hand is of much lower density (including vegetation and possible tufa used in its preparation). It had a mottled fabric, the product of crushed-up lumps of ceramic building material and paler rock types. More consideration had gone into the preparation of this material as shown by the variety of ingredients all geared towards producing a low density, homogeneous recipe. The presence of comb marks and a very thin dusting layer of crushed tile support this idea. Nevertheless, the absence of bright paint and plaster merely supports evidence from elsewhere in this report that this was a low-status bath-house building.

A tub of thick (120mm) waterproof, robust *opus signinum* flooring from sub-flooring (20240) laid within Room 5 during Phase 6 was found to be typically very hard and concretionary and comparable in colour to the salmon-pink hue of the wall plaster. These properties made it ideally suited to the paving of rooms where there was a great deal of moisture or water flow such as in a bath-house.

Painted wall plaster
Kayt M. Brown

A total of 125 fragments (2589g) were recovered, with a total estimated surface area of $0.1 m^2$ (e.g. 20cm by 50cm). Monochrome colours (white, red, blue, green, pink and black) accounted for just over 61% of the assemblage by fragment count, with white the single most dominant colour (21.6% of fragment count). Painted plaster was recovered from all three buildings; however the bulk of material (86% by count) was retrieved from a single layer of demolition debris (20626) within Building C.

Methodology

The whole assemblage was examined at the post-excavation assessment stage, during which all the wall plaster, painted and plain, was recorded by count and weight, with estimated surface area also calculated for painted pieces (mm^2). The ensuing data forms the basis

Table 3.11: Painted wall plaster type series

Colour Code	Description	Illustration, Fig. 3.43
1	Monochrome white	
2	Monochrome red	
3	Monochrome blue	
4	Monochrome pink	
5	Monochrome green	
6	Monochrome black	
7	Red with white expanse	
8	Red, white stripe 8mm thick, black band	No. 1
9	White stripe 8mm, red band 32mm	
10	Blue expanse, black band 6mm, green and white	No. 2
11	White base with black stripe, white stripe 4mm, light blue expanse	No. 3
12	Green and pink expanse	
13	Composite design: maroon, yellow and white and green motif	No. 4
14	Composite design: pink with black lines, blue, white, yellow	
15	Black, red over-painted with green/blue zone	
16	Blue/green expanse with red stripe 8mm, bordered by maroon stripes 2mm	
17	Degraded black/grey with 2mm stripe	
18	Maroon and pink, possibly part of design 14	
19	Degraded maroon with green	
20	White over-painted with red, black and blue/green expanse	

of this report. Given the fragmentary nature of the assemblage any speculation as to the original scale of the painted plaster is unhelpful, therefore no further reference is made in this report to the dimensions. A limited range of colours and colour combinations were observed, grouped broadly to form a simple type series presented in Table 3.11. For polychrome material the term 'stripe' is used to denote lines of less than 10mm thickness, 'band' for linear areas of defined width greater than 10mm, and 'expanse' for colour areas of indeterminate width. A quantification of these different types is summarised in Table 3.12, with a further quantification by context in Table 3.13. The plaster fragments recovered were in a highly comminuted state; although some surfaces were in relatively good condition, fragmentation levels were high and consequently only broad conclusions can be drawn concerning the decorative schemes employed.

Construction techniques

In terms of construction techniques, at least three layers were observed; two coarse layers of backing mortar (*arriccio*) were present on most fragments underlying a single plaster surface layer. The two mortar layers comprise a thick undercoat, or levelling layer of mortar, and a second, thinner and finer mortar layer applied at a relatively uniform thickness of 10mm. Based on examination by hand lens, both mortar layers appear to comprise a mix of local sand and lime and naturally occurring rock aggregates, the second layer containing a higher proportion of sand as is common in Roman Britain (Davey and Ling 1982, 54). Overlying this second mortar application was a single plaster or *intonaco* layer, approximately 0.25–0.5mm in thickness.

The plaster has been painted in the *fresco* style, the pigments applied to a layer of damp lime whitewash, becoming fixed in place as the lime dried (Mora *et al.* 1984, 10). Fragments from Building C show a relatively accomplished level of design and execution, more characteristic of 2nd-century painted plaster rather than the rougher techniques that appear in the 3rd and 4th centuries (Davey and Ling 1982, 59).

None of the pieces exhibited reed impressions or 'pecking' marks, necessary to ensure good adhesion to a surface; however, a rough masonry wall finish may have negated the need for such a bonding technique. One fragment from Building A (20461) was the only piece with evidence of possible moulding on the reverse surface, possibly from a door or window reveal.

Distribution

Building A

Nine painted and six unpainted plaster fragments were recovered from three contexts (20375; 20413; 20461). In addition to the monochrome red piece with possible moulding on the reverse, a red and white stripe fragment from rubble layer 20413 displayed evidence of possible repainting – the only example of this in the entire assemblage. The rough surface finish of the few red painted fragments from destruction layer 20375

Table 3.12: Painted wall plaster quantification of types by fragment count and estimated surface area

Colour Code	Count	Est. Surface Area (mm²)
1	27	27050
2	5	1867
3	25	6684
4	6	1988
5	5	1012
6	9	680
7	2	2042
8	10	2520
9	1	900
10	2	640
11	1	288
12	1	200
13	2	480
14	9	1616
15	2	288
16	1	40
17	5	480
18	3	360
19	1	80
20	1	140
Unpainted	7	51230
Total	125	100585

Table 3.13: Painted wall plaster quantification by context by count, weight and estimated surface area

Context	Feature	Count	Weight (g)	Est. Surface Area (mm²)
20298	Building B foundation	2	51	1840
20375	Building A demolition	9	1199	69626
20413	Building A rubble	1	44	1558
20461	Building A wall repair	5	229	1767
20556	Building C demolition	1	12	0
20626	Building C demolition	107	1054	25794
Total		125	2589	100585

Fig. 3.43 Painted wall plaster: 1 colour code 8; 2 colour code 11; 3 colour code 11; 4 colour code 13

are in contrast to the smooth finish of the plaster from Building C.

Building B
Just two fragments were retrieved (20298), both painted in monochrome white.

Building C
With the exception of a single fragment from 20556, all the remaining painted plaster fragments were recovered from context 20626; both are demolition layers. An indication of high-status decoration is implied by the quality of the wall plaster recovered; however, the small amount retrieved suggests that, in addition to the high levels of truncation encountered, much of the wall plaster may have already collapsed and been moved or cleared away prior to the final demolition of the building. It is, therefore, unclear whether the material recorded represents decoration from a single room scheme or, more likely, an accumulation from numerous rooms. With the exception of monochrome pink, possibly from a plain dado, the remaining fragments are likely to originate from middle zone panels; red, white and black panel schemes (Fig. 3.43, no. 1) are particularly characteristic of Flavian–Trajanic designs in Britain (Davey and Ling 1982, 33). A second scheme of blue panels delineated with black and white bands (Fig. 3.43, no. 2) may have contained figurative elements; several small fragments with blue brush strokes are reminiscent of garments (Fig. 3.43, no. 3). A further two further pieces decorated in yellow and white over maroon with possible green tendrils, suggest a foliate design rather than splashed dado (Fig. 3.43, no. 4) while small fragments of a composite pattern encompassing pink, black, blue and white offers a tantalising glimpse of a further design; however, these do not survive in sufficient size or quantity to allow any further elaboration or comparison.

Stone
Ruth Shaffrey

All worked, burnt and unusual stone was retained from contexts of likely archaeological significance. The collected remains comprise fragments of roofing and flooring as well as a spindlewhorl, a hone, lava quern fragments and a possible weight (Table 3.14).

Table 3.14: Stone catalogue

Function	Notes	Feature	Feature Period	Size	Lithology
Spindlewhorl	Neat disc with flat faces and straight vertical edges. Perforation measures 9mm at narrowest point and is not perfectly circular. Fine scratch marks are visible on all the surfaces from manufacture	Ditch L, 20213	Late Iron Age to Roman transition	Measures 10mm thick x 35mm diameter	Fine grained micaceous red sandstone
Possible floor stone	Large square slab - no perforation	Ditch DI, 20363	Early to Mid Roman	Measures 210mm x 199mm x 18mm thick	Lias
Possible weight or roof stone	Neatly shaped with slightly rounded base, straight sides and tapered top. Hole perforated from one side only and 3mm wide at narrowest point. Seems thick for a roof stone and sides are very straight (they are usually bevelled)	Ditch DI, 20364	Early to Mid Roman	Measures 205mm long x 125mm wide x 17mm thick	Lias
Possible flooring/ structural stone	Possible roofing or flooring	Quarry pit	Post-medieval	Measures 16mm thick	Fine grained micaceous red sandstone
Possible flooring/ structural stone	Straight edges - presumably broken deliberately	Quarry pit	Post-medieval	Measures 26mm thick	Lias
Roofing	Fragment of upper end of stone roof stone with slightly irregular circular hole of 6mm	Rubble layer 20556	Post-medieval	Measures 12mm thick	Lias
Hone (secondary whetstone)	Fragment with one worn surface with two deep sharpening grooves in it. The worn (and rounded) face suggests the stone functioned as something else first. A quern is a possibility	Oven 20600, 20601	Late Iron Age to Roman transition		Medium grained red sandstone, well sorted with occasional red siltstone pebble
Probable rotary quern fragments	Non-diagnostic	Pit 20802, 20801	Early to Mid Roman		Lava
Roof slates	See text for contexts with slate (probably roofing but not diagnostic)	Various			Slate

Fig. 3.44 Stone artefacts: 1 square Lias slab; 2 possible weight; 3 sandstone spindlewhorl

The single stone spindlewhorl, recovered from Late Iron Age Ditch L, is the only complete stone object and is of typical size and form, being a neat disc (Fig. 3.44, no. 3). Some small and worn fragments of lava, probably the remains of rotary querns, were recovered from Roman or later pit 20802. These are highly unlikely to pre-date the Roman period. A chunk of red sandstone from Iron Age pit 20600 has one worn face with two deep grooves across this face indicating its use as a hone. The worn face may also be associated with whetting, but seems more likely to indicate a previous function for the stone. It is possible it is from a quern, but the fragment is too small for any identification of function to be anything other than speculative. It is likely to be from the Otter Sandstone. A thick stone of rectangular form but with a rounded top and a perforation at this end is of uncertain function (Roman Ditch DI, fill 20364). It is similar in form to stone roofing; however, the edges are straight and thick, whilst those of stone roofing are typically tapered/bevelled to allow the stones to overlap neatly. A more likely function of this stone is as a weight perhaps for closing a door or gate (Fig. 3.44, no. 2). This context also produced a square piece of the same stone type, Lias limestone, a stone which is relatively straightforward to 'snap' into the straight-edged pieces (Fig. 3.44, no. 1). No *tesserae* were found during this fieldwork, but it is possible that the piece seen here relates to *tesserae* manufacture. Other stones certainly represent sandstone roofing (Building C demolition 20556) or likely roofing (post-medieval quarry 20442) and probable Lias flooring (Roman Ditch DI). With the exception of the lava quern, from Roman or later pit 20802, and probably from the Niedermendig source near Mayen in the Eifel region of Germany, all the stone types are thought to be local.

Metals
Katie Marsden

A total of 221 items of iron, copper alloy and lead or lead alloy were recovered. The large majority are structural nails and hobnails, and items too fragmentary or corroded for identification. The published catalogue is confined to items of significant interest in terms of dating or relating to activities taking place at the site (Fig. 3.45). The remainder of the assemblage is recorded for the archive and is summarised in Table 3.15.

Copper alloy

1   Demolition layer 20556 of Building C. Tweezers of Eckardt and Crummy's (2008) 'decorated blades' group. The tweezers comprise a strip bent to form a spring loop and two equal-sized blades. Both blades are decorated with multiple stamped rings. A similar example from Kingscote, Gloucestershire (ibid., 151, fig. 93, no. 1001), comes from a deposit dated to *c.* AD 353–360, although tweezers of this form are not well dated within the Roman period. Length: 52.9mm; width: 7.1mm; weight: 4g. Registered artefact (RA) 221.

2   Fill 20265 of Roman Hollow-way DD. Brooch of hinged Colchester Derivative form; Mackreth's (2011) type CD H 13b. This item has a wide, straight bow and narrow, cylindrical wings with double grooves at each end. The foot is decorated with lateral grooves and the catchplate is solid (the pin is missing). The head has the elaborately beaded moulding, or 'skeumorphic hook', which is the defining feature of Mackreth's sub-type 13b, the distribution of which is strongly south-western (ibid., 96). The available dating is variable (ibid.) but the type is probably mainly of 2nd-century date. Length: 45.2mm; width at wings: 26.1mm; width at foot: 4mm; depth: 13.7mm; weight: 9g. Registered artefact 210.

Iron

3   Fill 20378 of Roman Ditch DJ. Latch lifter, a simple form key of a type with Late Iron Age origins and continuing in use throughout the Roman period (Man-

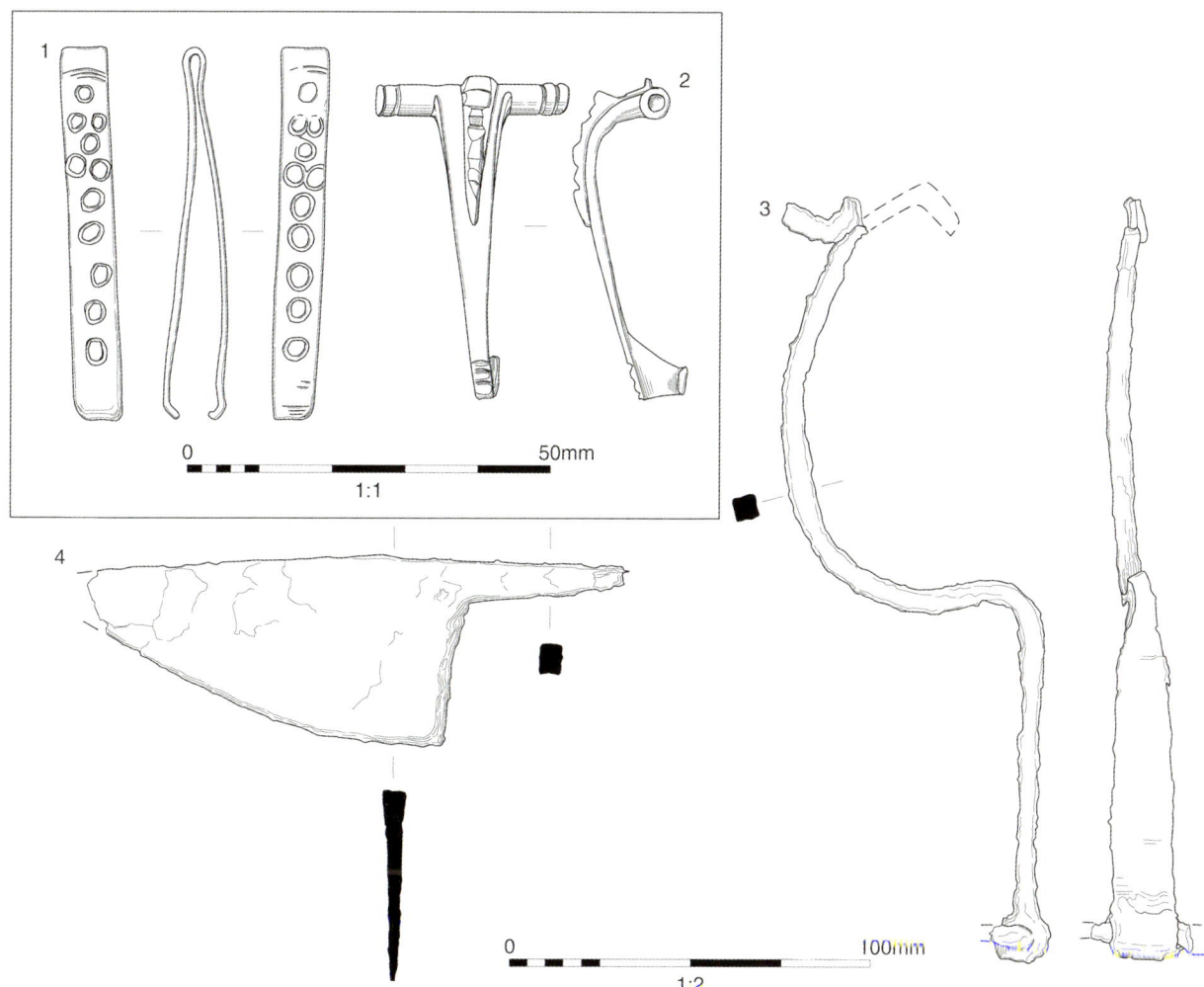

Fig. 3.45   Metal artefacts: 1 copper-alloy tweezers; 2 copper-alloy brooch; 3 iron latch lifter; 4 iron cleaver or knife

Table 3.15: Metalwork catalogue

Material	Feature Period	Context	Feature	RA no.	Type	X-ray ref.	Quantity
Cu. al.	Roman	20265	Hollow-way DD	210	T-shaped brooch	XRK15/107	1
Cu. al.	Roman	20556	Building C rubble	221	Tweezers	XRK15/107	1
Fe.	-	20001	Subsoil	-	Nail, square-sectioned shank, flat head	XRK15/107	1
Fe.	-	20001	Subsoil	-	Nails	XRK15/107	3
Fe.	Roman	20165	Ditch W	202	Manning type 12a knife or 2a cleaver	XRK15/110	1
Fe.	Roman	20165	Ditch W	203	Object	XRK15/110	1
Fe.	Roman	20165	Ditch W	201	Object	XRK15/111	2
Fe.	Roman	20165	Ditch W	-	10x nails (7 with square-sectioned shanks, 2 with circular-sectioned shanks and one shank undetermined), 3 pieces of possible industrial waste, one unidentified	XRK15/108	14
Fe.	Roman	20165	Ditch W	-	5x nails	XRK15/111	5
Fe.	Roman	20165	Ditch W	-	Square-sectioned nail with flat head	XRK15/111	1
Fe.	Post-medieval	20179	Quarry pit	-	Probable middle section of nail shank, breaks to both ends	XRK15/110	1
Fe.	Iron Age	20192	Ditch O	-	Nail	XRK15/110	1
Fe.	Roman	20198	Ditch W	-	Strip	XRK15/107	1
Fe.	Iron Age	20223	Ditch Z	214	Object - possible nail	XRK15/109	1
Fe.	Roman	20239	Building A	-	Nail, square-sectioned shank, flat head	XRK15/110	1
Fe.	Roman	20240	Building A	213	Nail with head missing	XRK15/110	1
Fe.	Post-medieval	20241	Quarry pit	-	2x nails	XRK15/110	2
Fe.	Roman	20257	Building B rubble	-	6x nails. 5x square-sectioned. 1x rectangular-sectioned	XRK15/115	6
Fe.	Roman	20262	Hollow-way DC	-	Nail	XRK15/110	1
Fe.	Roman	20266	Building A	-	Strip, rectangular in plan and section	XRK15/109	1
Fe.	Post-medieval	20283	Quarry pit	-	Nail	XRK15/108	1
Fe.	Post-Roman	20321	Layer	-	Nail	XRK15/110	1
Fe.	Roman	20334	Ditch W	-	Nails	XRK15/112	3
Fe.	Roman	20363	Ditch DI	-	Nail	XRK15/107	1
Fe.	Roman	20364	Ditch DI	-	Small hobnail or tack. Rounded head	XRK15/107	1
Fe.	Roman	20378	Ditch DJ	-	Latch lifter	XRK15/111	1
Fe.	Roman	20395	Hollow-way DH	-	2x nails	XRK15/110	2
Fe.	-	20401	Natural feature	-	Nail	XRK15/107	1
Fe.	Post-medieval	20405	Quarry pit	-	Nail	XRK15/107	1

Table 3.15 (cont.): Metalwork catalogue

Material	Feature Period	Context	Feature	RA no.	Type	X-ray ref.	Quantity
Fe.	Post-medieval	20412	Quarry pit	-	Strip, rectangular in plan with breaks at each end. Square-sectioned bar, tapering to each end terminating in probable breaks. *c.* 90 degree bend at one end and curve to middle	XRK15/110	2
Fe.	Iron Age or Roman	20444	Pit 20445	-	Nail, square-sectioned shank, flat head	XRK15/109	1
Fe.	Post-medieval	20451	Quarry pit	-	Objects, possibly nails	XRK15/111	11
Fe.	Roman	20470	Building A	-	Nail	XRK15/107	1
Fe.	Roman	20556	Building C rubble	-	2x nails	-	2
Fe.	Roman	20556	Building C rubble	-	17x nails, mostly complete and rectangular in section with heads. 1x strip, rectangular in plan and cross-section, 135 degree bend (probably modern damage). Three unidentified lumps (x-ray inconclusive)	XRK15/112	21
Fe.	Roman	20556	Building C rubble	-	13x nails, square-sectioned. One bent	XRK15/113	13
Fe.	Roman	20556	Building C rubble	-	28x nails, mostly complete and with square-sectioned shanks and flat heads. Of the group 1x nail has large, rounded head. 2x strips, rectangular in plan and section, one curving. 2x inconclusive fragments	XRK15/109	32
Fe.	Roman	20556	Building C rubble	-	2x nails	XRK15/107	2
Fe.	Roman	20556	Building C rubble	-	Nail	XRK15/107	1
Fe.	Post-medieval	20579	Quarry pit	-	Nails	XRK15/108	14
Fe.	Roman	20593	Building A	-	Large nail with heavy corrosion. Square-sectioned shank	XRK15/107	1
Fe.	Post-medieval	20599	Quarry pit	-	Nail, corroded but probably complete. Square-sectioned shaft and flat head	-	1
Fe.	Roman	20618	Building C rubble	-	Nail, square-sectioned shank, flat head	-	1
Fe.	Roman	20626	Building C rubble	-	Rod, circular section, possible nail shaft	XRK15/107	1
Fe.	Post-Roman	20628	Ditch DM	227	Rectangular in plan section and broadly rectangular in plan, tapering in thickness and width to narrowed, rounded end. Break to top. Possible tip of file	XRK15/109	1
Fe.	Post-Roman	20631	Ditch DM	-	Possible waste?	XRK15/109	1
Fe.	Post-Roman	20656	Ditch DM	246	Hobnails	XRK15/113	21
Fe.	Post-Roman	20656	Ditch DM	-	Nail, square sectioned shank, flat head	XRK15/109	1
Fe.	Post-Roman	20656	Ditch DM	224	Object - poss. brooch, buckle?	XRK15/107	1

Table 3.15 (cont.): Metalwork catalogue

Material	Feature Period	Context	Feature	RA no.	Type	X-ray ref.	Quantity
Fe.	Early medieval	20663	Building D	-	Probable middle section of nail shank, breaks to both ends	XRK15/110	1
Fe.	Roman	20673	Building C rubble	-	Hobnails, 1x nail	XRK15/107	23
Fe.	Early medieval	20733	Building D	-	Square-sectioned bar with circular-sectioned, narrowed bar extending from one end	XRK15/107	1
Fe.	Roman	20745	Fill of grave 20748	258	Hobnail	XRK15/112	1
Fe.	-	U/S	-	-	Bar/strip	XRK15/112	1
Fe.	-	U/S	-	-	Objects	XRK15/113	5
Pb.	Post-medieval	20262	Quarry pit	209	Lead pot repair	-	1
Pb.	Roman	20611	Building C	229	Object	-	1

ning 1982, 88–9). The tip is damaged, but appears to be sharply up-turned. The handle terminal has been folded under, securing a suspension ring, which is fragmentary. Length: 205mm; width: 65mm; thickness: 17mm; weight: 90g.

4 Fill 20165 of Roman Ditch W. Knife of Manning's (1982) type 12a, common throughout the Roman period. The knife comprises a wide, triangular blade, curving up to the tip. The back continues in line with the tang. Length: 145mm; width: 49mm; thickness: 6mm; weight: 94g. Registered artefact 202.

Metallurgical residues
Tim Young

A small assemblage (*c.* 890g) of metallurgical residues was recovered and assessed as part of the post-excavation process. This involved visual examination with a low-powered binocular microscope where required. No further analysis was recommended or carried out, and this report is a summary of the principal results (see CA 2016a for full report).

Smithing slags

There was a total of 710g of slag identified as smithing hearth cake (SHC), a residue indicative of blacksmithing. Six items were identified from the following contexts:

- 20107 (Iron Age pit 20106): 58g, SHC fragment
- 20055 (Iron Age Enclosure Ditch L): 46g, SHC fragment
- 20199 (Roman Enclosure Ditch W): 69g, SHC fragment
- 20239 (Building A construction cut 20341): 97g, small 50x50x30mm SHC
- 20656 (post-Roman Ditch DM): 160g, dense SHC resting on slag sheet
- 20334 (Roman Enclosure Ditch W): 280g, 161g, small SHC, 55x65x45mm 119g, fragmented SHC

In addition, a further 80g of dense iron slag and 84g of lining slag are also likely to have been produced during smithing whilst 19g of material derived from hearth linings.

Smithing microresidues

Very small quantities of hammerscale were recovered, none in sufficient quantities from a single context to indicate proximity to a smithy.

Coal and coke

Small particles of coal and partially burnt coal (coke) were found in small numbers across the site; the larger pieces came from post-medieval and later deposits. The use of coal during the Roman period is well established both for metallurgical and other purposes, so the fuel need not necessarily be uniquely associated with the blacksmithing activity. However, at least some of the material within Roman deposits might be intrusive from post-medieval activity.

Discussion

Most of the macroscopic metallurgical slags, except for those from Ditch L and pit 20106, both Iron Age features, occurred in Roman deposits. The residues are not associated with metallurgical features and presumably represent dispersal across the site. The residues comprise a small assemblage and no single context contained significant amounts of material, indicating that the focus of activity was either outside the investigated area or in a location destroyed by the later quarrying. However, the material is sufficiently concentrated within Roman deposits to be confident that blacksmithing was undertaken within or near to the Roman settlement.

Charred plant remains
Sarah F. Wyles

A total of 47 soil samples were taken and assessed from the Sandy Lane site. Of these, 11 samples were selected for detailed analysis on the basis of their quality. Four samples were taken from Late Iron Age/Roman transition Structure A and associated features, one each from Roman enclosure Ditch W and drain 20300, three samples from features associated with post-Roman Building D, and a sample each from post-Roman pits 20020 and 20625 (Tables 3.16 and 3.17). Methods follow those used for the Rodway Enclosure (Wyles, Charred plant remains, Chapter 2, this volume).

Late Iron Age–Roman transition

Structure A
A moderate charred plant assemblage was recovered from fill 20134 (sample 201), section 20133 of Ditch T. Charred hazel twig wood from fill 20134 was radiocarbon dated to 198–51 cal. BC (SUERC-69954). The cereal remains included emmer wheat, and chaff outnumbered grain. The weed seeds dominated the assemblage and included goosefoot (*Chenopodium* sp.), fat-hen, vetch/wild pea and common spike-rush (*Eleocharis* cf. *palustris*). These are generally species that favour grassland, field margins and arable environments. The assemblage may be a dump of crop-processing waste.

Feature group A
Fill 20601 (sample 234) and fill 20603 (sample 235) of pit 20600 produced a small and a moderate number of charred plant remains respectively. Charred fragments of hulled wheat grain from fill 20603 were radiocarbon dated to 50 cal. BC–70 cal. AD (SUERC-69953). The cereals included barley, emmer wheat and spelt wheat, with the grains being more numerous than chaff. Other potential crops were fragments of Celtic bean. The weeds included seeds of vetch/wild pea, black-bindweed (*Fallopia convolvulus*) and goosefoot. There was also a number of hazelnut shell fragments from deposit 20603. These assemblages may represent dumps of domestic settlement and crop-processing waste.

Pit 20324
The moderately large assemblage recovered from fill 20325 of pit 20324 was dominated by remains of bracken (*Pteridium* sp.) fronds. Charcoal roundwood fragments of indeterminate species from fill 20325 were radiocarbon dated to 198–47 cal. BC (SUERC-70708). The other remains included those of spelt wheat, sedge (*Carex* sp.), goosefoot and brome grass (*Bromus* sp.). The assemblage may be indicative of material used as tinder.

Early to Mid Roman

Enclosure Ditch W
Fill 20165 (sample 203) of cut 20304 of Ditch W contained a high number of charred plant remains. The assemblage was dominated by cereals, with grain fragments outnumbering chaff elements. The cereal remains included spelt wheat, free-threshing wheat (*Triticum turgidum/aestivum* type) and barley. A few of the hulled wheat grains showed traces of germination. Other potential crops included flax. The weed seeds included vetch/wild pea, oats (*Avena* sp.), brome grass, rye-grass/fescue (*Lolium/Festuca* sp.), curled dock (*Rumex crispus*) and bristle club-rush (*Isolepis selacea*). The assemblage may be representative of dumped domestic settlement and crop-processing waste.

Building B
A large quantity of charred plant remains were recorded from fill 20545 (sample 221) of cut 20301 of drain 20300. The assemblage was dominated by cereal remains, in particular those of spelt wheat. Remains of free-threshing wheat and emmer wheat were also recovered. Again, grain fragments outnumbered chaff elements. The weed assemblage, predominantly composed of the larger-seeded species, included seeds of oats, brome grass, vetch/wild pea, curled dock and brassica. There was also a triangular capsule fragment that may be from a flax capsule. This assemblage may be representative of remains from the processing of semi-cleaned stored grain and food production.

Early medieval

Building D
The large assemblage noted from fill 20667 (sample 249) of posthole 20666 and the moderate assemblage from fill 20672 (sample 251) of posthole 20671 were dominated by the weed seeds. Spelt wheat grains from fill 20667 of posthole 20666 were radiocarbon dated to 86–241 cal. AD (SUERC-69965) and spelt wheat grains from fill 20672 of pit 20671 were radiocarbon dated to 80–228 cal. AD (SUERC-69964). The cereal remains included spelt wheat and small quantities of free-threshing wheat and barley, with the chaff elements outnumbering those of grain. The chaff included coleoptile fragments, an indication of germinated grain. There were also remains of flax, possible Celtic bean, hawthorn (*Crataegus monogyna*) stones and Rosaceae-type thorns. The weed seeds included clover/medick, oats, brome grass, vetch/wild pea, curled dock, rye-grass/fescue, meadow grass/cat's tail (*Poa/Phleum* sp.), sedge, bristle club-rush, red bartsia (*Odontites vernus*), ribwort plantain (*Plantago lanceolata*) and stinking mayweed (*Anthemis cotula*). The weeds were mainly species which favour grassland, field margins and arable environments. These assemblages may represent waste from an earlier stage of crop processing, possibly from a sieving stage,

Table 3.16: Charred plant Identifications from Sandy Lane: Late Iron Age–Roman Transition features

Phase		LIA–RB Transition			
Group		Structure A	Feature group A		
Feature type/label		Ditch T	Pit		Pit
Cut		20133	20600		20324
Context		20134	20601	20603	20325
Sample		201	234	235	205
Vol (L)		32	7	10	2
Flot size (ml)		111	7	5	8.5
Cereals	**Common Name**				
Hordeum vulgare L. *s.l.* (grain)	barley	-	1	-	-
Triticum cf. *dicoccum* (Schübl) (grain)	emmer wheat	1	-	2	-
Triticum dicoccum (Schübl) (glume base)	emmer wheat	4	2	3	-
Triticum dicoccum (Schübl) (spikelet fork)	emmer wheat	3	-	1	-
Triticum spelta L. (glume bases)	spelt wheat	-	-	1	6
Triticum dicoccum/spelta (grain)	emmer/spelt wheat	1	1	12	-
Triticum dicoccum/spelta (spikelet fork)	emmer/spelt wheat	3	1	1	2
Triticum dicoccum/spelta (glume bases)	emmer/spelt wheat	3	2	5	4
Cereal indet. (grains)	cereal	2	3	7	-
Cereal frag. (est. whole grains)	cereal	1	1	2	-
Other Species					
Pteridium sp. Gled. Ex. Scop.	bracken frags> 2mm	-	-	-	25
Pteridium sp. Gled. Ex. Scop.	bracken < 2mm	-	-	-	50+
Corylus avellana L. (fragments)	hazelnut	1	-	17	-
Chenopodium sp.	goosefoot	10	1	3	2
Chenopodium album L.	fat-hen	5	-	-	-
Atriplex sp. L.	oraches	2	-	-	-
Persicaria lapathifolia/maculosa (L.) Gray/Gray	pale persicaria/redshank	1	-	1	-
Persicaria lapathifolia (L.) Gray	pale persicaria	-	-	-	1
Polygonum aviculare L.	knotgrass	-	-	1	1
Fallopia convolvulus (L.) À. Löve	black-bindweed	-	-	2	-
Rumex sp. L.	docks	-	-	-	1
Brassica sp. L.	brassica	-	1	-	-
Vicia L./*Lathyrus* sp. L.	vetch/wild pea	8	4	-	-
Vicia faba	Celtic bean	-	4	2	-
Plantago lanceolata L.	ribwort plantain	-	1	-	-
Sambucus nigra L.	elder	1	-	-	-
Eleocharis cf. *palustris* (L.) Roem. & Schult.	common spike-rush	1	-	-	-
Carex sp. L. (trigonous)	sedge	-	-	-	2
Lolium/Festuca sp.	rye-grass/fescue	1	1	-	-
Poa/Phleum sp. L.	meadow grass/cat's-tail	2	-	1	-
Avena sp. L. (grain)	oat grain	1	-	-	-
Avena L./*Bromus* L. sp.	oat/brome grass	1	1	1	1
Bromus sp. L.	brome grass	-	-	-	3
Monocot. stem/rootlet frag.		7	-	1	3

Table 3.17: Charred plant identifications from Sandy Lane: Roman and post-Roman features

Phase		Roman		Post-Roman				
Group		Enclosure ditch	Building B	Building D				
Feature type/label		Ditch W	Drain 20300	Postholes		Ditch DL	Pits	
Cut		20304	20301	20666	20671	20732	20020	20625
Context		20165	20545	20667	20672	20733	20019	20624
Sample		203	221	249	251	256	200	241
Vol (L)		32	9	36	8	10	36	18
Flot size (ml)		81	35	164	32	170	144	7
Cereals	**Common Name**							
Hordeum vulgare L. s.l. (grain)	barley	3	-	1	-	4	4	-
Hordeum vulgare L. s.l. (rachis frag.)	barley	-	-	-	-	3	-	-
Triticum dicoccum (Schübl) (glume base)	emmer wheat	-	1	-	-	13	-	-
Triticum dicoccum (Schübl) (spikelet fork)	emmer wheat	-	-	-	-	12	-	-
Triticum spelta L. (grains)	spelt wheat	9	58	-	-	2	-	-
Triticum spelta L. (glume bases)	spelt wheat	17	48	14	7	87	1	-
Triticum spelta L. (spikelet fork)	spelt wheat	-	-	-	-	1	-	-
Triticum dicoccum/spelta (grain)	emmer/spelt wheat	26	43	6	-	6	-	1
Triticum dicoccum/spelta (germinated grain)	emmer/spelt wheat	2	-	-	-	-	-	-
Triticum dicoccum/spelta (spikelet fork)	emmer/spelt wheat	3	15	1	-	19	1	-
Triticum dicoccum/spelta (glume bases)	emmer/spelt wheat	18	78	21	4	186	-	-
Triticum turgidum/aestivum (grain)	free-threshing wheat	9	3	6	1	2	6	-
Triticum turgidum/aestivum (rachis frags)	free-threshing wheat	7	4	-	-	2	-	-
Secale cereale (grain)	rye	-	-	-	-	-	3	-
Cereal indet. (grains)	cereal	25	50	18	4	29	10	2
Cereal frag. (est. whole grains)	cereal	13	20	4	1	10	8	-
Cereal frags (culm node)	cereal	-	-	1	-	2	1	-
Cereal frags (coleoptile)	cereal	-	-	2	-	1	-	-
Other Species								
Ranunculus sp.	buttercup	-	-	4	-	-	-	-
Corylus avellana L. (fragments)	hazelnut	-	-	-	-	2	1	1
Chenopodium sp.	goosefoot	3	-	4	1	1	6	2
Chenopodium album L.	fat-hen	-	-	2	-	-	3	-
Atriplex sp. L.	oraches	-	-	-	-	-	-	-
Stellaria sp. L.	stitchworts	-	-	-	-	2	2	-
Persicaria lapathifolia/maculosa (L.) Gray/Gray	pale persicaria/redshank	2	-	-	-	-	3	-
Persicaria lapathifolia (L.) Gray	pale persicaria	-	-	-	-	-	1	-
Polygonum aviculare L.	knotgrass	-	-	3	1	-	5	-

Table 3.17 (cont.): Charred plant identifications from Sandy Lane: Roman and post-Roman features

Phase		Roman		Post-Roman				
Group		Enclosure ditch	Building B	Building D				
Feature type/label		Ditch W	Drain 20300	Postholes		Ditch DL	Pits	
Cut		20304	20301	20666	20671	20732	20020	20625
Context		20165	20545	20667	20672	20733	20019	20624
Sample		203	221	249	251	256	200	241
Vol (L)		32	9	36	8	10	36	18
Flot size (ml)		81	35	164	32	170	144	7
Fallopia convolvulus (L.) À. Löve	black-bindweed	-	-	1	-	-	-	-
Rumex sp. L.	docks	3	2	8	2	2	70	10
Rumex crispus L. Type	curled dock	2	1	4	3	2	35	5
Malva sp. L.	mallow	-	-	-	-	-	17	3
Brassica sp. L.	brassica	4	2	-	-	-	2	-
Raphanus raphanistrum L.	runch	-	-	-	1	-	-	-
Rubus sect.2 Glandulosus Wimm and Grab.	bramble	-	-	-	-	-	-	8
Rubus sp. L.	brambles	-	-	-	-	-	-	11
Prunus spinosa L. (with holes)	sloe stone	-	-	-	-	-	-	4
Prunus spinosa L. (fragments)	sloe stone	-	-	-	-	-	-	28
Prunus domestica L.	wild plum	-	-	-	-	-	-	cf. 2
Prunus spinosa/ Crataegus monogyna (thorns/twigs)	sloe/hawthorn type	-	-	-	-	-	5	-
Crataegus monogyna Jacq.	hawthorn	-	-	2	-	-	-	2
Rosaceae type thorn		-	-	1	-	1	-	-
Vicia L./*Lathyrus* sp. L.	vetch/wild pea	27	6	14	3	2	6	-
Vicia faba	Celtic bean	-	-	cf. 1	cf. 1	cf. 1	-	-
Pisum sativum L.	pea	-	-	-	-	-	cf. 1	-
Medicago/Trifolium sp. L.	medick/clover	1	1	38	28	2	5	-
Linum usitatissimum L. (whole)	flax	1	-	4	1	-	-	-
Linum usitatissimum L. (frags est. whole)	flax	1	-	1	-	1	-	-
Plantago lanceolata L.	ribwort plantain	-	-	1	-	-	1	-
Odontites vernus	red bartsia	-	-	1	-	-	-	-
Galium sp. L.	bedstraw	-	-	-	1	-	-	-
Galium aparine L.	cleavers	1	-	1	-	-	-	-
Sambucus nigra L.	elder	-	-	-	-	-	-	-
Cardus/Cirsium sp.	thistle	1	-	-	-	-	-	-
Anthemis cotula L. (seeds)	stinking mayweed	-	-	1	-	-	-	-
Tripleurospermum inodorum (L.) Sch. Bip.	scentless mayweed	-	1	-	-	-	-	1
Eleocharis cf. *palustris* (L.) Roem. & Schult.	common spike-rush	-	-	-	-	1	-	7
Isolepis setacea (L.) R. Br.	bristle club-rush	1	-	2	-	-	-	-
Carex sp. L. trigonous	sedge	-	-	-	2	-	-	11
Lolium perenne L.	perennial rye-grass	1	-	-	-	-	-	-

Table 3.17 (cont.): Charred plant identifications from Sandy Lane: Roman and post-Roman features

Phase		Roman		Post-Roman				
Group		Enclosure ditch	Building B	Building D				
Feature type/label		Ditch W	Drain 20300	Postholes		Ditch DL	Pits	
Cut		20304	20301	20666	20671	20732	20020	20625
Context		20165	20545	20667	20672	20733	20019	20624
Sample		203	221	249	251	256	200	241
Vol (L)		32	9	36	8	10	36	18
Flot size (ml)		81	35	164	32	170	144	7
Lolium/Festuca sp.	rye-grass/fescue	4	1	4	3	8	-	-
Poa/Phleum sp. L.	meadow grass/cat's-tail	1	1	6	1	4	4	-
Avena sp. L. (grain)	oat grain	5	37	9	-	4	2	-
Avena L./*Bromus* L. sp.	oat/brome grass	3	48	11	-	7	-	-
Bromus sp. L.	brome grass	2	8	6	-	3	-	-
Sparganium erectum L.	branched bur-reed	-	-	-	-	-	-	-
Monocot. stem/rootlet frag.		1	5	4	3	4	25	1
Pod frag.		-	-	1	-	-	-	-
Bud		-	3	-	-	1	-	-
Parenchyma		-	-	-	-	-	-	-
Triangular capsule frag.		-	1	-	-	-	-	-
Tuber		-	-	-	-	-	1	-
Rodent faeces		-	-	-	-	-	-	35
Egg shell		-	-	-	-	-	-	-

after harvesting, winnowing and threshing, and prior to drying before storage (Hillman 1981; 1984). These assemblages are indicative of a Roman date.

Fill 20733 (sample 256) of cut 20732 (Ditch DL) contained a high number of charred plant remains, particularly chaff. Barley grains from this sample were radiocarbon dated to 134–326 cal. AD (SUERC-69955) and alder (*Alnus glutinosa*) charcoal fragments from the same deposit were dated to 658–769 cal. AD (SUERC-72472). The cereals included spelt wheat and lower numbers of emmer wheat, barley and free-threshing wheat. A coleoptile fragment was also recovered. There were also fragments of flax, possible Celtic bean, hazelnut shell and Rosaceae-type thorns. The weed seeds included oat, brome grass, rye-grass/fescue, clover/medick, curled dock, vetch/wild pea and common spike-rush. This assemblage may reflect waste material from the processing of semi-cleaned stored grain.

Pits

High numbers of charred remains, predominant weed seeds, were recovered from fill 20019 (sample 200) of pit 20020. Barley grains were radiocarbon dated to 665–853 cal. AD (SUERC-69963) and alder (*Alnus glutinosa*) charcoal fragments from the same deposit were dated to 682–866 cal. AD (SUERC-72475). The cereal remains included free-threshing wheat, barley, rye (*Secale cereale*) and spelt wheat. Other remains include a possible pea (*Pisum sativum*) and sloe/hawthorn-type (*Prunus spinosa/Crataegus monogyna*) thorn fragments. The weed seeds were dominated by docks and curled docks. Other seeds included those of mallow (*Malva* sp.), fat-hen, knotgrass, pale persicaria/redshank (*Persicaria lapathifolia/maculosa*), vetch/wild pea, clover/medick and meadow grass/cat's-tail. This assemblage may represent waste material from an earlier stage of crop processing.

A moderate assemblage was recorded from fill 20624 (sample 241) of pit 20625. Three radiocarbon dates were obtained on material from this deposit; hawthorn/rowan/crab apple (*Crataegus monogyna/Sorbus/Malus sylvestris*) charcoal fragments were radiocarbon dated to 407–538 cal. AD (SUERC-72467), sloe stone fragments to 667–770 cal. AD (SUERC-69961) and barley grains to 1042–1220 cal. AD (SUERC-72466). This assemblage was dominated by wild food, with fragments of sloe stones, possible wild plum (*Prunus domestica*) stones, hawthorn stones, a cherry pip, hazelnut shells, and seeds of brambles (*Rubus* sp.). A number of the sloe stones were whole with holes in and traces of rodent faeces were recovered from this deposit. The weed seeds included seeds of common spike-rush, sedge, curled docks and mallow. The weed assemblage appears to be indicative of an area of possible damp rough grassland in the vicinity. The assemblage may be representative of a dump of the waste from the exploitation of a local wild food resource from hedgerows/scrub and woodland edge environments.

Discussion

Late Iron Age–Roman transition

The samples richest in crop remains from deposits of this date were recovered from features around Structures A–C. There is an indication that crop processing, possibly the pounding of stored semi-cleaned spikelets to release the grains (Hillman 1981, 1984), took place in the vicinity of these structures. The unusual assemblage from pit 20324 within Structure B, dominated by bracken, may have come from a hearth.

The possible crops included spelt wheat, emmer wheat, barley and Celtic beans. Although spelt wheat was generally the predominant wheat during Iron Age and Roman times in southern Britain, remains of emmer wheat, along with spelt wheat, are also recorded (occasionally in relatively high numbers) in Iron Age and Roman assemblages from nearby sites such as Steart Point (Wyles 2017) and Huntworth (Stevens 2008), and from sites in the wider vicinity such as Aller (Simmons 2012), RNAS Yeovilton (Pelling 2005), Banwell Moor, North Somerset Levels (Jones 2000) and Avonmouth (Ritchie *et al.* 2007). It appears that emmer wheat has been recorded in more assemblages from this region, than from other regions such as the Thames Valley and Kent.

Again, the weed seed assemblages appear to be species typical of grassland, field margins and arable environments. The range of species is indicative of a number of different soil types exploited, with species such as ribwort plantain, clover and medick favouring lighter drier soils whereas sedge and common spike-rush are typical of wetter grassland areas and bracken of sandier or heath habitats. Oraches and fat-hen can be indicative of nitrogen-rich soils. There is an indication of the exploitation of wild foods, as shown by the presence of hazelnut shell. The crops may have been harvested low down by sickle as shown by the presence of a number weed species that twine around the crop, such as black-bindweed, and those which grow close to the ground, such as knotgrass and clover and medick.

Early to Mid Roman

The samples richest in crop remains of this date came from the enclosure ditch and Building B. There is an indication that crop processing, probably the dehusking of semi-cleaned grain and spikelets (Hillman 1981, 1984), took place in the vicinity of Building B, which replaced Structure A. Spelt dominated emmer wheat, while other possible crops included barley, free-threshing wheat and flax. This range of crops was recorded from Roman deposits at Steart Point (Wyles 2017).

The weed seed assemblages appear to be indicative of a variety of different environments, comprising mainly species typical of grassland, field margins and arable environments, but also including those which favour wetter grassland, such as sedge, curled dock and bristle club-rush.

Redeposited Roman material in post-Roman features

The cereal assemblages from postholes 20666, 20671 and Ditch DL are compatible with a Roman date and are likely to represent redeposited Roman material. The possible crops included spelt wheat, free-threshing wheat, emmer wheat, barley, flax and Celtic beans. There is an indication of a number of different stages of crop processing having taken place in the vicinity of post-Roman Building D; possibly the sieving stage prior to drying for storage in the vicinity of postholes 20666 and 20671, and the dehusking of semi-cleaned grain or spikelets in the vicinity of Ditch DL. It is probable that crop processing was taking place in this area of the site during the Roman period.

The weed seed assemblages appear to be generally typical of grassland, field margins and arable environments. The range of species indicate a number of different soil types being utilised, with species such as clover, medick and ribwort plantain favouring lighter, drier soils, while curled dock, sedge, bristle club-rush and common spike-rush are typical of wetter grassland areas, and stinking mayweed and red bartsia of heavier clay soils. The presence of low-growing weeds suggest that crops may have been cut low down.

Early medieval

The assemblages from pits around Building D are compatible with the post-Roman date of these features. There is evidence for an earlier stage of crop processing from the assemblage from pit 20020 near the Enclosure Ditch, whilst the assemblage from pit 20625 appears to be food waste.

The possible crops recovered from pit 20020 included spelt wheat, free-threshing wheat, barley, rye and possible pea. The combination of free-threshing wheat and rye is typically post-Roman. Assemblages dominated by free-threshing wheat came from post-Roman deposits at Aller (Simmonds 2012), and from medieval deposits at Steart Point (Wyles 2017), while an assemblage from a medieval ditch at Huntsworth contained remains of rye, free-threshing wheat and barley (Stevens 2008).

There is an indication of the exploitation of wild food, in particular from pit 20625, as shown by the presence of sloe, wild plum, brambles, hawthorn and hazelnut shell. Again the weed seed assemblages appear to be generally species typical of grassland, field margins and arable environments.

Charcoal
Sarah Cobain

A total of 50 bulk soil samples were taken and assessed for charcoal remains from a range of features at Sandy Lane dating from the Late Iron Age to post-Roman periods. Following assessment, 12 samples were deemed suitable for full analysis by reason of the quality and diversity of their assemblages. The aims of the analysis were to identify and record evidence for the sources of fuel, woodland management and the composition of the local woodlands and environment. Methods follow those used for the Bronze Age (Cobain, Charcoal, Chapter 2, this volume).

Subsequent to the analysis, radiocarbon dating from features associated with Building D indicated that the charred material was to a large extent, but not entirely, of Roman date and redeposited in early medieval features. It was therefore mixed to some degree and is misleading as an assemblage of either Roman or early medieval date. This material is omitted from the discussion here although the data are presented for comparative purposes (Tables 3.18 and 3.19).

Late Iron Age to Roman transition period

Curvilinear Ditch T; Structure A
Fill 20133 within Ditch T (cut 20134) (sample 201), part of Structure A, contained a large assemblage of moderately well-preserved charcoal identified as oak, viburnum (*Viburnum*), alder, hazel, alder/hazel, ash, hawthorn/rowan/crab apple and willow/poplar. This feature also contained a small assemblage of charred grain, chaff and weeds and together with the charcoal suggests dump of firing debris associated with crop-processing activities.

Early to Mid Roman

Feature Group A
Posthole 20169 (sample 202) contained a large assemblage of moderately well-preserved charcoal identified as oak and alder/hazel, with five fragments of alder/hazel further identified as hazel. This material perhaps represents a dump of firing debris into the posthole after the post had been removed.

Pit 20600 (sample 235) contained a moderate assemblage of well-preserved charcoal identified as alder/hazel, hazel, birch, maple, oak, ash, hawthorn/rowan/crab apple and cherry species. This pit also contained a small assemblage of charred grain and weeds waste, and together with the charcoal indicates a dump of firing debris associated with crop-processing/domestic activities.

Ditches DW, W and DI
Ditch DW (cut 20775, sample 261) contained abundant and well-preserved charcoal identified dominantly as ash, with quantities of oak, maple, hawthorn/rowan/crab apple, cherry species and blackthorn also recorded. Ditch W (cut 20304, sample 203) contained a large assemblage of well-preserved charcoal identified dominantly as oak and ash, with smaller quantities of alder, hazel, birch, hawthorn/rowan/crab apple and cherry species present. A moderate assemblage of moderately well-preserved charcoal was recovered from fill 20365 within Ditch DI (cut 20366; sample 206) and dominantly identified as oak, with small quantities of maple, alder/hazel, cherry species and willow/poplar present. The charcoal from all three ditches was relatively abundant and accompanied by small quantities of charred plant remains (Cobain 2016). This is indicative of dumps of firing debris, most likely associated with crop-processing and domestic food production activities taking place within and surrounding Buildings A, B and C.

Building B
Fill 20545 (sample 221) within drain 20301, part of Building B contained a large assemblage of well-preserved charcoal identified dominantly as oak and ash, with smaller quantities of alder, alder/hazel, hazel and willow/poplar also recorded. This fill also contained a large assemblage of charred cereal grains, and alongside the charcoal is indicative of a dump of firing debris associated with the processing of semi-clean grain and food production.

Early medieval

Pit 20020
Pit 20020 (sample 200) with two 7th to 8th-century radiocarbon dates, contained a large, well-preserved and diverse assemblage of charcoal identified as oak and willow/poplar, with smaller quantities of viburnum, alder/hazel, alder, hazel, birch, ash, hawthorn/rowan/crab apple and cherry species also recorded. Charred plant remains included cereal grains and weed seeds, and together with the charcoal are indicative of a dump of crop-processing waste.

Discussion

Late Iron Age to Roman transition and Roman
Charcoal analysed from features dating to the Late Iron Age to Roman transition and Roman periods comprises firing debris dumped in ditches, pits and postholes, originating from domestic use or crop-processing activities. Oak (38%) was the most common, although this represents a decrease from 81.8% in the Middle Bronze Age samples. The decrease in oak has mainly been replaced by the use of ash which increased significantly from 1.6% in the Middle Bronze Age, to 23.9% in the Late Iron Age/Roman. There is also an increase in the use of alder/hazel (from 7.9 to 21%), hawthorn/rowan/crab apple (from 2.1 to 4.1%), cherry species (from 3.7 to 5.3%), willow/poplar (from 0 to 2.9%) and birch (from 0.2 to 0.5%) (Figs 2.10 and 3.46).

Table 3.18: Late Iron Age/Early Roman and Roman charcoal identifications

Family	Species	Common Name	20133 / 20134 / Structure A; Ditch T / 201 / 111 / 32 / ++++ / Moderate	20169 / 20168 / Feature group A / 202 / 53 / 3 / ++++ / Moderate	20600 / 20603 / Feature group A / 235 / 5 / 10 / +++ / Good	20775 / 20773 / Ditch DW / 261 / 2383 / 32 / +++++ / Good	20304 / 20165 / Ditch W / 203 / 81 / 32 / +++++ / Good	20366 / 20365 / Ditch DI / 206 / 11.5 / 30 / +++ / Moderate	20301 / 20545 / Building B / 221 / 35 / 9 / +++++ / Good
Aceraceae	*Acer campestre* L.	Field maple	-	-	1	4	-	3	-
Adoxaceae	*Viburnum* L.	Viburnum twig	1	-	-	-	-	-	-
Betulaceae	*Alnus glutinosa* (L.) Gaertn.	Alder	1	-	-	-	4	-	2
	Alnus glutinosa (L.) Gaertn.	Alder r/w	1	-	-	-	-	-	-
	Alnus glutinosa (L.) Gaertn./*Corylus avellana* L.	Alder/Hazel	28	24	14	-	-	3	1
	Alnus glutinosa (L.) Gaertn./*Corylus avellana* L.	Alder/Hazel r/w	-	2	-	-	-	-	-
	Alnus glutinosa (L.) Gaertn./*Corylus avellana* L.	Alder/Hazel twig	-	-	5	-	-	-	-
	Betula L.	Birches	-	-	1	-	2	-	-
	Corylus avellana L.	Hazel	12	5	6	-	6	-	3
	Corylus avellana L.	Hazel r/w	1	-	4	-	1	-	-
Fagaceae	*Quercus petraea* (Matt.) Liebl./*Quercus robur* L.	Sessile Oak/Pedunculate Oak	20	34	2	15	25	35	26
	Quercus petraea (Matt.) Liebl./*Quercus robur* L.	Sessile Oak/Pedunculate Oak h/w	1	1	-	-	5	-	24
	Quercus petraea (Matt.) Liebl./*Quercus robur* L.	Sessile Oak/Pedunculate Oak r/w	14	5	1	1	5	10	1
Oleaceae	*Fraxinus excelsior* L.	Ash	7	-	2	51	38	-	-
	Fraxinus excelsior L.	Ash r/w	-	-	-	6	6	-	42
Rosaceae	*Crataegus monogyna* Jacq./*Sorbus* L./*Malus sylvestris* (L.) Mill.	Hawthorn/Rowans/Crab apple	3	-	3	8	3	-	-

Iron Age Settlement, Roman Villa and post-Roman Structure at Sandy Lane 101

Feature number			20133	20169	20600	20775	20304	20366	20301
Context number			20134	20168	20603	20773	20165	20365	20545
Feature Label			Structure A; Ditch T	Feature group A	Feature group A	Ditch DW	Ditch W	Ditch DI	Building B
Sample number (SS)			201	202	235	261	203	206	221
Flot volume (ml)			111	53	5	2383	81	11.5	35
Sample volume processed (l)			32	3	10	32	32	30	9
Charcoal quantity >2mm			+++++	+++++	++++	++++++	++++++	+++	+++++
Charcoal preservation			Moderate	Moderate	Good	Good	Good	Moderate	Good
Family	Species	Common Name							
	Crataegus monogyna Jacq./*Sorbus* L./ *Malus sylvestris* (L.) Mill.	Hawthorn/Rowans/Crab apple r/w	1	-	1	1	-	-	-
	Crataegus monogyna Jacq./*Sorbus* L./ *Malus sylvestris* (L.) Mill.	Hawthorn/Rowans/Crab apple twig	-	-	4	-	-	-	-
	Prunus L.	Cherries r/w	-	-	-	4	4	-	-
	Prunus L.	Cherries	-	-	7	8	1	1	-
	Prunus L.	Cherries twig	-	-	6	-	-	-	-
	Prunus spinosa L.	Blackthorn	-	-	-	2	-	-	-
Salicaceae	*Salix* L./*Populus* L.	Willows/Poplars	10	-	-	-	-	6	1
		Indeterminate	2	-	2	-	-	-	-
		Total (excluding indeterminate)	100	71	57	100	100	58	100

Table 3.19: Charcoal identifications from early medieval features

Feature number			20732	20644	20666	20671	20020
Context number			20733	20645	20667	20672	20019
Feature Label			Building D; beam slot DL	Building D; beam slot ED	Building D; beam slot DP	Building D; beam slot DP	Early med. pit
Sample number (SS)			256	245	249	251	200
Flot volume (ml)			170	21	164	32	144
Sample volume processed (l)			10	5	36	8	36
Charcoal quantity >2mm			+++++	++++	+++++	++++	+++++
Charcoal preservation			Good	Good	Good	Good	Good
Family	Species	Common Name					
Adoxaceae	*Viburnum* L.	Viburnum twig	-	-	-	-	1
Betulaceae	*Alnus glutinosa* (L.) Gaertn.	Alder	6	50	3	-	8
	Alnus glutinosa (L.) Gaertn.	Alder r/w	1	-	4	-	1
	Alnus glutinosa (L.) Gaertn./*Corylus avellana* L.	Alder/Hazel	3	10	5	-	7
	Betula L.	Birches	2	2	2	-	1
	Betula L.	Birches rw	-	-	1	-	-
	Corylus avellana L.	Hazel	6	5	6	-	11
	Corylus avellana L.	Hazel r/w	-	-	2	-	1
	Corylus avellana L.	Hazel r/w twig	-	-	-	-	4
Celastraceae	*Euonymus europaea* L.	Spindle	3	-	-	-	-
	Euonymus europaea L.	Spindle r/w	6	-	-	-	-
Fagaceae	*Quercus petraea* (Matt.) Liebl./*Quercus robur* L.	Sessile Oak/Pedunculate Oak	25	3	46	-	29
	Quercus petraea (Matt.) Liebl./*Quercus robur* L.	Sessile Oak/Pedunculate Oak h/w	-	-	-	-	4
	Quercus petraea (Matt.) Liebl./*Quercus robur* L.	Sessile Oak/Pedunculate Oak r/w	1	2	7	-	3
Oleaceae	*Fraxinus excelsior* L.	Ash	30	-	9	56	1
	Fraxinus excelsior L.	Ash r/w	4	-	8	3	-
Rosaceae	*Crataegus monogyna* Jacq./*Sorbus* L./*Malus sylvestris* (L.) Mill.	Hawthorn/Rowans/Crab apple	5	-	1	-	2
	Crataegus monogyna Jacq./*Sorbus* L./*Malus sylvestris* (L.) Mill.	Hawthorn/Rowans/Crab apple r/w	2	-	1	-	-
	Prunus L.	Cherries r/w	1	-	-	-	1
	Prunus L.	Cherries	2	-	-	-	1
Salicaceae	*Salix* L./*Populus* L.	Willows/Poplars	2	-	2	-	23
	Salix L./*Populus* L.	Willows/Poplars r/w	1	-	3	-	2
		Total	100	72	100	59	100

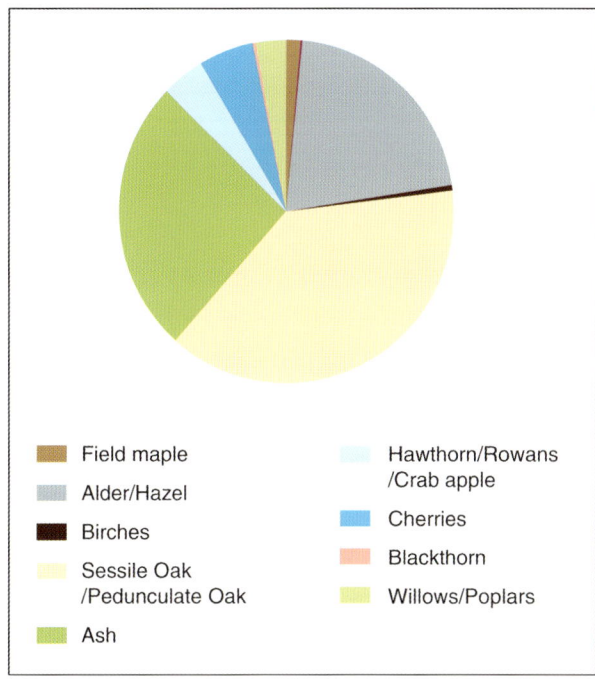

Fig. 3.46 Late Iron Age/Early Roman and Roman charcoal composition

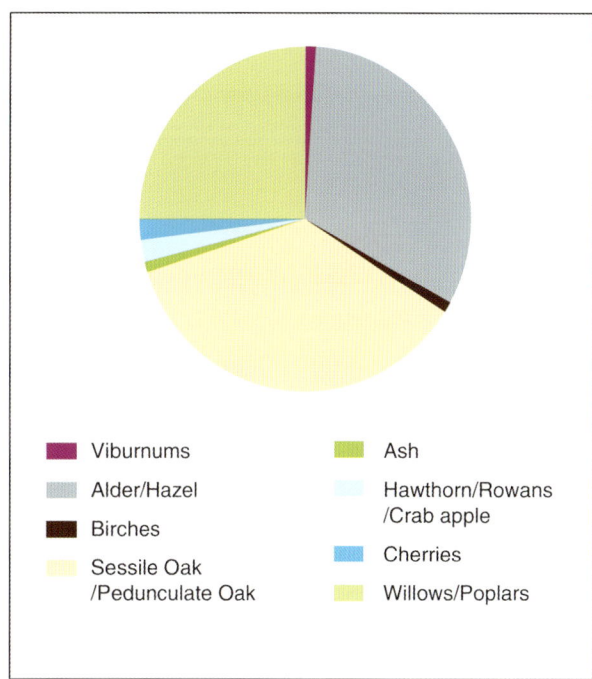

Fig. 3.47 Charcoal assemblage from early medieval pit 20020

The change in dominant fuelwood from oak to oak-and-ash is of interest. Deforestation would have been complete by the Iron Age period, and oak would have been less readily available. As oak is an efficient and highly calorific fuel, it is likely it would have been reserved for use within more specific industrial tasks which require fuels which burn to a high temperature (such as metalworking which was not observed on site). Oak (unlike ash) also has water resistant qualities which makes it valuable for construction. The increase in the use of scrub/hedgerow species (cherry, hazel, hawthorn/rowan/crab apple and birch) and species such as alder and willow/poplar which grow in wetland environments also indicates increased pressure on local woodlands. This trend has been observed in other sites and includes charcoal within a crop drier at Queen Camel, Somerset which was identified as ash, hawthorn/rowan/crab apple and maple (Challinor forthcoming) and can be seen in initial assessment results from charcoal within Iron Age and Roman settlement features (SPE 5) at Hinkley Point, Somerset (Cobain 2015).

Charcoal data suggests local woodlands consist of stands of oak, ash and small amounts of maple with shrubby species such as hazel, hawthorn/rowan/crab apple, cherry species and birch making up local hedgerows. Wetland areas are present nearby suggested by the use of alder and willow/poplar.

Early medieval

Charcoal dating to the early medieval period was recovered as part of domestic waste within pit 20020. The feature contains a slightly lower amount of ash and higher amount of willow/poplar and alder/hazel compared to the Roman features (Fig. 3.47). However, as only a single feature dating to this period was analysed, there is limited potential to compare fuel use and local woodlands with the Roman assemblage. The mixed assemblage from Building D is similar to the Roman charcoal profile (Fig. 3.48).

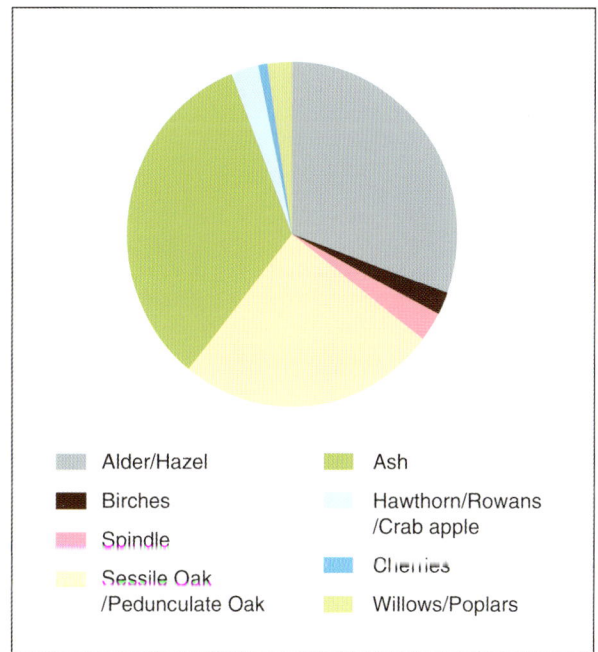

Fig. 3.48 Charcoal from Building D

Table 3.20: Summary counts of the identified animal bone elements/fragments (NISP). H = hand-collected; S = sieved samples. NISP data includes loose/isolated teeth and ABGs (associated/articulating bone groups)

Period	Late Iron Age to Roman transition		Early to Mid Roman		
	H	S	H	S	**TOTALS**
Mammals:					
horse *Equus caballus* (domestic)	7	-	32	2	**41**
cattle *Bos* (domestic)	89	1	222	1	**313**
sheep/goat *Ovis/Capra* (domestic)	112	5	339	13	**469**
pig *Sus* (domestic)	55	3	33	1	**92**
dog *Canis* (domestic)	1	-	78	1	**80**
cat *Felis* (domestic)	-	-	31	-	**31**
roe deer *Capreolus capreolus*	-	-	1	-	**1**
hare *Lepus capensis*	-	-	2	-	**2**
house mouse *Mus musculus*	-	-	3	24	**27**
wood mouse *Apodemus sylvaticus*	-	1	-	3	**4**
mouse *Mus/Apodemus sp.*	-	-	-	13	**13**
field vole *Microtus agrestis*	-	5	3	7	**15**
bank vole *Clethrionomys glareolus*	-	-	-	3	**3**
common shrew *Sorex araneus*	-	8	-	4	**12**
pygmy shrew *Sorex minutus*	-	1	-	1	**2**
shrew (sp. indet.)	-	5	-	-	**5**
small mammal (mouse/vole/shrew)	-	8	-	7	**15**
Subtotals	*264*	*37*	*744*	*80*	**1125**
Birds:					
domestic fowl *Gallus gallus* (domestic)	2	-	1	2	**5**
mallard/domestic duck *Anas platyrhynchos*/domestic	-	-	1	-	**1**
rock dove/domestic pigeon *Columba livia*/domestic	-	-	1	-	**1**
jackdaw *Corvus monedula*	-	-	-	2	**2**
magpie *Pica pica*	-	-	-	2	**2**
starling *Sturnus vulgaris*	-	-	2	2	**4**
indet. small wild birds	-	-	2	13	**15**
Subtotals	*2*	*0*	*7*	*21*	**30**
Fish:					
plaice *Pleuronectes platessa*	-	-	-	1	**1**
plaice/flounder *Pleuronectes platessa/Platichthys flesus*	-	-	-	2	**2**
freshwater eel *Anguilla anguilla*	-	-	-	1	**1**
Salmonid salmon/trout	-	-	-	1	**1**
Subtotals	*0*	*0*	*0*	*5*	**5**
Amphibian:					
common frog *Rana temporaria*	-	2	-	49	**51**
Anura (frog/toad)	-	5	-	7	**12**
Subtotals	*0*	*7*	*0*	*56*	**63**
Reptile:					
grass snake *Natrix natrix*	0	0	0	2	**2**
TOTALS	**266**	**44**	**751**	**164**	**1225**

Animal bones
Philip L. Armitage

The Iron Age and Roman settlements at Sandy Lane produced an assemblage of 1,225 animal bones, both hand-collected and recovered from sample processing. Species identifications were carried out using the author's modern comparative osteological collections and with reference to standard published works (Lawrence and Brown 1973; Sisson *et al.* 1975; Amorosi 1989; Bailon 1999; Tomek and Bocheński 2000; Wouters *et al.* 2007). Wherever possible, sheep and goat bones and teeth were differentiated following criteria in Boessneck *et al.* (1964) and Payne (1985). No positive identifications of goat were made and all elements with diagnostic features proved to be sheep, but it remains possible that goat remains are amongst the unidentifiable elements and so all *ovicaprid* material is therefore referenced as sheep/goat, except where positively identified as sheep.

Table 3.20 provides summary counts of the identified bone (number of identified specimens; NISP) by species and period. Overall, the species include mammals, birds, fish, amphibians and a reptile species. Overall, the state of preservation is moderate to good. Some bones exhibit attritional damage indicative of exposure before burial and this is also suggested by the occurrence of loose animal teeth (Table 3.21). Post-depositional abrasion caused by hydrodynamic action is also evident on the microfaunal remains. Seven associated/articulating bone groups (ABGs) were identified (Table 3.22).

Overall the incidence of burnt bone among the hand-collected material was very low and with no distribution pattern discernible. Burnt bone was recovered from 57 sieved samples but was not identifiable to taxa and has therefore been omitted from the results presented here, beyond the observation that most, if not all, probably derives from food scraps cast into cooking fires.

Results

Late Iron Age to Roman transition period

The Iron Age animal bone assemblage is of modest size. Cattle, sheep/goat and pigs are present, including young stock and with all skeletal parts represented. This indicates that these beasts were bred, slaughtered, butchered and consumed locally. The relative percentage

Table 3.21: Summary counts of numbers of loose animal teeth. H = hand-collected; S = sieved samples

	Late Iron Age to Roman transition		Early to Mid Roman		
	H	S	H	S	TOTALS
horse *Equus caballus* (domestic)			12		12
cattle *Bos* (domestic)	11		36		47
sheep *Ovis* (domestic)	11		49	9	69
pig *Sus* (domestic)	13	2	9		24
Totals	35	2	106	9	152

Table 3.22: Associated/articulating bone groups

Late Iron Age to Roman transition	Curvilinear Ditch T	Fill 20134: skull fragments/maxillae and jawbones of three subadult male pigs (14–21 months old)
Early to Mid Roman	Building A Phase 5	Rubble layer 20238 within hypocaust: part skeleton of an adult cat (NISP = 29)
		Rubble layer 20572 within hypocaust: parts of skeletons of three neonatal puppies (NISP = 54)
	Building C	Pit 20658 (fill 20659): skull and partial post-cranial skeleton of a 2- to 3-year-old sheep
		Pit 20729 (fill 20728): skulls, jawbones and metapodia of at least seven young sheep (NISP = 56)
	Ditch D1	Fill 20363: partial skeleton of a young dog aged under 1 year (NISP = 22)
		Fills 20364 and 20365: bones of right & left fore legs/feet of an adult horse (NISP = 8)

Table 3.23: Ages of the sheep mandibles (after Payne 1973)
ABG = Associated/articulated bone group

Stage	Age	Late Iron Age to Roman transition	Early to Mid Roman ABG pit 20658	Early to Mid Roman ABG pit 20729	Early to Mid Roman Other sheep
A	0 – 2 months	-	-	-	1
B	2 – 6 months	2	-	-	-
C	6 months – 1 year	-	-	5	2
D	1 – 2 years	2	-	-	-
E	2 – 3 years	1	1	-	-
F	3 – 4 years	1	-	-	5
G	4 – 6 years	2	-	-	-
H	6 – 8 years	1	-	-	-
I	8 – 10 years	-	-	-	-
Totals		**9**	**1**	**5**	**8**

frequencies based on the NISP data (Table 3.20) indicate that livestock husbandry was predominantly based on sheep with cattle in slightly lower numbers. However, cattle as the larger beasts would have provided a greater contribution to the overall meat diet. Pigs appear to have been kept in greater numbers than was the case in the Roman period. Few domestic fowl are represented and evidence for the exploitation of wild animals for food is absent. Horse and dog comprise the remains of the non-food domestic species, with the latter represented by a single adult scapula from Structure A Ditch T.

Sheep/goat
Only horned sheep are represented and these would have been small, slender-legged animals similar in appearance to Soay sheep. The small size is illustrated with reference to the withers height of 512mm calculated for a metacarpal bone from Structure B Ditch Q (method of Teichert referenced in von den Driesch and Boessneck 1974). An innominate bone from enclosure Ditch O belonged to a ewe. Table 3.23 summarises the mandibles that could be aged using the method of Payne (1973), although the small sample available prevents detailed interpretation.

Cattle
Enclosure Ditch O produced bones from two cows: the horn core and partial skull of a young adult short horned cow and a female innominate bone. Ditch O also produced a metacarpal bone from a young animal on which knife cutting marks provide evidence of skinning for hide removal. An adult metacarpus from pit 20600 near Structures A–C also displays knife marks suggestive of hide removal. A cattle skull found within pit 20106 was radiocarbon dated to 22 cal. BC–cal. AD 124 (SUERC-72465).

Evidence for the presence of plough oxen at Sandy Lane is indicated by an adult innominate bone identified as representing a castrate (Grigson 1982) from Ditch L. Two small-horned cattle represented by horn cores/part skulls from the same ditch include a young adult bull and an adult castrate.

Pig
All pig remains are from domestic beasts, with no wild pigs represented. Approximately a third of the total of the pig bones/teeth came from Structure A Ditch T, from which, based on the numbers of skulls and jawbones, three males are represented whose dental age ranges from one and a half to two years. Structure B Ditch S produced an unsexed pig aged 7 to 14 months and an unsexed pig aged 0 to 7 months.

Possible enclosure ditch 20580 produced part of a pig skull, along with an astragalus which derives from a pig whose withers height is estimated to have been 646mm (calculated from GLl 36.1mm x 17.9mm; Becker 1980, 27). Enclosure Ditch O contained bones from a male aged 14 to 21 months.

Horse
An equid metatarsal bone with unfused distal epiphysis from enclosure Ditch O is from an animal aged less than 16–20 months and suggests either that horse breeding was undertaken or that young animals were imported as replacement stock. From the same ditch there are jawbones from two adult horses aged 8 to 9 years and 11 to 12 years. Possible enclosure ditch 20580 produced the jawbone of another adult horse aged 11 to 12 years old, together with an adult horse scapula. Structure B Ditch Q produced a distal tibia.

Microvertebrates
Sieved sample 201 from Structure A Ditch T yielded

Table 3.24: Spatial distributions of the skeletal remains of small vertebrates. NISP = Hand-collected and sieved samples combined; (a) Small mammals = mice, voles, shrews (indet.)

	field vole	bank vole	wood mouse	house mouse	house/wood mouse	common shrew	pygmy shrew	shrew (indet.)	small mammals (a)	starling	jackdaw	cf.magpie	small wild birds	common frog	frog/toad	grass snake
Late Iron Age to Roman transition																
Ditch T (fill 20134)	5	-	1	-	-	8	1	5	8	-	-	-	-	2	5	-
Early to Mid Roman																
Building A																
Layer 20398	-	-	3	-	7	-	1	-	-	-	-	-	-	-	-	-
Layer 20238	2	-	-	2	-	-	-	-	-	2	-	-	2	-	-	-
Layer 20486	-	-	-	-	2	-	-	-	2	-	-	-	-	3	4	-
Building B																
fills inside drain 20301																
1st fill (20549/20550/20551)	-	2	-	3	6	-	-	-	-	-	-	2	-	24	-	-
2nd fill (20542) = (20534)	-	-	-	8	-	1	-	-	1	-	2	-	10	1	-	-
3rd fill (20535) = (20545)	-	1	-	4	-	1	-	-	-	-	-	-	-	17	-	-
Rubble layer 20257	1	-	-	1	-	-	-	-	-	-	-	-	1	-	-	-
Building C																
Rubble layer 20626	1	-	-	-	-	-	-	-	-	-	-	-	1	-	-	-
Grave 20697 (fill 20696)	1	-	-	-	-	-	-	-	-	-	-	-	-	-	-	-
Other features																
Posthole 20661 (fill 20663)	-	-	-	8	-	-	-	-	-	-	-	-	-	-	-	-
Ditch W (fill 20165)	2	-	-	-	-	-	-	-	-	-	-	-	1	-	3	-
Ditch W (fill 20199)	1	-	-	1	-	-	-	-	-	-	-	-	-	1	-	2
Ditch DI (fill 20365)	-	-	-	-	-	-	-	-	-	-	-	-	-	3	-	-
Early medieval																
Building D Ditch DL (fill 20733)	2	-	-	-	-	-	-	-	-	-	-	-	-	-	-	-

the remains of four small mammal species (Table 3.24). These comprised common shrew *Sorex araneus* (est. MNI = 4); pygmy shrew *Sorex minutus* (est. MNI = 1); wood mouse *Apodemus sylvaticus* (est. MNI = 1); and field vole *Microtus agrestis* (est. MNI = 2). Bones of common frog *Rana temporaria* (MNI indeterminate) were also present.

Early to Mid Roman

As for the Iron Age, cattle, sheep/goat and pig bones present represent the remains of animals bred, slaughtered, butchered and consumed locally. Numerically, sheep again predominate but, again, cattle would have contributed more to the meat supply, being individually larger. A few bantam-sized domestic fowl appear to have been kept, and there was evidence of breeding at the site provided by a neonatal/chick tarsometatarsal bone from ashy layer 20398 found between the Building A hypocaust pilae.

Evidence that the inhabitants supplemented their diet by hunting game is restricted to two hare bones (a humerus and a vertebra) from rubble layer 20257 associated with Building B. This is typical for the Romano-British period, during which wild animals do not appear to have been widely exploited for food, even on rural sites (Hammon 2011). A duck sternum from the same deposit may be from either a farmyard bird or a wild caught mallard. The exploitation of riverine fish also seems to have been limited, represented amongst the sieved material by only two bones: a vertebra from a very small freshwater eel from enclosure Ditch W and a precaudal vertebra of a *salmonid* (salmon/trout) from the backfill of grave 20748 (Sk 20746). Evidence for marine fish in the diet is also scanty, being restricted to a cleithrum from a plaice (Building B drain 20300) and a bone from a small flatfish (plaice/flounder) from enclosure Ditch W. The marine fish are species that may have been caught from the shore, or from fishing in deeper water.

Sheep

As for the Iron Age, the Roman period sheep would have been small, slender-legged animals similar to Soays. Only horned sheep were identified, including an old adult ewe represented by a horn core/part skull from Ditch W. The largest from Sandy Lane is represented by a metacarpal bone from enclosure Ditch W and would have had an estimated withers height of 590mm (method of Teichert referenced in von den Driesch and Boessneck 1974). This falls within the general Romano-British range of 480mm to 650mm.

Two deposits of sheep bones associated with Building C are worthy of special note. Pit 20658 contained the articulated remains of a two- to three-year-old sheep radiocarbon dated to cal. AD 70–221 (95.4% probability; SUERC-69974: Table 3.1). Owing to the high degree of fragmentation and incompleteness of the skull, it is not possible to say whether this animal was horned or polled (naturally hornless). Stature (withers height) was calculated from the greatest length measurements of the metacarpal (GL 111.5mm) and metatarsal (GL 121mm) bones (Teichert referenced in von den Driesch and Boessneck 1974), indicating that the living animal was 545mm tall. One of the three cervical vertebrae recovered had been chopped/sheared through transversely, perhaps indicating the manner of slaughter. No other evidence of butchery could be discerned and the absence of knife cut marks probably indicates that this sheep had not been skinned after killing.

Pit 20729 contained two skulls, five jawbones and lower leg/foot bones together representing at least seven young sheep; one of the leg bones was radiocarbon dated to cal. AD 230–381 (95.4% probability; SUERC-72468). Eruption and wear in the five mandibles present (after Payne 1973) indicate these sheep were aged six months to a year at time of death (Table 3.23). From the pattern of epiphyseal fusion in the associated metapodial bones and phalanges, a similar age range is determined; showing that all the seven individuals represented in this deposit probably were of the same age group. Owing to the degree of fragmentation and incompleteness of the two surviving skulls, only one animal was able to be identified with certainty and was a horned female. None of the limb bones appear to have been chopped, but superficial knife cut marks are evident on the shafts of two of the metatarsal bones. In addition to the sheep from pit 20658 and the five animals from pit 20729 documented above, the age of death in eight other sheep represented by mandibles from the Roman period are presented in Table 3.23. As with the earlier period the small sample size inhibits detailed analysis.

Cattle

All the cattle represented by mandibles seem to have been slaughtered as adults (Bond and O'Connor 1999, age category A3), probably between five and eight years of age. Such mature cattle would have been kept principally as plough animals and as breeding and milch cows, and only later in their lives killed for meat and hides. Supporting evidence for the presence of plough oxen and breeding/milking cows at Sandy Lane is indicated by an adult innominate bone identified as representing a castrate (Grigson 1982) from enclosure Ditch DI; a further example was recovered from a post-medieval quarry pit (20495). An adult metacarpal bone from enclosure Ditch DI is from a female with a withers height of 1.062m (calculated from GL 177mm by 6mm, method of Fock 1966 referenced in von den Driesch and Boessneck 1974). While there was a trend towards larger cattle during the Roman period, smaller livestock more typical of the Iron Age were still farmed into the Roman period and beyond, and the cow represented by the bone from Ditch DI may have been one such beast.

Pig

All of the pig bones come from domestic animals, with no wild pigs represented. A metacarpus IV from enclosure Ditch W represents a pig whose withers height is estimated to have been 661mm (calculated from GL 62.8mm by 10.53mm, method of Becker 1980, 27). Pit 20098, south of Building B, produced a tibia of a neonate/suckling piglet.

Horse

Applying the ageing method of Levine (1982), a jawbone from enclosure Ditch W is from a young horse five- to six-years-old at death. Enclosure Ditch DI yielded bones of the right and left forelegs of an adult horse of estimated stature (withers height) 1.22m (calculated from metacarpus III lateral length 191mm, method Kiesewalter 1888 referenced in von den Driesch and Boessneck 1974). Several superficial knife cut marks distally on the left radius of this horse indicate that it had been skinned.

An astragalus (foot bone) from trackway Ditch DJ exhibits distally extraneous bone outgrowths (exostoses) indicating that it comes from a horse afflicted with the pathological condition known as spavin. Heavy draught work can result in inflammation of the hock joint of the lower hind limb in horses, leading to inflammation and the fusion of the small bones (tarsals) comprising the joint. In advanced cases of spavin, even the astragalus can become involved (as seen in the Sandy Lane animal) and leads to lameness in the animal (Bartosiewicz 2013, 124–5).

Pit 20098 yielded a dog-gnawed shaft of a pony-sized

equid metacarpus III with exostoses distally and fused with part of the shaft of metacarpus II.

Dog
Among the dog remains are two ABGs. Fill 20363 of enclosure Ditch DI produced the partial skeleton of a young dog that at time of death was over six months but less than ten months old. The shoulder height is estimated (method of Harcourt 1974a) to have been at least 620mm, and the animal would probably have grown somewhat taller in adulthood, placing it well into the upper Romano-British range (230mm to 720mm) documented by Harcourt (ibid.). A dog of this size would have made either a good guard dog or useful hunting dog. The skeleton of this dog lacked the skull and jawbones, although whether or not this reflects decapitation, before or after the animal's death, is not apparent from the remains. The same deposit produced a radius of a second, smaller dog.

Rubble infill 20572 of the heating channel in Room 1 of Building A produced parts of the disarticulated and incomplete skeletal remains of three neonate puppies. Although these may have been natural birthing casualties there is the possibility that the remains derive from the killing and disposal/dumping of an unwanted litter.

Cat
Among the animal remains found in the rubble infills (20238 and 20486) of the heating channel in Room 1 Building A was the skeleton of an adult cat. The presence of a cat is not unusual and adds to examples from other excavated Romano-British villas, including Gadebridge Park, Hemel Hempstead (Harcourt 1974b, 260) and Frocester, Gloucestershire (Noddle 2000) as well as the Romano-British farmstead excavated at the Royal Naval Air Station site, Yeovilton (Hambleton 2005, 47). As observed by Kitchener and O'Connor (2010, 91–2), cats would have had a role as pest exterminators but their exact status at Roman sites is uncertain. There is evidence from the villa at Dalton-on-Tees, North Yorkshire that one Roman cat had been a cherished pet based on the evidence for healing of fractures on its limbs, indicating it had been cared for by humans (Buglass and West 2016). Whether or not the Sandy Lane cat was a household pet is unknown but its presence would no doubt have been useful to control the local mouse population, although it is equally possible that it had been a feral animal living in the vicinity of the building and feeding on small rodents.

Microvertebrates
Sieved samples yielded remains of microvertebrates (Table 3.24) comprising common shrew *Sorex araneus*; pygmy shrew *Sorex minutus*; house mouse *Mus musculus*; wood mouse *Apodemus sylvaticus*; field vole *Microtus agrestis*; bank vole *Clethrionomys glareolus*; common frog *Rana temporaria*; and grass snake *Natrix natrix*.

Birds
Three wild bird species are represented. From Building A Room 1, the Phase 5 rubble infills of the underfloor heating channels produced bones from starling *Sturnus vulgaris* (deposit 20238: one humerus and one tibiotarsus; deposit 20486 one scapula and one dorsal vertebra.

From Building B, the fills of drain 20300 produced the bones of *Corvid* cf. magpie *Pica pica* (fill 20549: one scapula; fill 20550: one carpometacarpus) and jackdaw *Corvus monedula* (fill 20534: one carpometacarpus and one scapula).

Discussion
The bulk of the hand-collected animal bone from the two periods at Sandy Lane is identified as discarded food debris from all stages of meat preparation (slaughtering, primary and secondary butchering) and consumption, revealing that the meat component of their diet was heavily dependent on locally bred livestock. Wild game and fowl and river and marine fish appear to have contributed little to the food supply.

Livestock economies
From the evidence, it is seen that sheep predominated over cattle at Sandy Lane during the Late Iron Age to Roman transition period (Table 3.25), a pattern

Table 3.25: Percentage frequencies of the cattle, sheep/goat and pig remains based on NISP data

	cattle	sheep/goat	pig	Total NISP
Hand-collected and sieved bones combined (omitting loose teeth)				
Late Iron Age to Roman transition	34.6%	46.5%	18.9%	228
Early to Mid Roman	37.0%	58.1%	4.9%	506
Hand-collected and sieved bones combined (including loose teeth)				
Late Iron Age to Roman transition	34.0%	44.0%	22.0%	265
Early to Mid Roman	36.6%	57.8%	5.6%	609

consistent with other Late Iron Age sites in Wessex and central-southern England where these animals would have helped maintain large-scale arable production (Hambleton 1998, 82). However, there is a relatively high percentage of pig bones in the same period when compared generally with the lower values at many other Late Iron Age southern British sites. This may be of relevance as it has been suggested by Grant (2002, 83) that in Britain there is a robust correlation between high-status Iron Age sites and relatively high pig percentages. Grant explains this with reference to cattle and sheep/goats not only producing meat but also milk, manure, hides and skins, whilst pigs were raised specifically for their meat and the only by-product would have been their manure, making them somewhat of a luxury animal (ibid.).

For the Roman period, the apparent decline in pig at Sandy Lane need not imply a lowering of status of the community as it is likely a greater emphasis was placed on sheep and cattle. An increase in arable production would have resulted in an increased requirement for plough animals and the pre-Roman pattern of predominance of sheep (valued for their manure, wool and milk) continued, both factors resulting in the decreased importance of pigs in the local farming economy. Contemporary rural sites like that of the Romano-British farmstead at Yeovilton, Somerset, present a similar picture to that seen at Sandy Lane, with sheep the most commonly exploited species (Hambleton 2005, 47). This is in contrast to the Roman roadside settlement at Fosse Lane, Shepton Mallet, Somerset, where cattle was the most abundant species, followed by sheep and then pig (Albarella and Hammon 2011). The pattern is in keeping with the usual regional prevalence of cattle in assemblages from towns, and sheep from rural farmsteads.

Building C sheep bones within pit 20729

This deposit, dominated by sheep metapodial bones and phalanges, could be explained as primary butchery waste (criteria of O'Connor 1993, 64–5) but also matches the anatomical profiles of deposits at other archaeological sites recognised as sheepskin-working waste (O'Connor 1984, Serjeantson 1989, Baxter 1998). The latter interpretation is perhaps supported by superficial knife cutting marks on two of the metatarsal bones, which are consistent with the skinning process as observed by O'Connor (1984, 56) in the case of sheep metapodials from 18th-century Walmgate, York. The lambs would have been killed and butchered elsewhere and their skins (retaining the feet and heads) brought to the site for processing.

A third interpretation is that this deposit is evidence of ritual activity. Although far smaller an assemblage, the anatomical representation and age profile of the Sandy Lane deposit matches very well the sacrificial deposit of lamb bones dominated by mandibles and also lower limbs discovered at the Roman temple site at Great Chesterford, Essex (Legge and Williams 2000 referenced by King 2005, 336–7). For both sites, there is evidence of the killing of lambs at the age of six to eight months (said for the Great Chesterford material to indicate autumn killing). Also, for both sites, there is the possibility that some of the lambs were skinned and in both cases meat probably had been removed for consumption elsewhere. The sheep in pit 20658, also buried within Building C, probably represents further ritual activity perhaps connected with the interment of the four infants in this room.

The farming landscape at Sandy Lane

Based on modern ecological studies of the habitat preferences and niche requirements of small wild mammal species (Lawrence and Brown 1973; Corbet 1977, 50; Evans 1977, 189; Flowerdew 1993) the microfaunal assemblages provide clues as to the nature of the vegetation in the surrounding landscape. At Sandy Lane, the macrofaunal remains suggest that the Late Iron Age and Roman settlements lay within a mosaic of pasture and arable fields, broken up by woodland, hedgerows, and water-filled ditches. This is illustrated with reference to the presence of common and pygmy shrews together with field vole, which indicate thick vegetation cover including rough ungrazed grassland, in the vicinity. Bank voles are timid creatures inhabiting hedgerows and woods, generally avoiding areas disturbed by people. Wood mice are the most common small rodent in woodland but also inhabit ploughed fields. House mice are commonly encountered in farm buildings but also occupy agricultural land, grassland and hedgerows. The ditches and any drains or water sources would have provided suitable wet habitats for the frogs and grass snake.

Building B drain 20300: the microvertebrate remains

Although a natural death accumulation may explain the presence of frog bones in the drain sediments, other explanations for the occurrence of the bones of small wild mammals and birds merit consideration. For example, it could be suggested that these represent the remnants of scats of foxes, dogs or cats, their faeces (containing bones) forming surface deposits nearby which subsequently washed into the drain. This seems unlikely, however, as none of the bones exhibit the severe degree of corrosion caused by digestive juices and fragmentation that is associated with the ingested/voided material of these mammalian predators as documented by Andrews and Nesbit Evans (1983, 297–301). Similarly, scats from mustelids (weasel, stoat or polecat) can be ruled out; bones from these again exhibit high levels of digestion and breakage (ibid., 301–2). An alternative possibility is that the bones derive from decayed owl pellets that had been washed into the drain. Prey bones in regurgitated owl pellets show far fewer effects from digestive juices or breakage, and skeletal elements are readily identifiable. Authors Dodson and Wexlar (1979), Yalden (1977) and Kusmer (1990) all identified distinctive patterns of skeletal element representation and bone fragmentation as useful attributes in identifying such assemblages. Unfortunately, the bias effects of post-deposition dispersal have meant that these patterns could not be applied to the Sandy Lane assemblage, leaving the question of whether they derived from owl pellets outstanding. However, one characteristic of the assemblage is the notable absence of bones from field voles *Microtus agrestis*: modern owl pellet analysis has shown field voles to be the frequent major prey item of both the barn owl *Tyto alba* and tawny owl *Strix aluca* (Southern 1954; Teagle 1963; Beven 1982). Evidence from other deposits at Sandy Lane shows that field voles were present, and so available as prey (Table 3.24), suggesting that, had the drain assemblage been derived from owl pellets, the bones of field voles would have been expected.

In conclusion, this leaves the possibility that the micromammals and small wild birds from the drain fills represent the dispersed remains of animals that had died in the immediate vicinity (natural death assemblage) and subsequently their carcasses washed into the drain. Although bank voles and shrews appear to be unlikely residents in a barn, or living in the immediate vicinity of the building, all of these creatures nevertheless could have been inadvertently brought onto the site from distant fields, in hay being transported to the barn for storing and feeding livestock.

Chapter 4
Discussion

Introduction

The excavations along Cannington Bypass investigated a tract of high ground overlooking the Parrett Valley to the north-east, with its former marshlands that form the edge of the Somerset Levels. Despite its imposing nature, the nearby Cannington Camp, an Iron Age hillfort also known as Cynwit Castle or Cannington Park Camp, has had little significant attention (Rahtz 1969). The only major archaeological works in the immediate vicinity, prior to those connected with the new bypass, were those of the Roman and later cemetery at Cannington Park Quarry, undertaken under salvage conditions in the 1960s (Rahtz *et al.* 2000). More generally, West Somerset has seen relatively little archaeological investigation as a result of planning conditions associated with modern development when compared, for example, with the areas around Ilminster and Shepton Mallet, where work ahead of modern development has revealed, amongst other discoveries, a dense distribution of villas and a Roman small town respectively (Holbrook 2011, 39). Development-led archaeological work in West Somerset has been largely in the environs of Taunton, with the Quantocks and the Levels, on the fringes of which Cannington Bypass is located, among the less well-investigated areas (ibid., 43–4). The notable recent exception is the work ahead of the construction of the new nuclear power station at Hinkley Point, a development covering 170ha, where remains have come to light spanning the prehistoric to modern periods (CA 2015; 2017a; 2017b). It is within this context that the new discoveries have made a significant contribution to knowledge.

Bronze Age settlement at Rodway in its context
Andrew Mudd and Jonathan Hart

The Middle Bronze Age settlement pattern in the South West, as elsewhere, shows small family or extended family farmsteads to have been typical. These are distinct from the class of larger enclosures which perhaps acted as regional centres, of which Norton Camp, Taunton, appears to be the closest (Fitzpatrick 2008, 118). In many parts of the country small groups of houses and other settlement features can be shown to have been dispersed around fields, sometimes part of large-scale co-axial systems, although there is currently no evidence for such land division in Somerset, except perhaps on Exmoor (ibid., 120). The evidence may, however, simply have been lost. The Middle Bronze Age settlement enclosures on Cranborne Chase, Dorset (South Lodge Enclosure and Down Farm), were situated among partly surviving lynchets of field systems (Barrett *et al.* 1991, 225). These may have been regularly cultivated plots extending over large tracts of countryside, and perhaps defined by hedgerows without ditches.

The Middle Bronze Age settlement at Rodway is tightly defined spatially and chronologically in an enclosure *c.* 30m by 25m in extent. The absence of identifiable earlier or later activity suggests that this represents a single-phase settlement compound, and it is similar in many respects to others in southern England, such as Thorny Down (Wiltshire), South Lodge Enclosure and Down Farm (both Dorset), and Irford Hill and Black Patch (both East Sussex) (Ellison 1987, 1978; Barrett *et al.* 1991; Drewett 1979, 1982). The similarities include houses with a lack of clear posthole patterns to suggest their form and structure. At Rodway it is suggested that there were two roundhouses of similar form, some 9–10m in diameter, and evidence from these other sites is compatible. The much nearer settlement at Brean Down, Somerset, may have had similarly paired roundhouses, although it is not clear how much of the settlement was revealed, and the houses excavated were smaller (*c.* 6m) as well as being different structurally (Bell 1990).

Roundhouse structure

The absence of most of the postholes that would have been needed to form walls made using wooden posts presents difficulties in determining the nature of the buildings at Rodway, as is the case elsewhere. At

Black Patch, Drewett suggested that the walls of the terraces into which the house platforms had been cut, augmented at the front of the terrace by low walls of the upcast stone, could have provided support for roof rafters (Drewett 1979, fig. 4). At Rodway, it can be suggested that the manner in which the enclosure ditch was modelled around rear of the roundhouses shows an intention to use the ditch upcast for the construction of mass-walling, although it is difficult to see how this would have been carried round the whole perimeter. The irregularity of the internal roof supports at Rodway, Black Patch, South Lodge Enclosure and, to a lesser extent, at Thorny Down gives an impression of somewhat *ad hoc* and impermanent structures. There is the suggestion of a more mobile population, or segment of population, than there was later in the Bronze Age. Evidence for seasonal activity comes from the relatively flimsy wooden rectangular 'longhouses' of the Severn Levels, such as at Redwick (near Caldicot, Newport), which can only have been occupied in the summer months and are convincingly seen as taking advantage of salt-marsh grazing (Bell 2013, 160–2). This suggests a pattern of flexible settlement in the Middle Bronze Age for which more substantial constructions were not suited, or were difficult to provide with the available labour. A low wattle-in-trench construction has been suggested for Structure 95 at Brean Down, perhaps without internal roof supports (Bell 1990, 52 and fig. 45).

Nature of the settlement

At Thorny Down the settlement, interpreted as two roundhouses and several ancillary structures, appeared to have occupied a banked enclosure, *c.* 40m in length (Fig. 4.1). The houses (I and V) were defined by irregular

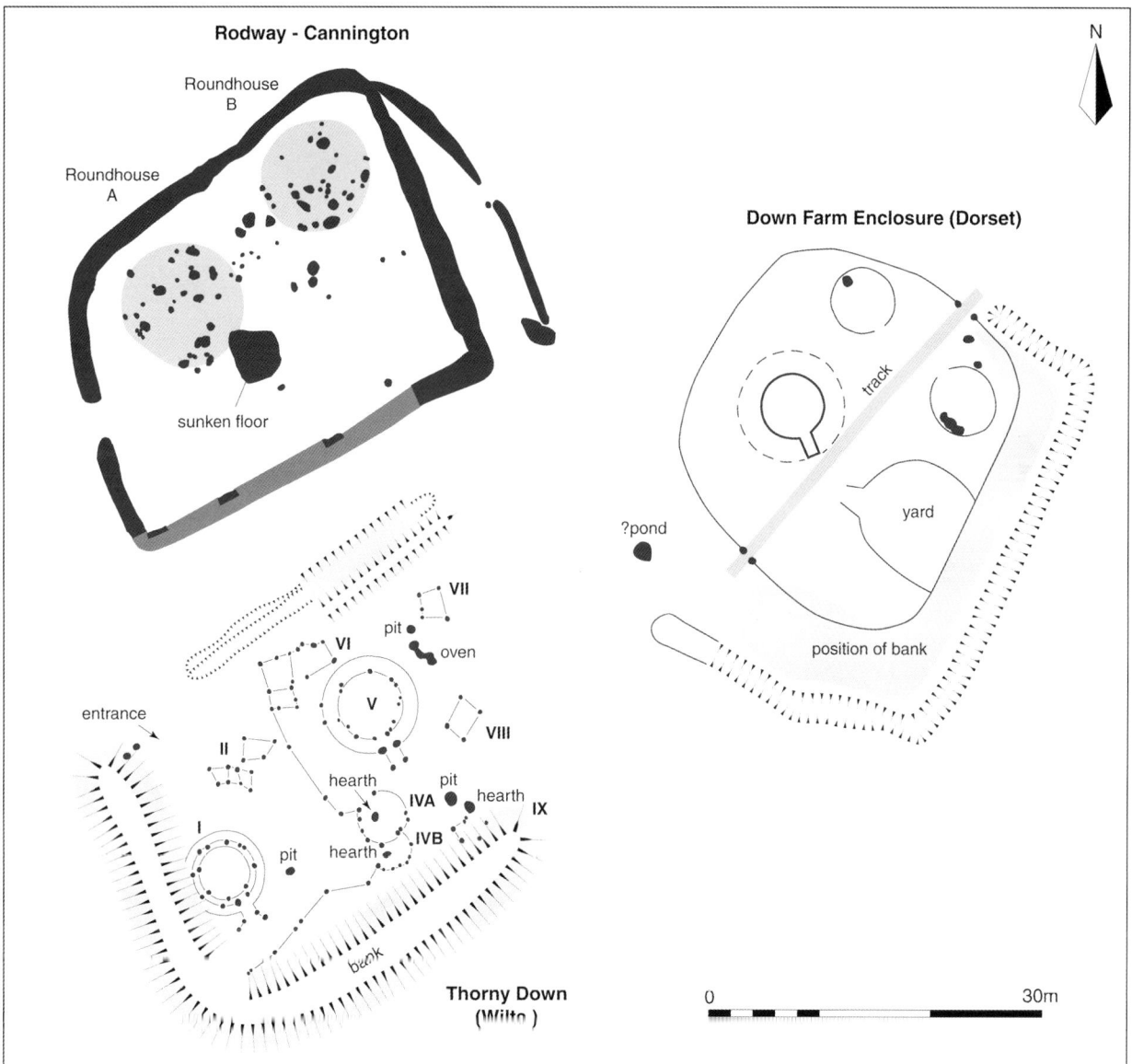

Fig. 4.1 Comparative plans of Middle Bronze Age settlements (Down Farm Enclosure after Barrett et al. 1991, fig. 5.41; Thorny Down after Ellison 1987, fig. 1)

double or triple rings of postholes. While wall lines are extremely speculative, the presence of more substantial entrance porches adds credence to this interpretation. Other structures there were defined by smaller arcs of postholes (Buildings IVA and IVB), in each case containing a pit interpreted as a hearth, and there were several irregular 'four-post' structures, which may have been raised grain stores. Finds distributions were used to suggest the presence of living quarters containing areas of food preparation and crafts, and ancillary buildings for cooking and storage (Ellison 1987, 391). The layout at Rodway is similar in some respects, although there is no clear evidence of above-ground storage or specific 'cooking huts'. It is possible that the sunken 'floor' 10083 with an 'entranceway' facing Roundhouse A has a corollary at Thorny Down, in hut IVA facing House V. A similar situation may be seen at Down Farm in its later phase, with the projecting entrance of the fenced 'yard' facing the principal dwelling on the other side of the enclosure (Fig. 4.1; Barrett *et al.* 1991, fig. 5.41). At South Lodge Enclosure, two structures were identified positioned at the back of a relatively large enclosure, with a possible cooking area to the west indicated by burnt flint (Fig. 4.2; Barrett *et al.* 1991, figs 5.12 and 5.13). Other structures may be suspected from the scatter of postholes and pottery.

Grain storage pits are not generally present in the Middle Bronze Age and large vessels are thought to have been used (Fitzpatrick 2008, 123). Raised granaries are also interpreted from a number of sites although the evidence seems equivocal. Relatively small storage pits are common if not ubiquitous, both inside and outside structures. Their specific purposes are not generally speculated upon, but may have been suitable for crops. Pits 10137 and 10263 in Roundhouse A at Rodway (Fig. 2.2) were steep-sided in the form of grain stores of Middle Iron Age type.

Ellison (1987, 391) saw Middle Bronze Age settlement in southern England as being structured around modules consisting of a major residential house, a smaller ancillary building, and external areas for storage and activity. The Rodway settlement appears broadly compatible with this model, although with relatively few ancillary features. It may best be seen as a single unit (with Roundhouse A or B as the 'major residence', and the other as ancillary) rather than two units as suggested for Thorny Down (Ellison 1987, fig. 2). Drewett's model for Black Patch also saw more than one residence in the typical settlement compound: in this case three of the larger buildings, while two smaller circular buildings were seen as adjacent animal huts (Fig. 4.2; Drewett 1979). Drewett also saw clear distinctions between 'hut 3', with evidence for storage (pits) and crafts (bronze tools, flint flakes, loom weights) and 'hut 1', without any evidence of crafts but with more pottery, perhaps indicating a location for food preparation (ibid., 7–10). The finds from Rodway are relatively meagre and there was no clear patterning, although the slightly higher quantity of pottery and charred botanical remains from Roundhouse A, together with its location closer to the compound entrance, may suggest seniority, if Ellison's model is followed.

The distribution of finds in Roundhouse A was dominated by sherds of a large biconical vessel and a large collection of charred emmer wheat from pit 10031. The sherds represent about a quarter of a vessel originally weighing about 8kg, and are unusual in combining Trevisker-related and biconical stylistic features more common in Dorset (Quinnell, Prehistoric pottery, Chapter 2, this volume). The grain is clean and had been burned following threshing and winnowing. It is difficult to see these deposits as occurring fortuitously and they seemed to have been placed deliberately in combination. It is hard to ignore the visual link between the decoration on the upper part of the vessel and the wheat it was associated with, and presumably would have contained in when in use. The perforation below the rim suggests that the vessel would have been suspended, perhaps a form of raised storage. There is a clear and growing body of evidence for the deliberate interment of materials on Middle Bronze Age sites, particularly in Cornwall where there is evidence of practices relating to the ritual closure of settlements (Nowakowski 1991; 2001). Intentional depositions are also known other parts of the country (Brück 2001b) including recently from Devon at Crablake Farm, Exminster, where a domestic site included a pit containing the body of a large Trevisker vessel (without rim or base) filled with dark earth (Mudd and Joyce 2014, 33–4; Quinnell 2014, 52–3). There are wider comparisons for the breakage, burning and burial of material goods at this time, including the breaking of pots and deliberate burning of grain, which Brück sees as related to commemorations of settlement lifecycles in some ways analogous to the cremation of individuals (Brück 2001b, 152–3). Representations of commemoration or closure rituals do not seem to have been recognised yet in Somerset, but this may well reflect the ambiguous formation processes of much deposited material as well as a lack of excavation on sites of this period. The deposit in pit 10031 at Rodway has a radiocarbon date on cherry wood which, if anything, is slightly earlier than the other dates, and so this particular deposit would not appear to represent a closure deposit for the house or settlement, although it could instead have been a foundation deposit. Another unusual deposit came from pit 10263, also within Roundhouse A, which contained a relatively large collection of burnt flax seeds. While flax must have been widely cultivated its rarity in the archaeological record is assumed to be because it normally did not come into close contact with fire. The deposit may therefore have been deliberately burned. The pit contained an eclectic mix of other botanical remains, including a range of woods (including a rare

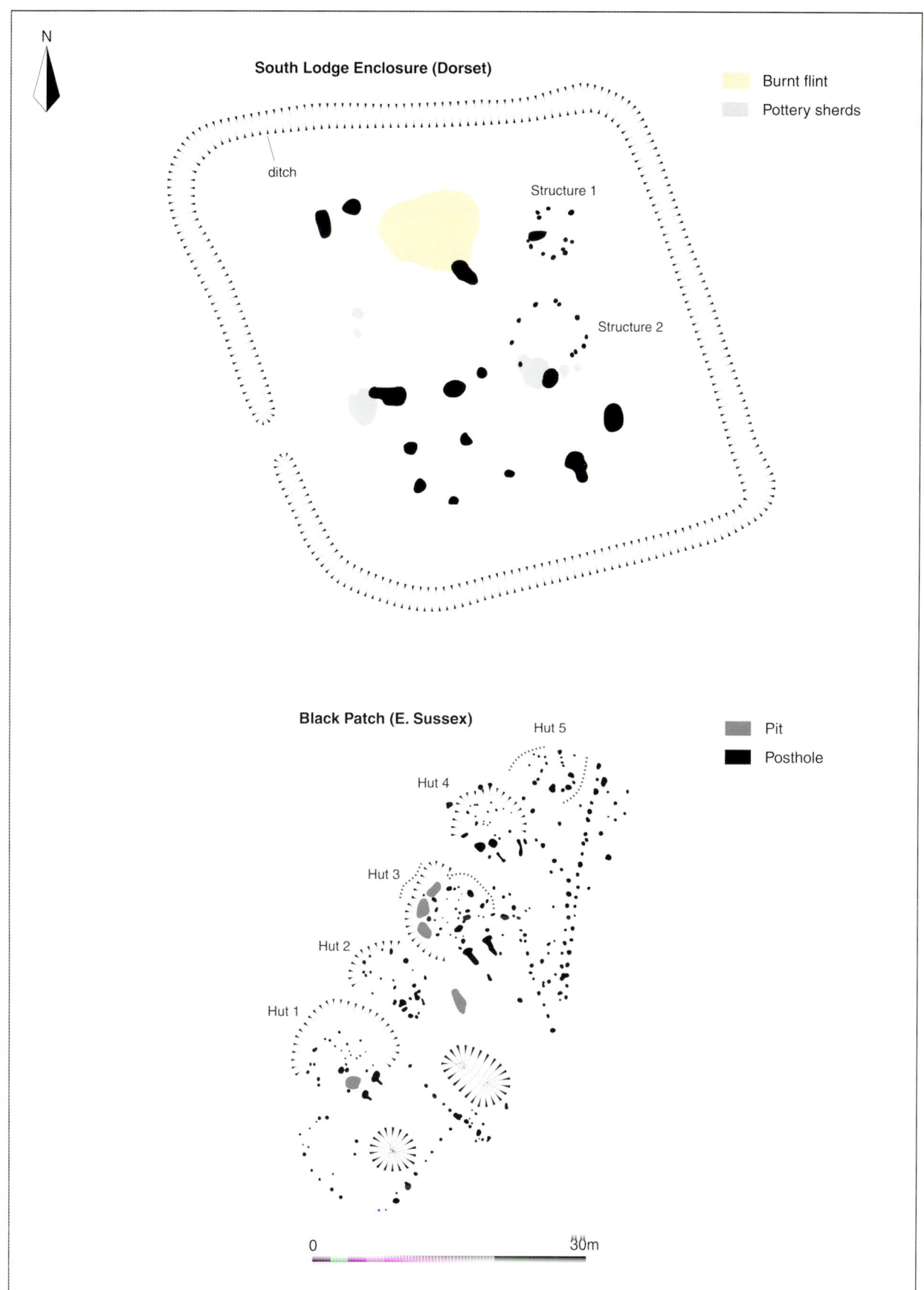

Fig. 4.2 Comparative plans of Middle Bronze Age settlements (South Lodge Enclosure after Barrett et al. 1991, fig. 5.13; Black Patch after Drewett 1979, fig. 1)

occurrence of ivy) and a number of wild plants such as medick/clover and vetch/wild pea. On the face of it, this does not seem to represent a deliberately selected assemblage and the pit perhaps included a mixture of accidently fired crops with weeds, and fuel.

The wider picture

There is little information about the wider pattern of land exploitation and contacts. Bone did not survive sufficiently well to enable an assessment of animal husbandry. There is good evidence that emmer wheat was the main crop grown, with barley also present, and flax and beans perhaps more common than the charred material might suggest. The range of wild plants potentially came from a variety of grasslands, arable fields and mixed woodlands/woodland margins, or perhaps hedgerows. The locally varied geology and landscape hinder an estimation of the range of land exploited, which need not have been particularly extensive despite wide botanical evidence. Similarly, the pottery fabrics, while showing a range of geological sources, may have been procured from deposits quite locally.

At Sandy Lane, 0.6km to the south-west, the rectangular pit or trough 20871 containing burnt stones has radiocarbon dates which overlap with those from Rodway and it may have been associated with the settlement in some manner (Fig. 3.10) The pit is characteristic of the kind of trough associated with burnt mounds, features that are frequently of this date but can be earlier or later. While the interpretations and associations of burnt mounds vary, it is generally accepted that the troughs held water into which stones, heated nearby, were put to produce hot water or steam. The absence of a mound of heated stones and of hearths for heating them at Sandy Lane is unsurprising on such a truncated site, but the siting on a hill-ridge is unusual because of an absence of an obvious water supply. It is possible that a local source of groundwater has since been extinguished. The provision, much later, of numerous land drains in this part of the site does suggest that the land was prone to wetness in more recent times.

The purpose of this type of site remains a matter of debate (for recent résumés of these see Ripper and Beamish 2011, 199–200; and Kenney 2012, 267–9). Theories include sites for cooking, brewing, crafts such as tanning or fulling, and steam bathing. Typically, these sites are poor in archaeological finds except charcoal, and clear evidence to support any interpretation has remained elusive. The siting of Bronze Age burnt mounds at distance from contemporaneous settlement suggests that they were associated with activities that fell outside normal settlement life. Such activities might have included the use of saunas during rituals such as rites of passage, or in relation to communal gatherings and trials of endurance using extreme steam bathing and/or narcotics (see Price 2010, 134, for an example of the former in a Viking funerary context; and Bucko 1998 for the use of sweat lodges during ritual activities amongst the Lakota Sioux).

The trough at Sandy Lane adds to the small corpus of burnt mounds and troughs known from the West Country, a region relatively sparsely represented by recorded examples when compared to others such as south-west Wales (Hart *et al.* 2014a). There are few in Somerset: a mound investigated at Spooner's Moor, in the Somerset part of Exmoor (Oakford Archaeology 2017) adds to those at Bos Swallet, Burrington (ApSimon 1997), and Hort Bridge, Ilminster (Wessex Archaeology 2009). An extensive spread of burnt stone at Cambria Farm, Taunton (SHER 28221), may represent a further example, but awaits full reporting. An example at Autumn Brook, Yate, remains the only example found to date in South Gloucestershire (Leonard *et al.* forthcoming), while known Devonshire examples appear restricted to those at Hayes Farm, Burlescombe and Woodbury Common, all near Exeter (Hart 2014b; Gent 2007; Tilley 2009), and Brendon Common, Exmoor (Wilson-North and Carey 2011).

The distribution of settlements of this date in the area remains unclear in the present state of knowledge. Unstratified, possibly Trevisker-related, pottery from Cannington Park Quarry (Quinnell, Prehistoric pottery, Chapter 2, this volume) suggests a settlement of some kind just 300m or so to the west (Fig. 1.4). A high density of small farmsteads may be expected if their distribution was similar to that in parts of the country where the land is known to have been allotted and densely settled, such as Dartmoor and South Devon, the Lower Exe and Otter valleys, Cranborne Chase and the Dorset Downs (Yates 2007, 110 and fig. 12.2). This kind of density of settlement is not ubiquitous, however, and the evidence from Somerset is at best sporadic (ibid., 71–2). A greater understanding of the context of the Rodway settlement must await further discoveries.

Iron Age and Roman settlement chronology
Andrew Mudd and Jonathan Hart

Aside from the Bronze Age trough and the few prehistoric flints, the earliest activity at Sandy Lane belonged to the later prehistoric enclosed settlement. The earliest radiocarbon dates, 198–47 cal. BC (SUERC-70708) and 198–51 cal. BC (SUERC-69954), came from pit 20324 within (but not necessarily part of) Structure B and from Ditch T of the adjacent Structure A. The dates, which were from charcoal from bulk soil samples, may have come from redeposited material and do not assuredly date the features themselves. These early dates, and the slightly later ones (22 cal. BC–cal. AD 124 (SUERC-72465) from a cattle skull in pit 20106; and 50 cal. BC–cal. AD 70 (SUERC-69953) from a cereal grain in pit 20600) accord with the later prehistoric pottery assemblage, comprising vessels in the south-western decorated style and in transitional plain bead-rim forms, together indicating dating from the earlier 1st century BC to the mid to late 1st century AD. There was no indication of any earlier (Early or Middle) Iron Age occupation.

There is no evidence for a hiatus between the Late Iron Age occupation and that of the Roman period. Although the settlement took on a Romanised appearance, it retained some of the layout apparent in the Iron Age, most notably in the location of the northern boundaries, but also in the choice of building locations, with Roman Building B and, possibly, Building A having overlain the footprints of former Iron Age structures. Roman finds from the upper fills of a number of the Iron Age boundary ditches demonstrate that these remained as earthworks, if not functional boundaries, into the Roman period. In contrast, Roman Building C, located on the southern side of the enclosure, seems to have been built on virgin ground, perhaps as much to make a conscious statement of Romanisation as to take advantage of the location's slightly elevated setting and panoramic views. Continuity is also indicated by the pottery assemblage. The significant proportion of Southeast Dorset Black-burnished ware (DOR BB1) pottery among the Roman ceramics includes forms dateable to the 1st century AD, providing an overlap with the latest 'transitional' pottery (handmade plain-style wares along with a few wheel-thrown 'Belgic' vessels) recovered from the Iron Age features. The indications of continuity are strengthened by those radiocarbon dates spanning the Late Iron Age and Early Roman periods (Fig. 3.36).

Occupation at Sandy Lane, which originated during the 1st or 2nd centuries BC, therefore continued without a break into the Roman period, as far as one can tell. The Roman buildings themselves are poorly dated. Closely dateable finds from foundation deposits associated with Buildings A and B were absent. The cattle skull in pit 20106 provides a general date for what is tempting to see as a foundation deposit for Building B, although it may have been deposited for other reasons.

The dating evidence for the construction of Building C is ambiguous. Layers filling the 'clearance cut' yielded pottery of broadly 2nd to 4th-century date. More precisely, the latest date from the foundation of the gallery suggests a construction in the mid 3rd century or later, although this, based on a single sherd, is unlikely given the consistent range of radiocarbon dates from the infant and sheep burials, whose modelled start date is weighted towards the mid or later 2nd century (Healy, Bayesian analysis, Chapter 3, this volume; Fig. 3.37). The burial deposits appear most unlikely to relate to an earlier building here for there is no trace of one, although it can be noted that the developed form of the villa residence, with an insistence on axial symmetry, is generally a later Roman phenomenon (Scott 1990, 162; de la Bédoyère 1993, 55–68), and from this standpoint the late dating would not be out of place. The other absolute dating for the use of this building comes from the burnt grain and charcoal in later features at the eastern end, and these dates are consistently earlier than the later 3rd century, and so it can be inferred that the building was not only in use by then but probably did not outlive the 3rd century to any significant extent. There are a few fragments of painted plaster of stylistically 1st-century AD date, but this appears anomalous in the context of Building C and the generally later development of villa elaboration in the region. The material is *ex situ* and it is possible that it derived from another building on the site, or that the style itself was old-fashioned at the time.

Abandonment

The latest Roman radiocarbon dates could be as late as the 4th century (cal. AD 217–384 (SUERC-69962) from a charred spelt wheat grain redeposited in a post-Roman ditch; and cal. AD 230–381 (SUERC-72468) from the pit in Building C containing young sheep). However, Oxfordshire and New Forest fineware pottery, wares dateable to the 4th century, were absent from the site and of the two identifiable coins recovered the latest was the radiate of Tetricus II, dateable to AD 270–274. Indeed, the very absence of large quantities of coins is suggestive of dating before the 4th century, after which coins would be expected to be present in significant quantities. Considered together, the evidence therefore suggests that the Roman occupation of the settlement had ceased by the start of the 4th century AD.

The dates of abandonment of individual elements of the villa are, like the founding dates, imprecise. Building A underwent several modifications throughout its life, which are themselves not closely dateable, and appears to have gone out of use by the end of the 3rd century, perhaps even by AD 260 to judge by a radiocarbon date from a puppy burial in the channel hypocaust backfill in Room 2 (SUERC-69960 at 77.4% probability; Table 3.1). This was one of the latest deposits associated with this building and the date is entirely compatible with the pottery from the rubble deposits across Building A, which contained nothing certainly dateable beyond AD 250. From Building B, an Oxfordshire mortarium fragment and an Oxfordshire red-slipped ware beaker, both dateable *c.* AD 240–300 and found within rubble layers associated with the building's disuse, suggest abandonment by AD 300 at the latest. Within Building C, the conical flanged DOR BB1 bowl from wall foundations 20610 indicates occupation (if not rebuilding) after *c.* AD 250. The Bayesian modelling of the human and animal burials along the corridor of Building C suggests that this activity ended *cal. AD 165–385 (95% probability), and more precisely AD 215–305 (68% probability)*, and while it cannot be assumed that this date range equates to the end of life of Building C, it does accord with the overall indications of abandonment by the 4th century (Fig. 3.38).

Design and purpose of the buildings
Andrew Mudd and Jonathan Hart

Later Iron Age Structures A, B and C
The form of Structures A, B and C is uncertain due to the extensive truncation. Only Ditch S of Structure B had a convincing terminal (Fig. 3.6); the other ditches might have terminated approximately as seen on site, or may have been more extensive prior to truncation. It does seem likely however that the ditches formed parts of structures, either as drainage gullies or wall foundation trenches, in either case relating to round or crescent-shaped structures. Taking the former possibility, the projected diameters of the ditches are approximately 14m for Structure A and 9m for Structures B and C, which suggests their sizes if these were wall foundation trenches. Alternatively, if these were eavesdrip gullies, then the wall lines might be expected to have been *c.* 1m inside the gullies. There was no strong evidence for either interpretation. All of these sizes compare well to other published examples of Iron Age roundhouses in Somerset and more widely. Four Middle Iron Age examples at Cannard's Grave, Shepton Mallet, ranged from 10m to 14m in diameter and survived as penannular ditches, although it was uncertain whether the ditches were foundation trenches or eavesdrip gullies (Birbeck 2002, 48–52, 110–11). The late prehistoric and Roman settlement at Huntworth, near Bridgwater, located on the edge of the River Parrett floodplain, was (as at Sandy Lane) highly truncated but included the remains of two to four Iron Age roundhouses dated to the Middle to Late Iron Age (Powell *et al.* 2008). These survived as curvilinear ditch arcs, none greater than *c.* 180° and with the shortest length comparable to the ditch of Sandy Lane Structure C, and were thought to represent the remains of roundhouses 6.5m–11m in diameter (ibid., 71, fig. 2), although it was again uncertain whether foundation trenches or eavesdrip gullies were represented.

The alternative interpretation for the curvilinear ditches at Sandy Lane is that they survived to more or less their full original extents and were the remains of crescent-shaped structures. These would presumably represent sheltered workshops, stores or animal pens, with the ditches having either supported walls, or having provided drainage against walls. Such structures might have been either open or closed-fronted. The finds assemblage from the structures was sparse and so offers little insight into the activities undertaken within them, even to the level of indicating whether these were domestic or working/storage areas, or a mixture of the two. The evidence for partly circular buildings on Iron Age and Roman sites was considered by Drury (1982, 10) with the conclusion that they were probably constructed as screens or fences for animals, or workshops where light and/or easy access were important. Numerous examples have been published since, although there seems to be little conclusive evidence as to the form of these structures or their purposes (Mudd *et al.* 1999, 254). An example from Birdlip Quarry (Glos.) was thought to have had a role in tending horses or cattle on account of the large number of 'hippo sandal' fragments found (ibid., 253 and fig. 4.108).

Structures A, B and C seem to respect one another's location, suggesting that all stood simultaneously. The series of intercutting ditches of Structure B suggests that it had been rebuilt on successive occasions on the same footprint, this in itself suggesting that space here was restricted, probably because Structures A and C were in existence at the same time. The suggestion that all three structures were contemporary is also raised by pit 20106 with the cattle skull (discussed above), which may have been deliberately placed centrally between the structures.

Later Iron Age Structure D
The suggestion that the two parallel features (20608 and 20751) beneath Roman Building A were part of a structure (Structure D) is clearly based on slight evidence, and they may relate to an early phase of Roman construction. Both features had profiles suggestive of beam slots or wall foundation trenches and the Late Iron Age to 1st-century AD pottery suggests, though not with any certainty, that they may relate to a Late Iron Age or Early Roman structure. In their location and dimensions they prefigured Building A and were probably its immediate precursor. There are numerous examples of timber buildings of Early Roman date, such as at Frocester (Glos.), where one apparently had opposed entrances almost centrally on the long side (Price 2000a, fig. 4.14, C4). The spacing of the beam slots for Structure D suggests a narrow central lobby (Fig. 3.9).

Later Iron Age Ditch I
The function of Ditch I, 11m south-west of Structures A, B and C (Fig. 3.6), is uncertain. Its flat-based profile suggests that it may have been a beam slot, comparable to the possible examples of Structure D, with all associated remains lost to quarrying. However, in the absence of associated features, this must remain speculative.

Roman Building A
For the Roman period, given the levels of truncation across the site, it is fortunate that three buildings partially survived, although only one of these, Building A, included anything significant above the lowest foundation courses.

In its original form Building A (Fig. 3.12) was a small rectangular building with a small heated room similar to examples such as the '2nd House' at Yewden, Buckinghamshire (Fig. 4.4). It was presumably for residential and/or agricultural use, and falls within the class of simple rectangular houses of which large numbers have been recorded (Hingley 1989, fig. 15).

Discussion 119

Fig. 4.3   Reconstruction of Sandy Lane Roman villa in its landscape

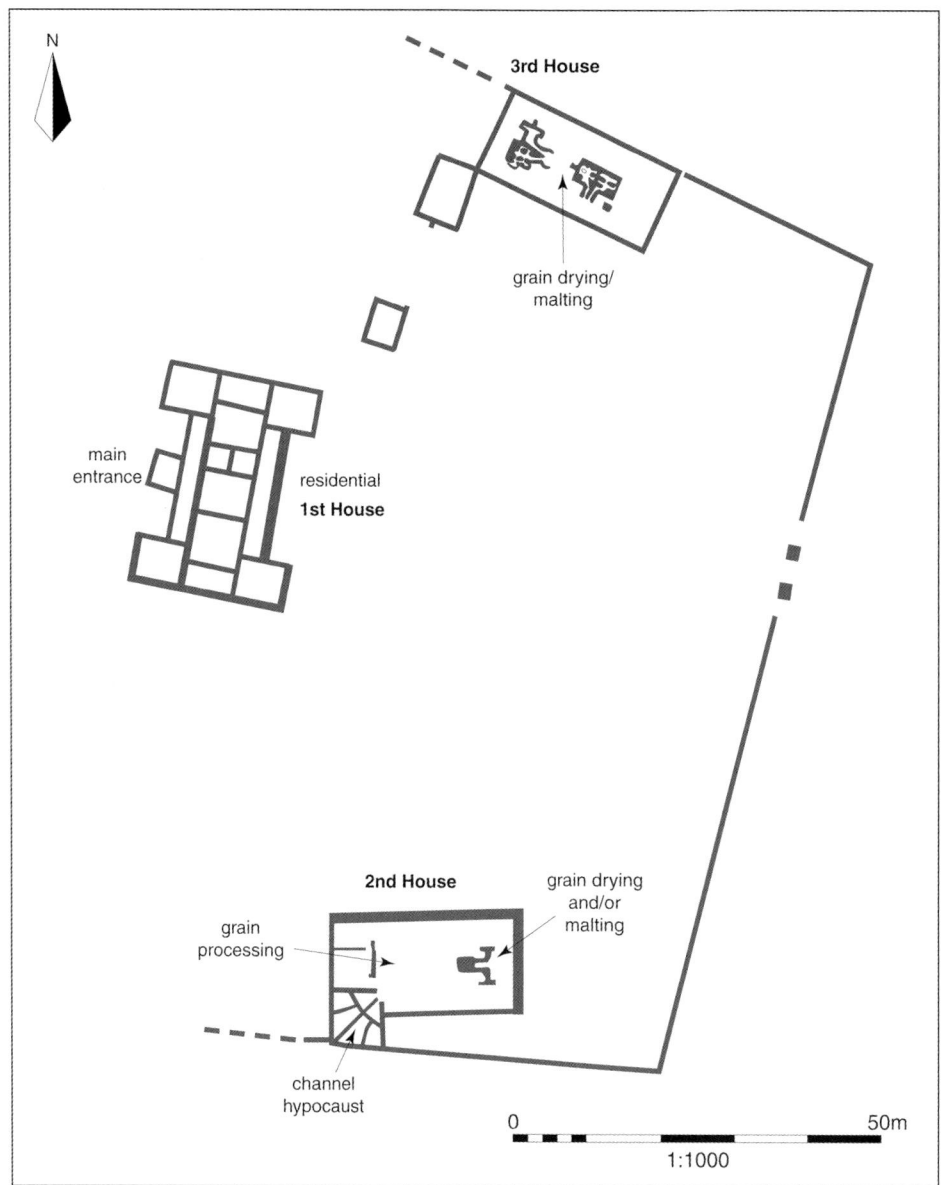

Fig. 4.4 Yewden, Hambleden Valley (Bucks.) Roman villa in 4th century (after Eyers 2011, fig. 3.40)

It may have been built on the footprint of the earlier building (Structure D, above, and Fig. 3.9), although now with shallow stone-rubble foundations probably supporting a timber superstructure. The small corner room may have been provided with heating from the outset, although the surviving channel hypocaust may have been an insertion, to judge by the type of mortar used. At Yewden, the later insertion of a grain drying or malting oven into the main room of the '2nd House' suggests that the building may always have had multiple functions as a residence and for agricultural tasks. The close association of living accommodation with equipment and space for production and storage was subsequently a characteristic of peasant houses in medieval times (Dyer 2013, 22–3).

The addition of Room 3 enlarged Building A to the south and west and it is possible that Room 4 was added to the north at the same time (Fig. 3.14). There was no evidence as to the function of Room 3. While the floor had been dug out to a greater depth than that in Room 1, there was no significant difference in their levels, and so it seems that the intention was to level the natural slope rather than create a sunken room. There was no indication of the room's construction, and this is significant for the overall interpretation of the building, which initially was thought to have included a bath-suite. It is possible that all traces of substructure and floors had been removed, but this would have been a fastidious undertaking. Bath buildings were often extremely solid constructions on stone foundations with

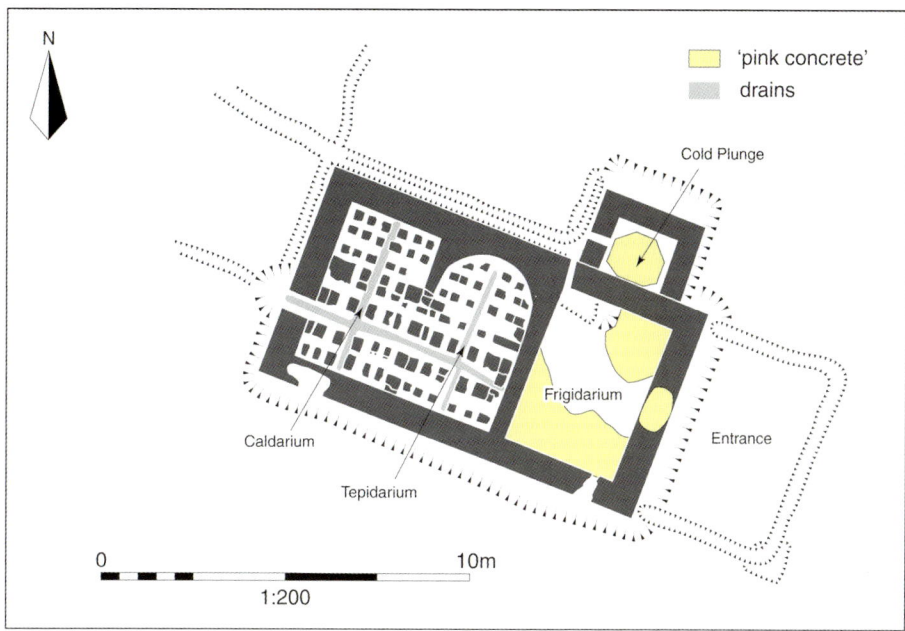

Fig. 4.5   Detached bath-house at Feltwell (Little Oulsham Drove), Norfolk (after Gurney 1986, fig. 10)

concrete floors; for example Building F at Winterton, Lincolnshire, was on rafts of pitched stones forming both floor and wall foundations, 0.76m (2ft 6ins) thick (Stead 1976, 53–4). The 'plunge bath' there had tiles set in *opus signinum* over layers of gravel and sand on heavy stone foundations. Perhaps more crucially the absence of sub-floor drains at Building A suggests that it never provided the full complement of bathing rooms, as prescribed by the Roman cultural norm, and bathing facilities may always have been limited. The small detached bath-house at Feltwell (Little Oulsham Drove) in Norfolk (Fig. 4.5) had drains surrounded by a layer of pink mortar, with tiles capping the drains and a further overlying layer of pink mortar on which the *pilae* were set (Gurney 1986, 13). The overall size of Building A with the addition of Rooms 3 and 4 can only be estimated from the absence of any trace of it north of the quarried area. This indicates that the building would have been no bigger than 11m square and Room 4 may have been quite narrow if its northern wall had been common to that of Room 3 (Fig. 3.14).

Later, Room 3 was shortened and a floor of *opus signinum* laid in the new smaller room (Room 5). It is perhaps significant that the new wall (20473) had been plastered down to the level of this *opus signinum*, indicating that it may have been originally used as a floor rather than simply as a base for the first hypocaust (Fig. 3.21). The insertion of the *pilae* indicates that the floor level was then raised, although it is not clear by how much and how it related to the rest of the building. For the hypocaust to have been accessible for maintenance the floor would have had to have been raised a metre or so, but it is not clear that this would have been considered necessary. There was no vent through from Room 1 into the hypocaust in Room 5 and it seems likely that the new hypocaust received heat from a now lost furnace at the northern end of the building. Another hypocaust in Room 6 to the north of Room 5, and a vent linking them, is perhaps an indication that Room 6 was a hot room (*caldarium*) with Room 5 the warm room (*tepidarium*) in the mode of Roman bathing culture. If the rooms had been kept humid there would presumably have been a boiler above the furnace to provide steam. Alternatively, dry heat only may have been provided (the room termed a *laconicum*). In either case bathing would have been completed with hot or cold water in some form of receptacle, if not in a pool or designated room. For this there is no evidence, although a simple basin (*labrum*) not requiring a drain and which would probably be archaeologically undetectable, may have been provided (Rook 1992, 25). The late 2nd/3rd-century phase of the Gorhambury villa bath-house in Hertfordshire may provide a parallel as this comprised just a furnace and three small rooms (2m to 3m square), two of them with hypocausts; two small later additions with drains were interpreted as 'plunge baths' (Neal *et al.* 1990, 65–6 and fig. 86A).

The superstructure of the heated rooms at Sandy Lane is likely to have been of stone if they were heated by cavity walls. Flue tiles indicate that the heat was carried through the walls to vents in the upper walls or roof, although the evidence is not entirely conclusive since flue tiles are known to have been used for other purposes such as floor supports (Allen 2016, 125–7). The floors were presumably tiled over, perhaps with a layer of concrete on top. There were no voussoirs and the roof is likely to have been tiled – a more straightforward construction than barrel-vaulting.

It is therefore possible that Building A provided a bath-house for at least part of its existence. If so, this seems likely to have been a simple affair, without all the provisions of a full suite of amenities that might be expected in a municipal bath-house or grand villa. The evidence is, however, equivocal since there is widespread evidence that rooms with hypocausts and concrete floors could be provided in a number of situations where heating and solid floors were needed (see Building C, below). There was no specific evidence that any of the rooms of Building A were for drying crops. The charred plant remains from the hypocausts comprised little more than charcoal, although the separation of the rooms from the furnace may have meant little opportunity for the contents to catch fire.

Evidence for the external appearance of Building A was provided by the 'bastard pointing' on the exterior of the surviving wall courses within the eastern part of the building. This decorative technique involves applying incised or impressed lines to the mortar or, as in this case, the render, in order to imitate regularly coursed stonework. Figure 3.18 shows this technique as applied to wall 20473 of Phase 3. Render was applied to the uppermost surviving course and into this a series of points were made, apparently by impressing the side of a trowel-type tool. The technique had been used rather crudely as the edging of the render was messy, and it was not known whether it originally completely covered the stonework, or left the central part of the face of each stone visible. Below the level of the upper surviving course, further pointing had been impressed into the mortar of the pitched stone course, including both pitched and vertical scoring, apparently made by drawing the blade of a trowel through the mortar. A lip at the base of the render above this suggested that the render thickened at the base of the wall, forming a small plinth that covered the pitched stones, indicating that these were used as a form of strong foundations rather than decoratively. The lines scored into the mortar of the pitched stones were therefore probably intended to help the render adhere, whilst that applied to the upper surviving courses was decorative and meant to be visible.

Examples of 'bastard pointing' have been recorded on Roman military and public buildings in Britain including the fort (established in the AD 70s) and amphitheatre (built *c.* AD 90) at Caerleon, where the masonry was dressed and bonded with fine mortar along which bastard joints were ruled with a rounded tool and then painted red (Fig. 4.6; Ward 1911, 257; Wheeler and Wheeler 1928, quoted in Blagg 1996, 14). Incised lines were scored along the pointing of the rear of the town wall at North Hill, Colchester (Hull 1958, quoted in Bidwell 1996, 20) whilst the basilica and forum

Fig. 4.6 Detail of amphitheatre at Caerleon, showing 'bastard pointing' picked out with red paint (from Archaeologia 78 (1928), plate XXXIV 1, by kind permission of the Society of Antiquaries)

at Leicester displayed similar decorative techniques (Hebditch and Mellor 1973, quoted in Bidwell 1996, 20). Given the villa's proximity to the port at Crandon Bridge, where goods (including pottery) may have shipped from Poole Harbour in Dorset to the fortress at Caerleon (Rippon 2008a, 93), it is possible that the owners of the Sandy Lane villa had seen this decorative technique at Caerleon, and had instructed their builders to reproduce the effect.

The final phase of Building A entailed the abandonment and infilling of the hypocaust and the creation of a new floor of *opus signinum* at the level of the floor of Room 1 (Fig. 3.22). The dividing wall between Rooms 5 and 6 was also covered in the process and this therefore seems to have created a single large room, perhaps with the channel hypocaust in Room 1 still functioning. There is no direct evidence for the reasons for this change, which may have been related to developments elsewhere, such as the provision of heated rooms in Building C.

Roman Building B

Although Iron Age Structure A had clearly been demolished in advance of the construction of Roman Building B, the superimposition of their ground plans was so close that some element of continuity, either relating to the use of physical space, or reference to memory, is surely implied.

Nothing survived of Building B above foundation level, and there were few associated finds. The somewhat speculative possibility that pit 20106 marked the foundation of Building B during 22 cal. BC–cal. AD 124 or AD 20–78 (68.2% probability) (SUERC-72465) has been raised above. At ground-floor level, Building B comprised two cells, accessed from the east via paired doors. The cross wall between the rooms might have included an access to the rear (western) room at floor level, and so not visible within the archaeological record. Equally though, the wall may have extended above floor level, providing the rear space with a raised wooden floor, and the few postholes in the northern part of the building closest to the entrance might have supported steps leading to this.

The build above ground level is uncertain but a timber-framed superstructure on stone sill beams and with wattle and daub or plank walls might be envisaged. Very small quantities of ceramic roof tiles might suggest a tiled roof was provided. A puzzling aspect of Building B is the disparity in the depths of the foundation trenches, the southernmost having been dug to some 0.25m greater depth in relation to Ordnance Datum than the rest of the foundations. There seems to be no structural benefit to this; the disparity might therefore simply reflect two different teams excavating the foundation trenches.

There is nothing about the architecture of Building B that gives a good indication of its function, and the singular arrangement of its foundations finds no ready comparisons. The open eastern side may indicate that there was a porch-like access on that side and the hardstanding adjoining the northern side may have been a threshing floor. The associated drain (20300) contained a large quantity of charred cereal remains, mainly of wheat but also oats. The presence amongst these of chaff suggests that they were the remains of semi-cleaned stored grain, conceivably derived from Building B. For these reasons the building is thought to have been a barn. This interpretation also finds support in the assemblage of small field rodents from the drain. Consideration has been given to the possibility that these were the remains of owl pellets, and therefore indicate the presence of roosting owls (Armitage, Animal bones, Chapter 3, this volume). While this neat support for the barn interpretation seems to be countered by the shortage of field voles, which comprise the bulk of the barn owl's diet in present times, it remains possible that the rodents were brought in with the harvest of hay and crops, or were attracted to the building's environment. The assemblage includes shrews, voles and mice, and is similar to that from among the crop of spelt wheat at Bredon's Norton (Gloucestershire) villa, found charred and in situ having collapsed from the upper storey of a sunken stone-floored building that had been destroyed by fire (Nicholson 2016, 1589).

A similar, although not identical, rodent assemblage from Ditch T of the preceding circular Late Iron Age Structure A, taken together with the clear superimposition of Building B, gives a suggestion of continuity of function, implying that Structure A may also have been a barn, of Late Iron Age form. This does not appear to be a recognised function of circular buildings, although there is a strong indication of one at Winterton (Building H) of a later (Early Roman) date (Fig. 4.9). The building, with a projected diameter of 15m, had a 4m-wide stoned entrance with wheel ruts, showing that loaded carts were taken as far as the pitched stone threshold. There was a surviving compacted clay and mortar floor surface and traces of internal plaster on the wall. The virtual absence of foundations to Building H at Winterton implies wooden or mass-walling higher up, which is presumed to have been the case for Structure A at Sandy Lane.

At Sandy Lane the possible threshing floor appears to have been outside Building B, and it is not clear if it was covered, although perhaps some sort of lean-to shelter was provided. The recognition of threshing floors does not seem common, although there was an extremely large one noted at Langton (East Yorkshire), which the rudimentary plan seems to indicate was uncovered, or perhaps within a building with insubstantial foundations (Fig. 4.7; Applebaum 1972, fig. 35, 1734). It is likely that any barn with a solid floor could have been used for threshing and there is a strong indication of one next to the granary at Pitney (Somerset) where the stone floor, 3m-wide doorway and projecting porch provide the important clues (Fig. 4.8).

The purpose of the L-shaped wall foundations immediately south of Building B is unknown (Fig.

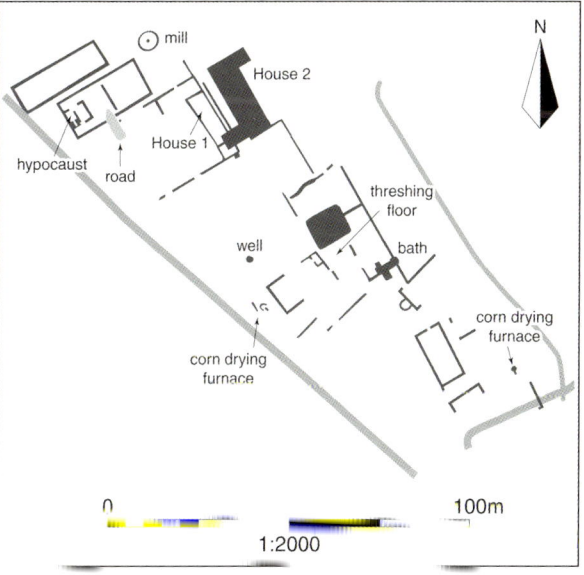

Fig. 4.7 Langton (East Yorkshire) Roman villa (after Applebaum 1972, fig. 35)

Fig. 4.8   Pitney (Somerset) Roman villa (after Applebaum 1972, fig. 38; Haverfield 1906 fig. 83)

3.23). They bore no resemblance to the well-formed walls of crop-drying ovens, and were not found with an associated cut providing a flue, oven and stoke hole.

Roman Building C

Building C, towards the southern edge of the villa compound, would seem to represent the surviving part of a domestic range and in plan is instantly recognisable as a villa residence with rooms attached to a corridor or gallery (Fig. 3.27). Given how little of Building C survived, its overall form, complexity and date range are unclear, and it is not even certain which way it faced. A broadly south-facing aspect might normally be considered as the frontage, maximising the use of light, in which case the square room (1) may have been the base of a grand porch leading to the corridor/gallery (Rooms 2 and 3), with domestic rooms behind, including Room 4 or, if Room 4 was a courtyard, flanking it. More probably, the residence faced northwards into the villa compound, with views towards the river, the sea and Cannington Camp hillfort. The views from a villa residence may generally be connected with the owner's sense of lordship (Smith 1997, 139). Other examples are known from Somerset (Rippon *et al.*, The Sandy Lane villa: its wider context, below) and this north-facing orientation is preferred in the reconstruction of the villa site (Fig. 4.3). The reconstruction also assumes that the villa was a 'hall' type with a front gallery.

As surviving, Room 4 was 12m long and at least 5m wide. While it may be suspected that internal divisions have been lost, and in its original form the building was designed as a 'row-house' comprising a line of smaller rooms, it is perhaps possible that this room was originally an open hall without subdivisions. The nature of the build above foundation level is uncertain. The scrappy nature of the stonework suggests that the walls were low ones supporting a timber superstructure, and there was no difference between the structures of Rooms 2, 3 and 4. In order for light to have entered Room 4 from the south, it is suggested that it would have had high 'clerestory' windows, even if it was not two floors high. The reconstruction therefore has Room 4 of greater height than the gallery rooms (Fig. 4.3). The roofing was wholly or partially of ceramic tiles, almost 10kg of which were recovered from associated deposits, despite the levels of truncation. Just a single stone roof tile was recovered from this building. The flue tile fragments from the building suggest that some rooms were heated, although only 3.6kg were found and no hypocausts survived in the area examined. A possible chimney pot fragment (Fig. 3.42) also suggests the heating of rooms, with its base suggestive of fitting a roof ridge, and its ornamental rim indicating a more decorative use than, for example, for a kiln or oven. Fragments of painted wall plaster suggest plain, foliate and figurative designs decorated at least some of the rooms, although none of these designs can be reconstructed due to the high levels of fragmentation. The fragments mostly came from dumped rubble deposits rather than *in situ* collapse; it is of course impossible to be certain that these deposits relate to the rooms in which they were found, but the largest number of plaster fragments came from a single dumped layer, 20626, in Room 4, suggesting either that these came from decorative panels within that room, or that they were a dump of fragments cleaned from robbed stonework by working parties using Room 4 as a convenient working area.

Room 1 appears to have been positioned centrally with respect to the southern façade, perhaps designed to emphasise its importance. Originally, the room was *c.* 2.2m by 3m internally but the southern wall was replaced, apparently entirely to judge by the internal facing stones on the new wall. This increased the size of the room to 3m square, providing minimal extra space for the effort involved, and it is possible that the reconstruction was a structural necessity, perhaps to provide or repair an upper storey. The purpose of this small room is not self-evident. In many of the larger villas the room occupies the position of what is seen as the dining room at the rear of the residential range, and often the location of elaborate mosaic floors. The size of Room 1 makes this interpretation unlikely in the extreme and its dating is also early for this kind of elaborate arrangement. At Yewden the 4th-century villa residence or '1st House' (Eyers 2011, fig. 3.40) had a room here of identical size to that at Building C, which was considered to have been an entrance porch or lobby (Fig. 4.4). This was interpreted as facing outwards, away from the farmyard, presumably to present a face to the outside world. A similar explanation is possible for the arrangement at Sandy Lane, although the room is large for an entrance porch, which in other villa contexts, are of more modest proportions, forming small adjuncts to the gallery without a dividing wall. There are examples at Gadebridge Park III, Hertfordshire (reproduced in Smith 1997, figs 13, 20), Bancroft, Milton Keynes (in de la Bédoyère 1993, fig. 57) and at Shakenoak, Oxfordshire (Brodribb *et al.* 2005, fig. 11.4). The difficulty of interpreting this room is shown at Gorhambury, Hertfordshire, where its interpretation as a central porch entailed re-orienting the building to face away from the courtyard that it had faced in the preceding phases (Neal *et al.* 1990, 57, fig. 73). Similarly, at Winterton Building G, this room was of identical size to those at Sandy Lane and Yewden, and slightly smaller than that at Gorhambury, and was the destination of a metalled roadway through the 'courtyard' (Fig. 4.9). The excavator considered this to have been an entrance porch, and it gave immediate access to a gallery linking what appear to have been a residential block to the south and a service area with ovens to the north (Stead 1976, 197). Subsequently, in Phase 2, the room was partly rebuilt with a larger apsidal addition nearly 6m by 9m in size, which the excavator interpreted as a conventional Roman *triclinium* (dining room). This interpretation demands that the room was now to the rear of the gallery, and therefore required that Building G now faced south-west, away from the courtyard. Such a re organisation is awkward and not entirely convincing, but of interest is the clear significance of this room which formed the original focal point for approaching and entering this villa building. J.T. Smith considered that it probably housed a shrine (Smith 1997, 166).

Room 1 is also similar in size to a small room at Pitney, located away from the villa residence, which has been seen as a grain store, mainly on the basis of external buttresses which suggest a military-style granary raised to two storeys (Applebaum 1972, 179–81 and fig. 38; Black 1981, 163; Fig. 4.8). There was a similar building at Gorhambury that was free-standing (Neal *et al.* 1990, fig. 52). It has been suggested Room 1 was two storeys high, perhaps made so by the rebuild of the southern wall, and there is an L-shaped beam slot that may have held a wooden stair, and so it is considered possible that this room was a granary with an upper floor.

In a wider discussion about agricultural storage, Black (1981) has drawn attention to the high structural specification recommended for agricultural stores in the Roman world, particularly for rooms at ground level, as opposed to raised stores. The former ideally required treated and sealed floors and walls. Columella, writing in around AD 60, describes the attention needed in the preparation of proper storage, which is worth considering in the light of what was undoubtedly one of the major concerns of farmers at this time, as in previous and subsequent eras:

> And I am not unaware that some consider the best place for storing grain to be a granary with a vaulted ceiling, its earthen floor, before it is covered over, dug up and soaked with fresh and unsalted lees of oil and packed down with rammers as is Signian work. Then, after this has dried thoroughly, it is overlaid in the same way with a pavement of tiles consisting of lime and sand mixed with oil lees instead of water, and these are beaten down with great force by rammers and are smoothed off; and all joints of walls and floor are bound together with a bolstering of tile, for usually when buildings develop cracks in such places they afford holes and hiding-places for underground animals … The walls are coated with a plastering of clay and oil lees, to which are added, in place of chaff, the dried leaves of the wild olive or, if these are wanting, of the olive. Then, when the aforesaid plastering has dried, it is again sprinkled over with oil lees: and when this has dried the grain is brought in. This seems to be the most advantageous method of protecting stored produce from damage by weevils and like vermin, and if it is not carefully laid away they quickly destroy it.
>
> Columella *De Re Rustica* Book 1

Black suggested that the Pitney granary, which was provided with a floor of *opus signinum* may well have followed the practice of raised and ground-floor storage in the same building. There are numerous examples of

126 *Cannington Bypass, Somerset: Excavations in 2014*

Fig. 4.9 Winterton Roman villa (Lincolnshire) (after Stead 1976; Hingley 1989, fig. 34)

villa rooms and buildings with raised and solid floors, among them those in Building A at Sandy Lane. It is clear that Columella's recipe need not have been carried out exactly, and olive oil would presumably have been unavailable in any quantity (notwithstanding the presence of Baetican amphorae among the limited imports at Sandy Lane), although the principle of making pest-proof floors, walls and the junctions between them may well have been followed in a number of ways within local capacities and traditions.

Black also drew attention to rooms at the southern end of the aisled building at Darenth (Kent) with massive 'corn dryers' (Rooms 3 and 4) occupying a space of about 7m by 8m, and a large (14m-long) adjacent room (Room 5) with a solid *opus signinum* floor and traces of *opus signinum* internally on one of the walls (Philp 1973, 128–30; Black 1981, 164). If the evidence is being read correctly, it implies the provision for the large-scale drying and storage of produce in this part of the villa complex. Similar kinds of evidence may be seen at the western end of Winterton Building B, where concrete floors were provided. In Room 2 an early concrete floor was dug through to hold joists for a raised timber floor, perhaps a storage area for crops (Morris 1979, 33) (Fig. 4.9). The hypocaust added in Room 6 was considered to have been used for drying grain (Black 1981, 165; Stead 1976, 92). At Langton, a barn, which was apparently larger than the main residence in the early phase of settlement, was provided with a hypocaust at the southern end (Fig. 4.7). This seems likely to have been for drying crops, brought in through the 3m-wide paved entrance, rather than for a bath-room (as suggested by Applebaum 1972, 171–4, fig. 35).

The efficacy of rooms with hypocausts and solid floors for the purpose of drying grain is far from clear. The Butser experimental grain-dryer showed that having an impermeable floor, obstructing the through-flow of air, made the operation very inefficient and doubts were raised as to whether it was ever practical (Reynolds and Langley 1979; Lodwick 2017, 57–8), although it did prove effective when the grain was spread thinly (Reynolds and Langley 1979, 39). Presumably manually turning the grain would also help and it is possible that a relatively large floor area was a solution to drying crops on a solid floor, and perhaps a reason for the construction of some exceptionally large dryers (e.g. Lodwick 2017, 57, figs 2.43 and 2.44). There is also evidence that floors of corn dryers were made of potentially more permeable material such as wood (Lodwick 2017, 57–8) although generally this evidence is lacking. In any case it seems that the advantage of increasing the permeability of a floor to circulate warm air would need to be balanced against the potential loss of the crop falling through it.

It may be considered that a solid floor with a hypocaust could also provide a place to store the crops as well as dry them, although storage would require cool as well as dry conditions (Morris 1979, 32) and one would need to assume that heating was used only sparingly to repel damp. There is a certain amount of evidence that grain was stored in (or perhaps above) rooms with hypocausts and solid, sometimes tessellated, floors (ibid., 35–6). Cellars are also sometimes seen as store rooms and suitable because of their coolness, and grain has been found in some. The cellar 'store room' at Barton Court Farm, Oxfordshire, had a tessellated floor (Miles 1986, fig. 10). Preserved grain at Bredon's Norton lay on a flagged floor having fallen from an upper storey when the building caught fire (Allen *et al.* 2016). While the building was seen as a bath-house reused as a barn or granary, the interpretation is not altogether convincing and it is perhaps possible that this was an agricultural complex. At Frocester Court, Gloucestershire, the late 3rd-century villa building had a probable buttressed tower at the north-east end of the gallery, originally with a floor of *opus signinum* through which a channel hypocaust had been inserted (Price 2000a, 99; Fig. 4.10). This was possibly a granary, originally with a ground floor designed to be pest-proof and later one with a capability of keeping produce dry. The corresponding room at the south-western end of the gallery at Frocester appeared to have been for crop processing and contained a 'drying kiln' (ibid., 95). The ground floor appeared to have been almost entirely given over to food production and other agricultural and related tasks, an arrangement that Price saw as being made possible by the provision of living accommodation on a 2nd and even 3rd floor, a possibility suggested by the extremely deep foundations (2.7m) of the central row of rooms. It seems, therefore, that in some cases the main residential building was the location of many activities associated with running the farm.

At Sandy Lane the evidence for grain processing at the eastern end of the gallery of Building C gives some indication that this was a part of the building dedicated to agricultural production in the 2nd/3rd centuries. While the grain came largely from features associated with Building D and phased to the post-Roman period, the radiocarbon dating shows that this material was largely redeposited from the earlier occupation (Wyles, Charred plant remains, Chapter 3, this volume; Fig. 3.36). The grain comprised mostly spelt wheat, but included free-threshing wheat, emmer, and barley in smaller quantities. They were found with large amounts of chaff, and reflect a range of processes undertaken close to or within Building C. These processes would have started with harvested crops being brought in and stored, before being threshed and winnowed, and then dried (Hillman 1981). The grain may then have been sieved and stored in a dry, probably raised area, within their spikelets (in the case of spelt and emmer). When these stored grains were required for cooking, they would have been pounded to release the grains from the glumes ready for grinding. All these stages are potentially represented by the grains and chaff found on that side of Building C. There is an alternative possibility, that the remains represent stored cereals charred in a house fire, rather than the occasional loss of produce during drying and cooking. However, there is a strong representation of weeds and chaff, which is similar to processing waste, and moreover, the wood charcoal shows a mixture of fuel-like species, rather than construction timbers. In either case, the implication of the charred cereal remains is that the eastern side of the villa range included crop

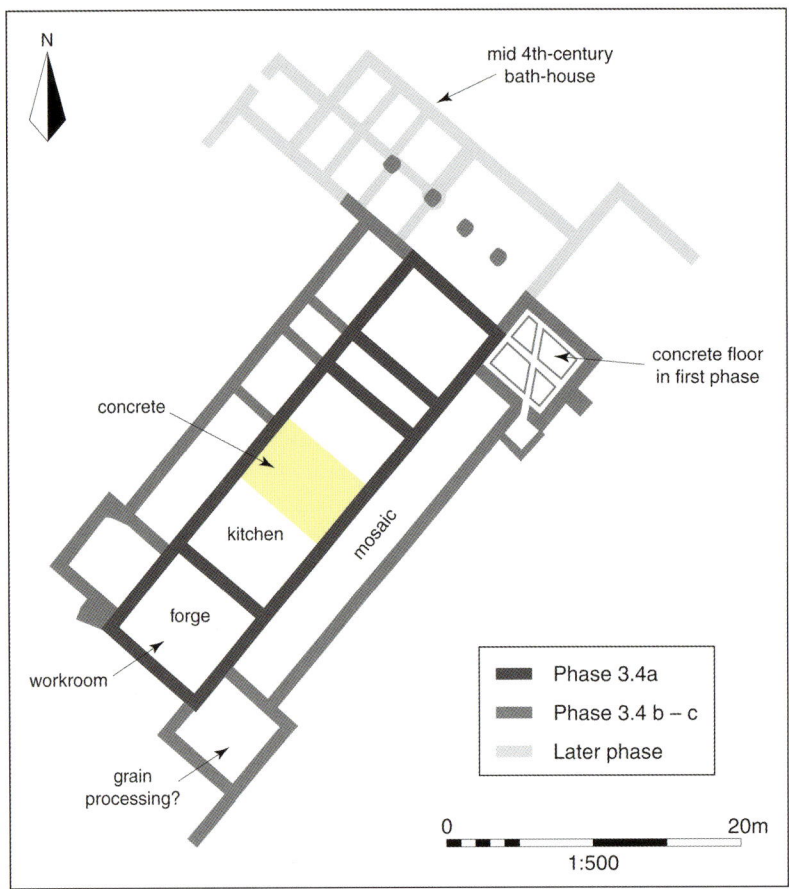

Fig. 4.10   Frocester Roman villa (Gloucestershire) (after Price 2000a, fig. 5.3)

storage areas along with crop-drying ovens and, probably, a kitchen. This probably corresponds to activities in a number of other villas such as Winterton Building G and Frocester (Figs 4.9 and 4.10).

This consideration of the function of Room 1 of Building C has led to the view that it may well have been a raised granary, designed to impress as well as to be functional. Its position with respect to the rest of Building C was conditioned by the architectural demand for symmetry, and, as with other villas, ergonomic convenience (in the form of interconnectedness with related agricultural processes) was to some degree sacrificed to the demand for architectural conformity. The architectural form of the villa should not, however, conceal its main functions which were connected with agricultural production, and reviewing some of the published evidence, it seems likely that many buildings and rooms can be viewed in this light, despite an adoption of Roman construction techniques that may suggest an aspiration to specifically Roman cultural practices. The demonstration of status was probably as much to do with the display of a successful farming enterprise as it was to the need to affiliate to the ruling elite. Villa display in the Roman world, with a concomitant provision of reception rooms, has been linked to the need for local elites to receive and entertain outsiders, and in particular officials assessing production and collecting taxes (Scott 1990, 164–5). This may have been a major motive behind the architectural conformity of Building C. As far as one can tell from their plans, Buildings A and B at Sandy Lane showed less concern with appearance, although Roman construction techniques were employed as needed. The bastard pointing on Building A may also be seen as imitating and thereby wanting to align with Roman authority, as exemplified in military and public constructions.

The character of the Iron Age and Roman occupation
Andrew Mudd and Jonathan Hart

The farm and economy
There is little direct information concerning the Late Iron Age occupation. The total area of the settlement and the number of structures it contained are not known, although the lack of Iron Age finds to the south of the quarry suggest that it was somewhat smaller than it became in the Roman period. There were no unusual finds to suggest a particular status, although the relatively frequent occurrence of pig bones

is noteworthy in the southern British Late Iron Age, where it has been strongly correlated with high status (Armitage, Animal bones, Chapter 3, this volume; Grant 2002, 83). This is one indication that the villa here developed from an establishment that belonged to a pre-Roman farmer of some rank; the enclosure itself may be another. The pigs were slaughtered during their prime meat-bearing years, between six and thirty months, the most economically viable period when the animals have reached a productive level of meat-bearing maturity but are killed off before requiring further feed (Hambleton 1999, 69). The consumption of pork has been seen as a Roman or 'gallicised' taste (King 1999; Cool 2006, 82–4). However, it may be more basically related to food supply and, in the present context, the social obligations of the owner to provide food for guests at any moment and thereby win clients, favours and prestige. An 8th-century Irish text, *Crith Gablach*, refers to the boar 'which removes dishonour at every season', while a 7th-century text *Andacht Morainn* describes a pig as 'the freeing of shame of every face' (Kelly 2000, 84). Both express the sentiment of being able to provide a feast when obliged to and thereby avoid dishonour (ibid.).

Typical of the southern British Late Iron Age pattern, the most common farm animals were sheep, although cattle were also a major component of the livestock. Cattle could also contribute a greater amount of meat, although those found were older animals, suggesting most were kept for dairying, breeding and traction rather than primarily for meat (Hambleton 1999, 87). The importance of other animal products, including milk, wool and hides, and manure to support arable farming, should not be overlooked. Cattle and sheep may have been grazed on the high ground of the Quantock fringe, but the Levels below would have been favourable to summer sheep-grazing, since the salt marsh would have helped prevent common ailments of sheep, such as liver fluke and foot rot because of the salt content of the soil (Thirsk 1967; Stallibrass 1996 quoted in Rippon 2008a, 133). A similarly high proportion of sheep was noted at the Roman settlement at Crandon Bridge (ibid., in Rippon 2008a, 133; Fig. 4.11). It is possible that this was a regional Iron Age pattern that became more widespread with later flood prevention and drainage projects, although at present firm evidence for this is lacking.

Crops included spelt wheat, emmer wheat, barley and Celtic beans, amongst which were the remains of cereal chaff, indicating that the grains were brought into the settlement in an unprocessed or semi-processed state. Charred weed seeds found alongside the cereals reflect the variety of areas exploited for arable production, including lighter drier soils, presumably from the higher ground, and wetter areas, perhaps along the valley floor. The varied topography and soils of the immediate area appear to be reflected in these remains. The presence of seeds from twining species, such as bindweed, and low-growing species such as clover, likely reflect the use of sickles to harvest the cereals and beans close to the soil surface, with the whole plant harvested.

The inhabitants also kept a few domestic fowl, but do not seem to have hunted or fished. A dog bone from Structure A reveals the presence of these animals as pets or working dogs, while the bone from a young horse suggests either breeding on site, or the importation of young animals. Other horse bones were from more mature animals which could have been used for draught or transport.

The economy of the Roman villa reflects continuity from the Iron Age settlement, with cattle and sheep/goat being bred, slaughtered, butchered and consumed. As before, the greater numbers of sheep would have been offset by the larger size (and therefore meat values) of the cattle, although many of the latter were again consumed in old age, having been kept primarily for dairying and breeding, with oxen (specifically identified) for draught. Horses were also used for draught/transport and one of these showed evidence of having been skinned, although gnaw marks on one horse bone suggest that parts were used as dog food. As before, a few fowl were kept, probably bantam-sized birds. The meat diet may have been supplemented on occasion by hunted game and fowl, and fish, but these seem to represent a negligible part of the diet, and these animals are probably more reflective of leisure or social pursuits of hunting and fishing. The dogs kept by the Roman period inhabitants might have been family pets or working/guard dogs. The cat found in Building A might also represent a family pet kept to reduce vermin attracted to farm buildings.

The pattern of animal husbandry is different to that in other parts of the country, where the accumulated evidence shows that cattle predominated almost everywhere (Smith *et al.* 2016), not only in the Central Belt but also the East and South (ibid., figs 5.50, 5.51, 6.34, 4.62). The dominance of cattle seems to be particularly marked on villas, and in the Central Belt cattle comprise 51% of bones of major livestock, with 32% sheep and 17% pig (ibid., fig. 5.51). By contrast the Sandy Lane assemblage comprises 36% cattle, 54% sheep and 10% pig (Armitage, Animal bones, Chapter 3, this volume), actually closer to the 'enclosed farmstead' than the 'villa' in that region. The proportions are closest to those found from the Cotswolds sub-region of the Central Belt (Smith *et al.* 2016, fig. 5.50) although the published data are not broken down by settlement type. The marked decline of pig at Sandy Lane is also similar to the trend in the Cotswolds where nearly 20% pig in the Late Iron Age falls to less than 10% in the 2nd/3rd century (ibid.). The fall elsewhere is less marked. The observed patterns are difficult to account for in any simple way, although it is clear that there was much variability of practice within modern categories of site type and region.

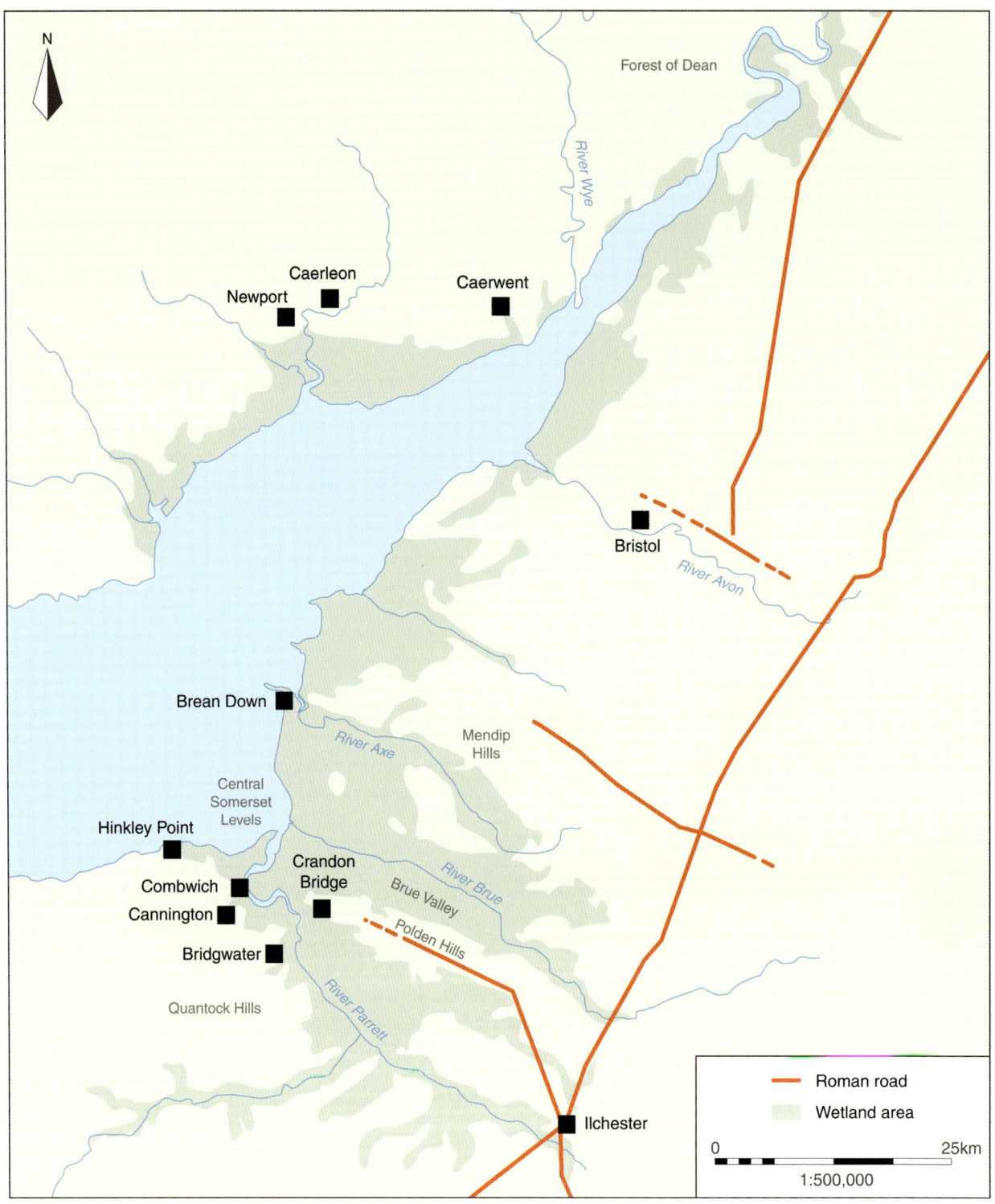

Fig. 4.11   Cannington in the context of Roman north Somerset

It is not known how much of the farm produce was sold, or where, but the nearest market may have been the Roman town of *Lindinis* (Ilchester). *Lindinis*, some 13km distant, could have been reached via the road leading from the Roman port at Crandon Bridge, which crossed the Levels along the higher ground of the Polden Hills (Fig. 4.11; Margary 1973, map 11 route 51). An additional important market may have been accessible across the Bristol Channel at Caerleon, where the legionary fortress was supplied with pottery from the Poole Harbour industries in Dorset via ships which may have sailed from Crandon Bridge (Rippon 2008a, 93).

The overall layout of the villa enclosure is not entirely clear, but it seems to have expanded from its Iron Age origins. Enclosure ditches were dug a little further down the slope on the north side, although they would have provided little more space. It is possible that the original banks were levelled as a requirement of the Roman administration (Scott 1990, 165) to be re-dug at a later date. The hollow-ways leading north would have continued to link grazing and other resources on the valley floor with the villa itself and farmland on the higher ground to the west. Enclosures to the south seem also have been used for livestock, as suggested by the possible stock race, a feature facilitating the inspection of sheep. The sheep may have been grazed on both grassland and cultivated fields, both of which would have benefited from their manure. As in the Iron Age, the fields produced spelt wheat, supplemented by emmer wheat and, possibly, barley with oats and free-threshing wheat also present. The Celtic beans may also have been a crop, with flax used for its seed, fibre or oil, although both less susceptible to preservation by being charred. This range is comparable to other southern British Roman sites, including Steart Point, 5.4km to the north-east (Higbee and Mepham 2017).

As elsewhere in southern Britain at this time, the land was probably highly managed, with arable and grazed fields demarcated with hedgerows and perhaps ditch/bank boundaries, the land dotted with small stands of woodland. There is some indication of this from the weed seeds and the small creatures found around the villa (voles, shrews and mice) which it is suggested may have arrived with the harvests of hay and crops. The various species included those of woodland, hedgerows and grassland, field margins and arable environments. Some associated with wetter environments may have derived from fields on the valley floor, or perhaps came from plants growing along ditched field boundaries. There is no evidence for the immediate farmed landscape, although south of Cannington geophysical survey and selected excavation in connection with the Cannington Flood Alleviation Scheme has revealed extensive fields and enclosures apparently on the margins of settlement, as well as probable 'ladder settlement' (Fig. 1.1) (CA 2018).

There was little evidence of industry and non-agricultural activities although the villa inhabitants undertook some blacksmithing, as indicated by both hammerscale and smithing hearth cakes. These residues were too dispersed to identify the locations of any smithies. It is worth noting that coal was widespread across the Roman (and later) deposits, albeit in small quantities which suggests intrusiveness, although coal may have been the fuel used for smithing. Coal is not uncommon on Roman sites and in this region may have been shipped from the Forest of Dean or the Somerset coalfields to Crandon Bridge (Rippon 2008a, 135).

The Sandy Lane villa was materially poor. The pottery (55kg including the Late Iron Age wares) comprised mainly jars, with coarseware bowls and dishes also noteworthy and perhaps suggesting the feeding of a workforce (McSloy, Iron Age and Roman pottery, Chapter 3, this volume). There were very few finewares or continental imports, although amphorae, made as wine and olive oil containers, were present. There were relatively few metal objects; 124 out of 217 iron objects were carpentry nails, and there were just three coins, and two other copper-alloy objects: a brooch and tweezers (Fig. 3.45). It is difficult to be sure how far this paucity can be attributed to the degree of truncation, although a comparison of the limited number of these finds with those from other sites in the Central Belt (Smith *et al.* 2016), expressed in numbers per hectare, shows that Sandy Lane is very unlike other villas (Table 4.1). The bald numbers make the site far more similar to a farmstead or enclosed farmstead. The villa at Gorhambury yielded around ten times the amount of pottery, and proportionally the numbers of other finds also appear to have been higher (Table 4.1). There were many other items from Gorhambury, replicated from many other villas, but not represented

Table 4.1: Quantity of object types by settlement category expressed as mean number of objects per hectare of excavation (from Smith et al. 2016, table 5.5, figures rounded to nearest whole number; with Sandy Lane and Gorhambury [Neal et al. 1990] for comparison). Both Sandy Lane and Gorhambury lie within the Central Belt defined in Smith et al. 2016. Gorhambury coins exclude 4th-century and Iron Age denominations. Areas of excavation: Sandy Lane 0.75ha (excluding quarrying); Gorhambury 1.8ha.

Object type	Roadside settlement (59 sites)	Villas (72 Sites)	All farmsteads (474 sites)	Complex farmsteads (98 sites)	Enclosed farmsteads (65 sites)	Sandy Lane villa	Gorhambury villa
coin	427	358	10	12	5	3	123
brooch	28	28	2	2	2	1	26
knife/tool	11	22	2	1	3	1	21
cosmetic/toilet item	9	11	<1	1	<1	1	22
pottery (kg)	-	-	-	-	-	73	717

at Sandy Lane at all – bracelets, pins, mounts, spoons, locks, keys, styli, glass vessels, and iron tools such as axes, chisels, ploughshares, goads and the like. While there are difficulties with strict inter-site comparisons (there are no quantifications of the volume of deposits excavated for example) the disparities are a strong indication that Sandy Lane was unlike most other sites in the category of villa. The shortage of coins is perhaps the greatest discrepancy seen from these figures, perhaps suggesting a lack of engagement in monetised trade. The shortage of all types of artefact, rather than simply what might be termed luxury items of dress and display, is curious but not unusual. Utilitarian agricultural and craft implements and tools (including querns) are also limited. It appears that the inhabitants made use of fewer material goods generally, and perhaps took more care of what they did have, with the recycling of iron a possible strategy.

Cannington villa overlooks an area used for salt production during the Roman period. This area, north of the River Parrett, along the marshes of the Huntspill River and the palaeo-river known as the *Siger* (Rippon 2008a, 92), has produced numerous archaeological remains of salt production sites and the salt may well have been transported along the River Parrett from Crandon Bridge (ibid., 136). Salt would have been essential for both the preparation and preservation of food and some of the locally produced salt would no doubt have been brought to Cannington villa. However, physical evidence for this was absent: briquetage, a ceramic type used in the production of salt, does not seem to have been used for its transportation, either in Somerset or more widely across the province, and so the use of some other vessel types must be suspected for its transportation. In north Kent, shell-tempered vessels may have been used initially, with BB2 jars perhaps used from the 2nd century onwards (Booth 2017, 73). At Cannington, it is not known what vessel types might have been used, and transport in non-ceramic containers is also possible.

Infant burials and symbolic deposition
The discovery of infant burials at Sandy Lane is unsurprising in view of their well-established association with Roman rural settlement where they are often located within and around buildings (Esmonde Cleary 2000; Pearce 2013; Millett and Gowland 2015). This contrasts with the burial locations of older children and adults, which tend to be at boundaries or in small burial plots towards the margins of settlement. It has been suggested that young infants were not accorded the same burial rites as adults because of their lack of a social persona (Esmonde Cleary 2000, 135), while Millett and Gowland (2015, 185) see the placement of infant burials within the settlement as reflecting a need to sustain the infant's link with the family. There is a continuing debate as to whether infant burials might be the result of selective infanticide, particularly where the numbers of neonatal/perinatal deaths are larger than would be expected from normal mortality, as suggested for the Yewden (Hambleden, Buckinghamshire) villa (Mays *et al.* 2011, 252). This view has been challenged, as has the notion that infants were simply disposed of, rather than being placed as the focus for commemorative rites (Millett and Gowland 2015; Scott 1991). The Sandy Lane perinatal infants can contribute little to the debate about infanticide, although the identification through aDNA of two boys and two girls suggests the expected ratio of a normal deceased population, rather than any selection against females, as has sometimes been claimed for Roman Britain and the wider Empire (Millett and Gowland 2015, 172).

There is difficulty in understanding the social rules governing infant burials. Their frequent location in and near buildings connected with agricultural production, and also near corn dryers and malting ovens, suggests some association with fertility and regeneration (Scott 1991, 118). There are also frequent associations with animal burials, and there are several cases similar to the association of sheep and infants at Sandy Lane. At Burnby Lane, Hayton (East Yorkshire) infant burials were associated with lamb and sheep burials suggesting feasting that marked stages in the human lifecycle (cited in Millett and Gowland 2015, 183–4). A similar situation might be envisaged for Sandy Lane, particularly with the seven or more lamb skulls and extremities from pit 20729 suggesting the special deposition of lamb skins in association with the infants, while the animals' body parts were taken elsewhere for consumption. The age at death of the lambs suggested that it was an autumn event and may therefore have been related to the harvest, although other explanations are possible. The radiocarbon modelling shows that this deposition, which was the latest of the burials here (Fig. 3.37), is most unlikely to have been directly related to commemorating the burial of any of the infants.

While the association of infants, sheep and other animals may be connected with fertility rites, the curious characteristic of Sandy Lane is their close association with the wall of a gallery room, or row of rooms, of what appears to have been the main residence. There is a possible likeness to the pattern of infant burials and cremated sheep at Winterton (Lincolnshire) where there seems to be a correspondence between the burials and the structure of Winterton Building B. Here a number of burials were apparently aligned along the postholes of the aisled building, perhaps mimicking the foundations of the building itself (Fig. 4.9). It is possible therefore that in these situations the burials and associated rituals can be seen as underpinning the success of the building and the social and agricultural enterprise which it housed. It is not clear that any specific burial or group of burials at Sandy Lane can be seen as a 'foundation' deposit. The difference in the radiocarbon dates of the infants is not statistically significant, meaning they could have died at the same time, but this ambiguity is inherent in the calibration curve in this period which makes the dating very broad. The slight differences in radiocarbon measurements and the observed stratigraphic relationships suggest the most likely sequence shown in Table 3.3. Thus the farmstead appears to have needed measures to ensure its prosperity conducted at intervals throughout its life at a lesser frequency than the annual cycle of agricultural production.

The special deposits here included an *in situ* pottery vessel of which the base survived, while other pits may have held organic remains that have not survived. The sheep in pit 20658 is of interest in that it seems to have been buried entirely, and possibly decapitated rather than being skinned or butchered. The burial of sheep remains in and around Roman buildings is not uncommon generally. At Nesley Farm, Tetbury (Gloucestershire), skulls buried with forelimbs were placed symmetrically next to a wall either side of the entrance to a Late Roman building (Roberts 2014, 28). At Doynton villa, also in Gloucestershire, similar combinations of sheep skulls and forelimbs were buried in various rooms of the villa (ibid., 29–30). There is no specific interpretation of these burials, although foundation deposits may be a reasonable supposition. One of the sheep deposits at Doynton was accompanied by two spindlewhorls, a symbolic combination showing the importance of cloth-making here.

None of the infants at Sandy Lane were certainly accompanied by finds, although a salmon/trout bone came from a soil sample associated with neonate girl Sk 20746. The burials must have been sealed by a floor, reducing the likelihood that this bone was intrusive, although it could have found its way into the grave among floor sweepings and infilling soils. However, it is possible that the fish bone represents food eaten as part of the funeral ceremonies, or placed as an offering. This suggestion is prompted by the extreme rarity of fish bone on the site, making any associations unusual, and the interpretation of fish bones found in burial contexts in Roman London's eastern cemetery. Here it was suggested that fish might represent a somewhat convoluted allusion to the *manes*, or spirits of the dead, amongst whom silence reigns, since a fish with its mouth sewn shut was an offering traditionally made to Tacita, the mute goddess (Barber and Bowsher 2000, 76).

The cattle skull, buried in small pit 20106 in the 1st century AD, appears to deliberately sited with reference to Late Iron Age Structures A–C or Roman Building B. It may be seen as a foundation deposit or the material evidence some kind of propitiation connected with the agricultural activities undertaken here. It falls within the category of special deposits recognised on Iron Age and Roman sites. In an Iron Age context animal skulls and other body parts are often found in grain storage pits and are seen as sacrifices linked to concerns over the success of the harvest (Cunliffe 2003, 147–49). At Barton Court Farm (Oxfordshire), one of a group of earlier 1st-century AD storage pits contained the mandibles of a dog and five cattle on its base (Miles 1986, 29). It is not clear how this pit may have related to the Early Roman 'six-posters' which are seen as replacing the Iron Age form of store on this site (ibid., 30), although the features were in approximately the same location and there may have been an intentional reference. The Sandy Lane pit may be equivalent to more formal shrines sometimes found on villa sites, such as the octagonal structure next to the granary at Stroud, Hampshire (Williams 1909; Fig. 4.12), containing a pit 'of a sacrificial nature', Applebaum 1972, 175). Typically, the antiquarian excavations provide little detail on its contents, although the plan (Williams 1909, plate 1) shows the octagonal structure in a late phase, and so perhaps formalising a location originally without an archaeologically recognisable structure. Polygonal structures have been recorded on a number of Roman rural settlements with the evidence of a ritual function sometimes convincing but generally highly variable (Smith 2018, 152).

The Sandy Lane villa: its wider context
Stephen Rippon, Stephen Armstrong and David Gould

The distribution of Roman villas across South West Britain
The villa at Cannington is of particular interest as it lies on the very western edge of those regions where such

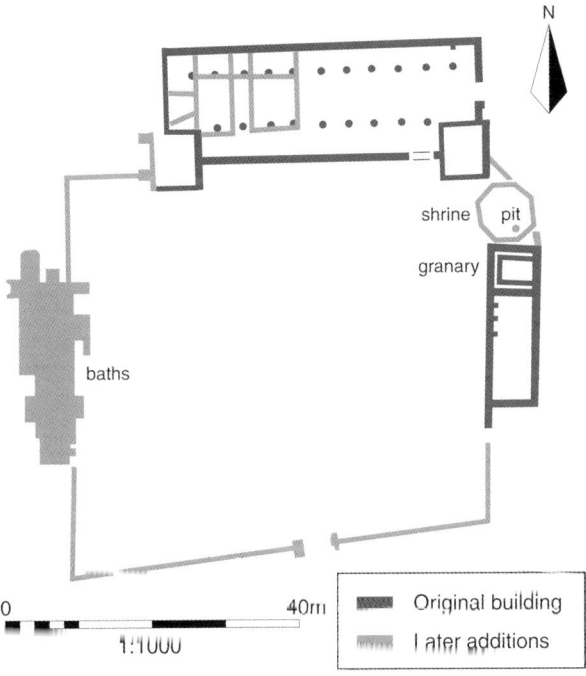

Fig. 4.12 Stroud Roman villa (Hampshire) (after Williams 1909, plate 1)

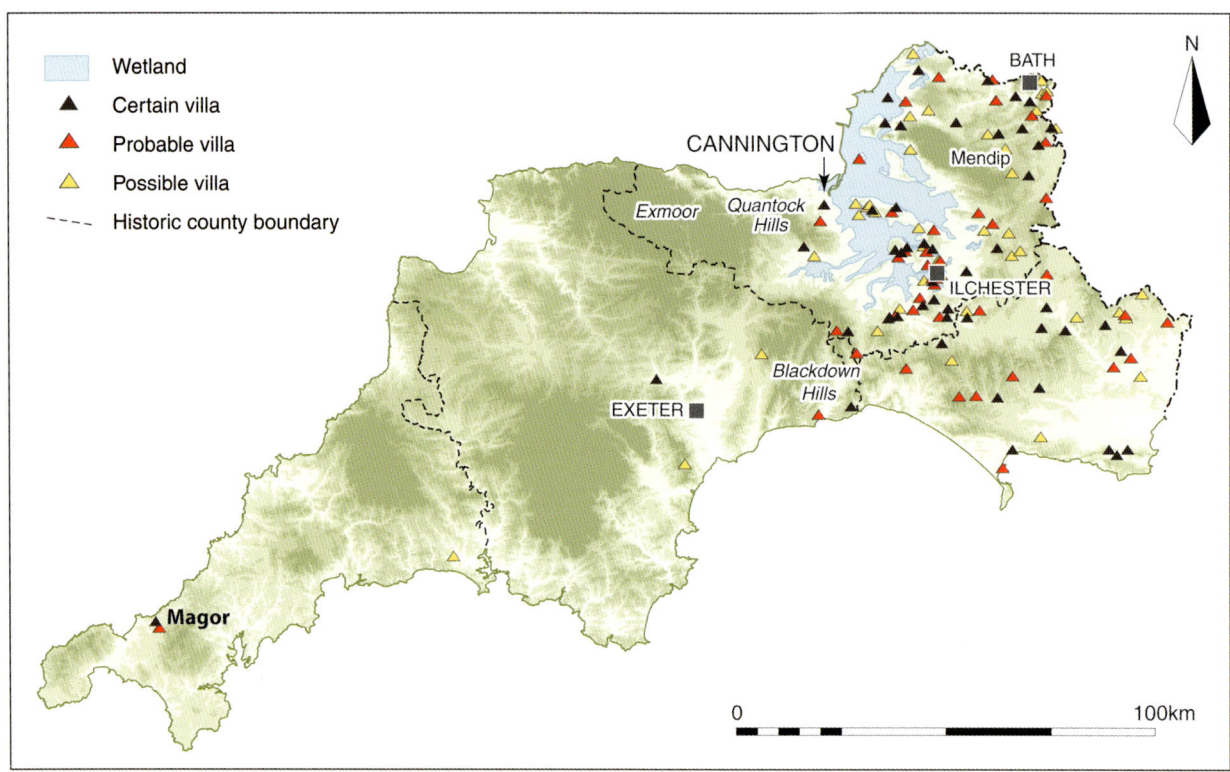

Fig. 4.13   Distribution of Roman villas across South West Britain (research and drawing by David Gould)

palatial country houses were a characteristic feature of the Roman countryside. Figure 4.13 illustrates our current understanding of the distribution of Roman villas across South West Britain (the historic counties of Cornwall, Devon, Dorset, and Somerset). Rather than simply recycling one of the many published maps of villa distributions – which often differ significantly with regard to which sites they include (e.g. Jones and Mattingly 1990, map 7.6; Millett 1990, fig. 48) – Figure 4.13 is based upon primary data obtained from Historic Environment Records and the published literature. Mapping 'villas' is, however, not an easy task which explains why published maps differ so much. There are two problems. Firstly, Roman Britain had a spectrum of rural settlement ranging from timber-built roundhouses through to palatial country houses, and so a judgement has to be made as to where on this spectrum a settlement can be regarded as a 'villa'. The definition used here is a residential building of Roman design (e.g. based upon rectangular modules), stone construction, and with a minimum of mortared floors, plastered walls, and a tiled roof. Cannington clearly exceeds those criteria – it also had underfloor heating in one of its buildings – but was still quite modest in that it lacked mosaic pavements (that are very common on other villas found right across central, eastern and northern Somerset).

A second problem with trying to map the distribution of Roman villas is the very incomplete archaeological record with which we have to work. The most problematic sites are those known only from surface scatters of material, or very fragmentary and/or antiquarian excavations. If a site has only produced unstratified ceramic roof and hypocaust tile then for the purposes of Figure 4.13 the threshold has not been crossed as it may have been brought to the site from elsewhere as rubble. If, however, there is a large unstratified assemblage of masonry building debris, hypocaust and roof tile, tesserae, and wall plaster then the site is classed as a 'probable' villa as even here there is the possibility that it comes from a temple, *mansio*, or roadside settlement. If there is relatively little material, or there is only *opus signinum* and painted wall plaster but no tesserae, then it is regarded as a 'possible' villa. The threshold for defining a villa, and the criteria for defining a site as certain, probable, and possible, have therefore been set fairly high but are designed to embrace the evidence from surface collection as well as aerial photography and excavation (for a fuller discussion see Rippon 2018).

Cannington within the Durotrigian civitas

Figure 4.13 shows that the greatest density of villas in the West Country has been recorded in central and eastern Somerset and northern Dorset, notably in the immediate hinterland of the small towns at Ilchester and Bath. The most westerly example in Somerset lies just 11km south-west of Cannington at Yarford, on the southern flanks of the Quantock Hills (King and Grande

2015). To the south, a small number of villas occupied the sheltered valleys within the Blackdown Hills, but to the west of these prominent uplands the Romano-British countryside had a very different character, with just two definite villas (Crediton in Devon, and Magor in Cornwall) and a small number of possible examples. It is likely that the Blackdown and Quantock Hills formed the boundary between the communities and *civitates* of the Durotriges (whose capital lay at Dorchester, *Durnovaria*) and the Dumnonii (whose capital lay at Exeter, *Isca Dumnoniorum*: Rippon 2012). Establishing the boundaries of the Romano-British *civitates* is extremely difficult, although a detailed study of the landscape of eastern Britain suggests that they generally ran through areas of sparsely settled land, most notably on high ground (Rippon 2018). It is, therefore, also possible that the boundary between the Durotriges and Dobunni lay along the Mendip Hills, in which case the northern part of Somerset will have lain within Dobunnic territory (as mapped by Jones and Mattingly 1990, map 5.11): the traditional view, that this area lay within the *civitas* of the Belgae (e.g. Millett 1990, fig. 16), gives rise to an utterly illogically shaped territory.

The layout of the villa at Cannington

That Cannington lay on the western edge of the heavily Romanised countryside of lowland Britain may explain some of its more curious characteristics, most notably its layout. It is increasingly recognised that there is marked regional variation in villa plans, with the classic winged-corridor layout for example being particularly common in the Dobunnic *civitas* (e.g. Frocester: Price 2000a). Barnsley Park and Kings Weston, in Gloucestershire, are two examples of villas with a winged-corridor façade, although the arrangement of their rooms is that of a hall-type plan (Smith 1985), a form that is also characteristic of this region. Another villa plan-type that included a large open space is the aisled hall; these are a particular characteristic of central-southern England and the south-east Midlands (Hadman 1978; Cunliffe 2013; Rippon 2018), and it is striking that they are absent in Somerset (the only aisled buildings being agricultural in character, such as Churchie Bushes near Bawdrip: Dewar 1957; Hadman 1978, 192).

Interpretation of the plan of Cannington villa is made difficult due to its very fragmentary preservation, although there appear to have been several buildings laid out in an exact rectangle around an open space. There is a large corpus of villa plans from elsewhere in Somerset with which we can compare Cannington's layout. As part of a University of Exeter and Cotswold Archaeology jointly funded Collaborative Doctoral Studentship, Stephen Armstrong has undertaken a comparative analysis of those sites for which there are partial or complete villa plans, of which there are 33: Banwell (Rippon 2006b, fig. 5.8), Blacklands (Lawes 2006, fig. 9, fig. 20), Bratton Seymour (Hughes and Lambert 2017, figs 2–3), Brislington (Branigan 1972, figs 1–2), Butleigh (Martin and Driscoll 2010, fig. 2, fig. 4), Sandy Lane, Cannington (this volume), Chew Park (Rahtz and Greenfield 1977, fig. 12), Dinnington (King and Grande 2015, figs 2–3), Durley Hill (Cox 1998, fig. 6), Ford Farm (Knibb 2009, fig. 26), Ham Hill (Hamilton Beattie and Phythian-Adams 1913, fig. 18), Hurcot (Gator *et al.* 1993, fig. 11), Ilchester Mead (Hayward 1982, fig. 4, fig. 12), Littleton (Haverfield 1906, fig. 81), Lopen (Lopen Villa Website 2017), Low Ham (Goodburn *et al.* 1976, fig. 21), Lufton (Hayward 1972, fig. 2), Newton St Loe (Stanton 1936, fig. 4) (Owen 1968, fig. 4), Paulton (Haverfield 1906, fig. 75), Pitney (Haverfield 1906, fig. 83), Queen Camel (Graham 2010, fig. 1), Seavington St Mary (Graham and Mills 1996, fig. 2, fig. 6), Somerdale (Bulleid and Ethelbert 1925, fig. 12), Spaxton (Wallace 1977), Star (Barton 1964, fig. 2, plates 1–2), Stawell (Ellson 2001, fig. 4), Wadeford (Anon. 1865, 65), Wellow (Haverfield 1906, fig. 69), Wemberham (Reade 1885, 65), Westland (Radford 1928, Plate K), Whatley Combe (Stead 1970, fig. 2), Wraxall (Sykes and Brown 1961, plate 1), and Yarford (King and Grande 2015, fig. 13).

Four villas comprise small, free-standing, winged-corridor buildings, all of which are in the north of Somerset (Blacklands, Brislington (Fig. 4.14), Chew Park, and Somerdale), while the main domestic block within the courtyard villa at Wellow (Fig. 4.14), and one of the two houses at Newton St Loe (Fig. 4.14), both near Bath in northern Somerset, are also of winged-corridor form. Villas of this plan probably lie within the cores of Wemberham and Whatley Combe, and while Skinner's sketch plan of the villa at Paulton, near Camerton (also in northern Somerset) has to be viewed with caution, it too appears to show a winged-corridor layout. That these classic winged-corridor forms are so characteristic of northern Somerset (north of Mendip) but not areas to the south may just be the product of the small sample size and the rather fragmentary nature of some villa plans, or it may be another example of regional variation in villa architecture. Although several of the larger, more complex courtyard villas in southern Somerset may have contained residential blocks with elements of this architectural form (e.g. Bratton Seymour, Ham Hill and Westland), the more common layout was for there to have been a longitudinal corridor either just at the front of the main domestic range (e.g. the southern end of the western range at Dinnington (Fig. 4.14), Ilchester Mead, Littleton and Pitney) or at both the front and the back (e.g. Hurcot).

And so we turn to the very fragmentary plan of Cannington, where we must remember that extensive later quarrying has removed all evidence from large parts of the site. It is a common feature of villas in Somerset to have buildings arranged around a courtyard, which is seen at seven other villas in Somerset: Banwell, Dinnington (Fig. 4.14), Durley Hill, Ilchester Mead,

136 *Cannington Bypass, Somerset: Excavations in 2014*

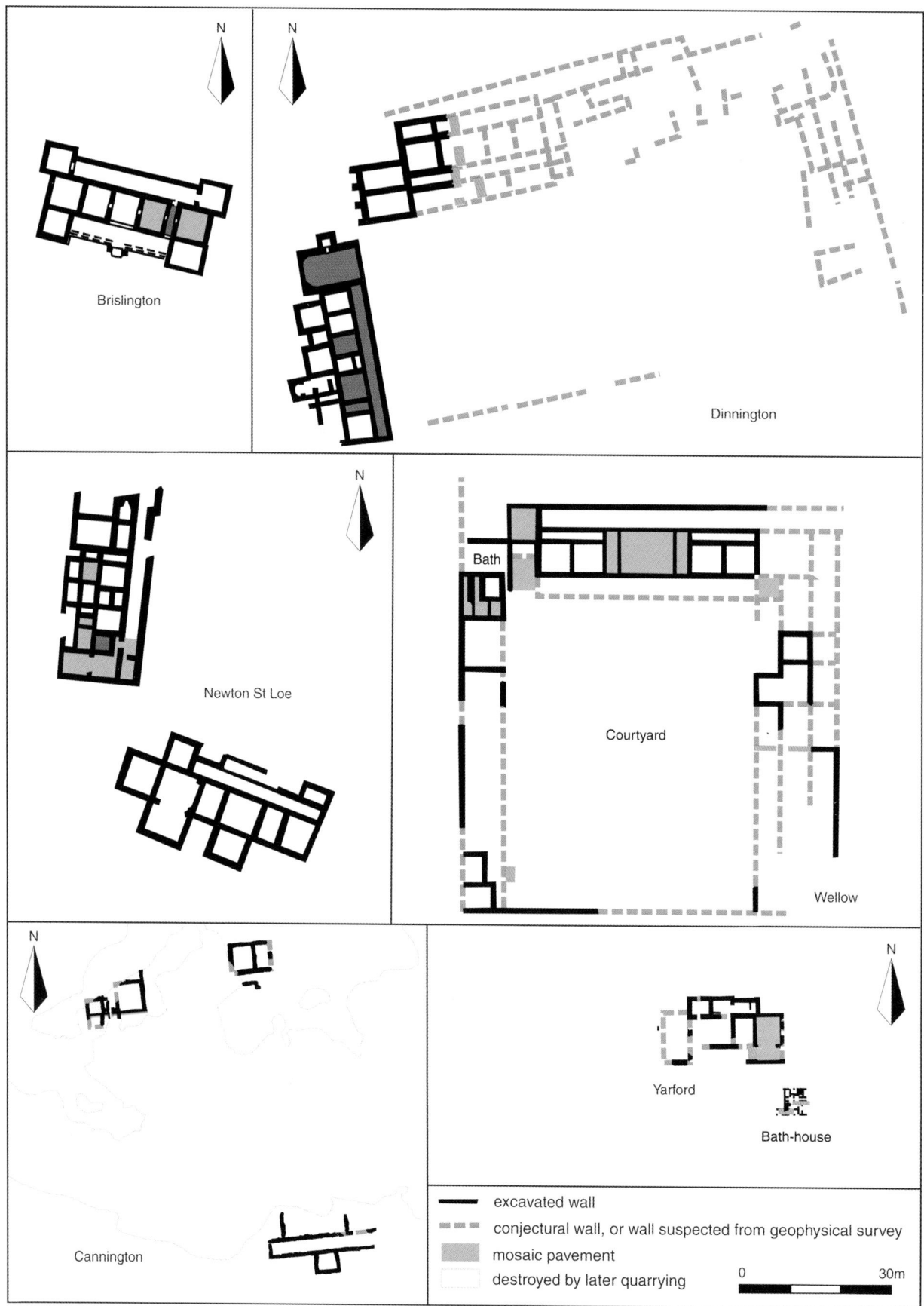

Fig. 4.14   Plans of selected villas from Somerset, all redrawn at the same scale. Note – the orientation of Wellow is not known (research and drawing by Stephen Armstrong)

Pitney, Wellow (Fig. 4.14), and Westland. The most common arrangement in these courtyard villas is for the main residential block, usually with an attached bath-house, to fill one side of the courtyard, and for there to be subsidiary wings creating a U-shaped arrangement. The villa complex can be regarded as facing the direction that the main residential wing looked, and conversely the direction that it will have been approached from, although villas such as Newton St Loe (Fig. 4.14) were of the unit-type plan with two domestic blocks facing onto the courtyard and so the direction which it faced is less clear. There is in fact a lot of variation in the direction in which villas faced with Blacklands looking west (Wessex Archaeology 2007), Banwell and Ilchester Mead facing south-west, Brislington and Yarford facing south (Fig. 4.14), Chew Park facing south-east, Lufton facing directly east, and (crucially for our interpretation of Cannington) the villa at Whatley Combe and the southern house at Newton St Loe facing north (Fig. 4.14).

Cannington shows some similarities to these other villa layouts in Somerset in that Buildings A, B and C are all on exactly the same east–west orientation (i.e. Building C to the south is exactly parallel to Buildings A and B to the north). The size of the open area between Buildings A–C at Cannington is also very similar to Banwell, Dinnington, Pitney, Wellow (Fig. 4.14), and Westland. What is unusual about Cannington, however, is the way that rather than having long ranges of buildings that extended the full length of a courtyard, relatively small, discrete buildings may have been spread around the edges of a central open area (although it must be stressed that most of this was destroyed by later quarrying). That what appears to be the main residential wing (Building C) faces north is not without precedent (e.g. Newton St Loe), although the apparent absence of a range of buildings down the western side (i.e. south of Building A, the possible bath block) is curious. Although large areas have been lost to later quarrying, there are undisturbed areas to the south of Building A, yet no traces of stone buildings were found in this area. Perhaps there were timber structures here whose ephemeral remains have not survived.

Could it be that in fact Building C at Cannington faced south and not north? There is very little evidence to go on, although topographically this will have made little sense as the ground rises up to the south: there will have been far better views looking north, including towards the hillfort at Cannington Camp which may still have had some psychological significance for the residents. The key architectural feature in Building C is the projecting Room 1 that appears to have been rebuilt/strengthened sometime after its initial construction. In most of the Somerset villas projecting rooms, or blocks of rooms, were at the back of a domestic range, seen most clearly with the bath-houses at villas such as Dinnington (Fig. 4.14), Lufton, and Wemberham. The single projecting room at Ilchester Mead (6m by 4.5 m) was also clearly at the back of the house, and comparable in size to Cannington Building C Room 1 (*c.* 7.6m by 5.9m). At Littleton there were similarly a series of rooms projecting from the back of the house, but also a small structure at the front that was interpreted as a porch (Haverfield 1906, fig. 81) although this measured *c.* 3.7m by 2.4m, making it considerably smaller than Cannington Building C Room 1.

Another distinctive feature of the site at Cannington is the way that the domestic buildings lay within a ditched enclosure. In many cases it is simply not possible to say whether other villas in Somerset lay within ditched enclosures as the early excavations were restricted to the stone buildings themselves, and relatively few sites have seen geophysical survey and/or excavations beyond the main residential buildings. With these caveats in mind, the only examples of a Roman villa in Somerset lying within a fully excavated, substantial ditched enclosure is Blacklands, and there the enclosure was rectilinear. Other excavated examples of ditches in association with villas include Ilchester Mead and Chew Park, although in all these examples the full extent of the ditches was not uncovered making it difficult to say whether they related to villa boundaries or were to aid drainage as at Wraxall.

Overall, the Romano-British villa at Cannington is a difficult one to find local parallels for. There are some elements of the overall layout (its rectilinearity, with buildings arranged around a yard) and the architecture of individual buildings (mortared painted-plaster walls, underfloor heating, *opus signinum* floors, tiled roofs) that are typical, whereas the layout of the site - with three individually small buildings, here spread around sides of an extremely large open space - is without precedent in Somerset.

The post-Roman occupation
Andrew Mudd and Jonathan Hart

The early medieval remains were identified only as a result of radiocarbon dating, artefacts of this date being absent, a reminder of how archaeologically invisible this period can be. This is particularly the case in Somerset and Devon, which were largely aceramic at this time apart from small amounts of Mediterranean imports that are restricted in their distribution. Inevitably, given this paucity of material remains, questions as to the nature, duration and intensity of the early medieval use of the site persist. The post-Roman radiocarbon dates include one of cal. AD 426–582 (SUERC-69956) on oak twig charcoal from the upper fill of Roman Ditch DW (Fig. 3.36). The charcoal-rich deposit may have related to burning activity nearby and which had been dumped into the remnant of the ditch. A wood charcoal fragment from medieval pit 20625, dug into the floor of Roman Building C, was radiocarbon dated to cal. AD

407–538 (SUERC-72467) and was found alongside later-dated material, but hints that some of this early post-Roman activity focused on the villa, although what form this took, and whether the villa was reoccupied in any way, are unclear. The reuse of existing enclosure earthworks in the post-Roman period is well-attested in the West Country (Dark 2000, 136–49; Webster 2008, 174), although in this case there is insufficient evidence to suggest that the earthworks were refurbished. It is more probable that this was simply an opportunistic reuse of the visible earthwork enclosure. It appears that this may have taken place a hundred years or so after the villa was abandoned and no form of direct continuity is implied from the evidence found, although the extent of later quarrying means that any assertions about the duration of occupation need qualification.

Structure D is suggested to be of 7th to 8th-century date on the basis of a date on charcoal from Ditch DL (cal. AD 658–769; SUERC-72472). The radiocarbon dated grain from this feature and others associated with this building formed a coherent group in the 2nd to 3rd centuries AD, a consistency implying that they represent redeposited material from earlier Building C, with which Building D cannot be contemporary on stratigraphic grounds. The alignment of the walls of Building D does, however, indicate recognition of the villa building, which was presumably still evident as a ruin.

The levels of truncation mean that the ground plan of this building can be only partially reconstructed. A building c. 9m long by 5m or more wide, formed of two cells either side of a 2m-wide corridor, seems the most likely interpretation. Houses, and settlements generally, are poorly attested in Somerset for the 5th to 7th centuries AD (Costen 2011, 51). In part, this may reflect a decline in population following plague outbreaks during the 6th and 7th centuries (ibid., 51), but it is also true that settlement remains from this period often produce little by way of dateable finds, meaning that unless they conform to a recognised site or feature type, or are scientifically dated, they are at risk of remaining undated, or being wrongly assigned to a different period of activity. Precise comparanda for Building D from Somerset therefore appear to be lacking, although a 7th to 8th-century timber building at Church Field, Shapwick survived as postholes forming a trapezoid plan 17m long and 7m wide, with evidence for internal subdivision (Gerrard 2007, 418–23, fig. 9.16).

Further afield at Frocester (Glos.) there may be a more precise comparison with post-Roman timber Building E (Price 2000a, 115 and fig. 6.4). This appears to have been constructed using earth-fast posts and ground beams, forming a structure c. 12m long and 7m wide, of three bays, although the precise form of the structure is not clear (Fig. 4.15). The dating is given as 5th century or later (ibid.) and therefore not necessarily contemporary with Building D at Sandy Lane. More generally across Britain, early medieval houses are characterised by subdivision either side of doorways placed centrally along each long axis (Gardiner 2000, 168; Hamerow 2004, fig. 2.8), and this may be analogous to the hall/corridor of Building D. The post-Roman Poundbury (Dorset) settlement had hall-like timber buildings, apparently constructed using combinations of ground beams and posts, dated somewhat approximately to the 5th to 6th centuries (Sparey Green 1987). Poundbury Building PR2a was c. 8m long and 5m wide, perhaps constructed using a line of ridge posts (Fig. 4.16). There is a hint of a three-fold division of the space with a 2m-wide central bay, making it similar to Building D at Sandy Lane. There was a potentially much larger building to the north, PR3, although the remains of it were slighter and its interpretation more conjectural (Fig. 4.17). This is interpreted as an aisled hall, perhaps a barn (ibid., 151) c. 11m long and 7m wide, with two lines of roof supports 2m apart. A similar reconstruction would make Building D 9m wide and of unknown length, making it of unusual size, but perhaps equivalent to the largest of the Poundbury buildings. The architecture of the Poundbury buildings is thought to be characteristically sub-Roman, rather than Anglo-Saxon, with possible comparisons in western Britain (ibid., 152), although all the evidence for this period is slight.

Further dating of this period came from pit 20020, cut into the edge of the western ditch (W) of the villa

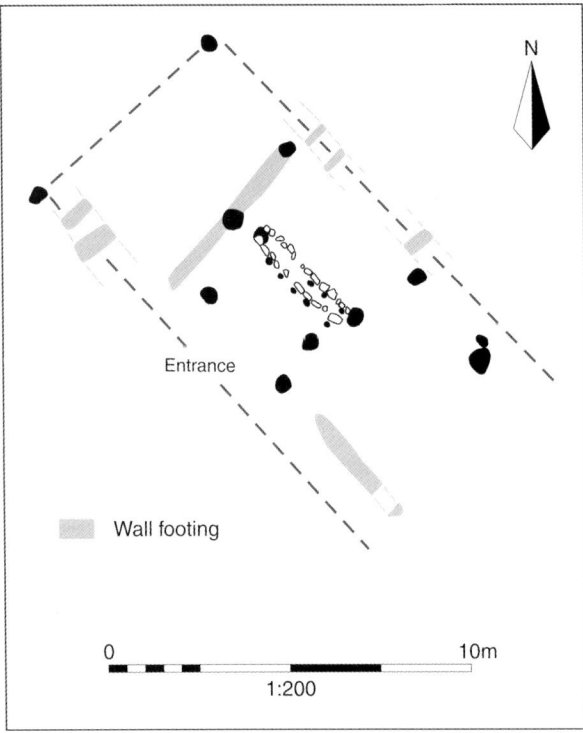

Fig. 4.15   Frocester (Gloucestershire) Building E, 5th century or later (after Price 2000a, fig. 6.4)

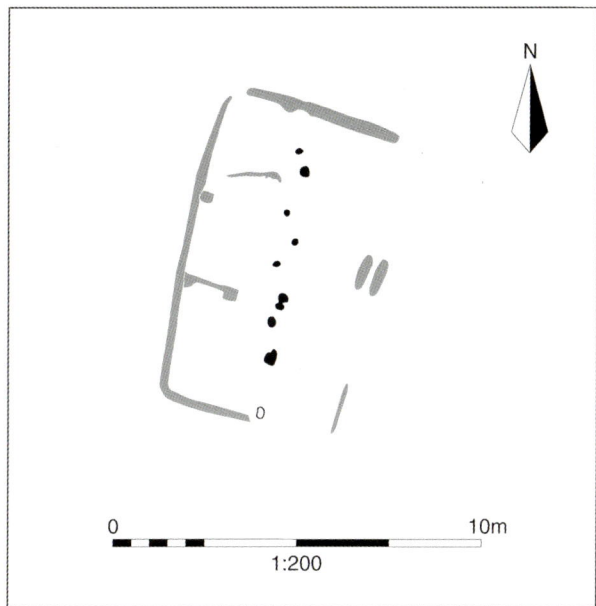

Fig. 4.16 Poundbury (Dorset) Structure PR2a, 5th–6th century (after Sparey Green 1987, fig. 55)

enclosure, which yielded two radiocarbon dates, cal. AD 665–853 (SUERC-69963) and cal. AD 682–866 (SUERC-72475) (Fig. 3.36) on a charred barley grain and an alder charcoal fragment respectively. This provides more consistent evidence of activity during the mid/later 7th to later 9th centuries AD, a good 70m

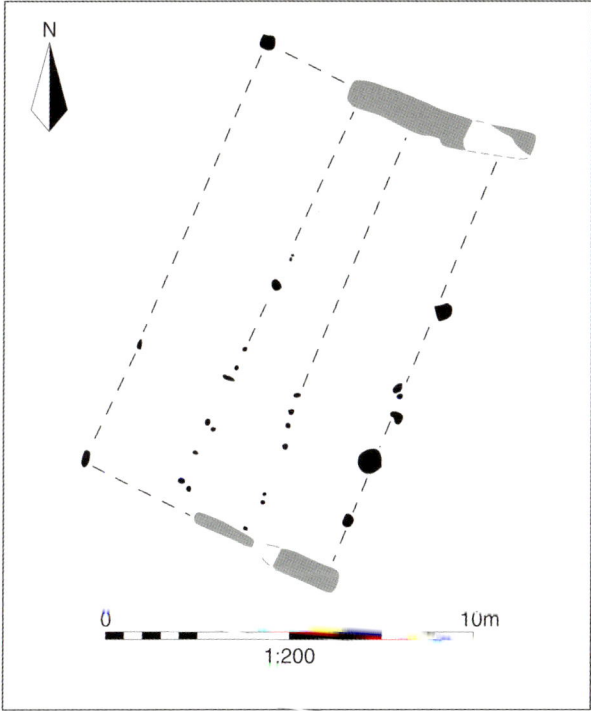

Fig. 4.17 Poundbury (Dorset) Structure PR3, 5th 6th century (after Sparey Green 1987, fig. 56)

Discussion

from Building D. A similar date range (cal. AD 667–770; SUERC-69961) was obtained on a charred cherry pip from pit 20625 dug through the floor of Roman Building C, although this seems to have been residual as there was also a medieval radiocarbon date from this pit.

While the nature of the post-Roman activity at Sandy Lane is not known, and even the dating ambiguous, it is possible that the site had some significance in the wider settlement context. The question brings into focus the status of the Roman and post-Roman Cannington Park Quarry cemetery site at this time. There is certainly evidence that it was important beyond its role as a burial ground for a widely scattered community. There is material dating from the 1st to 7th/8th centuries (independent of the grave goods), including ferrous and non-ferrous metals and metalworking residues, glass and pottery (Rahtz *et al.* 2000, 397). Structures include a possibly Late Roman temple, shrine or mausoleum on the summit of the hill, a large wooden structure (?church) towards which many of the burials were aligned and a unique slab-lined grave approached by a made pathway ('pilgrimage grave') (ibid., 413). The cemetery site has therefore been seen as a place for repeated visitation, participation in ritual, and social activity, with crafts supporting a resident and transitory population (ibid., 400). Several sites of supposed high status, such as Cadbury Congresbury and Glastonbury Tor, have associations with metalworking, and Cannington Park Quarry may have been of comparable importance. The post-Roman finds include imports of gabbro-gritted, grass-marked pottery manufactured in Cornwall, two sherds of 5th/6th-century Bii amphora from the eastern Mediterranean and two sherds of 6th-century African red-slipped ware.

Cannington was a royal ecclesiastical centre for the kings of Wessex from the mid 7th century (Costen 2011, 58) and so this would seem to have been a time of significant settlement in the area. Settlement may still have been dispersed at this time, and so, while 800m or so from the core of the present village, Sandy Lane may have formed part of a pattern of settlement which, within a century or so had coalesced on the lower ground to the south by Cannington Brook. There is as yet no evidence for settlement this early under the village; the present church of St Mary has fabric dating from the 12th century and may have been the church of the Benedictine nuns who occupied the nearby priory at this time (HER 15702, 15704) or alternatively the site of an early medieval minster. Certainly, the size of the Roman and later cemetery at Cannington Park Quarry, which may have contained as many as 5,000 graves (Rahtz *et al.* 2000, 56) (although other assessments tend to be more conservative and estimate *c.* 2000 graves) suggests that the area already had political importance by the early medieval period. Burial there had ceased by around the mid 7th century (ibid.), around the time when the West Saxons took political control. Following the general model of changes in early medieval burial practice (Webster 2008, 185), it may have been replaced by a burial ground in a churchyard in the valley where the present village lies, although there is currently no evidence for this.

The similarities between Cannington and Dorchester may be worth noting although advocating parallel developments is speculative in the present state of knowledge. The dating of the post-Roman settlements appears to be at odds, with that at Poundbury next to the hillfort outside Dorchester perhaps ending suddenly in the middle of the 7th century with the arrival of the Saxons (Sparey Green 1987, 153). The best estimate for the Sandy Lane building is 7th to 8th century and it may have been contemporary with Saxon, rather than sub-Roman, settlement in the area. Nonetheless the similarities extend to the coincidence of a hillfort, a Late Roman cemetery just outside it, the post-Roman reuse of a Roman site and by, the 8th century, the siting of a royal residence nearby somewhere on the lower ground. It seems that the importance of the later Saxon settlements may have been connected with Iron Age centres of power which were transmitted into the Roman period and after. It is interesting to note that Building D at Sandy Lane appears to have been aligned on the main villa residence (Building C) even though the latter had long gone out of use. If it had been a large aisled building like Poundbury PR3, it may even have imitated the form of the villa building. The Poundbury settlement, like that at Sandy Lane, was also within an enclosure and it is suggested the settlement followed a layout around a courtyard (30m by 40m) (ibid., 151). It seems possible that this owed something to the form of the villa compound, memorialised in a sub-Roman architectural tradition.

The early medieval territory associated with Cannington
Stephen Rippon

During the early medieval period Cannington appears to have been the centre of a territory that extended from the Parrett Estuary up onto the Quantock Hills (Fig. 4.18). Territories of this type have been recognised across Britain, and are occasionally recorded in contemporary documents as *pagi* or *regiones* (see Rippon 2012, chapter 8 for a historiography of research into them). Perhaps the most familiar term for these territories is 'multiple estate' (e.g. Jones 1979), although that phrase is flawed as 'estate' implies the ownership of land, and 'early folk territory' is perhaps a better reflection of the kin-based social structure that lay behind them. Early medieval territorial arrangements can be reconstructed using a wide variety of sources including place-names, contemporary documents such as charters, and the relationship of parish boundaries to the historic landscape (e.g. see Rippon 2008b, 95–102; Rippon 2012, 151–64), and the Cannington area provides a particularly clear example.

Cannington itself was a hundredal centre, ancient royal manor (Thorn and Thorn 1980: *DB Som.* 1,6), and minster church. It was included in King Alfred's will of 873–88 (Sawyer 1968, no. 1507), when it was spelt *cantūctūn* ('the tun by the Quantocks'). The name *cantūc* may be derived from the British **cantaco* (whose earliest form is not known), meaning 'a district divided off', referring to the way that the hills separate this area of land from the rest of Somerset (Costen 1992, 63; Watts 2004, 113). The close proximity of the hillfort at Cannington Camp (which shows signs of occupation in the Roman period), the Sandy Lane villa, the late and post-Roman cemetery at the nearby Cannington Quarry (Rahtz *et al.* 2000), and the nearby royal manor and minster church provide the intriguing possibility of continuity in this locale as an estate centre. The parishes within Cannington Hundred were characterised by complex boundaries that zig-zag through field systems, with many parishes having detailed parcels elsewhere, a pattern that suggests they were once part of a single territory. Another territorial connection was that Idstock was a chapelry of Cannington (*DB Som.* 1,6; 16,3; Youngs 1980, 420), something that is suggestive of Cannington having once been a minster church. Over time, early folk territories were divided up, and one such subdivision may have been centred on Stogursey that was a very large parish (8,893 acres) and had a chapelry at Lilstock (Youngs 1980, 437) which again suggests that it was a former minster. It is noticeable that none of the territorial links that bound the parishes within Cannington Hundred together extended west of the Quantock Hills (Fig. 4.18).

South of Cannington Hundred lay the small hundred of Andersfield (that included just the four parishes of Broomfield, Durleigh, Enmore, and Goathurst) and North Petherton Hundred. Once again, this was an area with a network of interlocking parishes and detached parcels such as Chilton Trinity (in North Petherton Hundred) having a detached parcel called Huntstile in Goathurst (in Andersfield Hundred). It is noteworthy that the web of territorial connections that binds this area together does not extend to the south of the northern boundary of the very large parish of North Petherton. The river+ton place-name of North Petherton is in itself indicative of an important early medieval centre, and this is confirmed by it having been an ancient royal manor with a church in Domesday (*DB Som.* 1,3; 16,7). Its former minster status is reflected in the large size of its parish (10,336 acres in the Tithe survey) and its having chapelries at Chedzoy (an island in the Somerset Levels), Durston, Huntworth, Michael Church, Newton Comitis, Newton Regis, Sherston, and Woolmersdon (Aston 1986, 75). Although later in Whitley Hundred, the island-based estate of Sowy (which was later divided into the parishes of Othery,

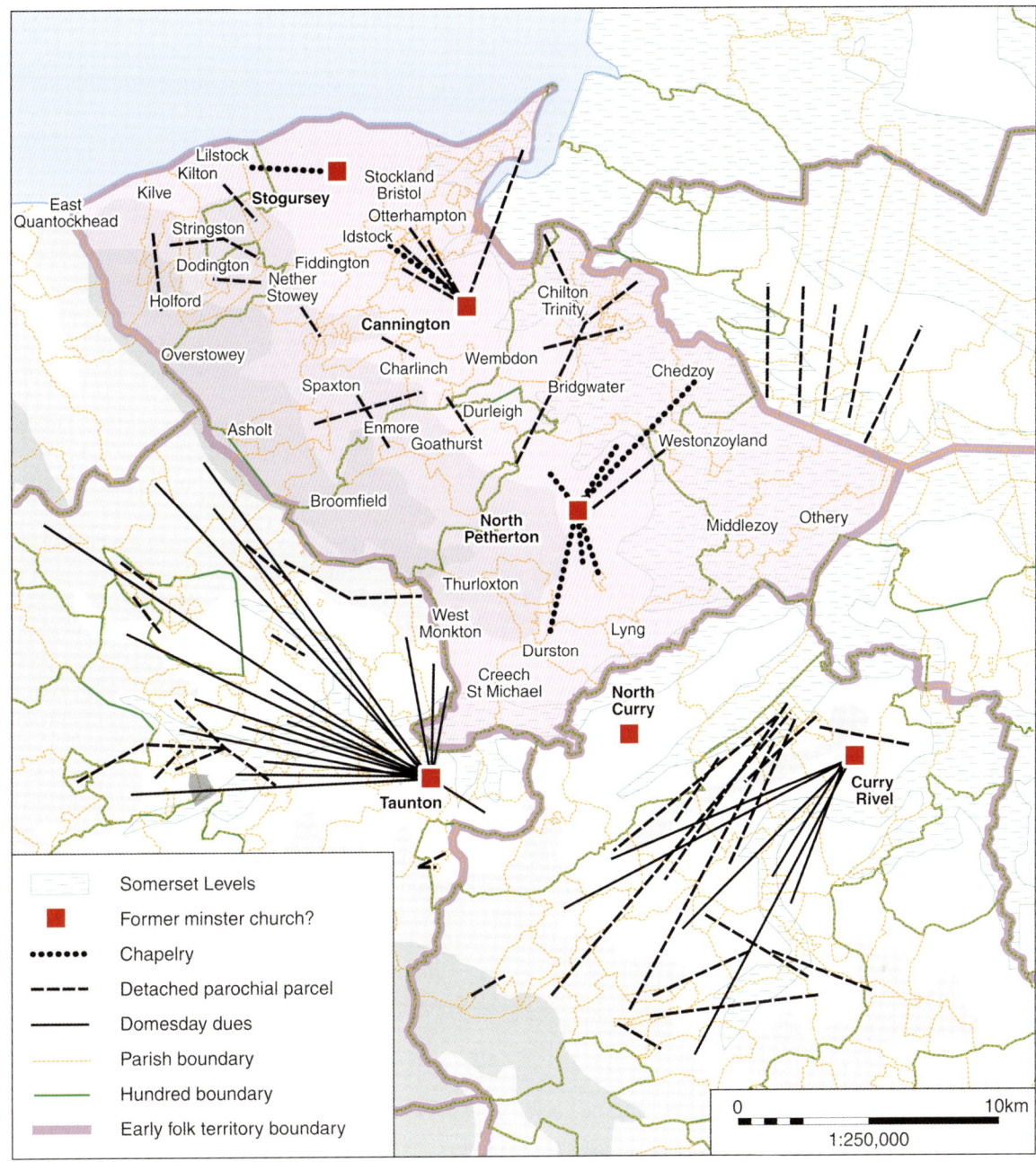

Fig. 4.18 The early folk territory between the Quantock Hills and Parrett Estuary (research and drawing by Stephen Rippon)

Middlezoy and Westonzoyland) appears to have been carved out of the south-east corner of the Cannington early folk territory and it was probably transferred to Whitley when 12 *manentes* (an early medieval unit of assessment probably equivalent to the 'hide', or area of land sufficient to support a thane) were granted to Glastonbury Abbey in 725 (Finberg 1964, no. 379; Sawyer 1968, no. 251; Abrams 1996, 218–20). Another early charter, that is 'only available in a later copy and while thought to include the substance of an original may include so material that is spurious, substituted or interpolated' records a grant in 682 by Centwine, king of the West Saxons, to Haemgils, abbot of Glastonbury, of 23 *mansiones* (another early medieval unit of assessment probably equivalent to the 'hide') 'by the wood called *Cantucwdu* (Quantock Wood)' and three *cassati* (also probably the equivalent to a 'hide') 'in the island by the hill which the British call *Cructan* and we *Crycbeorh*': the boundaries of this estate are described and show that it included the whole of West Monkton and the western part of Creech St Michael (Finberg 1964, no. 361; Sawyer 1968, no. 237; Abrams 1996, 99–100). Both Sowy and *Crycbeorh* were at the very edges of the putative early folk territory based at Cannington and as such provide examples of how peripheral areas were often the earliest to be given away by early medieval kings.

Figure 4.18 shows how a web of territorial connections bind this putative early folk territory together, and how this is mutually exclusive to the connective webs that help in the reconstruction of two other early folk territories to the south. To the south-east lay the Curry Valley where a large number of parishes had detached parcels, and Domesday records how various places paid dues to other centres: Cricket (St Thomas) paid (South) Petherton six sheep with as many lambs and one bloom of iron from each free man (*DB Som*. 1,5); Ashill ought to pay Curry (Rivel) 30 pence (*DB Som*. 19,18), while the two manors of Bradon each paid Curry (Rivel) one sheep and a lamb (*DB Som*. 19,17; 19,23); Bickenhall paid Curry Rivel five sheep and as many lambs, while each freeman owed a bloom of iron (*DB Som*. 19,27); and Seaborough paid Crewkerne 12 sheep with their lambs, a bloom of iron from every freeman (*DB Som*. 3,1) (see Rippon 2008b, 98 for a full discussion). To the west, Domesday also records that Taunton received customary dues from a large number of places *(DB Som*. 2, 1–2,5)*.

These various strands of evidence suggest that there was an early folk territory bounded by the unenclosed uplands of the Quantock Hills to the west, the Bristol Channel to the north, the Parrett Estuary to the east, and the wetlands of the Somerset Levels and west Sedgemoor to the south. There appear to have been two major royal estate centres – Cannington and North Petherton – with another probable minster at Stogursey. In total this putative territory covered around 350km².

Conclusions
Andrew Mudd

The much-needed bypass around Cannington was constructed over a relatively short distance of 1.6km but all the same fortuitously coincided with virtually the entire surviving remains of two important archaeological sites, both of which were excavated ahead of the construction of the road. At the same time the project was also successful in engaging the local community through museum displays, an open day, short films and video diaries, arranged through South West Heritage Trust. The video records are available to view on the YouTube channels of Cotswold Archaeology and South West Heritage Trust (www.youtube.com/c/Cotswoldarchaeology; www.youtube.com/c/SouthWestHeritageTrust).

The site at Rodway, the remains of a small Middle Bronze Age settlement consisting of a pair of houses within an enclosure, is unusual for Somerset, although similar examples have been found in Dorset and further east, while the pottery has affinities to that in the South West peninsula. The remains from Rodway included evidence for the production and storage of wheat. The site appears to be a component of a social and agricultural system that exploited the landscape in varied and particular ways – a system that included the use of 'burnt mounds' for separate but unknown purposes, one of which was found in isolation at Sandy Lane.

The Roman villa at Sandy Lane is the first discovered in the environs of Cannington and provides support for the notion that Cannington was a significant focus of population and perhaps also political power in the Roman period – a status already suggested by the large Roman and early medieval cemetery at Cannington Park Quarry. The Late Iron Age presence at Sandy Lane provides grounds for arguing that the villa's status was inherited from its Iron Age predecessor, although Cannington Camp Iron Age hillfort nearby, while lacking detail of chronology and status, was perhaps not coincidentally located in the same area and may reflect an earlier centre of power.

The villa compound within its inherited ridge-spur boundaries was poorly preserved due to later quarrying and the remains, lacking close comparisons within the local repertoire of villa buildings, were in many ways unusual both individually and in combination. An examination of the buildings and associated material remains, including the botanical and environmental evidence, has indicated that interpretations are not self-evident and that there are several possible explanations of individual buildings and rooms. Comparisons with other villas, both regionally and nationally, following in particular the examples that Applebaum (1972), Morris (1979) and Black (1981) drew attention to, suggest that similar evidence is to be found elsewhere. Sub-floor heating for example, may have been used for the specifically Roman cultural practice of bathing, or in other cases for purposes of agricultural processing and storage. Despite common assumptions that the use of new building techniques using brick, tile, cement and plaster were signals of aspirations to a Roman cultural norm, it is perhaps just as likely that they were an investment directed at immediate farming concerns, as some of the examples presented indicate.

It can therefore be suggested that, rather than indicating a relatively poorly executed project to become Roman, the evidence reflects ideas and practices that were important to the agricultural community itself. It has been suggested that the villa's role evolved from the status of the local lord in the pre-Roman Iron Age whose obligations included the requirement to provide food for kin and guests when called upon. From this it may be argued that display and competitive emulation within the social circles of the villa owners were more to do with the success of their farming enterprise and the skills needed to achieve it than with Roman cultural accomplishments (Taylor 2013). This enterprise may well have been directed at a great uplift in demand for grain, in particular, to supply the Roman armies, and it is possible that villas more generally provided central processing and storage facilities for a wider network of farms (Lodwick 2017, 67–8). Materials introduced as an outcome of Roman political control enabled the construction of better means of harvesting and storing agricultural products, and the use of these new construction techniques are all interpretable in these terms. It did not noticeably result in the consumption of a range of other goods normally associated with villas. The pottery was largely sourced from regional centres such as Dorset and there were few exotic items and virtually none that could be ascribed to specifically Roman-inspired cooking and eating practices. It seems therefore that the inhabitants had little interest in Roman-style dining, the pottery profile instead showing a uniformity that might suggest a preference for communal food sharing. The lack of coins may imply barter or other, socially embedded, means of exchange. It is possible that the agricultural surplus was something that could be exchanged for labour service and allegiance, and also a way of displaying success and showing generosity.

The demise of the villa by the 4th century happened for reasons that are unclear. Whether this was part of the particular biography of this settlement, with the social structure failing to reproduce itself perhaps through death and emigration, or whether it was part of a wider dislocation caused or influenced by political authority, such as a greater centralisation through the amalgamation of landed estates, is not apparent. The destruction of some West Country villas in the 4th century has been attributed to the attacks by Irish pirates recounted by Ammianus Marcellinus (Branigan 1976, 136–9). While such a possibility is worth bearing in mind the archaeological evidence is seldom precise enough to support such a specific cause and, in any case, the Sandy Lane villa would seem to have been abandoned half a century or more earlier. Certainly, the 4th century in the West Country is the period of greatest elaboration of villas generally, both in their size and visual splendour. This suggests a progressive concentration of wealth in fewer hands and the Sandy Lane inhabitants may have dispersed and become attached to larger, more viable, farms.

The reoccupation of the villa in the post-Roman period adds to the regional picture of the sporadic reuse of Roman and earlier sites at this time. This occupation consisting of no more than the traces of a timber building and a few pits, is hard to define or understand, and even its date is uncertain. The most parsimonious explanation sees this as a somewhat expeditious reuse of a site defined by at least partly extant earthworks, and perhaps other remains, acting as a template. This was perhaps part of a dispersed settlement pattern which later coalesced into the familiar village-centred rural landscape. On the other hand attention has been drawn to the importance of Cannington as a royal demesne by the 8th century, and its probable status as the centre of an early folk territory. It is possible, therefore, that the settlement at Sandy Lane was originally far more extensive and lay at the local centre of power in this period before a shift in focus moved the settlement to its present location in the valley to the south.

References

Website resources

Cotswold Archaeology website, Archaeological Reports Online, http://reports.cotswoldarchaeology.co.uk/ (accessed 5 June 2018)

Lopen Villa website, http://www.lopen.btck.co.uk/LopensRomanMosaic/11Whatwasfound (accessed 30 July 2017)

Must Farm website, http://www.mustfarm.com/ (accessed 2 May 2018)

OxCal website, https://c14.arch.ox.ac.uk/oxcal.html (accessed 29 June 2018)

The Genealogist website, https://www.thegenealogist.co.uk/ Cannington Tithe Map (1839) (accessed 4 March 2018)

Bibliography

Abrams, L. 1996 *Anglo-Saxon Glastonbury: Church and Endowment* Woodbridge, Boydell Press

Albarella, U. and Hammon, A. 2011 'The animal bone', in Ellis, P. and Leach, P. 'The Roman settlement at Fosse Lane, Shepton Mallet: The Tesco excavation, 1996–7', *Somerset Archaeol. Natur. Hist.* **155**, 1–38, W37–W43

Alexander, M. and Adam, N. 2013 'Bronze Age and later archaeology at Wick Lane, Norton Fitzwarren', *Somerset Archaeol. Natur. Hist.* **156**, 1–17

Allen, J.R.L. 1998 'Late Iron Age and earliest Roman calcite-tempered ware from sites on the Severn Estuary Levels: character and distribution', *Studia Celtica* **32**, 27–41

Allen, L. 2016 'Ceramic building material', in Allen *et al.* 2016, 121–7

Allen, M. and Smith, A. 2016 'Rural settlement in Roman Britain: morphological classification and overview', in Smith *et al.* 2016, 17–43

Allen, T., Brady, K. and Foreman, S. 2016 *A Roman Villa and other Iron Age and Roman discoveries at Bredon's Norton, Fiddington and Pamington along the Gloucester Security of Supply Pipeline*, Oxford Archaeology Monograph **25**

AMEC 2010 *Cannington Bypass Associated Development: Cultural Heritage Desk-Based Assessment,* Unpublished AMEC typescript report ref. **15928TR00043**

AMEC 2011 *Hinkley Point C Associated Development Cannington Bypass: Written Scheme of Investigation for Archaeological Mitigation-Set-Piece Excavation,* Unpublished AMEC typescript report ref. **15928/TR/00132**

Amorosi, T. 1989 *A Postcranial Guide to Domestic Neo-Natal and Juvenile Mammals,* Brit. Archaeol. Rep. Internat. Ser. **533**

Anderson, F.W. 2000 'The geology', in Rahtz *et al.* 2000, 9

Andrews, P. and Nesbit Evans, E.M. 1983 'Small mammal bone accumulations produced by mammalian carnivores', *Paleobiology* **9(3)**, 289–307

Anon. 1865 'Roman remains at Wadeford', *Somerset Archaeol. Natur. Hist.* **13**, 61–5

Applebaum, S. 1972 'The Roman period', in Finberg H.P.R. (ed.) *The Agrarian History of England and Wales, I.II* Cambridge, Cambridge University Press, 3–277

ApSimon, A.M. 1997 'Bos Swallet, Burrington, Somerset; boiling site and Beaker occupation site', *Proc. Univ. Bristol Spelaeol. Soc.* **21(1)**, 43–82

ApSimon, A.M. 2000 'The Neolithic, Bronze Age and Iron Age pottery', in Rahtz *et al.* 2000, 282–90

Aston, M. 1986, 'Post Roman central places in Somerset', in Grant, E. (ed.) *Central Places, Archaeology and History* Sheffield: University of Sheffield, 49–77

Bailon, S. 1999 *Différenciation ostéologique des Anoures (Amphibia, Anura) de France*. Fiches D'Ostéologie Animale Pour L'Archéologie Serie C: Varia **1**. Centre de Recherches Archéologiques

Barber, B. and Bowsher, D. 2000 *The Eastern Cemetery of Roman London. Excavations 1983–1990,* Museum of London Archaeology Service Monograph **4**

Barrett, J., Bradley, R. and Green, M. 1991 *Landscape, Monuments and Society: the Prehistory of Cranborne Chase* Cambridge, Cambridge University Press

Barton, K.J. 1964 'Star Villa, Shipham, Somerset', *Somerset Archaeol. Natur. Hist.* **108**, 45–93

Bartosiewicz, L. 2013 *Shuffling Nags, Lame Ducks. The Archaeology of Animal Disease* Oxford, Oxbow Books

Baxter, I.L. 1998 'Late medieval tawyers' waste and pig skeletons in early post-medieval pits from Bonners Lane, Leicester, England, U.K.', *Anthropozoologica* **28**, 55–63

Bayliss, A., van der Plicht, J., Bronk Ramsey, C., McCormac, G., Healy, F. and Whittle, A. 2011 'Towards generational time-scales: the quantitative interpretation of archaeological chronologies', in Whittle, A. Healy, F. and Bayliss, A. *Gathering Time: Dating the Early Neolithic Enclosures of Southern Britain and Ireland* Oxford, Oxbow Books,16–60

Becker, C. 1980 *Untersuchungen an Skelettresten von Haus- und Wildschweinen aus Haithabu* Neumunster, Karl Wachholtz Verlag

Bell, M. 1990 *Brean Down: Excavations 1983–1987,* English Heritage Archaeological Report **15**. London

Bell, M. 2013 *The Bronze Age in the Severn Estuary,* Counc. Brit. Archaeol. Res. Rep. **172**

Berry, R. and Berry, A. 1967 'Epigenetic variation in human cranium', *J. Anatomy* **101**, 361–79

Beven, G. 1982 'Further observations on the food of Tawny owls in London', *The London Naturalist* **61**, 88–94

BGS (British Geological Survey) 2017 *Geology of Britain Viewer* at http://mapapps.bgs.ac.uk/geologyofbritain/home.html (accessed 19 December 2017)

Bidwell, P. 1996 'The exterior decoration of Roman buildings in Britain', in Johnson with Haynes (eds) 1996, 19–29

Birbeck, V. 2002 'Excavations on Iron Age and Romano-British Settlements at Cannards Grave, Shepton Mallet', *Somerset Archaeol. Natur. Hist.* **144**, 41–116

Black, E.W. 1981 'An additional classification of granaries in Roman Britain', *Britannia* **12**, 163–5

Blagg, T.F.C. 1996 'The external decoration of Romano-British buildings', in Johnson with Haynes (eds) 1996, 9–18

Boessneck, J., Müller, H-H. and Teichert, M. 1964 'Osteologische Unterscheidungmerkmale zwischen Schaf (*Ovis aries* Linné) und Ziege (*Capra hircus* Linné)', *Kühn-Archiv* **78**, H.1–2

Bond, J.M. and O'Connor, T.P. 1999 *Bones from Medieval Deposits at 16–22 Coppergate and Other Sites in York*, The Archaeology of York **15/5**. York, York Archaeological Trust and Council for British Archaeology

Booth, P. 2017 'Kent Roman rural settlement', in Bird, D. (ed.) *Agriculture and Industry in South-Eastern Roman Britain* Oxford, Oxbow Books, 55–83

Borlase, W.C. 1872 *Naenia Cornubiae* London, Longmans

Brailsford, J.W. 1958 'Early Iron Age C in Wessex', *Proc. Prehist. Soc.* **24**, 101–9

Branigan, K. 1972 'The Romano-British Villa at Brislington', *Somerset Archaeol. Natur. Hist.* **116**, 78–85

Branigan, K. 1976 'Villa settlement in the West Country', in Branigan, K. and Fowler, P.J. (eds) *The Roman West Country: Classical Culture and Celtic Society* Newton Abbott, David and Charles, 120–41

Brickley M. and McKinley, J. 2004 *Guidelines to the standards for recording of human remains,* Chartered Institute for Archaeologists Paper No. **7**

Britnell, W.J. and Silvester, R.J. (eds) 2012 *Reflections on the Past. Essays in Honour of Frances Lynch* Welshpool, Cambrian Archaeological Association

Brodribb, G. 1987 *Roman Brick and Tile* Stroud, Alan Sutton Publishing

Brodribb, A.C.C., Hands, A.R. and Walker, D.R. 2005 *The Roman Villa at Shakenoak Farm, Oxfordshire: Excavations 1960–1976*, Brit. Archaeol. Rep. Brit. Ser. **395**

Bronk Ramsey, C. 2009 'Bayesian analysis of radiocarbon dates', *Radiocarbon* **51**, 337–60

Bronk Ramsey, C. 2017 'Methods for summarizing radiocarbon datasets', *Radiocarbon* **59(2)**, 1809–33

Bronk Ramsey, C. and Lee, S. 2013 'Recent and planned developments of the program OxCal.', *Radiocarbon* **55(2–3)**, 720–30

Brück, J. (ed.) 2001a *Bronze Age Landscapes, Tradition and Transformation* Oxford, Oxbow Books

Brück, J. 2001b 'Body metaphors and technologies of transformation in the English Middle and Late Bronze Age', in Brück (ed.) 2001a, 149–60

Buck, C.E. and Juarez, M. 2017 '*Bayesian radiocarbon modelling for beginners*', https://arxiv.org/abs/1704.07141 (accessed 10 December 2017)

Bucko, R. 1998 *The Lakota Ritual of the Sweat Lodge. History and Contemporary Practice,* Studies in the Anthropology of North American Indians. Lincoln, University of Nebraska Press

Buglass, J. and West, J. 2016 'Of mousers and men. Exploring the archaeology of the domestic cat', *Curr. Archaeol.* **27(6)**, 36–8

Bulleid, A. and Ethelbert, H. 1925 'The Roman House at Keynsham, Somerset', *Archaeologia* **75**, 109–38

Butler, C. 2005 *Prehistoric Flintwork* Stroud, Tempus Publishing

CA (Cotswold Archaeology) 2011 *Cannington Bypass, Somerset: Archaeological Evaluation*, Cotswold Archaeology typescript report **11008**

CA (Cotswold Archaeology) 2015 *Hinkley Point C, Somerset. Archaeological Works: Post-Excavation Assessment SPE1–SPE5 (Task 10.2),* Cotswold Archaeology typescript report **13432**

CA (Cotswold Archaeology) 2016a *Hinkley Point C Associated Development: Cannington Bypass, Somerset. Archaeological Works: Post-Excavation Assessment*, Cotswold Archaeology typescript report **16141**

CA (Cotswold Archaeology) 2016b *Hinkley Point C Associated Development: Cannington Bypass, Somerset. Archaeological Works: Updated Project Design and Publication Proposal*, Cotswold Archaeology typescript report **16287**

CA (Cotswold Archaeology) 2017a *Hinkley Point C, Someret. Archaeological Works: Post-Excavation Assessment SPE 6 and SPE 7,* Cotswold Archaeology typescript report **17308**

CA (Cotswold Archaeology) 2017b *Hinkley Point C, Somerset. Archaeological Works: Post-Excavation Assessment SPE 8 Burials Site* Cotswold Archaeology typescript report **17402**

CA (Cotswold Archaeology) 2018 *Cannington Flood Alleviation Scheme, Cannington, Somerset; Post-Excavation Assessment and Updated Project Design,* Cotswold Archaeology typescript report **16262**

Calkin, J.B. 1962 'The Bournemouth area in the Middle and Late Bronze Age with the Deverel-Rimbury problem reconsidered', *Archaeol. J.* **119**, 1–65

Challinor, D. forthcoming 'Charcoal', in Newton, L. 'Middle Bronze Age settlement and a Romano-British Villa at Queen Camel, Somerset', *Somerset Archaeol. Natur. Hist.*

CIfA 2014 *Standard and Guidance for the Creation, Compilation, Transfer and Deposition of Archaeological Archives* Chartered Institute for Archaeologists

Cobain, S. 2015 'Plant macrofossils and charcoal', in CA 2015

Cobain, S. 2016 'Plant macrofossils and charcoal', in CA 2016a

Coles, J.M. and Minnitt, S. 1995 *'Industrious and fairly civilised' The Glastonbury Lake Village* Exeter, Short Run Press, Somerset Levels Project and Somerset County Museums Service

Columella *De Re Rustica Book 1,* Vol. 1 of the Loeb Classical Library edition 1941, http://penelope.uchicago.edu/Thayer/E/home.html (accessed February 2018)

Context One Archaeological Services 2011 *Cambria Farm, Taunton, Somerset: excavation within a late prehistoric and Romano-British settlement in the Tone Valley,* Draft report

Cool H.E.M. 2006 *Eating and Drinking in Roman Britain* Cambridge, Cambridge University Press

Corbet, G.B. 1977 'Common shrew *Sorex araneus*', in Corbet and Southern (eds) 1977, 46–54

Corbet, G.B. and Southern, H.N. (eds) 1977 *The Handbook of British Mammals* 2nd edition. Oxford, Blackwell Scientific Publications

Costen, M. 1992, *The Origins of Somerset* Manchester, Manchester University Press

Costen, M. 2011 *Anglo-Saxon Somerset* Oxford, Oxbow Books

Cox, A. 1998 *Keynsham Cemetery, Durley Hill, Keynsham, Bath and North East Somerset. Archaeological Evaluation Project,* Bristol, Avon Archaeological Unit, https://doi.org/10.5284/1029136 (accessed 14 October 2017)

Crawford, A. and McSloy E. forthcoming 'The Roman Pottery', in Mudd *et al.* forthcoming *Excavations at Hinkley Point, Somerset* (working title)

Cunliffe, B. 2003 *Danebury Hillfort* Stroud, Tempus Publishing

Cunliffe, B. 2013 '"For men or rank ... basilicas": British aisled halls reconsidered', in Eckardt, H. and Rippon, S. (eds) *Living and Working in the Roman World: Essays in Honour of Michael Fulford on his 65th Birthday,* J. Roman Archaeol. Supp. Ser. **95**, 95–109

Dark, K. 2000 *Britain and the End of the Roman Empire* Stroud, Tempus Publishing

Davey, N. and Ling, R. 1982 *Wall-painting in Roman Britain,* Britannia Monograph Series **3**. London, Society for the Promotion of Roman Studies

de la Bédoyère, G. 1993 *Roman Villas and the Countryside* London, B.T. Batsford

Dewar, H.S. 1957 'Churchie Bushes', *J. Roman Stud.* **45**, 221–2

Dodson, P. and Wexlar, D. 1979 'Taphonomic investigation of owl pellets', *Paleobiology* **5(3)**, 275–84

Drewett, P. 1979 'New evidence for structure and function of Middle Bronze Age round houses in Sussex', *Archaeol. J.* **136**, 3–11

Drewett, P.L. 1982 'Later Bronze Age downland economy and excavations at Black Patch, East Sussex', *Proc. Prehist. Soc.* **48**, 321–400

von den Driesch, A. and Boessneck, J. 1974 'Kritische Anmerkungen zue Widerristhöhenberechnung aus Langenmassen vor-und frühgeschichlicher Tierknochen', *Saugetierkundliche Mitteilungen* **22**, 325–48

Drosou, K. and Brown, T. 2017 *Ancient DNA analysis of skeletons from Hinkley Point and Cannington Bypass,* Manchester Institute of Biotechnology, University of Manchester, typescript report for Cotswold Archaeology

Drury, P.J. 1982 'An interpretation of the structures', in Jackson D.A., 'Great Oakley and other Iron Age sites in the Corby area', *Northamptonshire Archaeol.* **17**, 3–23

Dunbar, E., Cook, G.T., Naysmith, P., Tripney, B.G., and Xu, S. 2016 'AMS 14C dating at the Scottish Universities Environmental Research Centre (SUERC)', *Radiocarbon* **58(1)**, 9–23

Dyer, C. 2013 'Living in peasant houses in late medieval England', *Vernacular Architect.* **44**, 19–27

Eckardt, H. and Crummy, N. 2008 *Styling the body in Late Iron Age and Roman Britain; a contextual approach to toilet instruments,* Monographies Instrumentum **36**. Montagnac

Edmonds, E.A. and Williams, B.J. 1985 'Geology of the country around Taunton and the Quantock Hills', *Memoir of the British Geological Survey, Sheet 295 (England and Wales)* London, HMSO

Ellis. P. (ed.) 1989 'Norton Fitzwarren Hillfort: a report on the excavations by Nancy and Philip Langmaid between 1968 and 1971', *Somerset Archaeol. Nat. Hist.* **133**, 1–74

Ellison, A. 1978 'The Bronze Age of Sussex', in Drewett P.L. (ed.) 1978 *Archaeology in Sussex to AD 1500*, Counc. Brit. Archaeol. Res. Rep. **29**, 30–7

Ellison, A. 1987 'The Bronze Age Settlement at Thorny Down: pots, post-holes and patterning', *Proc. Prehist. Soc.* **53**, 285–392

Ellson, P. 2001 *A Romano British Villa found at Stawell* Bridgwater and District Archaeological Society

English Heritage, 2002 *Environmental Archaeology: A guide to the theory and practice of methods, from sampling and recovery to post-excavation* Centre for Archaeology Guidelines 2002:01

Esmonde Cleary, S. 2000 'Putting the dead in their place: burial location in Roman Britain', in Pearce J., Millett M. and Struck M. (eds) *Burial, Society and Context in the Roman World* Oxford, Oxbow Books, 127–42

Evans, D. 1977 'Field vole *Microtus agrestis*', in Corbet and Southern (eds) 1977, 185–93

Eyers, J.E. (ed.) 2011 *Romans in the Hambleden Valley. Yewden Roman Villa. High Wycombe* J. Eyers and Chiltern Archaeology

Finberg, H.P.R. 1964, *The Early Charters of Wessex* Leicester, University of Leicester Press

Fitzpatrick A.P. (ed.) 2008 'Later Bronze Age and Iron Age', in Webster (ed.) 2008, 117–50

Flowerdew, J. 1993 *Mice and Voles* London, Whittet Books Ltd

Fulford, M.G. 2000 *New Forest Pottery: manufacture and distribution with a corpus of pottery types*, Brit. Archaeol. Rep. Brit. Ser. **17**. Oxford

Gale, R. and Cutler, D.F. 2000 *Plants in Archaeology; Identification Manual of Artefacts of Plant Origin from Europe and the Mediterranean* Otley, Westbury and the Royal Botanic Gardens Kew

Gardiner, M. 2000 'Vernacular buildings and the development of the later medieval domestic plan in England', *Medieval Archaeol.* **44**, 159–79

Gator, J., Leech, R.H. and Riley, H. 1993 'Later Prehistoric and Romano-British settlement sites in Somerset: some recent work', *Somerset Archaeol. Natur. Hist.* **137**, 41–58

Gent, T. 2007 'Bronze Age burnt mounds and early medieval wells at Town Farm Quarry, Burlescombe,' *Proc. Devon Archaeol. Soc.* **65**, 35–46

Gerrard, C. 2007 'Excavations at and near Church Field', in Gerrard with Aston 2007, 405–47

Gerrard, C. with Aston, M. 2007 *The Shapwick Project, Somerset. A rural landscape explored*, The Society for Medieval Archaeology Monograph **25**. Leeds, Society for Medieval Archaeology

Goodburn, R., Wright, R.P., Hassall M.W.C. and Tomlin R.S.O. 1976 'Roman Britain in 1975', *Britannia* **7**, 290–392

Graham, A. 2010 'A Romano-British building at Queen Camel', *Somerset Archaeol. Natur. Hist.* **153**, 158–60

Graham, A.H. and Mills, J.M. 1996 'A Romano-British building at Crimbleford Knap, Seavington St Mary', *Somerset Archaeol. Natur. Hist.* **139**, 119–34

Grant, A. 2002 'Scales of reference: archaeozoological approaches to the study of behaviours and change', in Dobney, K. and O'Connor, T. (eds) *Bones and the Man. Studies in Honour of Don Brothwell* Oxford, Oxbow Books, 79–87

Green, H.S. 1980 *The Flint Arrowheads of the British Isles: A detailed study of materials from England and Wales with comparanda from Scotland and Ireland. Part I,* Brit. Archaeol. Rep. Brit. Ser. **75(i)**

Greig, J. 1991 'The British Isles', in van Zeist, W., Wasylikowa, K. and Behre, K-E. (eds) *Progress in Old World Palaeoethnobotany* Rotterdam, Balkema, 229–334

Grigson, C. 1982 'Sex and age determination of some bones and teeth of domestic cattle: a review of the literature', in Wilson *et al.* (eds) 1982, 7–23

Gurney, D. 1986 *Settlement, religion and Industry on the Fen-edge; Three Romano-British Sites in Norfolk,* East Anglian Archaeology Report **31**. Dereham, Norfolk Archaeological Unit

Hadman, J. 1978 'Aisled buildings in Roman Britain', in Todd, M. (ed.) *Studies in the Romano-British Villa* Leicester, Leicester University Press, 187–95

Hambleton, E. 1998 *A Comparative Study of Faunal Assemblages from British Iron Age Sites*. Unpublished PhD thesis for the University of Durham, http://etheses.dur.ac.uk/ (accessed 7 June 2108)

Hambleton, E. 1999 *Animal Husbandry Regimes in Iron Age Britain. A comparative study of faunal assemblages from British Iron Age sites*, Brit. Archaeol. Rep. Brit. Ser. **282**

Hambleton, E. 2005 'Animal bone', in Lovell 2005, 44–7

Hamerow, H. 2004 *Early Medieval Settlements. The Archaeology of Rural Communities in North-West Europe 400–900* Oxford, Oxford University Press

Hamilton Beattie, I. and Phythian-Adams, W.J. 1913 'Romano-British house near Bedmore Barn, Ham Hill, Somerset', *J. Roman Stud.* **3**, 127–33

Hammon, A. 2011 'Understanding the Romano-British–early medieval transition: a zooarchaeological perspective from Wroxeter (*Viroconium Cornoviorum*)', *Britannia* **42**, 275–305

Harcourt, R.A. 1974a 'The dog in prehistoric and early historic Britain', *J. Archaeol. Sci.* **1**, 151–75

Harcourt, R.A. 1974b 'Animal bones', in Neal, D.S. *Excavations of the Roman Villa in Gadebridge Park Hemel Hempstead,* Reports of the Society of Antiquaries of London **31,** 256–61

Harris, F., Harris, J. and James, N.D.G. 2003 *Oak, a British History* Oxford, Oxbow Books

Hart, J., Rackham, J., Griffiths, S and Challinor, D. 2014a 'Burnt mounds along the Milford Haven to Brecon gas pipeline, 2006–07', *Archaeol. Cambrensis* **163**, 133–72

Hart, J., Wood, I., Barber, A., Brett, M. and Hardy, A. 2014b 'Prehistoric land use in the Clyst Valley: Excavations at Hayes Farm, Clyst Honiton, 1996–2012', *Proc. Devon Archaeol. Soc.* **72**, 1–56

Hartley, K. 2001 'Shepton Mallet Mortaria', in Leach, P. and Evans, C.J. *Fosse Lane, Shepton Mallet: Excavations in 1990,* Britannia Monograph Series **18**. London, Society for the Promotion of Roman Studies,130–2

Haverfield, F. 1906 'Romano-British Somerset', *Victoria County History of Somerset* **1**, 207–372

Hayward, L.C. 1972 'The Roman Villa at Lufton, near Yeovil', *Somerset Archaeol. Natur. Hist.* **116**, 59–77

Hayward, L.C. 1982 *Ilchester Mead, Roman Villa*, Ilchester and District Occasional Papers **31**. Guernsey, Toucan Press

Higbee, L. and Mepham, L. 2017 *Living on the Edge. Archaeological investigations at Steart Point, Somerset*, Wessex Archaeology Occasional Paper. Salisbury, Wessex Archaeology

Hillman, G.C. 1981 'Reconstructing crop husbandry practices from charred remains of crops', in Mercer, R. (ed.) *Farming practice in British prehistory* Edinburgh, Edinburgh University Press, 123–62

Hillman, G.C. 1984 'Interpretation of archaeological plant remains: the application of ethnographic models from Turkey', in van Zeist, W. and Casparie, W.A. (eds) *Plants and Ancient Man. Studies in Palaeoethnobotany* Rotterdam, Balkema, 1–41

Hillson, S. 1996 *Dental Anthropology* Cambridge, Cambridge University Press

Hingley, R. 1989 *Rural settlement in Roman Britain* London, Seaby

Holbrook, N. 1991 'Axminster Woodbury Close Excavations 1990: The Roman Pottery', *Exeter Museums Archaeological Field Unit Rep.* **91.17**

Holbrook, N. 2011 'Assessing the contribution of commercial archaeology to the study of Roman Somerset, 1990–2004', *Somerset Archaeol. Natur. Hist.* **154**, 35–52

Holbrook, N. and Bidwell, P.T. 1991 *Exeter Archaeological Reports Vol. 6; Roman Finds from Exeter* Exeter, Exeter City Council and University of Exeter

Hughes, V. and Lambert, P. 2017 *Roman Villa - Cattle Hill, Bratton Seymour, Hadspen, Somerset, Archaeological Interim Report*, Draft Oxford Archaeology report

Johnson, P. with Haynes, I. (eds) 1996 *Architecture in Roman Britain*, Counc. Brit. Archaeol. Res. Rep. **94**

Jones, B. and Mattingly, D. 1990 *An Atlas of Roman Britain* Oxford, Blackwell

Jones, G.R.J. 1979, 'Multiple estates and early settlement', in P.H. Sawyer (ed.) *English Medieval Settlement* London, Edward Arnold, 9–34

Jones, J. 2000 'Plant macrofossils', in Rippon, S. 'The Romano-British exploitation of the coastal wetlands: survey and excavation on the North Somerset Levels 1993–7', *Britannia* **31**, 69–200, 122–56

Kelly, F. 2000 *Early Irish Farming* School of Celtic Studies, Dublin Institute for Advanced Studies

Kenney, J. 2012 'Burnt mounds in north-west Wales: are these ubiquitous features really so dull?', in Britnell and Silvester (eds) 2012, 254–79

King, A. 1999 'Diet in the Roman world: a regional inter-site comparison of the mammal bones', *J. Roman Archaeol.* **12**, 168–202

King, A. 2005 'Animal remains from temples in Roman Britain', *Britannia* **36**, 329–69

King, A.C., and Grande, C.M. 2015 *Dinnington and Yarford, Two Roman Villas in South and West Somerset,* Winchester, Department of Archaeology, University of Winchester, http://www.academia.edu/13097905/Dinnington_and_Yarford_two_Roman_villas_in_south_and_west_Somerset (accessed 15 August 2017)

Kitchener, A.C. and O'Connor, T. 2010 'Wildcats, domestic and feral cats', in O'Connor, T. and Sykes, N. (eds) *Extinctions and Invasions. A Social History of British Fauna* Oxford, Oxbow Books, 83–94

Knibb, P. 2009 *What does the excavation at Ford Farm tell us about the settlement there in the Roman Period? A Reassessment of the finds.* Unpublished University of Bristol B.A. Dissertation

Kusmer, K.D. 1990 'Taphonomy of owl pellet deposition', *J. Paleontology* **64(4)**, 629–37

Lawes, J. 2006 *Blacklands: a Landscape. Excavation of a Late Iron Age and Romano-British Settlement, near Frome, Somerset* Bath and Camerton Archaeological Society

Lawrence, M.J. and Brown, R.W. 1973 *Mammals of Britain Their Tracks, Trails and Signs* Revised edition. London, Blandford Press

Leach, P. 1982 *Ilchester Volume 1: Excavations 1974–5*, Western Archaeological Trust, Excavation Monograph **3**

Leonard, C., Hart, J. and Cobain, S. forthcoming 'The Excavation of a Burnt Mound at Autumn Brook, Yate. A summary report', *Trans. Bristol Gloucestershire Archaeol. Soc.*

Levine, M.A. 1982 'The use of crown height measurements and eruption-wear sequences to age horse teeth', in Wilson *et al.* (eds) 1982, 223–50

Lewis, M. 2007 *The bioarchaeology of children: perspectives from biological and forensic anthropology* Cambridge, Cambridge University Press

Lodwick, L. 2017 'Arable farming, plant foods and resources', in Allen, M., Lodwick, L. Brindle, T., Fulford, M. and Smith A. *New Visions of the Countryside of Roman Britain. Volume 2: The Rural Economy of Roman Britain*, Britannia Monograph Series **30**. London, Society for the Promotion of Roman Studies, 11–84

Lovell, J. 2005 'Excavation of a Romano-British farmstead at RNAS Yeovilton', *Somerset Archaeol. Natur. Hist.* **149,** 7–70

Mackreth, D.F. 2011 *Brooches in Late Iron Age and Roman Britain* Oxford, Oxbow Books

Manning, W.H. 1982 *Catalogue of the Romano-British Iron Tools, Fittings and Weapons in the British Museum* London, British Museum Publications Ltd

Margary, I.D. 1973 *Roman Roads in Britain* 3rd edition. London, John Baker

Martin, P. and Driscoll, S. 2010 *Excavation of a Romano-British Site, Butleigh, Somerset: Season One 2009.* Copy in Somerset HER. File Number 22193

Mason, C. 2010 *Archaeological evaluation at Nerrols Farm, Taunton, Somerset TTNCM:108/2010*, Northamptonshire Archaeology Report **10/108**

Mays, S. Brickley, M. and Dodwell, N. 2004 *Human bones from archaeological sites-Guidelines for producing assessment documents and analytical reports* Swindon, English Heritage

Mays, S., Vincent, S., Robson-Brown, K. and Roberts, A. 2011 'Chapter 6 The Human Remains', in Eyers (ed.) 2011, 247–54

McKinley, J. 2004 'Compiling a skeletal inventory; disarticulated and co-mingled remains', in Brickley and McKinley 2004, 13–16

Miles, D. (ed.) 1986 *Archaeology at Barton Court Farm, Abingdon, Oxon,* Oxford Archaeological Unit Report **3**, Counc. Brit. Archaeol. Res. Rep. **50**

Millett, M. 1990 *The Romanization of Britain* Cambridge, Cambridge University Press

Millett, M. and Gowland, R. 2015 'Infant and child burial rites in Roman Britain: a study from East Yorkshire', *Britannia* **46**, 171–89

Mora, P., Mora, L. and Philippot, P. 1984 *Conservation of wall paintings* London, Butterworths

Morris, E.L. 2007 'Prehistoric pottery', in Gerrard with Aston 2007, 565–71

Morris, P. 1979 *Agricultural Buildings in Roman Britain,* Brit. Archaeol. Rep. Brit. Ser. **70**, Oxford

Mudd, A. and Joyce, S. 2014 *The Archaeology of the South-West Reinforcement Gas Pipeline, Devon. Investigations in 2005–2007,* Cotswold Archaeology Monograph **6**. Cirencester, Cotswold Archaeology

Mudd, A., Williams, R.J. and Lupton, A. 1999 *Excavations alongside Roman Ermin Street, Gloucestershire and Wiltshire: The Archaeology of the A419/A417 Swindon to Gloucester Road Scheme, Volume 1: Prehistoric and Roman Activity* Oxford Archaeological Unit

Neal, D.S., Wardle, A. and Hunn, J. 1990 *Excavation of the Iron Age, Roman and Medieval Settlement at Gorhambury, St Albans* London, Historic Buildings and Monuments Commission for England

Nicholson, R. 2016 'Small mammal remains', in Allen et al. 2016, 158–60

Noddle, B.A. 2000 'Large vertebrate remains', in Price (ed.) 2000b, 217–44

Nowakowski, J.A. 1991 'Trethellan Farm, Newquay: the excavation of a lowland Bronze Age settlement and Iron Age cemetery', *Cornish Archaeol.* **30**, 5–242

Nowakowski, J.A. 2001 'Leaving home in the Cornish Bronze Age: insights into planned abandonment processes' in Brück (ed.) 2001a, 139–48

Oakford Archaeology 2017 *Archaeological evaluation on Spooner's Moor, Exmoor, Somerset,* Oakford Archaeology typescript report **1210**

O'Connor, T.P. 1984 *Selected Groups of Bones from Skeldergate and Walmgate. The Archaeology of York* **15**: *The Animal Bones* Council for British Archaeology and York Archaeology Trust

O'Connor, T.P. 1993 'Process and terminology in mammal carcass reduction', *Internat. J. Osteoarchaeology* **3**, 63–67

Owen, M.B. 1968 'Excavations at Newton St Loe Roman Villa', *Somerset Archaeol. Natur. Hist.* **112**, 104–5

Parker Pearson, M. 1995 'Southwestern Bronze Age pottery', in Kinnes, I. and Varndell, G. (eds) *'Unbaked Urns of Rudely Shape' Essays on British and Irish Pottery for Ian Longworth*, Oxbow Monograph **55**, 89–100

Patchett, F.M. 1944 'Cornish Bronze Age pottery', *Archaeol. J.* **101**, 17–49

Payne, S. 1973 'Kill-off patterns in sheep and goats: the mandibles from Aşvan Kale', *Anatolian Studies* **23**, 281–303

Payne, S. 1985 'Morphological distinctions between the mandibular teeth of young sheep, *Ovis*, and goats, *Capra*', *J. Archaeol. Sci.* **12**, 139–47

Peacock, D.P.S. 1969 'A contribution to study of Glastonbury ware in south-west Britain', *Antiq. J.* **49**, 41–61

Pearce, J. 2013 *Contextual Archaeology of Burial Practice. Case studies from Roman Britain,* Brit. Archaeol. Rep. Brit. Ser. **588**. Oxford, Archaeopress

Pearce, S.M. 1973 'Bronze Age Pottery from Barrows at Berrynarbor, Nymet Tracey and Lovehayne', *Proc. Devon Archaeol. Soc.* **31**, 45–51

Pelling, R. 2005 'Charred plant remains', in Lovell 2005, 49–55

Philp, B. 1973 *Excavations in West Kent 1960–1970* Dover, Kent Archaeological Rescue Unit

Powell, A.B., Mepham, L. and Stevens, C.J. 2008 'Investigation of later Prehistoric and Romano-British settlement at Huntworth, 2006', *Somerset Archaeol. Natur. Hist.* **151**, 69–81

Powell, A.B. and Barclay, A.J. forthcoming, *Between and Beyond the Monuments: Prehistoric activity on the downlands south-east of Amesbury*, Wessex Archaeology Monograph **36**. Salisbury, Wessex Archaeology

Price, E.G. 2000a *Frocester. A Romano-British Settlement its Antecedents and Successors. Volume 1. The Sites,* Stonehouse, Gloucester and District Archaeological Research Group

Price, E.G. (ed.) 2000b *Frocester. A Romano-British Settlement its Antecedents and Successors. Volume 2. The Finds,* Stonehouse, Gloucester and District Archaeological Research Group

Price, N. 2010 'Passing into poetry: Viking-Age mortuary drama and the origins of Norse mythology', *Med. Arch.* **54**, 123–56

Quinnell, H. 2012 'Trevisker pottery: some recent studies', in Britnell and Silvester (eds) 2012, 147–71

Quinnell, H. 2014 'Neolithic and Bronze Age pottery', in Mudd and Joyce 2014, 45–55

Rackham, O. 2001 *Trees and Woodland in the British Landscape. The complete history of Britain's trees, woodland and hedgerows* New York, Phoenix Press

Radford, R. 1928 'The Roman site at Westland, Yeovil', *Somerset Archaeol. Natur. Hist.* **74**, 122–43

Rahtz, P. 1969 'Cannington Hillfort 1963', *Somerset Archaeol. Natur. Hist.* **113,** 56–68

Rahtz, P.A. and Greenfield, E. 1977 *Excavations at Chew Valley Lake, Somerset* London, HMSO

Rahtz, P., Hirst, S. and Wright, S.M. 2000 *Cannington Cemetery,* Britannia Monograph Series **17**. London, Society for the Promotion of Roman Studies

Raymond, F. 2012 'Bronze Age pottery', in Gilbert, D. 'A Bronze Age Enclosure with Extramural Structures and Field System on Land to the North of Old Rydon Lane, Exeter', *Proc. Devon Archaeol. Soc.* **70**, 76–80

Reade, R.C. 1885 'The Roman Villa at Great Wemberham in Yatton', *Somerset Archaeol. Natur. Hist.* **31**, 64–73

Reimer, P.J., Bard, E., Bayliss, A., Beck, J.W., Blackwell, P.G., Bronk Ramsey, C., Buck, C.E., Cheng, H., Edwards, R.L., Friedrich, M., Grootes, P.M., Guilderson, T.P., Haflidason, H., Hajdas, I., Hatté, C., Heaton, T.J., Hoffmann, D.L., Hogg, A.G., Hughen, K.A., Kaiser, K.F., Kromer, B., Manning, S.W., Niu, M., Reimer, R.W., Richards, D.A., Scott, E.M., Southon, J.R., Staff, R.A., Turney, C.S.M., and van der Plicht, J. 2013 'Intcal13 and marine13 radiocarbon age calibration curves 0–50,000 years cal BP', *Radiocarbon* **55**, 1869–87

Reynolds, P.J. 1995 'The life and death of a post-hole', in Shepherd L. (ed.) *Interpreting Stratigraphy 5. Proceedings of a Conference held at Norwich Castle Museum on Thursday 16th June 1994,* Norwich, 21–5

Reynolds, P.J. and Langley, K.J. 1979 'Romano-British corn-drying oven: an experiment', *Archaeol. J.* **136**, 27–42

Ripper, S. and Beamish, M. 2011 'Bogs, bodies and burnt mounds: Visits to the Soar Wetlands in the Neolithic and Bronze Age', *Proc. Prehist. Soc.* **78**, 173–206

Rippon, S. 1997 *The Severn Estuary: Landscape Evolution and Wetland Reclamation* Leicester, Leicester University Press

Rippon, S. 2006a 'Landscapes of pre-medieval occupation' in Kain, R. (ed.) *England's Landscape: The South West* London, Collins, 41–66

Rippon, S. 2006b *Landscape, Community and Colonisation: The North Somerset Levels during the 1st to 2nd millennium AD,* Counc. Brit. Archaeol. Res. Rep. **152**

Rippon, S. 2008a 'Coastal trade in Roman Britain: the investigation of Crandon Bridge, Somerset, a Romano-British trans-shipment port beside the Severn estuary', *Britannia* **39**, 85–144

Rippon, S. 2008b, *Beyond the Medieval Village* Oxford, Oxford University Press

Rippon, S. 2012 *Making Sense of a Historic Landscape* Oxford, Oxford University Press

Rippon, S. 2018, *Kingdom, Civitas, and County* Oxford, Oxford University Press

Ritchie, K., Barnett, C., Barclay, A., Scaife, R., Seager-Smith, R.H. and Stevens, C.J. 2007 'The Upper and Middle Wentlooge Formation and a Romano-British settlement: Plot 4000, the Western Approach Distribution park, Avonmouth, South Gloucestershire', *Archaeology in the Severn Estuary* **18**, 19–58

Roberts, T. 2014 'Observations on ritual sheep burials in Roman buildings', *Glevensis* **47**, 28–31

Rook, T. 1992 *Roman Baths in Britain* Shire Archaeology

Rouillard, S. 1987 'The Iron Age pottery from Meare Village East', in Coles, J.M. (ed.) 'Meare Lake Village East', *Somerset Levels Paper* **13**, 183–221

Saville, A. 1990 'The flint and chert artefacts', in Bell 1990, 152–7

Sawyer, P.H. 1968, *Anglo-Saxon Charters: An Annotated List and Bibliography* London, Royal Historical Institute

Schoch, W., Heller, I., Schweingruber, F.H. and Kienast, F. 2004 *Wood anatomy of Central European species,* www.woodanatomy.ch (accessed November 2017)

Schwartz, J.H. 1995 *Skeleton Keys: An Introduction to Human Skeletal Morphology, development and analysis* Oxford, Oxford University Press

Scott, E. 1990 'Romano-British Villas and the social construction of space' in Samson R. (ed.) *The Social Archaeology of Houses* Edinburgh, Edinburgh University Press, 149–72

Scott, E. 1991 'Animal and infant burials in Romano-British Villas: a revitalization movement', in Garwood, P. Jennings, D. Skeates, R. and Toms, J. *Sacred and Profane: Proceedings of a Conference on Archaeology, Ritual and Religion, Oxford 1989,* Oxford University Committee for Archaeology Monograph **32**, 115–21

Seager-Smith, R. and Davies, S.M. 1993 'Black burnished ware and other Southern British coarsewares', in Woodward *et al.* 1993, 229–84

Serjeantson, D. 1989 'Animal remains and the tanning trade', in Serjeantson, D. and Waldron, T. (eds) *Diet and Crafts in Towns. The Evidence of Animal Remains from the Roman to the Post-Medieval Periods,* Brit. Archaeol. Rep. Brit. Ser. **199**, 129–46

Simmons, E. 2012 *Charred plant macrofossils and wood charcoal, Aller, Somerset*, Somerset County Council **44/2012**

Sisson, S., Grossman, J.D. and Getty, R. 1975 *Sisson and Grossman's The Anatomy of Domestic Animals* Philadelphia, Saunders

Smith, A. 2018 'Chapter 5: Religion and the rural population', in Smith, A., Allen, M., Brindle, T., Fulford, M, Lodwick, L. and Rohnbogner, A. *New Visions of the Countryside of Roman Britain. Volume 3: Life and Death in the Countryside of Roman Britain*, Britannia Monograph Series **32**. London, Society for the Promotion of Roman Studies (Draft)

Smith, A., Allen, M., Brindle, T. and Fulford, M. 2016 *New Visions of the Countryside of Roman Britain. Volume 1: The Rural Settlement of Roman Britain*, Britannnia Monograph Series **29**. London, Society for the Promotion of Roman Studies

Smith, J.T. 1985 'Barnsley Park villa: its interpretation and implications', *Oxford Journal of Archaeology* **4**(3), 341–51

Smith, J.T. 1997 *Roman Villas: a study in social structure* London, Routledge

Southern, H.N. 1954 'Tawny owls and their prey', *Ibis* **96**, 384–410

Sparey Green, C. 1987 *Excavations at Poundbury, Dorchester, Dorset 1966–1982. Volume 1: The Settlements*, Dorchester, Dorset Natural History and Archaeological Society Monograph **7**

Stace, C. 1997 *New Flora of the British Isles*. 2nd edition. Cambridge, Cambridge University Press

Stanton, G.R. 1936 'The Newton St Loe pavement', *Journal of Roman Studies* **XXVI**(i), 43–6

Stead, I.M. 1970 'Roman Villa at Whatley Combe', *Somerset Archaeol. Natur. Hist.* **114**, 37–47

Stead, I.M. 1976 Excavations at Winterton Roman Villa, and other Roman sites in North Lincolnshire 1958–1967, Department of the Environment Archaeological Reports **9**. London, HMSO

Stevens, C.J. 2006 'The charred plant remains from Saltwood Tunnel, Kent', CTRL Specialist Report Series, Archaeology Data Service 2006, http://archaeologydataservice.ac.uk/archives/view/ctrl/reference.cfm (accessed 8 June 2018)

Stevens, C.J. 2008 'Environmental evidence', in Powell *et al.* 2008, 77–9

Stevens, C.J. 2014 'Charred and mineralised plant remains', in McKinley, J.I., Leivers, M., Schuster, J., Marshall, P., Barclay, A.J. and Stoodley, N. *Cliffs End Farm Isle of Thanet, Kent, A Mortuary and ritual site of the Bronze Age, Iron Age and Anglo-Saxon period*, Wessex Archaeology Report **31**, 193–9

Straker, V. 1990 'Charred plant macrofossils', in Bell 1990, 211–19

Stratascan 2010 *Geophysical Survey Report, Hinkley Off Site Developments*, Unpublished typescript report **J2676**

Stratascan 2013 *Geophysical survey report: Cannington* Stratascan Report **J5754**, in CA 2018, *fig. 2*

Stratascan 2015 *Geophysical survey report: Cannington* Stratascan Report **J8273**, in CA 2018, *fig. 2*

Sykes, C.M. and Brown, A. 1961, 'The Wraxall villa', *Somerset Archaeol. Natur. Hist.* **105**, 37–51

Taylor, J. 2013 'Encountering Romanitas: characterising the role of agricultural communities in Roman Britain', *Britannia* **44**, 171–90

Teagle, W.G. 1963 'Analysis of Barn owl pellets from Claremont, Esher, Surrey', *The London Naturalist* **41**, 59–61

Thirsk, J. 1967 'Farming techniques', Chapter III, in Thirsk, J. (ed.) *The Agrarian History of England and Wales. IV. 1500–1640* Cambridge, Cambridge University Press, 161–97

Thorn, C. and Thorn, F. 1980 *Domesday Book, Somerset* Chichester, Phillimore

Tilley, C. 2009 'Jacob's Well, Black Hill: a Bronze Age water shrine on Woodbury Common', *Proc. Devon Archaeol. Soc.* **67**, 23–38

Timby, J. 1989 'The Roman pottery', in Ellis (ed.) 1989, 53–9

Tomber, R. and Dore, J. 1998 *The National Roman Fabric Reference Collection: a handbook* London, Museum of London Archaeology Service

Tomek, T. and Bocheński, Z.M. 2000 *The Comparative Osteology of European Corvids (Aves: Corvidae), with a Key to the Identification of Their Skeletal Elements* Kraków, Polska Akademia Nauk

Treasure, E.R. and Church, M.J. 2016 'Can't find a pulse? Celtic bean (*Vicia faba* L.) in British prehistory', *Environmental Archaeol.* **22(2)**, 113–27, http://www.tandfonline.com/doi/abs/10.1080/14614103.2016.1153769 (accessed 7 June 2018)

Usher, G. and Lilly, D. 1964 'A Romano-British pottery kiln site at Venus Street, Congresbury', *Somerset Archaeol. Natur. Hist.* **108**, 172–4

Wallace, D.W. 1977 *1:48 Spaxton Excavation Plan*. Drawing HBC 1/45/1. Copy in Somerset HER, File Number 10802

Ward, G.K. and Wilson, S.R. 1978 'Procedures for comparing and combining radiocarbon age determinations: a critique', *Archaeometry* **20**, 19–31

Ward, J. 1911 *Romano-British Buildings and Earthworks* London, Methuen and Co.

Warry, P. 2006 Tegulae: Manufacture, typology and use in Roman Britain, Brit. Archaeol. Rep. Brit. Ser. **417**

Watts, V. 2004, *The Cambridge Dictionary of English Place-Names* Cambridge, Cambridge University Press

Webster, P.V. 1976 'Severn Valley ware: a preliminary study', *Trans. Bristol Gloucestershire Archaeol. Soc.* **94**, 18–46

Webster, C.J. (ed.) 2008 *The Archaeology of South West England. South West Archaeological Research Framework, Resource Assessment and Research Agenda* Taunton, Somerset Heritage Services

Wessex Archaeology 2007 *Blacklands, Upper Row Farm, Laverton, Somerset: Archaeological Evaluation and Assessment of Results*, Wessex Archaeology typescript report **62504.01**, https://doi.org/10.5284/1030416 (accessed 7 June 2018)

Wessex Archaeology 2008 *Land at Hartnell's Farm, Monkton Heathfield, Taunton, Somerset. Phase 1: Evaluation Report*, Wessex Archaeology typescript report **66312.03**

Wessex Archaeology 2009 *Land at Hort Bridge, Ilminster, Somerset: Archaeological Field Evaluation Report*, Wessex Archaeology typescript report **72011.03**

Wheeler, E.A., Baas, P. and Gasson, P.E. 1989 'IAWA list of microscopic features for hardwood identification', *IAWA Bulletin ns* **10**, 219–332

Williams, A.M. 1909 'The Romano-British establishment at Stroud, near Petersfield, Hants', *Archaeol. J.* **66**, 33–52

Williams, D.F. 1987 *Petrological Examination of Bronze Age and Iron Age Pottery from Norton Fitzwarren, Somerset* Ancient Monuments Laboratory Report **46/87**

Willis, S. 2005 'Samian pottery, a resource for the study of Roman Britain and beyond: the results of the English Heritage funded Samian project. An e-monograph', *Internet Archaeology* **17**, https://doi.org/10.11141/ia.17.1 (accessed 6 November 2017)

Wilson, B., Grigson, C. and Payne, S. (eds) 1982 *Ageing and Sexing Animal Bones from Archaeological Sites*, British Archaeol. Rep. Brit. Ser. **109**

Wilson-North, R. and Carey, C. 2011 'A burnt mound on Brendon Common, Exmoor', *Proc. Devon Archaeol. Soc.* **69**, 9–22

Woodward, A. 1989 'The Prehistoric pottery', in Ellis (ed.) 1989, 39–53

Woodward, A. 1990 'The Bronze Age pottery', in Bell 1990, 121–45

Woodward, A. and Cane, C. 1991 'The Bronze Age pottery', in Nowakowski 1991, 103–31

Woodward, P.J., Davies, S.M. and Graham, A.H. 1993 *Excavations at Greyhound Yard, Dorchester 1981–4*, Dorchester, Trust for Wessex Archaeology, Dorset Natural History and Archaeological Society Monograph **12**

Wouters, W., Muylaert, L. and van Neer, W. 2007 'The distinction of isolated bones from plaice (*Pleuronectes platessa*), flounder (*Platichthys flesus*) and dab (*Limanda limanda*): a description of the diagnostic characters', *Archaeofauna* **16**, 33–72

Wyles, S.F. 2017 'Charred plant remains', in Higbee and Mepham 2017, 59–67

Wyles, S.F. and Stevens, C.J. forthcoming, 'Charred plant remains', in Powell and Barclay forthcoming

Yalden, D.W. 1977 *The Identification of Remains in Owl Pellets* Occasional Publication of the Mammal Society

Yates, D.T. 2007 *Land, Power and Prestige; Bronze Age Field Systems in Southern England* Oxford, Oxbow Books

Young, C.J. 1977 *Oxfordshire Roman pottery*, Oxford, Brit. Archaeol. Rep. Brit. Series. **43**

Youngs, F.A. 1980, *Guide to the Administrative Units of England. Volume 1: Southern England* London, Royal Historical Society

Zohary, D., Hopf, M. and Weiss, E. 2012 *Domestication of plants in the Old World: the origin and spread of cultivated plants in West Asia, Europe, and the Nile Valley* 4th edition. Oxford, Clarendon Press

Index

Illustrations are denoted by page numbers in *italics* or by *illus* where figures are scattered throughout the text. Places are in Somerset unless indicated otherwise..

agriculture
   Bronze Age 116
   Iron Age–Roman 109–10, 128–32
Alfred, king of Wessex 6, 140
Aller 98
Ammianus Marcellinus 143
Andersfield Hundred 140
animal bones, Iron Age–Roman
   assemblage 104, 105
   discussion 37, 109–11
   results
      Late Iron Age–Roman 105–7
      Early–Mid Roman 107–9
arrowhead, barbed and tanged 21, *22*
Ashford Farm 5
Ashill 142
Autumn Brook (S. Glos.) 116
Avonmouth (Bristol) 98

Bancroft villa (Milton Keynes) 125
Banwell (N. Som.)
   Banwell Moor 98
   villa 135, 136
bar, iron 92
barn 123
Barnsley Park villa (Glos.) 135
Barton Court Farm (Oxon) 127, 133
'bastard pointing' 43, 45, *46*, 122, *122*, 128
bath-house 120–2, 142; *see also* Building A
Belgae 135
Bickenhall 142
Birdlip Quarry (Glos.) 118
Black Patch (E. Sussex) 112, 113, 114, *115*
blackberries (*Rubus* sp.) 98
Blacklands villa 135, 137
Bos Swallet (N. Som.) 116
Bradon 142
Bratton Seymour villa 135
Brean Down (N. Som.)
   lithics 21–2
   plant remains 24
   pottery 19, 20
   radiocarbon dates 27
   roundhouses 112, 113
Bredon's Norton villa (Glos.) 123, 127
Brendon Common (Devon) 116
brick, Roman 80
Brislington villa (Bristol) 135, *136*, 137
brooch 89, *89*, *90*, 131
brooch/buckle 91
Broomfield 140
Building A
   animal bones 107, 109
   discussion 117, 118–22, 128, 137
   excavation evidence (illus) 29, 40–50
   pottery 75
   radiocarbon dates 63
   wall plaster, painted 85–7
Building B
   animal bones 107, 109, 110–11
   charcoal 99
   discussion 117, 122–4, 128, 137
   excavation evidence 50–3, *51*, *52*, *53*
   plant remains 93, 98
   pottery 75
   wall plaster, painted 87
Building C
   animal bones 107, 108, 110
   discussion 117, 124–8, 137
   excavation evidence 53–9, *54*, *55*, *57*, *58*
   human bones 61–2, *62*
   pottery 75
   wall plaster, painted 86, 87
Building D
   charcoal 103, *103*
   discussion 138, 140
   excavation evidence 59–61, *59*, *60*
   plant remains 93–7, 98
   radiocarbon dates 63
buildings, design and purpose
   Iron Age 118
   Roman 118–28
   see also Buildings A–D; Structures A–D
Burnby Lane (E. Yorks.) 132
burnt stones 14–15, 116
Butleigh villa 135

Cadbury Congresbury (N. Som.) 139
Caerleon (Newport) 122, *122*, 130
Cambria Farm 20, 27, 116
Cannard's Grave 118
Cannington
   church 139, 140
   early medieval territory 140–2, *141*, 143
   royal estate 1, 6, 139, 140, 142, 143
Cannington Bypass excavations
   archaeological background 3–7, *6*
   discussion (illus) 142–3
      Bronze Age 112–16
      Iron Age–Roman 116–37
      post-Roman 137–42
   environmental evidence *see* animal bones; charcoal; human bones; plant remains
   excavation evidence *see* Rodway; Sandy Lane
   finds *see* ceramic building material; lithics; metal objects; metallurgical residues; mortar; plaster; pottery; stone; wall plaster, painted
geology 3, 4

Cannington Bypass excavations (cont.)
    location 2, 3
    methods and standards 7–8, 7
    project background 1–3
    topography 2, 3, 3
Cannington Camp (Cynwit Castle) hillfort
    excavations 5, 112
    location 1, 2, 30, 30, 124, 137, 142
    post-Roman period 6–7, 140
Cannington Flood Alleviation Scheme 5, 131
Cannington Park Quarry
    caves 5
    cemetery 1, 5–6, 112, 139–40, 142
    pottery 17, 20, 116
Castle Hill Quarry 1, 5
Celtic beans (*Vicia faba*)
    Bronze Age 12, 24
    Iron Age–Roman 93, 97, 98, 129, 131
cemetery, Roman *see* Cannington Park Quarry
Centwine, king of West Saxons 141
ceramic building material 53, 79–82, *81*, *82*
charcoal
    Bronze Age 25–7, 27
    Iron Age–post-Roman period 99–103
        Late Iron Age–Roman 99, 100–1, 103
        Early–Mid Roman 99, 100–1, 103
        early medieval 99, 102, 103
Chedzoy 140
cherry (*Prunus* sp.) 98
Chew Park villa (B.& N.E.S.) 135, 137
Chilton Trinity 140
chimney pot 61, 81–2, *82*, 124
Churchie Bushes 135
cleaver *see* knife/cleaver
Cliffs End Farm (Kent) 24
coal 92, 131
coins 117, 131, 132
Colchester (Essex) 122
Columella 125–6
Combwich 5, 6
Congresbury (N. Som.) 74
corn dryers 127
Crablake Farm (Devon) 114
Cranborne Chase (Dorset) 112, 116
Crandon Bridge 5, 122, 129, 130, 131, 132
Crediton villa (Devon) 135
Creech St Michael 141
Crewkerne 142
Cricket St Thomas 142
crop-processing evidence
    Bronze Age 24
    Iron Age–Roman 93, 98, 99, 127
Crycbeorh 141
Curry Rivel 142
Cynwit Castle *see* Cannington Camp

Dalton-on-Tees villa (N. Yorks.) 109
Darenth villa (Kent) 127
diet 128–9; *see also* animal bones; plant remains
Dinnington villa 135, 136, 137
ditches *see* enclosures; field boundaries; Structures A–C
Dobunni 135
Dorchester (*Durnovaria*) (Dorset) 135, 140
Down Farm (Dorset) 112, 113, 114
Doynton villa (Glos.) 133

drain 52, 123
Dumnonii 135
Durleigh 140
Durley Hill villa 135
Durotriges 135
Durston 140

economy 128–32
Edward the Elder 6
enclosures
    Bronze Age
        charcoal 25–7, 27
        discussion 112, 113
        excavation evidence 9–14, 9, 10, 12, 13
        lithics 21–2, 22
        plant remains 22–5
        pottery 15–17
        radiocarbon dates 14, 27–8
    Iron Age 30–6, 32, 33
    Roman 37–40, 39, 137, 138
Enmore 140
Exeter (*Isca Dumnoniorum*) 19, 135

Feltwell (Norfolk) 121, *121*
fence-line 11
field boundaries 40, 131
file tip 91
fish bones 107–8, 133
flax (*Linum usitatissimum*)
    Bronze Age 24–5, 25, 114
    Iron Age–Roman 93, 97, 98, 131
floor stone 87, 88, *88*
Ford Farm villa 135
Frocester Court villa (Glos.)
    animal bones 109
    buildings 118, 127, 128, *128*, 135, 138, *138*
furnace 41, 42, 44

Gadebridge Park villa (Herts.) 109, 125
Glastonbury Abbey 141
Glastonbury Tor 139
Goathurst 140
Gorhambury villa (Herts.) 121, 125, 131–2
grain stores 36, 53, 128
Great Chesterford (Essex) 110
Gwithian (Cornwall) 20

Haemgils 141
Ham Hill villa 135
Hartnell's Farm 20
Hayes Farm (Devon) 116
hazelnut (*Corylus avellana*) 22–4, 93, 97, 98
hearth 61
Hinkley Point 103, 112
hobnails 89, 90, 91, 92
hollow-ways 40, 131
hone 87, 88
Hort Bridge 116
human bones 61–2, *62*
Huntspill, River 132
Huntworth 98, 118, 140
Hurcot villa 135
hypocaust
    ceramic building material 80–1, *81*
    discussion 120, 121–2, 142
    excavation evidence 42, 47–9, 49

Idstock 140
Ilchester (*Lindinis*) 5, 74, 130
Ilchester Mead villa 135, 137
industry 92, 131
infanticide 132
inhumations, Roman
   discussion 132–3
   excavation evidence 54–6, 55, 62
   human bones 61–2
   radiocarbon dates 63, 66–7, 66
   see also sheep/lamb burials
iron smithing 92, 131
Itford Hill (E. Sussex) 112

Kings Weston villa (Bristol) 135
knife/cleaver 89, 90, 92

Langton villa (E. Yorks.) 123, *123*, 127
latch lifter 89–92, *89*
Leicester (Leics.) 122
Lilstock 140
lithics 21–2, *22*
Littleton villa 135, 137
Lopen villa 135
Low Ham villa 135
Lufton villa 135, 137

Magor villa (Cornwall) 135
metal objects 89–92, *89*
metallurgical residues 92
Michael Church 140
Middlezoy 141
mortar 82–3, 84
Must Farm (Cambs.) 25

nails 89, 90, 91, 92, 131
Nerrols Farm 20
Nesley Farm (Glos.) 133
Newton Comitis 140
Newton Regis 140
Newton St Loe villa (B.& N.E.S.) 135, *136*, 137
North Petherton 140, 142
North Petherton Hundred 140
Norton Camp 112
Norton Fitzwarren 17, 19, 20, 74

Odda, Eolderman of Devon 7
opus caementatum 83
opus signinum 46–7, 48, 49, 83–4, 121, 122
Othery 140

pagi 140
Parrett, River *2*, 3, 5, 6, 132
Paulton villa (B.& N.E.S.) 135
paving *see* floor stone
pea (*Pisum sativum*) 97, 98
pilae
   ceramic building material 80–1
   discussion 121
   excavation evidence 47–9, *49*, 49
pilgrimage grave 139
Pitney villa 123, *124*, 125, 135, 137
pits
   Bronze Age 11, 12, 13–14, 114
   Iron Age 35–6

   Roman 37, 40
     Building B 52–3, 123
     Building C 54, 56
     Building D 61
   see also trough
plant remains
   Bronze Age 12
   Iron Age–Roman
     discussion 98–9
     results 94–7
       Late Iron Age–Roman transition 93
       Early–Mid Roman 93
       early medieval 93–8
     samples and methods 93
plaster 83, 84; *see also* wall plaster, painted
Poole Harbour (Dorset) 122, 130
Porthleven (Cornwall) 20
postholes
   Bronze Age 11–12, 12–13, 14
   Iron Age 35, 36
   Roman 52–3, 54, 60
pot repair, lead 92
pottery, Bronze Age
   assemblage 15
   discussion 17–21, 18–19
   fabrics 15–17
pottery, Iron Age–Roman
   assemblage and methodology 68–9
   discussion 36–7, 117, 131, 143
   late prehistoric
     assemblage 69
     dating/discussion 71
     fabrics 69
     forms and decoration 69–71
   Late Iron Age–Early Roman 71–3, *73*
   Roman
     assemblage 74
     composition 74–5
     dating summary and discussion 77–9, *78*
     samian 75
     stratigraphy 75–7
Poundbury (Dorset) 138, *139*, 140

Queen Camel
   Bronze Age site 27, 103
   villa 135
quern fragments 87, 88–9

radiocarbon dates
   Bronze Age
     enclosure 11, 12, 13, 14, 27–8
     trough 14, 15, 27–8
   Iron Age–Roman, settlement 62–8, 63, 66
Redwick (Newport) 113
RNAS Yeovilton 98, 109, 110
roads
   Roman 5, 130
   Saxon 6
rod, iron 91
Rodway
   charcoal 25–7, *27*
   discussion 112–16, 113, 115, 142
   excavation evidence 9–15, 9, 10, 12, 13, 14
   lithics 21–2, 22
   plant remains 22–5

Rodway (cont.)
   pottery 15–21, 18–19
   radiocarbon dates 14, 27–8
roofing stone 87, 88
roundhouses
   discussion 112–14
   Roundhouse A
     discussion 114
     excavation evidence 10, 12, 13
     plant remains 22, 23, 24
   Roundhouse B
     charcoal 25
     discussion 114
     excavation evidence 10, 12–14, 13

sacrifice 133
salt production 132
Saltwood Tunnel (Kent) 24
Sandy Lane, Bronze Age trough
   charcoal 25–7, 27
   discussion 116
   excavation evidence 14–15, 14
   lithics 21–2, 22
   radiocarbon dates 14, 27–8
Sandy Lane, Iron Age–post-Roman settlement
   background and location 29–30, 29, 30, 31
   discussion 142–3
     buildings (illus) 118–28
     character of occupation 128–33, 130
     context 133–7, 134
     layout 135–7, 136
     settlement chronology 116–17
     post-Roman occupation 137–40, 138, 139
   environmental evidence
     animal bones 104–11
     charcoal 99–103
     human bones 61–2
     plant remains 93–8
   excavation evidence
     Late Iron Age–Roman transition period 30–6, 32, 33, 34, 35
     Early–Mid Roman 36–59, 38
     early medieval–medieval 59–61, 59
     post-medieval–modern 61
   finds
     ceramic building material 79–82, 81, 82
     metal objects 89–92, 89
     metallurgical residues 92
     mortar and plaster 82–4
     pottery 68–79
     stone 87–9, 88
     wall plaster, painted 84–7, 86
   radiocarbon dating 62–8, 63, 66
Seaborough 142
Seavington St Mary villa 135
settlement *see* Sandy Lane, Iron Age–post-Roman settlement
Shakenoak villa (Oxon) 125
Shapwick 138
sheep/lamb burials 54–6, 66, 108, 110, 132, 133
Shepton Mallet 74, 110; *see also* Cannard's Grave
Sherston 140
Siger 132
skinning, evidence for 106, 108, 110, 129
slag, Sandy Lane 92
sloe (*Prunus* sp.) 97–8

Somerdale villa (B.& N.E.S.) 135
South Lodge Enclosure (Dorset) 112, 113, 114, *115*
South Petherton 142
Sowy 140–1
spacer bobbin 80–1, *81*
Spaxton villa 135
spindlewhorl, stone 87, 88, *88*
Spooner's Moor 116
Stawell villa 135
Steart Point 98, 131
stock race 40, 131
Stogursey 140, 142
stone 87–9, *88*
strips, iron 90, 91
Stroud villa (Hants.) 133, *133*
structural stone 87
Structure A
   charcoal 99
   discussion 116, 118, 122, 123
   excavation evidence 34, 34
   plant remains 93, 98
   pottery 71
   radiocarbon date 63
Structure B
   discussion 116, 118
   excavation evidence 34, 35–6, 35
   plant remains 93, 98
   pottery 71
Structure C *34*, 36, 118
Structure D 36, *37*, 118, 138
structured deposition
   Bronze Age 17, 24, 114–16
   Iron Age 36, 117, 118, 133
   Roman 54–6, 55, 110, 132–3

Tacita 133
Taunton 142
temple/mortuary enclosure 5, 139
territories, early medieval 140–2, *141*, 143
tesserae manufacture 88
Thorny Down (Wilts.) 112, 113, *113*, 114
threshing floor 123
tiles 79–82
tree-throw hole 11, 22, 23, 24
trough *see* Sandy Lane, Bronze Age trough
tweezers 58–9, 89, *89*, 90, 131

villa, Roman
   discussion
     buildings (illus) 118–28
     character 128–33
     context 130, 133–7, 134, 136
     reconstruction 119
   excavation evidence (illus) 36–59

Wadeford villa 135
wall plaster, painted
   assemblage 84
   construction techniques 85
   discussion 124–5
   distribution 85–7, 86
   excavation evidence 40, 57–8
   methodology 84–5
weight 87, 88, *88*
Wellow villa (B.& N.E.S.) 135, *136*, 137

Wemberham villa 135, 137
West Monkton 141
Westland villa 135, 137
Westonzoyland 141
Whatley Combe villa 135, 137
Whitley Hundred 140–1
wild plum (*Prunus* sp.) 98
Winterton villa (Lincs.) 121, 123, 125, *126*, 127, 128, 132

Woodbury Common (Devon) 116
Woolmersdon 140
Wraxall villa (N. Som.) 135, 137

Yarford villa 134, 135, *136*, 137
Yewden villa (Bucks.) 118, 120, *120*, 125, 132
York (Yorks.), Walmgate 110